The Complete
Vampire Companion

The
Complete

Companion

Rosemary Ellen Guiley

with J. B. Macabre

MACMILLAN • USA

For Sue and Doug Hobart

Vitam impendere vero

and For Edward Stark, Rosalind Stark Mauceri,
and Joseph Mauceri, Jr.

MACMILLAN • USA
A Prentice Hall Macmillan Company
15 Columbus Circle
New York, NY 10023

Library of Congress Cataloging-in-Publication Data

Guiley, Rosemary.
The complete vampire companion : legend and lore of the living
dead / Rosemary Ellen Guiley with J. B. Macabre.
p.   cm.
Includes bibliographical references and index.
ISBN 0-671-85024-5
1. Vampires.   I. Macabre, J. B.   II. Title.
BF1556.G85   1994
133.4'23—dc20   94-10737
CIP

Book design by Richard Oriolo

Manufactured in the United States of America

First Edition

10 9 8 7 6 5 4 3 2 1

page ii: Original art by Christiane Raymond

Acknowledgments

hearty thanks and heartfelt gratitude are extended to the experts on various aspects of the vampire myth, who supplied either art or information, granted interviews, or wrote essays.

In particular, a round of applause goes to J. B. Macabre, an expert on the horror genre, who took on the daunting task of collaborator, and who toiled away for months, chasing down and writing up material.

The guest essayists turned in some engrossing reading: author Joanne P. Austin on Bram Stoker and Anne Rice; author and literary critic Margaret Carter on the vampire as villain and hero; author and novelist Les Daniels on comics; author, publisher, and critic Robert Eighteen-Bisang on vampires in literature; author and editor John Gilbert on Brian Lumley and the "Vampire Poets"; Allen J. Gittens, founder and president of The Vampyre Society, England, on vampire fan clubs; music critic Lawrence Greenberg on music; and author and vampire researcher Martin V. Riccardo on vampire haunts around the world, and vampirism in magic and psychic attack.

The appendices at the end of the book should serve every vampire fan well. Robert Eighteen-Bisang compiled a terrific bibliography of works of vampire fiction and nonfiction to appear in print, listing nearly 700 works. J. B. Macabre assembled an equally comprehensive lists of films plus a list of fan clubs. With the help of Eric S. Held, founder and president of the Vampire Information Exchange, Brooklyn, New York, J. B. also created a perpetual calendar "vampire datebook."

I would also like to thank some other artists who made special contributions to the book. Christiane Raymond, who edits the journal for the Miss Lucy Westenra Society of the Undead, is a talented artist who created the stunning frontispiece for this book. Fred Berger, founder and publisher of *Propaganda* magazine, a remarkable photographer who captures the eerie and macabre, supplied some captivating photographs with vampire themes.

I am also especially grateful to Jeanne Keyes Youngson, founder and president of the Count Dracula Fan Club, New York City, who is a dear friend as well as a colleague. Jeannie generously opened her files and museum collections for the research on this book. Numerous times, her headquarters served as Vampire Command Central—a place to interview, a place to study, a place to party, a place for respite.

In addition, I would like to thank author Vincent Hillyer and Bernard Davies, co-founder and honorable secretary of The Dracula Society, London, for their assistance.

Thanks also to all the fans of the vampire myth, who made this book possible.

—Rosemary Ellen Guiley

I've dedicated this book to Edward Stark, my grandfather, who taught me how to turn my nightmares into dreams . . .

And to my mother, Rosalind Stark Mauceri, who allowed me the freedom and space to pursue these macabre flights of fancy . . .

Most of all, this book is dedicated to my son, Joseph Mauceri, Jr., in hopes that one day he may also learn about the magic of his dreams and nightmares and how to put them to good uses!

No truer words were ever spoken than that the ability for one to succeed depends upon the shoulders he is allowed to stand on. In my case, it has been many. So it is with my sincere thanks and love that I wish to thank my father Joseph V. Mauceri, my sister Roselle Mauceri, Mark Gallagher, Kevin Lindenmuth, Al Shevy, Anthony Sloan, Joe Citro, Joe Lansdale, Steve Jones, Clive Barker, and all the directors, contributors, and authors who helped to add to the wealth of this book.

A very special thanks to Dr. Jeanne Youngson, for her support and for granting me access to her inner sanctum of the undead.

Finally, to my good friend and colleague, Rosemary Ellen Guiley, who not only allowed my to stand on her shoulders for a while, but put out her hands and gave me a boost up.

Best blood ya'll,
—Joseph B. Mauceri —J. B. Macabre

Contents

II. *Ars Moriendi:*
The Entertaining Vampire

III. Fans and Fang Gangs:
Vampires in Real Life

IV. Appendices

"May the earth not receive you!"
—GREEK CURSE

Introduction

The vampire has fascinated us more than any other monster or supernatural creature perhaps since the beginnings of myth and storytelling. In mythologies around the world, demonic beings and half-humans who suck off the vital life force of the living, robbing them of health, wealth, and life itself, have been held in fear and dread.

This terror holds elements of both repulsion and attraction. Since the Eastern European vampire cult entered Western arts as a literary device in the eighteenth century, we have become less repulsed and more attracted to the vampire. The vampire of the arts is slick and more humanlike than his folklore counterpart, and has been endowed with numerous attractive characteristics. This vampire is the modern Devil, who uses our fatal attraction to him to try to seduce and trick us out of our souls.

The vampire myth has stimulated a steady creative outpouring for more than a century, and especially since the publication of Bram Stoker's *Dracula* in 1897. There have been cyclical waxings and wanings, but by and large the vampire myth has held steady in our interest, and has in fact grown to the point where in arts and entertainment it can be considered a genre unto itself, not a subgenre of horror.

The Complete Vampire Companion is intended to have a little something for every fan of the vampire myth. It covers folklore, literature and pop fiction, films, stage dramas, radio, television, music, comic books, and, yes, real life.

I've been a fan of the vampire myth since I was an adolescent, when I first read Bram Stoker's compelling novel. Though tame by present vampire standards, it terrified me then, and I was hooked. My particular interest is vampire folklore, and how the arts and entertainment fields have drawn on and mutated the lore—and, in fact, have created a whole new vampire myth. My first book devoted solely to vampires was published in 1991 as *Vampires Among Us*. It concerns the Eastern European vampire cult and its influence on vampires in arts and entertainment and pop culture, especially the "wanna-be-a-vampire" syndrome.

In tackling this much broader project, I was delighted to work with J. B. Macabre, a New York writer and critic who is tremendously well versed in the arts and entertainment industry, and is a veritable storehouse of information on the horror genre in general. We tapped some of the best talent on both sides of the Atlantic for material and interviews, and we called upon various experts to contribute essays. The result is a collection that has both depth and diversity. Yet, the book is easy to read and is great for browsing.

The Complete Vampire Companion is organized into three sections, each with a different theme. Each section comprises numerous articles on various aspects of the theme. The first, "The Dead Shall Rise Again: The True Vampire," concerns vampire folklore, the discovery of the rural Eastern European vampire cult by the industrialized West, and the begin-nings of the popular vampire myth. The second section, *"Ars Moriendi:* The Entertaining Vampire," covers the evolution of the vampire myth in arts and entertainment. The third section, "Fans and Fang Gangs: Vampires In Real Life," covers people who want to be vampires (or think they are vampires), the role of vampirism in magic, the habits of "living vampires," criminal vampires of history, and vampire fan clubs.

Finally, there are four appendices. The bibliography of fiction and nonfiction works is probably one of the finest ever assembled, thanks to Robert Eighteen-Bisang, a leading authority on vampires. J. B. Macabre compiled a comprehensive biobliography of vampire films, a directory of fan clubs, and a "vampire datebook"—an annual calendar, compiled with the help of Eric S. Held, founder and president of the Vampire Information Exchange in Brooklyn, New York.

I hope this book delights, entertains, and informs, and serves as a faithful armchair companion to the devoted vampire fan. Now, on to an exploration of the vampire's *pallida mors*—the "pale death."

Rosemary Ellen Guiley
Baltimore, 1994

I.

The Dead Shall Rise Again: The True Vampire

What's a Vampire
Like You Doing in a Cape
Like That?

In 1931, a little-known Hungarian actor named Bela Lugosi flashed onto the silver screen as the vampire Dracula. The character and story were based on the 1897 novel, *Dracula*, by Irish writer Bram Stoker. As Dracula, Lugosi cut a sinister but exotic figure, sweeping about the streets of Victorian London in the full evening dress of tails, cape, and top hat. He glowered at the lesser mortals he met, seductively drank the blood of young women, and mesmerized everyone—on- and off-screen—with his intense gaze and dramatic accent.

Vampirism has never been the same since.

Thanks largely to Stoker's novel and Lugosi's performance, we have come to view vampires as creatures far different from the true vampires who exist in the shadowy, occult world of myth and folklore. Yes, true vampires do exist. However, they are quite unlike anything we encounter in movies or in the pages of a novel.

True vampires do not wear fancy clothes, lead sophisticated immortal lives, command armies of the so-called undead, or wander among humans looking for their lost loves from past lives. Those are storybook vampires.

True vampires occupy another, alternate reality. They do not have physical forms like ours. They molest and harass. They sustain themselves by drawing off the vital juices and life forces of various living things, including the blood of animals and people.

True vampires are far more fearsome than their fictional counterparts. They are the dread and terror of the night, the fear of death, and the helplessness in the face of the Unknown. They are the evil of hell and the Dark Side of the Universe.

Vampires have existed since human consciousness emerged from the Dreamtime and created mythologies to explain the order and disorder of the cosmos. Vampires have been

A nightmare demon sits astride a sleeping victim

among us for thousands of years. Real vampires are among us today, though in guises we might not readily recognize. They are not the people who dress in black, wear fangs, drink blood, and tell television talk show hosts they are vampires.

If we close our eyes and let our thoughts soar beyond the physical plane, we'll find ourselves in the Land of Myth and Legend. It's a place that exists in its own right, yet we cocreate our vision of it, and our experiences in it, with our collective unconscious. All our hopes, dreams, and fears are projected here, to coalesce in a menagerie of beauties and beasts,

who in turn come back to visit us in our world for better or worse.

In this Land of Myth and Legend is a place called Vampire Reality. It's here that we can discover the story of the true vampire—how it emerged out of darkness and took shape, how it has interacted with humanity in the past, how it has been subverted by fiction, and how it continues to interact with humanity in the present.

Vampires are predatory entities. They come in a variety of guises and behave in a variety of ways. They exist universally in mythologies— in fact, vampires, along with werewolves, are among the oldest figures in mythology. Most commonly, vampires are conceived as demonic beings, having either the bodies of monsters or the shapes of half-humans, halfanimals. Some of them are winged, such as the lamiae of Greece. Generally, they are night demons who descend upon sleeping victims, attacking them to drain off the vitality of the living in order to sustain themselves. This vitality can be: blood; good health and resistance to disease; milk (from both women and female animals); and sexual fluids. Vampires also sap the life force of fields by destroying crops through natural disaster, drought, and disease. Although most vampire attacks occur during the night, the vampire is capable of doing its dirty work during the day as well. And, although most vampires are ascribed some kind of shape, they also can be invisible, or appear as ghosts of the human dead.

The lore of vampires is often vague, contradictory, and overlapping of the lore of other supernatural entities. For example, incubi and succubi are male and female demons, respectively, who attack humans for sex, but vampires also can attack victims for sex. This contradicts our pop culture vampire, who is sexually alluring but impotent—an image handed down to us through fiction, then film, courtesy of Victorian morals. Gypsy vampires in particular have voracious sexual appetites.

The Ultimate and Ubiquitous Vampire

Move over, Dracula and the walking Undead—the "vampire's vampire" is a tiny creature that exists everywhere in the world. This little-known tale was discovered by Dr. Jeanne K. Youngson, founder and president of the Count Dracula Fan Club, during a trip to the Yukon. There she made a brief acquaintance with two Tlingits, Donald Crowe and Ben Gates. Upon finding out about her vampire interests, they relayed a Tlingit myth to her. In Dawson, Canada, Youngson was able to find a written account in a library. Here is her adaptation of the tale:

Once upon a time there was a Tlingit woman who wanted children more than anything else in the world, but was unable to conceive. She was the sister of the chief of her people.

After she had given up hope of ever becoming a mother, she found herself pregnant with a child that grew unnaturally fast, leaping from her womb just weeks after the pregnancy was discovered.

He continued to grow quickly, his body covered with hair while still a child; sharp, pointed teeth in place from birth.

It was whispered that the child was not human at all but an evil spirit, and it was said that the unnatural child hunted, not for food or fur, but for the joy of watching creatures die. It was said that the child killed not only animals but other children as well, and delighted in drinking their blood.

Because he was the chief's nephew, no one dared touch him. People in the community kept disappearing and there was great fear among the tribe. The chief himself finally realized that his sister's son—now fully grown—could no longer stay among his people.

He went to his nephew and ordered him to leave. When the vampire only grinned his razor-sharp smile, the chief drew his knife and prepared to drive him away by force.

Slashing at the vampire's arm, the chief watched the knife cut the skin—but to his amazement, there was no blood.

The chief knew the creature was not human and tried to kill him, but he possessed superhuman strength. All night they wrestled, and it often seemed that the monster would sink his teeth into the chief's throat. At last, during a struggle to the death, the chief managed to get a hold on the creature. He threw him into the flames of the campfire.

The vampire burned and crackled like dry wood, and then from the flames came his voice, crying: "You're not rid of me this easily. I will drink your blood for a thousand years!"

As his voice died away, his ashes rose from the fire and formed a swirling cloud in the night air—and each ash became a mosquito.

ROSEMARY ELLEN GUILEY

The *mara*, or nightmare hag, is an entity that sits on the chest at night, paralyzing and suffocating its victim, leaving him or her exhausted. The vampire also is capable of such behavior. Poltergeists are spirits that harass by moving objects about, making terrible noises, pulling off bedclothes, and pinching and biting. The vampire does those things as well.

A Silesian case from the late sixteenth century concerns a vampire who exhibited characteristics of the incubus and poltergeist. (Although the mischief was blamed on the vampiric spirit of a dead man, in modern times we would probably blame it on a demon.)

The vampire was the returning ghost of a man named Johannes Cuntius of Pentsch in Silesia (parts are now Poland, Czechoslovakia, and Germany). Upon his deathbed, he proclaimed that his sins were too grievous to be pardoned by God, and that he had made a pact with the Devil. When he died, his eldest son observed a black cat running to his body and violently scratching his face. A great tempest arose and did not subside until he was buried. Friends of Cuntius prevailed in persuading the church to bury him on the right or "good," side of the altar.

Cuntius was dead only one or two days when rumors circulated around the village that an incubus in his form was forcing itself upon women. Sexual molestations continued after burial, as well as poltergeistlike disturbances. Trampling noises resounded throughout his house at night so severe that the entire house shook. Objects were flung about. Sleeping persons were beaten. Dogs barked all over town. Strange footprints, unlike those of man or beast, appeared around the house.

The list of disturbances was long. The Cuntius specter demanded conjugal rights with his widow and molested other women. It strangled old men, galloped around the house like a horse, wrestled with people, vomited fire, spotted the church's altar cloth with blood, bashed the heads of dogs against the ground, turned milk into blood, drank up supplies of

milk, sucked cows dry, threw goats about, devoured chickens, and pulled up fence posts. Terrible smells and the sensation of foul, icy breath permeated the Cuntius house.

Signs of vampirism were visible around the grave: mouse-size holes went all the way down to the coffin. If they were filled, they reappeared. The villagers at last had the body of Cuntius dug up. According to Montague Summers in *The Vampire in Europe* (1929, p. 142):

His Skin was tender and florid, his Joynts not at all stiff, but limber and moveable, and a staff being put into his hand, he grasped it with His fingers very fast; his eyes also of themselves would be one time open, and another time shut; they opened a vein in his Leg, and the blood sprang out as fresh as in the living; his Nose was entire and full, not sharp, as in those that are ghastly sick, or quite dead: and yet *Cuntius* his body had lien [sic] in the grave from *Feb.* 8 to *July* 20 which is almost half a year. . . .

His body, when it was brought to the fire, proved as unwilling to be burnt, as before to be drawn; so that the Executioner was fain

---

with hooks to pull him out, and cut him into pieces to make him burn. Which, while he did, the blood was found so pure and spiritous, that it spurted into his face as he cut him; but at last, not without the expense of two hundred and fifteen great billets, all was turned into ashes. Which they carefully sweeping up together . . . and casting them into the River, the *Spectre* never more appeared.

The vampire also bears a strong resemblance to various birth demons. These are monstrous entities, usually female, who prey upon pregnant women, women who have just given birth, and their young offspring. Birth demons tear out entrails, devour flesh, suck off milk, and drink blood. Perhaps the best known are the strigae and lamiae of Greco-Roman lore: female demons who assume the forms of birds and prey upon human victims at night. The most terrifying, however, are the viscera suckers of Southeast Asian lore: bodiless flying heads with streaming entrails.

In Western lore, vampires are most associated with the restless spirits of the dead, who, as revenants, return to harass and attack the living. The fear of the dead, and especially of the ability of the dead to vampirize the living, is ancient and universal. Anthropologist Sir James Frazer stated that fear of the dead, not reverence for the dead, has inspired throughout history the range of practices associated with death, especially the postdeath treatment of the corpse and its burial. In Greece and parts of Eastern Europe, the dead are dug up three to five years after burial, and the bones are examined to ascertain whether or not the soul has found peace. According to lore, if the body has not entirely decomposed, if the bones are dark and not white, or if bits of hair cling to the skull, the soul is not at rest.

The ancient Egyptians believed the souls of the dead could return as vampires. And a Chaldean epic of the third millenium B.C. portrays the goddess Ishtar, who goes to the underworld to find her son/lover Tammuz, declaring, "I will cause the dead to arise and devour the living." The devouring most likely means destruction through a wasting illness.

Similarly, Chinese lore offers "hungry ghosts," voracious spirits of the dead who have no one living to feed them with the proper postmortem rituals and offerings.

Virtually all societies have established rituals to prevent the return of the dead (usually through certain funeral and burial procedures), or to dispatch them should they find their way back to the living (usually by mutilating or burning the corpse, believed to be the vehicle that sustains the revenant). The dead come back for various reasons: they committed suicide or were murdered; they died unrepentant of sins; they were victims (especially the first victims) of plagues or epidemics; they were not properly buried; or they had unfinished business with the living. The returning dead usually plague their immediate families first and then spread their mischief to the community at large.

It is also possible to be a vampire while still alive. Generally, such persons are witches, wizards, and sorcerers. In Africa, folklore holds that witches frequently indulge in vampirism, as well as in cannibalism and necrophagy. The witches leave their bodies and fly about in search of victims. They enter houses through the roofs and then enter the stomachs of sleeping persons. Inside, they wound the vital organs—especially the heart, liver, and lungs—with "secret spears" or else they suck out the heart. They also suck off the essence of the victim's blood. The victim immediately becomes ill and ulcerated and then dies.

African vampire witches also drink a brew in their rites that is the essence of human blood. According to M. J. Field in *Religion and Medicine of the Ga People* (1937, pp. 142–43):

When the witches meet they are believed to gather 'round a pot called baisea. . . . The pot is often supposed to contain the "blood"

Gypsy Vampires

Eastern European beliefs about vampires have been influenced by Gypsies, nomadic, dark-complected people who probably emerged out of northern India and spread throughout Europe, the British Isles, and eventually America. Gypsy tradition is steeped in magic and superstition. Gypsies have various beliefs about the dead and vampires. Generally, they view the world of the dead as nothing more than the grave itself. Consequently, the cult of the dead imposes special burdens upon the living and has special terrors as well—especially the threat of vampirism.

Little is known about the origins of the Gypsies. The first record of them in Europe is in 1417 in Germany. It is likely that they arrived much earlier, perhaps as early as the tenth century; reasons for their migrations are not known. They came as Christian penitents and claimed to be exiles from a land called "Little Egypt." Europeans called them "Egyptians," which derived into "Gypsies." Their language, Romany, is related to Sanskrit, and many of their customs are similar to Hindu customs. They brought Indian beliefs about gods and the dead to the Balkans and, in turn, absorbed the local pagan and Christian beliefs.

A Turkish legend explains the Gypsies' lack of a specific religious credo: When religions were given to the peoples of the earth a long time ago, each wrote them down to preserve them. Rather than write in books or on wood or metal, the Gypsies recorded their religion on a cabbage. A donkey came along and ate the cabbage.

The Gypsy universe is populated with various deities and spirits. *Del* is both God and everything that is above—the sky, heavens, and heavenly bodies. *Pharaun* is a god said to have once been a great pharaoh in the Gypsies' long-lost Little Egypt. *Beng* is the Devil, the source of all evil. He is ugly and reptilian in appearance and has the power to shape-shift. The cult of *Bibi* concerns worship of a lamialike birth demon goddess who strangles *gorgio*, or non-Gypsy,

of the victims. This "blood" appears to ordinary eyes as mere water, but it contains the vitality of the victim. And though the victim has lost none of his tangible blood and bleeds in the normal way when cut, the essential properties of his blood have been "sucked" and transferred to the pot to be drunk by the witches. Occasionally when a witch is arrested, confesses, and consents to reform, she begins by vomiting all the "blood" she has ever sucked.

Similarly, in Eastern European and Russian lore, a chief occupation of certain witches, wizards, and sorcerers is to suck off the blood essence of humans and animals. Some of these magical adepts have the power to shape-shift into animal forms. In Romania, the term *strigoi* applies to both living witches and the vampiric dead. Among the Karachay, the *oburs* are shape-shifting witches or wizards who smear themselves with a magical salve, mount brooms, fly up chimneys in the form of cats, and go in search of victims for blood. Once children by infecting them with cholera, tuberculosis, and typhoid fever. The Gypsies consider fire divine, with the ability to heal, protect, preserve health, and punish evil.

Gypsies have a strong fear of death and the dead, and numerous taboos govern the way they deal with the dead and dying. All of a dead person's possessions, including his animals, are considered polluted and will haunt the living unless they are destroyed or buried with him. This practice has lessened since the nineteenth century, due to economic factors and the fact that Gypsies are not as nomadic as in previous times. In addition, there are taboos associated with a dead person's favorite foods and pastimes. The living also make regular trips to grave sites to whisper messages to the dead through cracks in the earth and to offer presents and feasts of food and drink intended for the dead to share with the living.

A great fear exists that the dead, trapped forever in their grave-world, are angry at being dead and will return as vampires, or *mullos*, to avenge their deaths. This view is characteristic of primitive concepts that death itself is unnatural—that there is no logical reason why life, with all its pleasures, should ever end. Death, then, must be caused by evil. The dead, who come under the influence of evil, are likely to become restless and vampiric.

Corpses are considered highly dangerous to the living until they have completely decayed. The most dangerous corpses are those of persons who died unnaturally, by violence, suicide, or sudden accident; who were evil or ill-tempered in life; and who were stillborn or died right after birth. In the cases of infants, it is believed that they continue to grow in the grave, until they reach either their eighth year or adulthood, when they become restless and want to leave their grave-world.

The *mullo* is feared with the greatest horror. It is full of hatred and seeks revenge against those who caused his death, those who kept his possessions instead of destroying them, and those who failed to observe the proper burial and graveside respect.

Mullos also return to satisfy their prodigious sexual appetites, either with their spouses, women or men they were never allowed to marry in life, or, for that matter, anyone they choose. They may be invisible

sated, the *oburs* return home by descending the chimneys on their brooms and resuming human form. In Russia, the term *eretik* is applied to both sorcerers and religious heretics who are fated to become vampires after death.

The vampire fate of heretics raises an interesting matter. As Christianity spread through pagan lands, church officials made use of local vampire beliefs as part of their conversion efforts. The church stressed that the unconverted and the unrepentant would become vampires after death. Likewise, murderers, arsonists, and other criminals were doomed to postmortem vampirism. In Eastern European lore, we find a particular connection between alcoholism and vampirism. Perhaps it was believed that the addiction to drinking would not be stopped by death and that the restless soul would turn to drinking blood as a substitute.

We also find in Eastern European lore a strong link between the vampire and the werewolf, a human who lives under a curse of involuntary shape-shifting every full moon, going on a rampage of killing and destruction.

to all but their lovers; it is dangerous to speak of them to others. While having sex with a vampire, it is permissible only to scream. *Mullos* may ask their lovers to marry them or come to the grave with them. They are so insatiable that their human partners are likely to weaken and become ill from exhaustion. It is possible for a widow to become pregnant by her vampire husband. Among the Slavs, the resulting child—which can only be male—is called a *dhampir*. The *dhampir* has supernatural powers for detecting vampires and is useful in hunting them down. Unfortunately, he is likely to have a short life, for he is born with a fragile, jellylike body.

Like Balkan natives, the Gypsies have different beliefs concerning the appearance of the *mullo*. Some regard it as having the same form as when it was buried; the corpse remains undecayed. The *mullo* rises at midnight to strangle people and animals and fill itself up with blood. Some Slavic and German Gypsies believe the blood-filled vampire has no use for bones and leaves them behind in the grave. Others believe that vampires have monstrous appearances: ragged hair that touches the ground; flaming yellow hair; skin the color of congealed blood; tusk-like fangs; missing middle fingers on both hands; animal feet.

Still others believe that the vampire always is invisible, and will reveal itself only to its victims. The vampire can be seen by looking under one's own arms, under the arms of a witch, or by performing certain magical charms, though to do so invites the risk of illness and death.

The *mullo* also can shape-shift to a wolf, dog, or cat; Swedish Gypsies believe it can take the form of a bird or horse.

If human vampires weren't enough, some Gypsies, such as Moslem Gypsies in parts of Europe, also believe that certain animals, vegetables, and even tools can become vampires. The most likely animal candidates are snakes, dogs, cats, sheep, horses, and chickens, but any animal can become a vampire under certain conditions, especially if it jumps over a human corpse prior to burial or if another animal jumps over the animal's corpse. Large fur-bearing animals are not hunted by some Gypsies out of fear that they will return as avenging vampires.

Vegetable vampires are more annoyances than dangers. Pumpkins and watermelons kept longer than ten days, or kept after Christmas, will show traces of blood on them and will go about on their own noisily disturbing people and animals. Tool vampires are similar. Wooden knots for yokes and wooden rods for binding wheat sheaves

Among the Southern Slavs, the term *vudkolak* ("wolf's hair") refers to both a vampire and a vampire-werewolf—the latter being a sort of two-for-the-price-of-one creature. In parts of Europe, especially Romania, Greece, and East Prussia, folklore beliefs hold that when werewolves die, they become vampires.

Vampires come in various shapes and guises, with various patterns of behavior, but all vampires seem to share two things in common: they exist in myth and folklore to explain (or take blame for) the terrible things that happen to the living and they are expressions of human fears about those terrible things. The most terrible fear, of course, concerns death, the greatest Unknown. The birth demons such as the lamiae and viscera suckers explain miscarriage, the pregnancy- and childbirth-related deaths of women, and the early deaths of newborns and infants. The postmortem will become vampires if left undone for more than three years and will make disturbances on their own.

Preventive measures against vampires are similar to those practiced by others. Fences of iron—an amulet against evil—are constructed around graves to keep the *mullo* from escaping. Corpses are pierced with a steel needle through the heart before burial or are buried with bits of steel or iron in the mouth, ears, nose, and between the fingers. The heels of shoes are removed to prevent walking, or hawthorn is placed in a sock or driven through the legs.

Gypsies also seek to appease a vampire god by leaving out rice balls and bowls of milk or animal blood. The names of the dead, which are believed to have magical power, are used in oaths and invocations to ward off their return. Homes can be protected with fishing nets—vampires must stop to count every knot before entering—or a sprinkling of thorns or the posting of rosaries, crosses, and pieces of wood feared by vampires. One of the most unique charms against vampires is to live in a home with a twin brother and sister who were born on Saturday and who wear their underwear inside out. Just to see them will send a vampire screaming. Saturday is a magical day in folklore, bestowing upon people the ability to see ghosts and spirits. Saturday is the one day that vampires must rest in their graves. The benefit of inside-out underwear remains a puzzle, but twins wearing it cut quite a figure as vampire busters.

Mullos can be destroyed in a variety of ways. One can shout a Romanian curse, "God send you burst!" The vampire will oblige and explode, leaving behind a puddle of blood. The vampire also can be struck in the stomach with an iron needle or doused with holy water. It can be shot or knifed, preferably by a *dhampir*. It can be destroyed by black dogs, black cocks, or white wolves. If the vampire's left sock is in one's possession, the sock can be filled with rocks or earth from the vampire's grave and tossed into running water. The vampire will wander off in search of its sock and accidentally drown itself. Of course, the vampire's body also may be disinterred and staked, mutilated, doused with boiling oil, cut up, or burned.

Despite the Gypsy belief that the dead stay forever in their graves, the threat of a *mullo* is not unending. *Mullos* are believed to have limited life spans of destruction, from forty days after burial to three to five years, after which time they will sink back into their graves forever. Taking measures against them prior to their demise depends on the extent of their damage to the living.

ROSEMARY ELLEN GUILEY

vampire that rises from the grave as the restless, demonized spirit of the dead is an expression of the fear and incomprehension of the finality of death. The world of the dead is seen as being jealous of the world of the living; its demonic denizens will, whenever given the opportunity, avenge themselves on the living by sucking off their life forces, be they blood, health, milk, or the life force of crops. Thus the vampire, as the specter of death and representative of the land of the dead, is blamed for a host of evils that befall humans from beyond their control: death (especially untimely) due to illness, plague, accident, or violence; misfortune; blighted crops and sick livestock; and natural disaster.

This vampire bears little resemblance to the vampire that entertains us in our modern popular culture. Today's fictional vampire is contaminated with the romantic hero: a Beast in

The Yellow Cat Vampire

A Gypsy tradition called Sari Kedi, which means "Yellow Cat," concerns a comely vampire maiden who has the power to shapeshift into a yellow cat and victimize young men for their blood. The true origins of the Yellow Cat legend are lost, but it is reminiscent of the legends of the dangerous Lorelei and the sirens, whose singing lured sailors to wreck their ships, and of the seductive harlot in Proverbs in the Bible. Essentially, it expresses the theme of man who is powerless in the face of the eternally feminine.

Traditionally, the Yellow Cat ballad is sung without accompaniment as a semi-recitative by a maiden about fifteen years old. Ideally, she has waist-length, raven-black hair and a grey cat's-eye glint to her eyes. The rendering of the ballad is entertainment done for profit. It is the Gypsy girl's specialty and is designed to extract as much money as possible from the audience. In the light of the fire, her eyes blaze and she makes people look over their shoulders in fear that the Yellow Cat is creeping up silently behind, ready to pounce in lethal strike. On moonless nights pierced by howling winds and screeching owls, it is whispered that the girl who sings the ballad is truly the Yellow Cat herself. Young men, beware!

The ballad, recorded by Englishman W. V. Herbert in his book, *Bypaths in the Balkans* (1906), is as follows:

> The Yellow Cat on the hilltop stood,
>   With her eyes of glittering grey.
> She longed for a drink of purple blood,
>   For the noise and joys of the fray.
> And all ye good people, remember that:
> Beware, if you dare, of the Yellow Cat.
>
> The Yellow Cat is a maiden bold,
>   A maiden fair and frail;
> Her hair has the color of burnished gold;
>   'Twas pressed to her breast in the gale.
> And all ye good people, remember that:
> Beware, if you dare, of the Yellow Cat.
>
> The Yellow Cat can purr and kiss,
>   And sing a wonderful tune.
> The Yellow Cat can scratch and hiss

search of his Beauty, looking for redemptive love. To learn more about how this metamorphosis took place, it is instructive to trace the development of the vampire myth in Eastern Europe, for it is the Slavic vampire that provided the genesis of our modern-day vampire.

It cannot be said for certain exactly when the Slavic vampire came into being. Some historians trace the beginnings to the mythology of the ancient Slavs, who were sun worshipers. They believed in a rather vague, vampiric demon who lived in the sky and vampirized the sun and moon by eating them, that is, by causing eclipses. This demon also chased rain clouds and drained them of moisture, which literally is the lifeblood of the sky. It wasn't until about the ninth century that a term for vampire entered the Serbian language, helping to formalize a type of demonic entity that sustained itself from the life force of others.

The concept of vampirism was further aided by a comingling of religions, chiefly the early Slavic paganism, called Bogomilism, and Christianity. Bogomilism was a dualistic sect founded in the tenth century by a Bulgarian

She chanted divinely of earthly bliss,
  And heavenly joys ere long,
    With a wile and a smile and a lying kiss,
    And the call and the thrall of her song.
And all ye good people remember that:
Beware, if you dare, of the Yellow Cat.

They found the young man, white and stark,
  As the morn dawned in gold and in rose.
What are they whispering? What talking of?
  —Hark!
  " 'Tis he whom the she-devil chose."
And all ye good people, remember that:
Beware, if you dare, of the Yellow Cat.

"What has felled him, sturdy and good?"
  "What smote him, passing fair?"
"What is become of his purple blood?"
  "What blanched his nut-brown hair?"
Oh, all ye good people, just think of that:
His blood quenched the thirst of the Yellow
  Cat.

ROSEMARY ELLEN GUILEY

And bite and strike in the moon.
And all ye good people, remember that:
Beware, if you dare, of the Yellow Cat.

The young man saw the yellow-haired maid,
  And heard her entrancing wail.
She purred and fawned and kissed and bade
  Him come to her home in the dale.
And all ye good people, remember that:
Beware, if you dare, of the Yellow Cat.

priest. The Bogomils believed that God had two sons: Jesus, the good one, and Satan, the evil one. They equated the body and matter with the forces of evil. The body was the tomb of the soul, and they believed that after death, demons could invade the corpse and cause it to reanimate and wreak evil against the living. The Bogomils had strict procedures for handling and burying corpses, lest the living be contaminated by the demonic forces that endangered the vulnerable corpse. The body was believed to be especially vulnerable during the time of decomposition, until the flesh was en-

tirely wasted away.

The Slavic vampire cult grew until it reached its peak in about the fifteenth and sixteenth centuries. The growth was fueled in part by conversion to Christianity, which used vampirism as a threat to the unconverted and unrepentant; the Inquisition, which focused attention on demons; and epidemics of black plague. It was believed that the first victims of the plague in a community became vampires and infected others, who died and also became vampires.

While circumstances varied from village to

The Anne Rice vision of the "beautiful vampire" (In *Propaganda* magazine. Model: Scott Crawford.
Copyright © Fred S. Berger. Used with permission)

village, vampire attacks generally manifested in the following way: After a person died, the living, usually his immediate family, would experience his presence among them. Quite often, the revenant would be invisible; sometimes it would appear as an apparition. The apparition might seem to be as real as a flesh body. The revenant was a menacing presence, directly attacking the living by making noises, moving objects, and physically assaulting and sexually molesting them. The victims invariably reported feeling drained of energy by these attacks. Sometimes the attacks stopped by themselves, but other times they escalated to include distant relatives and the community at large. The victims suffered misfortune, illness, and death.

The only remedy was to dig up the body of the vampire or the suspected vampire and check for signs of vampirism. (In the cases of plague, many bodies might have to be dug up before one was found in the "vampire condition.") Telltale signs were a shifting of the corpse in the coffin; open eyes; a ruddy appearance; what appeared to be new growth of hair and nails; and streams of blood from the body orifices, among others. These signs have natural explanations, but the peasants then, who knew little about decomposition, took them as supernatural symptoms.

Sometimes, almost any sign of decomposition was greeted as a sign of vampirism, as we see in this account by Georg Tallar, an eighteenth-century German physician who attended a grave opening in Wallachia (*Vampires, Burial and Death*, by Paul Barber, 1988, p. 40)

We opened the coffin, and, to be sure, with most of the dead, one saw that a foaming, evil-smelling, brown-black ichor welled out of their mouths and noses, with the one more, with the other less. And what kind of joy did this cause among the people? They all cried, "Those are vampires, those are vampires!"

Once identified, the vampire corpse was mutilated so that its spirit could not wander the earth. Mutilation practices are a form of sympathetic magic in the belief that what is done to the body also is done to the spirit. Thus, corpses were slashed, staked, and cut up. This usually was an unhappy task on the part of the living, for corpses that are filled with decomposing gases will gush forth the most foul contents when violated. Numerous accounts exist of onlookers becoming violently ill or losing consciousness when blasted with the stench of gases, decaying matter, and rotting blood. One wonders at the fortitude and perseverance of peasants back then: they were so fearful of the vampire that they were willing to repeatedly subject themselves to the most revolting and vile of experiences.

In 1672 a man named Giure Grando died near Laibach, Istria. The dead man was seen immediately after his burial sitting behind the door in his house. Thereafter, he appeared at night to have sexual relations with his widow. He also ran up and down the village streets knocking on doors, whereupon someone inside died. His distressed widow appealed to the village mayor for help, and the mayor found several brave men to open Grando's grave. An account, written by Baron Jan Vajkart Valsovar in 1689 and published in *The Vampire in Europe* (1929) by Montague Summers (pg. 156), continues:

In it they found Giure Grando intact. His face was very red. He laughed at them and opened his mouth. At first [the mayor's] companions fled, but soon they came back again and set about driving a sharpened hawthorn stake through the belly of the corpse, which recoiled at each blow. Then the priest exorcised the spirit with a cruci-fix, "Behold you vampire (*strigon*), here is Jesus Christ who has delivered us from hell and has died for us; and you, vampire (*strigon*) can have no rest, etc." At these words tears flowed from the corpse's eye. Finally they cut off the dead man's head with one blow, at which he let out a cry like a living person and the grave was filled with fresh blood.

In extreme cases, the vampire corpses were burned. If not cremated, the mutilated body would be reburied. This was risky, because the peasants believed the vampire might find a way to revive itself in spite of the damage.

Sometimes these remedial measures did not work the first time, and vampire attacks did continue. Incredible stories have been recorded in which staked European vampires turned their stakes into their own weapons of destruction. A Bohemian vampire staked in the 1300s not only failed to expire but exclaimed that the stake would be useful in fending off dogs. An abbot named Neplach recorded the story in a chronicle dated 1336:

In Bohemia near Cadanus a league from a village called Blow a certain shepherd called Myslata died. Rising every night he made the rounds of the villages and spoke to people, terrifying and killing them. And while he was being impaled with a stake, he said, "They injured me severely, when they gave me a stick with which to defend myself from dogs." And when he was being exhumed for cremation, he had swelled like an ox and bellowed in a dreadful manner. And when he was placed in the fire, someone, seizing a stake, drove it in him and immediately blood burst forth as from a vessel. Moreover, when he was exhumed and placed on a vehicle, he drew in his feet as if alive, and when he was cremated, all the evil ceased, and before he was cremated, whomever he called by name at night died within eight days.

Chroniclers of the Undead

If there were a Vampire Hall of Fame, a special place would have to be set aside for two of the greatest writers of vampire lore: Dom Augustin Calmet (1672–1757) and Montague Summers (1880–1948). Both were clergy and thus might be surprised to find themselves in a hall of fame devoted to a being they considered under the dominion of Satan. They were on opposite sides: Calmet was a disbeliever in vampires; Summers a believer. Nonetheless, both produced prodigious works on vampirism that comprise the best collections of lore and actual cases. Both Calmet and Summers have been criticized for their interpretations of cases, and Summers in particular for his credulity. However, their works remain indisputable classics, the gold in them far outweighing the dross.

Dom Augustin (sometimes spelled Augustine) Calmet was born on February 26, 1672, at Mesnil-la-Horgne in Lorraine, France. In 1688, he joined the Benedictine order at Saint Mansuy Abbey in Toril and was ordained in 1696. Calmet devoted most of his life to studying the Bible and presiding over an academy at the abbey of Moyen-Moutier. During his life, he was one of the best-known biblical scholars of his time.

News of the vampire cult in Eastern Europe intrigued Calmet, and he began collecting information on it. In 1746, he published a two-volume work, *Traite sur les Apparitions des Esprits, et sur les Vampires, ou les Revenans de Hongrie, de Moravie, etc.*, concerning the vampire cult largely in Hungary, Moravia, and Silesia. The work was an instant best-seller for the times and was published in three editions in three years. In 1759, it was translated into English. The English edition was republished in 1850 under the title *The Phantom World*, edited by Reverend Henry Christmas.

Calmet approached vampirism with an open-mindedness that earned him criticism from skeptics. Still, he found vampires a mystery and sought to find the answers to that mystery. The questions that obsessed him the most concerned whether vampires were really dead, and how they managed to exit and reenter their graves. If vampires were dead, and not persons buried alive who somehow found their way out of their graves, then humanity was forced to consider what power reanimated the corpses. If demons were responsible, they could not do so on their own power, but only with the permission of God. Therefore, God was responsible for unleashing vampires upon the living, but why he did so remained a mystery.

"We must then keep silence on this article, since it has not pleased God to reveal to us either the extent of the demon's power, or the way in which these things can be done," Calmet wrote. "There is very much the appearance of illusion; and even if some of the reality were mixed up with it, we may easily console ourselves for our ignorance in that respect, since there are so many natural things which take place within us and around us, of which the cause and manner are unknown to us."

As for the matter of how the vampire exits and reenters his grave, Calmet gave consideration to a prevailing belief that demons essentially dematerialized the physical corpse and turned it into spirit, which enabled the vampire to pass through matter. He rejected this notion, commenting that "We cannot even conceive that an earthly body, material and gross, can be reduced to that state of subtilty and spiritualization without destroying the configuration of its parts and spoiling the economy of its structure; which would be contrary to the intention of the demon, and render this body incapable of appearing, showing itself, acting and speaking, and, in short, of being cut to pieces and burned, as is commonly seen and practiced in Loravia, Poland, and Silesia." Calmet concluded that it was impossible for the vampire to leave the grave. "No one has ever replied to this difficulty, and never will," he wrote. "To say that the demon subtilizes and spiritualizes the bodies of vampires, is a thing asserted without proof or likelihood."

Calmet also was troubled about the incorruption of the vampire corpse. The incorrupt condition was, in the eyes of his church, a state enjoyed by deceased saints—a testament by God to the degree of their sanctity. He recognized that the Eastern church viewed incorruptibility differently, asserting that sinners and the excommunicated would not enjoy dissolution into the earth, but would become vampires. If all excommunicated did not decay, he said, then "all the Greeks towards the Latins, and the Latins towards the Greeks, would be undecayed, which is not the case. That proof then is very frivolous, and nothing can be concluded from it. I mistrust, a great deal, all those stories which are related to prove this pretended incorruptibility of excommunicated persons. If well examined, many of them would doubtless be found to be false."

Ultimately, Calmet found himself forced to reject the notion of vampires on intellectual grounds. He could not reconcile the claims about the vampire with the teachings of the Western church. He could not transcend the limits of those teachings or the limits of the prevailing thought of the time that vampires, like other supernatural entities, had to exist in, and behave according to, the terms of the physical world.

Montague Summers was born Alphonsus Joseph-Mary Augustus Montague Summers on April 10, 1880, in Clifton, near Bristol, England. He was raised an Anglican, but later converted to Catholicism. He graduated from Clifton College and Trinity College in Oxford and from Lichfield Theological College, earning both bachelor and master of arts degrees by 1906.

In 1909, Summers left the Church of England and entered the Roman Catholic Church and became a priest. From 1911 to 1926, he taught at various schools and collected information for books on literature, drama, witchcraft, vampires, and werewolves. His first book on the supernatural, *The History of Witchcraft and Demonology*, appeared in 1926 and became a best-seller in England. In his later years, Summers lived and studied at Oxford, where he worked at the Bodleian Library and pored over the thousands of books he had collected over the years. His peers considered him an odd man, and rumor circulated that he had, while living abroad on the Continent for a period, become involved in occult and black magic practices. The rumors were never substantiated.

Summers devoted most of his time to an intense study of witchcraft, which he felt had been neglected by serious English history writers. He published a second book on the subject, *The Geography of Witchcraft*, in 1927. Summers acknowledged that he had "a complete belief in the supernatural, and hence in witchcraft," which prompted at least one reviewer of *Geography* to comment that he "is amusing us at our expense." Reviewers greeted Summers' other supernatural works with the same skepticism. His books on vampires and werewolves were blasted by critics as filled with unsubstantiated old wives' tales: *The Vampire: His Kith and Kin* (1928); *The Vampire in Europe* (1929); and *The Werewolf* (1933). In these books, he attempted to trace the traditions to their earliest inceptions and to examine the folklore and superstitious practices that arose around them.

Summers opined that vampires do exist. "Cases of vampirism may be said to be in our time a rare occult phenomenon," he wrote in *The Vampire in Europe*. "Yet whether we are justified in supposing that they are less frequent to-day than in past centuries I am far from certain. One thing is plain—not that they do not occur but that they are carefully hushed up and stifled."

Criticisms of both Calmet and Summers are justified, especially in the hindsight of modern times. However, credit must be given where credit is due. Regardless of their opinions, both writers have given us a legacy of vampire treasure: tremendous collections of lore and cases for future generations to examine and ponder.

ROSEMARY ELLEN GUILEY

Another persistent vampire plagued the town of Lewin in 1345. A witch died, and her body, which could not be buried in the consecrated earth of a churchyard, was dumped into a ditch. She turned into a vampire, roaming about in the forms of various unclean beasts, attacking and killing people. When disinterred, she was found to have chewed and swallowed one-half of her facecloth, which, when pulled from her throat, was bloody. She was staked in the heart, but this measure failed to stop her. She continued to roam the night-time countryside, now with stake in hands, using it to kill more people. The witch was dug up again and was burned; this stopped her vampirism.

If vampire attacks persisted, bodies were sometimes disinterred again and mutilated more; or, like Myslata and the witch from Lewin, they were burned and the ashes scattered or thrown in a river. If those measures didn't work, new vampires were sought out through divination and trial-and-error digging.

These vampire beliefs and practices went on in the darkness of geographical remoteness and lack of communication. Then, in the late seventeenth and early eighteenth centuries, the Slavic vampire cult was unearthed, so to speak, by the West. The Austro-Hungarian empire launched a military campaign against the Muslim Turks who occupied large parts of the Balkan Peninsula. The soldiers sent into remote parts came upon village after village where peasants feared the walking dead, and dug up decomposing bodies to mutilate them to stop the dead from walking. The vampire cult at once horrified and fascinated the Austro-Hungarian soldiers and prompted a horde of researchers, some of them theologians, to travel to the Balkans to investigate these outrageous practices.

By 1732, numerous books and reports had been published on vampirism for the Western audience. In that year, fourteen books on the subject were published in Germany alone. Also in 1732, an Austrian surgeon, Johann Flückinger, published a report on his observations of the vampire cult in Serbia. The report received wide distribution in the West, quickly undergoing several translations. His German report was written up in a French newspaper article, which was translated into English and republished, thus finally giving the West the English term *vampire*. In 1749, Westerners were given a huge work on the subject of vampires, authored in French by Dom Augustin Calmet, a Benedictine abbot. The work appeared in English in 1759.

The vampire seized the fancy of both artists

and populace. Romantic writers and poets used the vampire as a metaphor for the irresistible but sinister and all-consuming lover. The vampire also became a popular villain in cheap thrillers. The notion of the living dead, or the undead, was embellished and changed to suit the fictional needs of artists and to meet the tastes of their audiences. Vampires were portrayed as inhabiting undead but real flesh-and-blood bodies and mingling in the world of the living. The fictional vampire thus took on a life of its own, pursuing its own mutations and enduring and growing in strength over the decades as the real vampires of folklore receded in Eastern European popular belief in the face of the advances of science and technology.

The pop culture vampire has become so strong that there are no signs of us tiring of it or letting go of it—despite the periodic gloomy prognostications of critics and observers who deplore the vampire's romantic evolution from villain to antihero to hero. Meanwhile, the real vampire—the demonic entity that sucks off the vital forces of the living—has not vanished. True to its shape-shifting nature, it has changed its form to suit our modern, high-tech times. We're still afraid of darkness and death, though that fear takes more sophisticated forms. To find the modern vampire, we must look not down into the earth but up into the skies. We have transferred our collective fear of the vampirizing Unknown to the extraterrestrial.

The transference of a collective belief in vampires to the extraterrestrial encounter is a phenomenon with which we have yet to come to terms due to conflicting beliefs about space aliens and arguments over their objective reality. When it comes to vampires, we remain preoccupied with the fictional creation, an increasingly beautiful creature clothed in lace with the sophisticated manners of High Court. Bram Stoker gave us the blueprint; Anne Rice has given us perhaps the epitome of the Beautiful Vampire. These fictional vampires may be beautified and their evil neutralized, but, like their folklore counterparts, they reflect our deep concerns with eternal issues: fear of death, fear of darkness, and desire for eternal life and eternal youth.

ROSEMARY ELLEN GUILEY

E.T.: A Vampire for the New Age

Our collective fear of the vampire as the agent of Darkness, Death, and the Unknown has shape-shifted venues, from the walking undead of yore to the alien visitor from another planet. Belief in extraterrestrials who come in spaceships has been on the rise since 1947, when a group of "flying saucers" was reported near Mt. Rainier, Washington, by Kenneth Arnold, a pilot. The "extraterrestrial hypothesis," as it is called, has been hotly debated since. Skeptics discount the possibility of the objective reality of alien beings from elsewhere in the universe. Believers embrace a range of hypotheses, from objective reality to paraphysical reality, including the idea that E.T.s may be, at least in part, projections from the collective unconscious of humanity.

Those arguments aside, an examination of the E.T. myth shows many similarities and parallels with the vampire myth. There may be real aliens—just as there are real vampires—but our encounters with them may involve projections of our own fears, thus creating collective beliefs and expectations that in turn create the myths and the creatures in them.

Encounters with vampires—and indeed with many other supernatural entities, such as demons, fairies, nature spirits, and pagan deities—may take place in an alternate reality that seems to be as real and as valid as waking life. The concept of an alternate reality, a kind of "middle plane" between heaven and earth where human beings can meet supernatural entities, is an ancient and universal one. Plato called this place the "between place." It is also the land of dreams. Many societies consider the events in dreams to be real and to have their own validity. It is important to note that in earlier centuries the Slavs considered dreams to be real. Possibly, vampire attacks occurred in the dream state (most did happen at night) and were reported as real events because no distinction was drawn between dream and waking lives.

Similarly, modern encounters with E.T.s often have a dreamlike quality to them. Most occur at night, especially when the victim is alone or in a remote location. Sometimes, the victim is awakened from sleep to find E.T.s present in the bedroom. Both vampire and E.T. encounters are described as involving feelings of terror and paralysis on the part of the victim. In both cases, there is paranormal movement of objects: vampires jerk off bedclothes and violently move household objects; E.T.s move and levitate themselves, objects, and victims.

E.T. encounters usually are not recalled until the victim undergoes hypnosis or begins having nightmares about them. Perhaps our ancestors, being more open to the supernatural, did not repress supernatural experiences the way we might today.

But, like the vampire that comes from beyond the grave, the E.T. comes from beyond the earth to victimize human beings and animals. The vampire does so by draining off the vital fluids—blood, milk, and life energies. E.T.s take their victims away to a spaceship, where they vampirize them for body tissue and fluids, especially blood samples, semen, ova, and even fetuses. Both vampire and E.T. cases can involve eroticism and sex; however, in the case of vampires, it concerns the vampire's spouse or lovers, whereas in the case of E.T.s, it concerns strange and unknown life-forms. The taking of ova and fetuses by E.T.s is reminiscent of the activity of vampiric birth demons.

Some beliefs about E.T.s posit that aliens seeded the human race eons ago, for the express purpose of eventual enslavement of mind, body, and soul—perhaps even to serve as a source of food. The aliens also are said to be intent upon vampirizing the resources of the earth for their own needs.

Like vampires, E.T.s seem to be interested in blood. For decades, animals have been found dead in pastures and remote locations from mysterious, vampiric mutilations. Cows, sheep, dogs, horses, and other animals have been completely drained of blood, with tongues, eyes, and vital organs removed with surgical precision. Predators and humans are not satisfactory explanations. It is not possible to completely exsanguinate a body, for capillaries collapse at some point and retain blood. Also, the wounds left on the carcasses show signs of intense heat, as though lasers were used. There is no conclusive link between mutilations and E.T.s, but UFO sightings and encounters usually are reported in the areas where mutilated animals are found.

John A. Keel, one of the world's leading authorities on UFOs and anomalies, became interested in the vampiric nature of E.T.s while researching mysterious events in West Virginia in 1967. Besides UFOs, phenomena included sightings of a large, bat-winged man (dubbed "Mothman"); phantom dogs; mysterious creatures; phantom people; and sinister "men in black." The latter are dark, mechanical-like men who harass victims and threaten them to keep silent. Some are cadaverous in appearance; they seem to appear and vanish mysteriously.

In his account of his research, *The Mothman Prophecies* (1975), Keel gives his first-person report of a bizarre incident where a UFO chased down a Red Cross bloodmobile loaded with blood:

On the night of March 5 [1967], a Red Cross Bloodmobile was traveling along Route 2, which runs parallel to the Ohio River. Beau Shertzer, twenty-one, and a young nurse had been out all day collecting human blood and now they were heading back to Huntington, West Virginia, with a van filled with fresh blood. The road was dark and cold and there was very little traffic. As they moved along a particularly deserted stretch, there was a flash in the woods on a nearby hill and a large white glow appeared. It rose slowly into the air and flew straight for their vehicle.

"My God! What is it?" the nurse cried.

"I'm not going to stick around to find out," Shertzer answered, pushing his foot down on the gas.

The object effortlessly swooped over the van and stayed with it. Shertzer rolled down his window and looked up. He was horrified to see some kind of arm or extension being lowered from the luminous thing cruising only a few feet above the Bloodmobile.

"It's trying to get us!" the nurse yelled, watching another arm reach down her

side. It looked as if the flying object was trying to wrap a pincerlike device around the vehicle. Shertzer poured on the horses but the object kept pace with them easily. Apparently they were saved by the sudden appearance of headlights from approaching traffic. As the other cars neared, the object retracted its arms and hastily flew off.

Both young people rushed to the police in a state of hysteria. The incident was mentioned briefly on a radio newscast that night but was not picked up by the newspapers.

In cases like this we have to ask: Did the UFO really intend to carry off the Bloodmobile? Or was it all a sham to "prove" the UFO's interest in blood. Later I tried to check to find out if any Bloodmobiles had actually vanished anywhere. The Red Cross thought I was a bit nuts.

But I often found myself seriously wondering if we only hear about the people who get away!

There are more similarities between E.T.s and vampires. E.T.s "mark" their victims, coming again and again over years to take more samples. Knowledge of these attacks on the part of the victims can result in stress and psychological disorder. Vampires repeatedly visit their victims, too, until they sicken and sometimes die.

E.T.s communicate with their victims by telepathy. Vampires are reported to communicate as well; they speak with their voices, however.

While the similarities are marked, there are significant differences:

■ E.T.s do not seem to be the reanimated dead, but seem very much alive. However, they do have some associations with corpses and the underground. Some people believe they reside in underground bases deep within the earth, and that these bases contain alien bodies and body parts.

- E.T.s don't seem to kill their victims; they just monitor them.
- E.T.s arrive in brilliant light; vampires arrive in darkness and remain invisible or apparitional.
- E.T.s communicate messages of global concern; vampires seem preoccupied with themselves and their former lives.
- E.T.s fly about in spaceships; vampires travel in their own forms.
- Not all E.T. encounters are terror-filled. Some victims report feelings of awe, ecstasy, and pleasure, and even feel that the E.T.s are benevolent and helpful. While vampire encounters are usually characterized by pain and terror, some extant accounts report the victims feeling no particular distress by the appearance of the vampire.

The E.T. myth contains elements not restricted to the vampire myth. Researchers have compared UFO encounters with anecdotal testimony given over the centuries concerning encounters with demons, fairies, elves, trolls, and other supernatural creatures. UFO investigator Jacques Vallee presented compelling comparisons between E.T.s and fairies, elves, and demons in his 1969 book, *Passport to Magonia*. The saucer myth, Vallee points out, bears a remarkable resemblance to the fairy-faith of Celtic countries.

Similarly, Thomas Bullard, a folklorist at Indiana University who has written extensively on UFOs and folklore, finds similarities between E.T.s and fairies and demons. Bullard and Kenneth Ring, an expert on the near-death experience, and others also find similarities between the E.T. encounter and the shamanic initiation. The shamanic initiation takes places in the dark underworld and involves torment and dismemberment by horrible beings.

Some UFO experiencers draw parallels between E.T.s and angels; however, they are out-numbered by experiencers who find E.T.s to be more of a demonic—and vampiric—nature.

What is going on here? No one can say for certain. Supernatural encounters seem to involve archetypal elements that have to do with our collective consciousness, especially our collective fear of the Unknown. Vallee opined in the conclusion of *Passport to Magonia* (pg. 163) that the solution may forever lie beyond our grasp: "Perhaps what we search for is no more than a dream that, becoming part of our lives, never existed in reality. We cannot be sure that we study something real, because we do not know what reality is; we can only be sure that our study will help us understand more, far more, about ourselves."

ROSEMARY ELLEN GUILEY

According to some European folk beliefs, witches, shown here paying homage to the devil, are vampire-like in their ability to drain the blood essence from their victims

A Glossary of Vampires from Around the World

Here are some of the vampire entities who appear in folklore around the world:

- **Afrit.** In Arabian lore, an *afrit* is the vampiric spirit of a murdered man who seeks to avenge his death. The demon rises up like smoke from the blood of the victim. The *afrit* can be stopped by driving a nail into the blood-stained ground.

- **Aswang manan.anggal.** Shape-shifting Philippine viscera suckers, *aswang mananunggals* fly about as bodiless heads with trailing entrails and feed on human flesh, blood, organs, and mucus, especially that of fetuses and newborns. They are accompanied by small birds who act as familiars and reconnaissance, locating prey. By day, *aswang mananunggals* are either men or women who are likely to be respected members of their communities.

- **Bhuta.** In India a *bhuta* is a malignant spirit or demon or a spirit of the dead. If the latter, they usually are the restless souls of men who died untimely deaths. *Bhutas* are flesh eaters who haunt forests and empty dwellings by day and night. They are flickering lights or misty apparitions that cast no shadows and hover above the ground. Thus, they can be avoided by lying flat on the ground. In particular, they plague living people who do not perform the proper funerary rights for the dead. Like the European vampire, *bhutas* are blamed for blighted crops, diseased livestock, natural and domestic calamities, accidents, illness, plagues, and insanity. They can enter human bodies and make victims sicken and die.

- **Brahmaparusha.** Indian vampire similar to the *bhuta* (above), the *brahmaparusha* is commonly depicted as a male demon wearing a wreath of intestines around his head, gnawing the flesh off a man's head, and drinking blood from the skull.

- **Ekimmu.** In Babylonian and Assyrian demonology, an *ekimmu* is the restless spirit of the dead denied entry to the underworld that is forced to prowl the earth. It is created through lack of burial, improper burial, or lack of proper attention by the living, especially the leaving of food and liquids intended to sustain the spirit on its journey to the underworld. The *ekimmu* vampirizes humans not by preying on their blood or flesh but by entering their households at night and causing misfortune and destruction.

- **Empusa.** A Greek demonic vampire spirit, the *empusa* has no shape of its own, but appears as a foul phantom in a myriad of guises, sometimes in the form of an alluring young woman. It enters the body of its human prey to consume its flesh and drink its blood.

- **Eretik.** In Russian lore, an *eretik* is a heretic who becomes a vampire after death, sucking blood and eating human flesh. Heretics include Old Believers (the keepers of the old religion) as well as wizards and sorcerers.

- **Hantu langsuir (langsuyar).** In Malayan lore, a *hantu langsuir* is the spirit of a woman who died in childbirth, becoming a demon that subsists on the blood, milk, and entrails of newborns, nursing mothers, and pregnant women. The *hantu langsuir* drains its victim's blood through a hole at the base of its neck. It sometimes shape-shifts into the form of an owl.

- **Hantu penanggalan.** A Malaysian viscera sucker that is usually female, the *hantu penanggalan* flies about as a bodiless head with trailing entrails. Like other birth demons, it preys upon pregnant women and newborns, sucking their blood and eating their viscera.

- **Krasyy.** In Thai and Laotian demonology, *krasyys* are old women who shape-shift into viscera suckers and fly about on moonless nights. They particularly like infants, but will feast on human excrement as a substitute.

- **Lamia.** A class of monstrous female birth demons, *lamiae* are named after Lamia, a destroyer deity in Babylonian and Assyrian lore, and Lamia, a goddess who was the mistress of Zeus. Hera, the wife of Zeus, was so enraged by the liaison that she killed the offspring that resulted from the union. In revenge, Lamia swore to kill the children of others. *Lamiae* became female demons with deformed lower limbs who preyed upon newborns, drinking their blood and consuming their flesh. In Hebrew lore, *lamiae* are represented by Lilith, Adam's first wife, who was punished for leaving her husband.

- **Loogaroo.** A West Indies vampire, a *loogaroo* is an old woman who has made a pact with the Devil. She shape-shifts by first removing her skin and becoming a blob of light. The *loogaroo* likes to suck human blood. Her name bears a strong resemblance to the French term for werewolf, *loup garou*. If the *loogaroo* is injured while in her shape-shifted form, she will, like the werewolf, show her wound when she changes back to human form.

- **Mullo.** A Gypsy vampire whose name literally means the "living dead," *mullos* are restless spirits of the dead who rise from the grave to avenge their deaths, wreak havoc upon those persons they disliked in life, and indulge in their insatiable sexual appetites. In particular, they strangle animals and humans for their blood. They appear in human form, except that they have no bones, leaving them behind in their graves. Some of them have hair so long it touches the ground. Indian Gypsies see vampires with flaming yellow hair, flesh the color of congealed blood, and tusklike fangs.

A lamia attacks a man

- **Nachzehrer.** A *nachzehrer* is a Silesian revenant who vampirizes its relatives. While in the grave, it first eats its own clothing and flesh, which causes its nearest relatives to sicken and die. The *nachzehrer* then leaves its grave at midnight every night to search out remaining family members and suck their blood.

- **Obayifo.** In Ashanti lore, an *obayifo* is a witch, or sometimes a wizard, who sucks the blood of children, causing them to pine and die. It also saps the vitality from crops, blighting them.

- **Pijawica.** A *pijawica* is a Croatian vampire whose name comes from the root *pit*, meaning "to drink." The name refers less to blood drinking than to alcoholism, which is associated with vampirism in Eastern European folklore.

- **Pisaca.** A flesh-eating Indian demon, a *pisaca* haunts cremation grounds, doorways, royal roads, and deserted houses. Seeing one means death will come within nine months. *Pisacas* can become invisible and enter the bodies of the living through their mouth. Once inside, they feed on intestines and feces.

- **Polong.** A Malaysian vampire in the shape of a tiny person, either male or female, who has the ability to fly, a *polong* is made by collecting the blood of a man who has been murdered. The blood is left in a bottle for two weeks, and magical incantations are said over it. The *polong* grows in the blood and chirps when ready to emerge. Its human creator then must cut a finger daily for the *polong* to suck. The *polong* then can be dispatched to attack enemies by burrowing into them and making them sicken and die. It travels with its familiar, a *pelesit*, a cricketlike demon with a sharp tail. The *pelesit* burrows its tail into the victim, making a tunnel by which the *polong* enters the body to suck blood.

- **Pontianak.** An Indonesian viscera sucker that is the spirit of a woman who died in childbirth, a *pontianak's* favored prey are pregnant women. She kills both woman and fetus by stabbing the woman in the abdomen with her talons.

- **Raksasa.** In Indian lore, a *raksasa* is a type of vampiric demon that operates at night, especially during the dark and new moons. Like the Greek birth demons, *raksasas* attack the vulnerable, especially children and women at their weddings. They also attack men while they eat and drink, entering their bodies and driving them insane. *Raksasas* usually appear as humans with fiery eyes and abnormally long tongues. They also can shape-shift into dogs, eagles, vultures, owls, and cuckoos and can masquerade as dwarfs, husbands, and lovers.

Vampire Vocabulary

The English word *vampire* is derived from a wide range of similar-sounding words such as the Hungarian *vampir*, Polish *upior*, and Russian *wampira*. In addition, the Romanian word *nosferatu*, which means "undead," has become a synonym for *vampire*. The etymology of these words reflects the fact that most of the vampires with which we are familiar are descended from Eastern European folk vampires.

ROBERT EIGHTEEN-BISANG

■ **Sarkomenos.** With a name meaning "the fleshy one," a *sarkomenos* is a ghoulish vampire of Crete and Rhodes.

■ **Striga (strix).** In Greco-Roman lore, *striges* are females who can shape-shift into voracious birds of prey—usually owls—and, like *lamiae*, feast upon the blood and flesh of children. They are particularly fond of livers and internal organs. *Striges* fly at night, and no locks or barriers can keep them out. Ovid said *striges* use their beaks to pick out a child's milk-fed bowels.

■ **Strigoi.** A Romanian term for *vampire*, the name *strigoi* is almost exclusively applied to the returning dead. When applied to the living, it refers to a witch or wizard. Living *strigoi* who perform magical work-for-hire are held in good regard.

■ **Talamaur.** In Melanesian lore, a *talamur* is the soul of a dead person that sustains itself by vampirizing the last sparks of strength of the dying and just dead.

■ **Tanggal.** An Indonesian sorceress who detaches her head and bowels from her body and flies about at night looking for human prey, the *tanggal* uses her large ears or lungs to fly.

■ **Tengu.** A *tengu* is a Japanese vampire demon in the shape of a bird.

■ **Vetala.** In Hindu lore, the *vetala* is a class of ghouls or vampires that lurk about cemeteries and reanimate the dead. They have human bodies that have the hands and feet turned backward. They live in stones, and their eerie singing is often heard in cemeteries. They enjoy playing nasty tricks on the living.

■ **Vieszcy.** A Kashub vampire, the telltale sign of the *vieszcy* is that the left eye remains open after death.

■ **Vukodlak.** A southern Slavic vampire-werewolf, the *vukodlak*'s name literally means "wolf's hair." Most often male, the *vukodlak* is created forty days after death by the entry into the corpse by a demonic spirit that reanimates the body. The *vukodlak* leaves its grave to drink human blood and have sexual relations with its former wife or girlfriends or young widows.

■ **Vyrkolakas.** The Greek term for *vampire*, a *vyrkolakas* is generally the revenant of a man that rises from the grave, preys upon humans and animals for their blood, and tears out the livers of its victims.

■ **Xiang shi (ch'iang shih).** In Chinese demonology, a *xiang shi* is a vampire created from the *po*, the power of the two souls possessed by every human. Either the *po* or the *hun*, the higher soul, can remain with the corpse, but only the *po* has the power to become an evil spirit in the form of the *xiang shi*. The vampire, which has red, staring eyes and long, crooked talons, lives inside the corpse and keeps the host alive by preying on other corpses or living people.

ROSEMARY ELLEN GUILEY

How to Recognize a Vampire: Then and Now

The peasants of medieval Europe had a list of criteria by which to judge corpses as potential vampires. The telltale signs were actually changes in the corpses due to the natural process of decomposition. The peasants didn't know that, however, and so staked or dismembered the unfortunate bodies found to be in the "vampire condition." Key signs were:

1. **Bloating.** A puffy corpse signaled to the investigators that a vampire was sating itself on the blood of the living. Bloating really was caused by a buildup of gases, mostly methane, in the tissue and cavities.

2. **Oozing blood.** Trickles of blood from the body's orifices, especially the mouth and nose, were another guarantee that a vampire had been discovered. Because it was believed that corpses could not bleed, the blood had to have come from the living—

thus accounting for the notion that vampires suck blood. However, blood inside a corpse coagulates and can sometimes reliquify, especially if death was sudden. And, the gases of decomposition are capable of forcing the corpse's own blood up through the mouth and nose. If the body was buried face-down—a common preventive measure against postmortem vampirism—then the body's blood would naturally follow gravity to the mouth and nose.

3. **Bright red blood.** The exuding blood usually was observed—to the horror of the peasants—to be a fresh-looking red. A corpse's blood usually darkens as the oxygen in the blood is consumed. But some postmortem conditions, such as low temperatures, can prevent all the oxygen from being used up, thus giving the blood a brighter red color.

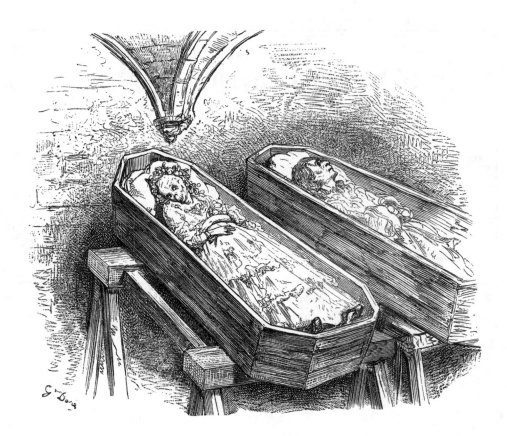

4. **Ruddiness of skin.** Immediately after death, flesh assumes a bluish-gray color, and gums become pale. Thus, when weeks-old corpses were disinterred and found to be pink and red in complexion, as though in the blush of health, it was a dead giveaway for a vampire. No one knew that ruddiness is a natural phase of decomposition, caused by the pooling of the body's blood in capillaries.

5. **Flaccid limbs.** Burial in earlier times usually was swift, especially if the dead were victims of plague or other illness. Consequently, bodies were interred while still stiff from rigor mortis. Unbeknownst to the peasants, rigor mortis is only a stage, followed by flaccidity once again. If a flaccid

corpse was handled—as it often was by the investigators—it might appear to move of its own accord, when actually it was being shifted by gravity.

6. **Movement in the coffin.** Naturally, a vampire corpse was thought to move about in its coffin. However, corpses naturally shift due to the expanding gases of decomposition. Some researchers have suggested that premature burial accounted for the shift in positions found in some disinterred bodies—victims awoke in their graves and attempted to claw their way out. This may account for a small number of vampire cases, but the most likely explanation is natural decay.

7. Incorruption. Bodies found not decomposed—or not decomposed enough—upon disinterment were branded vampires. The question is, how much decomposition is enough for any given time in the ground? Rates of decomposition vary significantly due to a number of factors, such as the means of death, the health of the victim at the time of death, the season (cold slows the process), and the presence of insects, microorganisms, air, and moisture. Interestingly, some accounts tell of bodies found with few obvious physical signs of decomposition, yet giving off a tremendous stench—surely an obvious sign of the normal decomposition process.

Barnabas Collins is a most sartorially correct vampire (Copyright © 1991 MGM-Pathe Communications Co. Used with permission)

8. "New" skin and nail growth. A vampire corpse was observed to sport new growth of skin and nails, thus proving an unnatural life beyond death. This new growth was found beneath skin and nails that had sloughed off. The sloughing off was a normal phase of decomposition, and merely exposed raw areas of skin and nail beds that appeared fresh.

9. Chewed shrouds and limbs. The undead were believed to chew on their shrouds or on their own limbs. In Slavic lore, vampires, whose teeth are like steel, will gnaw through anything. A shroud is a mere appetizer. As the vampire eats his hands and feet, his living relatives and neighbors sicken and die. The vampire then goes forth to attack cattle, babies, and other living next of kin.

Natural explanations can be found for chewed shrouds and limbs, however. A "chewed" shroud may have been nothing more than a bit of the cloth clinging to the mouth. "Chewed" limbs were merely partially decomposed.

10. Noises. When staked, vampire corpses were reported to make noises in protests—even shrieks according to the story of Arnod Paole, an ex-soldier from Serbia who died after falling off a hay wagon in the early 1700s. Noises thought to be shrieks and groans most likely were gases forced by the pressure of staking through the glottis, the slitlike opening between the windpipe and pharynx.

Fortunately, no one these days has to dig up a foul corpse to recognize a vampire. Today's vampires have the good graces to walk about in living bodies and even exhibit some fashion sense. Consequently, recognizing one can be a bit tricky. But the "living vampires" who have styled themselves after the fictional vampires of Dracula, the Lost Boys, Barnabas Collins, and Lestat have adopted some giveaway signs:

1. **Black.** All-black clothing is a *must* for the serious living vampire. The black clothing is accented with silver studs, chains, and jewelry—even crucifixes, which modern-day vampires fear not. Some modern vampires also dye their hair black. The use of black extends as well to home decorating—rooms or entire dwellings are done over in black for the appropriate funereal touch.

2. **Paleness.** No ruddy complexions for modern vampires! These folks are ultra-pale. If nature didn't provide a fair complexion, whiteface makeup does the trick. Both male and female modern vampires sometimes paint their nails and lips blood red or black.

3. **Sunglasses after dark.** Buried vampires didn't have to worry about fearing the sun—that problem was left to the devices of fiction writers, who allowed vampires to roam only at night. Modern vampires feel obliged to uphold the fictional tradition by being nocturnal in habit. Some develop a hypersensitivity to the sun.

4. **Coffins.** If they can afford it, the conscientious modern vampires will buy a coffin. Some even sleep in them. Others, who prefer the comforts of mattresses, use coffins as coffee tables.

5. **Aversion to garlic.** Bram Stoker's Dracula was kept at bay by wreaths of garlic. This is a bit of modern wisdom that does derive from folklore, for garlic is an ancient weapon against vampires, ghosts, demons, and anything supernatural or of malevolent intent. Fictional vampires avoided garlic for decades following the publication of Stoker's *Dracula*, but later authors have allowed their fictional vampires to break away from a monotonous habit. Consequently, living vampires are free to choose pro or con on the issue of garlic, depending on their personal tastes.

Mesmerizing vampire eyes in *Innocent Blood.* (Courtesy Warner Bros., Inc.)

The art of elegant coffin lid raising (In *Propaganda* magazine. Model: Tia Giles. Copyright © Fred S. Berger. Used with permission)

6. **Fondness for bats.** Bats make a weak appearance in vampire folklore. They were added rather late—in the sixteenth century—following news of Cortez's discovery of the blood-sucking bat in the New World. A Romanian superstition holds that bats flying over a grave will turn the corpse into a vampire. Nonetheless, modern lore has the vampire regularly shape-shifting into a bat to travel, flee persecutors, and gain access into the bedrooms of victims. We can give Bram Stoker the most credit for entrenching bats in modern vampire lore, with his dramatic descriptions of Dracula transforming himself into a bat.

Most living vampires have the good sense not to claim to be able to shape-shift into bats, but many love to use bats in their decorating themes.

7. **Supernormal strength.** Real vampires, those bloated corpses, lay in their coffins upon discovery, meekly awaiting their fate. The strongest protest was a "groan" upon being staked. Modern living vampires will have none of that behavior. Instead, they claim to possess astounding strength—able to hurl boulders and bodies with a flick of the wrist. Most, however, do not feel inclined to demonstrate their prowess for the curious.

8. **Immortality.** Real vampires unfortunately had to first die and mold away before turning into vampires. Thanks to fiction, modern vampires can enjoy immortality in their own living bodies. This is a tough one to prove to the skeptic.

9. **Fangs.** A vampire's teeth are seldom mentioned in folklore. Russian vampires are among those that puncture the skin of their victims with sharp, pointed tongues. Montague Summers, that credulous vampirologist, commented once upon a vampire's long, gleaming, razor-sharp teeth, which probably gave rise to the fictional trait of nasty vampire canines (teeth designed to tear flesh, not puncture for sucking). Not every modern vampire sports fang canines because good fangs are expensive. Being a living vampire unfortunately does not make one's canines grow into fangs. To remedy this problem, some vampires use a plastic variety for occasional impact. However, the truly serious vampires go to a dentist to have bridgework done or, better yet, have permanent fang caps put on their canines. The results may look spectacular, but they're hard to manage when it comes to eating. But what's a vampire doing eating food, anyway?

10. **Blood-drinking.** This seemingly obvious vampire trait is at the end of the list because few living vampires drink blood in large amounts. And no one but fictional vampires guzzle an entire human body's worth of blood. Rather, modern living vampires discover, ironically, that drinking a lot of blood makes them ill. Most settle for token amounts—a few spoonsful here, a wine glass or two there—and claim that modern vampires need only partake of symbolic blood drinking on an occasional basis. Modern vampirism is an invent-it-yourself-as-you-go-along myth, so who's to challenge the claim?

ROSEMARY ELLEN GUILEY

An Ounce of Prevention Is Worth a Bite on the Neck

It's reasonable to ask why, if the European peasants of yore were anxious about corpses turning into vampires, they didn't prevent vampirism rather than wait for it to occur. In fact, the peasants took numerous preventive measures at death and burial, especially with deceased who were high on the list of vampire suspects. It's not known how efficacious these measures were, based on surviving accounts of vampire exhumations. However, there are accounts of measures taken to kill vampires that were not successful; hence we can assume that preventive measures sometimes did not work, either.

Preburial and burial precautions against vampirism were:

1. **Weight the corpse's eyelids with coins.** This was considered "payment" for the transport of the soul to the afterworld. Once there, the soul could not return to the world of the living.

2. **Tie the mouth closed.** The soul was believed to escape from the mouth at death. Consequently, if the soul lingered and returned to the body to subsist as a vampire, tying the mouth was one way to prevent it from leaving the grave.

3. **Stuff the mouth with garlic, coins, or dirt.** Garlic was believed to ward off vampires. Stuffing the mouth thus prevented vampirism as well as stopped any vampire soul from leaving the corpse. It also prevented the corpse from chewing on itself, a sure sign of vampirism.

   In China, jade was used to fill a corpse's mouth to keep the soul from becoming restless, while elsewhere in the world plant fibers and wool were used.

4. **Cover the mirrors in the house upon death.** According to widespread lore, mirrors are soul stealers. If a corpse was seen in a mir-

ror, the soul would have no rest and thus was at risk to return as a vampire.

5. **Stop the clocks in the dead person's house upon death.** Stopping time at the moment of death put the corpse into a sort of suspended, protected state until its safety was attained by interment. Thus, the corpse had some measure of protection from invasion by demonic forces.

6. **Put a lighted candle near the corpse or in its hands.** Souls get lost in the dark, so a lighted candle would prevent the soul from wandering away and becoming a vampire. Instead, the light would help the soul get to heaven.

7. **Keep a vigil over the corpse.** Watching a corpse until burial would prevent such unlucky occurrences as animals stepping over it or under it, which would doom the corpse to vampirism.

8. **Paint a cross in tar on the door of the deceased's house.** Tar remedies abound in magical lore for stopping all manner of evil entities from crossing a threshold. The time

between death and burial is a dangerous one, when the corpse is vulnerable to contamination by evil. The cross shape reflects the influence of Christianity, which grafted itself onto the vampire cult.

9. **Remove the corpse from the house carefully.** A corpse should never be taken out through the front door, which enables the revenant to return to plague the living. Corpses should be removed through the back door, or out a window or a hole in a wall cut especially for the purpose. Also, corpses should always be taken out feet first.

10. **Bury the corpse face-down.** This was believed to prevent the vampire from finding its way to the surface. Also, this protected the living who had to bury the corpse or perhaps deal with it later as a vampire in exhumation. The gaze of a vampire was considered fatal, so turning the corpse face-down prevented its baleful glance from falling upon the living.

11. **Bury the corpse at a crossroads, boundary, or remote location.** The vampire would be

trapped by the unhallowed ground of a crossroads and could not wander among the living. Boundaries provided the least offensive neutral zone for unwanted corpses. Perhaps the easiest solution was to bury the body as far away from the village as possible.

12. **Stake or mutilate the corpse.** Why wait until a vampire began its attacks before staking it or cutting it up? Instead, stake it first, through the shoulders, heart, belly, or head. Or, decapitate it, remove the heart, or cut off the limbs. Other measures were to slit the soles of the feet and the palms of the hands or to insert nails into the feet.

13. **Wrap the corpse in a net.** Superstition held that a vampire would be forced to untie all the knots before being able to leave the grave. According to German lore, the vampire could untie the knots only at the rate of one per year.

14. **Tie body parts together.** Binding the feet, knees, or hands together would imprison the vampire in the grave.

15. **Weight the corpse, coffin, or grave with stones.** Stones would prevent the vampire from escaping the grave. The purpose of the tombstone is less to record the names and ages of the dead than to prevent them from becoming restless and leaving their graves.

16. **Fill the coffin with sand or seeds.** Likewise, the vampire would be forced to collect all the grains of sand or all the seeds—or eat all the seeds—at a rate of one per year before he would be able to leave the grave. Favored seeds were poppy (which has a narcotic effect and might have been intended to put the corpse to sleep), mustard, linen, and carrot. Millet and oats served the same purpose.

17. **Place food in the coffin.** A well-fed corpse would not feel the need to leave as a vampire and suck the blood of the living. This practice ties in with ancient and widespread beliefs that the soul required food, water, and money to make its journey to the next world.

18. **Place an object on the corpse, especially its midsection.** Sharp objects such as needles, skewers, spikes, thorns, daggers, nails, and sickles, as well as tin plates and crucifixes, were buried with corpses to prevent vampirism. Metal objects sometimes were heated first. In Romania, the sickle was placed around the neck, so that if the vampire tried to rise from the grave it would decapitate itself. Sickles also were embedded in the heart, believed to be the seat of the soul.

19. **Drive stakes into the grave.** Once again, Romania takes the honors for do-it-yourself vampire slaying. Three stakes were driven into the grave of a suspected vampire. If the vampire tried to leave the grave, it would automatically impale itself on the stakes.

20. **Cremate the body and scatter the ashes.** The most certain way to prevent vampirism was to annihilate the revenant's physical vehicle beyond repair. Cremation, however, was not always easy because bodies are difficult to burn. A contradictory superstition holds that the ashes of a cremated vampire hold the power to cure terrible illness and should be fed to the sick.

ROSEMARY ELLEN GUILEY

How to Find and
Kill a Vampire

If a vampire is stalking the land of the living, he must be found and dispatched, which is no mean feat. Fortunately, various tried-and-true methods have been developed over the centuries. None is for the weak of body or the faint of heart.

Finding a real vampire is relatively easy—they're all dead, so hunts can be confined to suspect cemeteries. If the identity of the vampire is known (in earlier times, the first person to die of an epidemic was automatically a vampire), then go straight to the grave and get the gruesome job done.

If the identity of the vampire is not known, try scattering ash or salt about the graves. The vampire will leave telltale footprints as he exits and enters the grave. It is advisable to keep a hidden, all-night vigil nearby, to rule out the possibility of footprints left by people who like to stroll around graveyards at night.

Still better is to find a horse—either uni- formly white or black, depending on the lore of the area—and lead it around the graves. Horses are sensitive to spirits and the supernatural; thus, the horse will refuse to step over the grave of a vampire. The best equine candidates for the job are ones that have never stumbled. If a virgin boy can be found to ride the horse, the task will be even easier. The purity in both boy and horse will recoil in horror in the presence of the evil of the vampire.

Sometimes the vampire's grave will give itself away by the presence of an eerie, bluish flame at night. In European folklore, the blue glow is the soul. (The glow often is associated with buried treasure, since many people were buried with their valuables).

Other signs to look for are graves that have holes in them, graves that are sunken in, and graves that have crooked crosses or tombstones. All of these indicate that a vampire is dwelling underneath.

If none of these efforts is successful, then a vampire hunter must face the necessity of digging up bodies until the right one is found. In southern Europe, the search is best done on a Saturday because that is the only day of the week that vampires are obliged to lie in their graves.

In Slavic lore, the only certain ways to destroy vampires are these:

1. **Drive an aspen stake through the corpse's heart with a shovel.** Certain variations are allowed. For aspen, one may substitute ashwood, hawthorne, maple, blackthorn, or whitethorn, as well as spades, thorns, sharp pieces of iron, nails, or needles. It is also permissible to aim for the head, belly, or navel. According to lore, the impalement pins the soul to the corpse and prohibits it from further wanderings.

As an extra precaution, it is advisable to wash the staked corpse with boiling wine, scorch it with a hot iron, or fill the coffin with garlic or poppyseeds.

2. **Decapitate the corpse with a shovel belonging to either a grave digger or a sexton.** Hardware store shovels simply won't do. A grave digger's shovel possesses a certain supernatural potency from its association with

The hard work of vampire hunting (From *Captain Kronos Vampire Hunter*, Hammer Film Productions Ltd. Courtesy Paramount Pictures)

the dead. A sexton's shovel possesses the holy power of God. Before you slice, cover the corpse with a cloth to avoid being sprayed by the vampire's blood. If you're splashed, you'll either go mad or die instantly.

Stuff the severed head with garlic, coins, or stones. Place the head under the corpse's arm, at its buttocks, or at its feet. You may rebury the pieces, but put a little extra dirt between the head and the torso. It is better to rebury the pieces at a crossroads or dispose of the head and body separately, by reburying them in separate locations, throwing them into a river, or burying them.

3. **Burn the body.** This method may sound the easiest, but it's probably the most difficult—unless you have handy access to a crematorium. Bodies don't burn very well due to their high water content. Furthermore, bodies don't burn on the sides on which they lie because of a lack of sufficient oxygen for combustion. The peasants of earlier centuries discovered these grim facts when they sought to destroy vampires by fire. They also couldn't stoke wood fires hot enough to burn bodies completely to ash (an adult body will burn to ash in about forty-five minutes in a fire of 1,600 °F). As a result, the village hangmen usually were left with the unhappy task of chopping the

Warding Off Vampires

The crucifix is a potent weapon against the dreaded vampire (From *Bram Stoker's Dracula: The Film and the Legend.* Copyright © 1992 Columbia Pictures Industries, Inc. Used with permission)

Suppose you suddenly find yourself under threat of a vampire attack. If no stakes are handy, what do you do to keep the monster at bay? Take a tip from these European folklore remedies.

Ditch high-priced perfume in favor of garlic, green nutshells, or cowdung found under a hawthorn bush. Wreaths of garlic—or even wolfbane—can be worn instead.

Carry a bagful of salt, sand, or tiny seeds. In a pinch, you can hurl a handful in the path of your pursuer, who is obliged by the Rules of Folklore to stop and pick up every grain one by one.

Use the same goods to protect your bed. Scatter granules around the bed, on windowsills, and at thresholds. Or, recycle your newspapers by laying them out around the bed. Vampires in today's times are literate, but they are still bound by the Rules of Folklore—they must stop and read every word before they can pounce on you.

Other bedside protections include crucifixes and garlands of garlic, which should be nailed over the head of the bed, and silver knives, which should be slipped under the mattress or pillow. Silver is effective against supernatural agents of evil, and a knife is a handy thing to have if the vampire is a speed reader and makes it through all those newspaper pages.

It doesn't hurt to keep a large mirror hung over the bed. Mirrors do not stop vampire attacks, but, as Bela Lugosi dramatically demonstrated in the movie version of *Dracula* (1931), a vampire recoils violently upon not seeing his own reflection. The recoil might give you time to get away!

ROSEMARY ELLEN GUILEY

A vampire is put out of commission with a stake (From the made-for-television movie *'Salem's Lot*)

partially burned bodies into bits that were small enough to burn more easily. Sometimes a hangman had to labor away for an entire day to dispatch a single vampire. In some cases, it was a preferred alternative to burn only body parts, especially the heart or the head. Losing either would put an end to the revenant. It's not surprising that the failure of bodies to burn well only reinforced the belief in vampires.

If a vampire is successfully cremated, the ashes should be scattered. The vampire cannot survive without a physical vehicle for sustenance.

What if none of these measures works, and the vampire still stalks the land? Such determined, Rasputinlike creatures have been documented in European folklore. The only solution is to try different tactics, until the job is done.

ROSEMARY ELLEN GUILEY

Crossroads: The Twilight Zone

The intersections of roads and pathways are dark and dangerous places, according to widespread and ancient superstitions. Crossroads are unhallowed ground; here one meets vampires, demons, witches, fairies, ghosts, and a host of supernatural creatures, such as trolls and spectral hounds. Spirits who like to lead travelers astray also haunt crossroads.

Crossroads are no place to be after midnight, when vampires rise from their graves. According to some superstitions, they take their shrouds with them and station themselves at crossroads, looking for victims.

Crossroads also play roles in various funeral and burial rites designed to keep the dead from returning to harass or attack the living. An old Welsh custom calls for corpses to be laid down at every crossroads and prayed over as they are carried from house to graveyard to protect the corpse from the evil spirits and to prevent the return of the dead. In Hessen, Germany, the return of the dead was prevented by smashing the pottery of the deceased at a crossroads. In many locales, victims of murder and suicides traditionally were buried at crossroads. Suicides were sinners and were not allowed to be buried in the consecrated ground of churchyard cemeteries. Some murder victims were taken to crossroads because it was feared their spirits would be troubled and restless and would return to the living to take revenge. Burial at a crossroads would keep them in place.

Superstitions are often contradictory from place to place, and so it is with the supernatural nature of crossroads. As mentioned earlier, some believe vampires stalk their victims at crossroads, their place of power. Conversely, others contend that crossroads neutralize magic and malevolent beings.

The safest approach when traveling is to always know where you are going. Don't hesitate at crossroads—especially at night—where spirits and vampires wait to pounce on travelers who are uncertain about their direction.

ROSEMARY ELLEN GUILEY

Vampires Stalk New England

News of the European vampire cult leaked out to the West in the early eighteenth century and swept on to infect the American colonies in New England, especially Connecticut and western Rhode Island. There, deaths due to highly virulent diseases such as tuberculosis, measles, and smallpox were blamed on vampirism, and bodies were exhumed and mutilated in the same fashion as had been done for centuries in the rural parts of the Balkans. The nature of infectious disease was not understood, and vampirism was an easy culprit, especially when people died of tuberculosis, a disease that literally wastes the body.

The Mercy Brown vampire case of Rhode Island, in the late nineteenth century, is perhaps the most famous of the vampire episodes, but in 1990, evidence was discovered in Connecticut that the vampire cult probably was more extensive during the eighteenth and nineteenth centuries than had been previously believed.

A gravel pit excavation in the town of Griswold, Connecticut, exposed two human skulls from an old abandoned family cemetery. A subsequent archaeological investigation revealed that twenty-nine people had been buried there. The seven men, seven women, twelve children, and three babies were all members of the Walton family, who had moved from Massachusetts to Connecticut in 1690 and had farmed land in Griswold until 1830, when the family moved to Ohio. The family cemetery, used from 1740 to about 1830, was a small, sixty- by fifty-foot plot.

The remains discovered showed signs of the victims having died of tuberculosis, which was the leading cause of death in adults until about the 1860s. Some of the children buried together may have died in measles or smallpox epidemics, which swept the area in 1759 and 1790, respectively. Some of the remains showed signs of mutilation.

One of the Walton adult men, who died of

Newspaper article about a late nineteenth-century vampire scare in Rhode Island

tuberculosis at about age forty, was dug up about ten years after burial. His chest cavity was cut open, and probably what remained of his organs, if anything, was removed for cremation. It was believed that if the heart or other organs of a vampire were cremated—and possibly eaten by the sick—then a cure would be effected for the individuals stricken but still living.

Vampirism was blamed by members of the Ray family of Griswold, when three family members died of tuberculosis between 1845 and 1851 and a fourth became infected. The corpses of the three dead victims were exhumed by surviving members of the Ray family and their neighbors and were cremated in the cemetery. This measure did the trick, and the fourth Ray recovered.

Vampire fears extended to other parts of New England as well, infecting Manchester, Vermont. In 1790, Captain Isaac Burton married Rachel Harris. Shortly after their wedding, she came down with tuberculosis and died. In 1791, Burton married Hulda Powel, and she, too, came down with tuberculosis. As she lay near death in 1793, Burton organized a ceremony at the cemetery where Rachel Harris was buried. There, before a frightened crowd of one thousand onlookers, Rachel's remains were exhumed. What was left of her heart, liver, and lungs was removed, taken to a blacksmith's forge, and burned. Alas, the measures failed to help Hulda Powel, who died shortly thereafter.

In Rhode Island, the vampire cult started during the Revolutionary War days, according to legend. A well-to-do farmer named "Snuffy" Stukeley, who had fourteen children, began to suffer a horrible and recurring nightmare, in which he would witness half of his orchard wither and die before his eyes.

Soon after these dreams began, Stukeley's oldest child, Sarah, became ill and died, probably of tuberculosis. Then five more children sickened and died, one by one. Stukeley was convinced that his dream was a prophecy of tragedy. The deaths were made even more ominous by the complaints of the five children who died that they were visited nightly by Sarah, who was returning from the dead. Even Mrs. Stukeley began complaining of nocturnal visits from Sarah. Stukeley consulted his neighbors and learned about vampirism by the dead.

The six children then were dug up. Five were in stages of decomposition, but Sarah, legend has it, was uncorrupt. She exhibited some of the classic signs of vampirism: her eyes were open, her hair and nails seemed to have grown, and there was evidence that fresh blood still flowed in her veins. Horrified,

Stukeley cut out her heart and burned it on a rock. Only one more child, who was already ill, died, but the rest remained untouched by disease and death.

In the late 1800s, the George Brown family of Exeter, Rhode Island, were stricken with tuberculosis. Brown's wife, Mary, died, followed by their daughter, Mary Olive. Four daughters and a son remained. Four years later, Edwin, the son, became ill. He and his bride left for Colorado, where Edwin sought treatment at a mineral springs. During his absence, daughter Mercy became sick and died on January 18, 1892. She was nineteen years old. Edwin then returned home, and his condition worsened.

It is probable that Brown was aware of the Stukeley vampire case and so decided to dig up the bodies of Mary, Mary Olive, and Mercy to save his son. The medical examiner, Dr. Harold Metcalf, was on hand at Chestnut Hill Cemetery during the exhumations. The corpses of Mary and Mary Olive were well decomposed, but the body of Mercy was determined to be in surprisingly good condition. Witnesses who had been at her wake swore that her body had shifted in the coffin.

Brown instructed Dr. Metcalf to remove Mercy's heart and liver. All present were astonished when blood dripped from the organs—a sure sign of vampirism. Brown took the organs to a rock and burned them. The ashes were saved. Dr. Metcalf told Edwin to take the ashes and mix a tiny amount in medicine he'd prescribed and drink the mixture. Edwin followed the instructions, but died soon thereafter. The story received sensational treatment in the local newspaper.

Over the years, the story has been retold and embellished. It has been claimed that six or seven girls in the Brown family died before Mercy was exhumed, and they all bore "the mark of the vampire" on their throats when they died (the vampire bite on the throat was popularized in fiction). Mercy's grave continues to attract visitors. People report seeing a blue light or a glowing ball of light hovering over the grave, and other visitors claim they can hear a girl's voice whisper, "Please help me. Let me out." It may be imagination, or the sighing of the wind—or perhaps the spirit of Mercy Brown still lies restless in her grave.

Vampire Haunts

Thousands of sites around the world are known for their restless spirits and ghosts, but barely a handful of places are reputed to harbor real vampires. As might be guessed, cemeteries are the most often-reported habitat for these elusive creatures, followed by remote areas. The following are accounts of real vampires encountered around the world—including one vampire that enjoyed a tropical beach in Brazil. Like all tales of hauntings, human nature tends to exaggerate the facts. Therefore, all accounts should be taken with a grain of salt . . . or perhaps a clove of garlic.

We tend to think of old-world places like Transylvania as the classic breeding ground for vampires, not modern countries like the United States. Yet, right in the middle of America's breadbasket, some people claim to have sensed the blood-chilling presence of a being that is vampiric and grotesquely evil. The stories center around the Free Thinkers Cemetery in the town of Spring Valley, Illinois, which is in the north central area of the state about eighty miles southwest of Chicago. The cemetery was established in the 1920s, and in the 1960s it acquired a reputation for the ghoulish.

There is only one aboveground crypt in the entire cemetery. Built in the 1950s, it holds the bodies of three bachelors, the Massock brothers, who accumulated a sizable fortune from their work as butchers. In a gruesome prank, two teenagers broke into the crypt in 1967 and stole the head of one of the brothers, Anton Massock.

The crime was discovered, the teenagers were apprehended and punished, and the head was returned to the crypt. Yet, the belief persisted that something unearthly was released by the grisly incident. Stories have circulated that dead dogs, drained of their blood, have been found in the cemetery. Stranger still are the stories of something seen in the

Graveyard at St. Mary's Church in Whitby, England (Photo by Rosemary Ellen Guiley)

cemetery—something weird and mysterious resembling a vampire.

In the early 1980s, a Vietnam veteran who lived in Spring Valley heard these stories and decided to check them out. He and a few friends from Chicago went to the cemetery one night. None of them expected to find anything unusual as they wandered the grounds.

To their astonishment, they suddenly saw standing before them a ghastly figure. It was gaunt and pale and seemed to radiate a sensation of horrendous evil. They stopped in their tracks. Was this the reputed vampire? The veteran had brought a gun with him and instinctively aimed it at the creature. He fired five bullets into the thing at close range without effect. It moved toward them. The men turned and ran at top speed.

Not long after the incident, a writer from Chicago visited the cemetery with a friend to investigate. The writer walked up to the crypt, rapped on its door, and poked a stick into a small ventilation hole. Without warning, "something" shot out from the hole and fell to the ground. It was black and wormy in appearance and was coiled in a ball. That was enough to make them leave and get holy water.

By the time they returned, the sun was going down. Using the vents of the crypt, they threw the holy water on the coffins within. A noise sounding like a "painful groaning" issued from the crypt. Hastily, they left the grounds.

Also in the Midwest, marauding vampires have gained notoriety at Graceland Cemetery in Mineral Point, Wisconsin, more than a hundred miles west of Milwaukee. Early in 1981, a police officer was shining his light on cemetery grounds when he saw a huge figure draped in a long black cape. It seemed to be over six feet tall, with a hideous face as white as death. The officer chased the entity, but it vanished into the depths of the cemetery.

After that, a rash of vampire sightings were reported to the police in Mineral Point. Citizens approached police on the streets to describe macabre encounters at the cemetery. They gave accounts of weird entities with white faces popping out of the shadows at them. It was suspected that pranksters who heard about the first encounter were now out to scare up some fun at the expense of the gullible. Yet, not everyone fully accepted that explanation. One police lieutenant admitted to the press that officers were not eager to return to the cemetery.

In California, folklore has laid claim to a vampire said to be real and not of the Hollywood variety. Between Los Angeles and Santa Barbara is the quiet, beautiful community of Ojai, popular with artists and members of the New Age community. The area's serenity,

A spooky setting for vampires

however, might be marred by a dark denizen who is more down-to-earth, so to speak.

Legend has it that in the 1980s, local ranchers discovered their cattle were being decimated. The carcasses were found with their throats slashed and the bodies drained of blood. A vampire was the suspected predator.

The ranchers combed through the property of a new landowner in the area, of whom they were suspicious. They spotted something in the distance that looked like a large stone box near a crossroad off Creek Road. As they walked toward it, they heard a deep, ferocious growl. A black dog of tremendous size jumped out of the brush and blocked their path. Snarling and glaring at them, it stood guard over the vampire lying in his daylight sanctuary.

One of the ranchers pulled out a large crucifix made of silver, and with this as protection they were able to keep the hellish canine at bay as they moved forward. When they reached the vampire's sarcophagus, the animal lunged at them. Their guns at the ready, they fired into the beast, but to no effect. Fortunately, one of the men had the foresight to bring holy water from the local mission. When the spray of holy water hit the creature, it let out a bloodcurdling shriek and ran off whimpering.

The men approached the sarcophagus, which was surrounded by tall weeds under the tree. They pried the lid open and found within it the cadaverous body of a nobleman—the vampire. Dusk was approaching, so they made haste and staked the creature, replaced the lid, and left the scene. They were so unnerved by the experience that they never made any further effort to destroy the vampire's body.

The tale sounds like the kind of yarn locals might spin for their own amusement, especially in light of the inclusion of some of the most common pagan, Christian, and fictional elements of the vampire myth: the crossroad, the spectral black dog, the nobleman, the silver crucifix, and the approaching dusk. Nonetheless, the wild, open areas around Creek Road

Capital Vampires

According to lore, vampires once prowled America's capital, Washington, D.C. The stories began to circulate several years after publication of Bram Stoker's *Dracula* (1897). It's more than likely that the popular book gave rise to similar tales with a local twist.

The story tells of a girl from a well-respected family who fell in love with a European prince in the 1850s. She met him at an embassy party and was immediately entranced by his stunning good looks and his piercing black eyes. He romanced her and beguiled her and her family. One night—under a full moon, of course—he secretly drained her blood, and her pale corpse was found the next morning in a clearing a few miles from her home. Her long hair hid the vampire's fang marks on her neck. The prince mysteriously disappeared.

The girl was buried in a white lace dress that was to have been her wedding gown. She was laid to rest in her family vault, only to rise herself as a vampire. People began to whisper about a white-clad girl or woman whose face was hideously distorted by wolf-like fangs.

In 1923, a writer for the *Washington Post*, Gorman Henricks, published a long account of the vampire girl's terrorizing. A woodcutter, enroute home one night, saw her specter float through the sealed vault door. He told others, but no one believed him. And then one day, he was found dead, drained of blood, with fang marks on his neck.

The woodcutter's death started a panic, and people began protecting their homes and themselves with huge bunches of garlic. Armed guards were posted at the girl's burial vault.

She did not appear again until the eve of St. George, during a thunderstorm. The guards heard the sound of squeaking hinges and saw a ghostly figure glide out and disappear into the nearby woods. The guards fled.

The next morning, a group of citizens inspected the vault, and found that a huge stone slab that had been placed over the coffin had been moved. The girl was in the coffin, her blood-red lips parted by wolflike fangs. The terrified people had the presence of mind to replace the slab, but they did nothing else—certainly nothing traditional, such as driving a stake through her heart.

The vampire specter continued to haunt the area. One male witness described it as floating through trees near the vault, emitting a maniacal laugh and smelling like a charnel house. He died a week later.

Meanwhile, the girl's distressed family moved away. No one would buy their house, and it and the burial vault fell into ruin. The hauntings seem to have ended with Hendricks' story, and the tales undoubtedly were more fiction than fact.

in Ojai still create a sense of dread and uneasiness, especially at night. It is said that a gruesome black dog is sometimes seen in the area and that a stone coffin is occasionally rediscovered beneath an overgrowth of weeds. It is also said that one can see the remains of the undead through a window in the lid of the coffin.

The haunts of reputedly real vampires are found elsewhere around the world. In the 1960s, police in Brazil were apprehensive about a vampire reported on a beach near

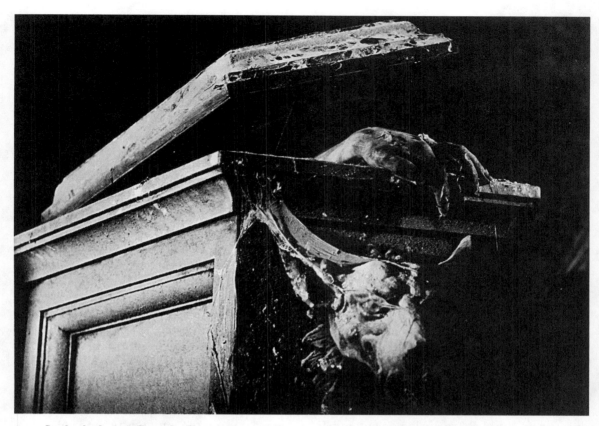

Do the dead rise? (From *Dr. Terror's House of Horrors*, Amicus Productions Ltd./Paramount Pictures Corp.)

Manaus, a city on the Amazon, deep in the interior of the country. Beaches are normally a place for sun worshipers—not the logical haunt for a vampire. However, this alleged undead had a flair for the unusual.

In 1967, residents told police they were being terrorized by a female vampire stalking the beach at night. A child said to be a victim had two small round wounds near the jugular vein. Newspaper accounts quoted eyewitnesses who described the vampire as a "blond woman with sharp and pointed teeth, wearing a miniskirt and black stockings." This sexy vampire was making no effort to be inconspicuous! While it might seem easy to track down and apprehend such an alluring and fashion-conscious predator, the creature remained at large. Public fear rose to such a pitch

at one point that seventeen of the thirty policemen assigned to the case refused to participate in the investigation.

In Italy, where dozens of vampire movies have been filmed and the city of Padova was once famed for its Vampire Festival, a real vampire was reported in the press in April 1970. The location was Lerici, a village near La Spezia in the northwestern part of the country. There, in an olive grove, a sinister figure in a long black cloak was seen on numerous occasions. Frightened villagers described it as having a thin and ashen face that was contorted "in a snarl disclosing two protruding, long, and pointed teeth." The mystery remained unsolved.

It's not surprising that many claims of real vampires are suspect. Dudley Wright, a compiler of vampire lore, wrote in the 1920s about a small graveyard in Ireland that, according to legend, held a "beautiful female vampire still ready to kill those she can lure thither by her beauty." Wright claimed the graveyard was at Waterford "under a ruined church near Strongbow's Tower." A few years later, vampire researcher Montague Summers retorted in his own writings that there was no "Strongbow's Tower," and that Reginald's Tower, the most likely possibility, merely had a legend of a frog entombed within it. It definitely was not a vampire frog!

Similarly, Highgate Cemetery, on the outskirts of London, was the subject of an inordinate amount of media attention in the 1970s as the alleged stomping grounds of a murderous vampire. The cemetery had been a favored burial ground of the Victorian rich. The old section is full, but a newer section is still open for burials. The vampire supposedly haunted the older section of the cemetery, a spooky place of tilting tombstones and vaults.

However, most of the vampire reports were given to the media by self-appointed vampire hunters who probably were looking for publicity. These poor imitations of Dr. Van Helsing, the vampire hunter in Bram Stoker's *Dracula*, built up dubious reputations with unauthorized intrusions into cemetery grounds. The media had a field day. The stories of the vampire continue to be discounted by the Friends of Highgate Cemetery, an organization that operates the cemetery.

The Greek island of Santorini has for centuries been given an unfair reputation as a place rife with *vrykolakas*, the Greek term for vampire. The reputation might be due to the island's volcanic soil, which preserves the dead perhaps too well. It might also be due to the Greek tradition of removing suspected vampire corpses to distant islands in the belief that vampires could not travel over water. Santorini, one of the southernmost of the Greek Cyclades Islands and a popular vacation place, supposedly became a favorite dumping ground.

It is true that legends of the *vrykolakas* have been strong on Santorini, as they have throughout Greece well into the twentieth century. Montague Summers claimed that around 1906, he was shown a suspected vampire cadaver being prepared for exorcism in a Santorini church. Yet, there is no cemetery—or any other place on the island—that claims to have a real, active vampire.

Rumors of vampires often have been created out of flimsy evidence. For example, mere ornate images of bats and skulls at a family gravesite in Kitzingen, Germany, triggered a devout belief among some American servicemen stationed there that the gravesite harbored a vampire—even the fictional Dracula himself was suspected! And, a cemetery in Coventry, Rhode Island, generated stories of a vampire in the 1960s on the basis of the words on one person's tombstone: "I am waiting and watching for you." The inscription actually refers to the anticipation for a heavenly reunion—not the ominous warning of a vampire.

Obviously, the power of suggestion plays a big role in any locality where a belief in vampires starts to take root. When three strangers wearing white robes were spotted after dusk in Anson County, North Carolina, in 1980, rumors spread like wildfire that vampires were abroad. Nothing came of it, but the incident shows how fear and imagination can create a panic out of anything even slightly unusual. With this knowledge, should anyone bother to stake out a cemetery in pursuit of real vampires? Should we be wary of some immortal undead out for a bite in our own neck of the woods? Taking these things too seriously would be a grave mistake.

MARTIN V. RICCARDO

II.

Ars Moriendi: The Entertaining Vampire

Sinking Teeth into the Literary Vampire

The vampire is the most popular monster in horror fiction. Images of the vampire rising from its coffin, changing into a bat or a wolf, sinking its fangs into its victim's neck, cringing at the sight of a cross before it is staked, shrieking in its coffin, or dissolving in sunlight, are familiar to everyone in the modern world. Thus, when a recent study asked a four-year-old girl if she knew what a vampire was, she replied, "It's a scary bat" (Norine Dresser, *The American Vampire*, 1989).

Many men admire the way the vampire conquers his enemies and "seduces" so many beautiful women in an ongoing series of adventures, while women tend to see him as a manifestation of the proverbial tall, dark, handsome stranger of romantic fiction. In the same vein, both men and women are fascinated by the irresistible, deadly charm of the vampiress. In all of its guises, the vampire offers us an escape from the routines and con-straints of daily life. Like the serpent in the Garden of Eden, it tempts us with the lure of the forbidden and holds forth the promise of Genesis 3:5 that, "You will not die . . . but will become like God."

Vampire stories have been popular for thousands of years and have been told and retold in every part of the world. Many primitive societies believed that hunger and thirst could compel the dead to arise from their graves in search of nourishment. Virtually every society has myths about angels, witches, and vampires. These creatures take many different forms. For instance, the *penanggalan* of Malaysia is a flying head whose digestive organs trail from its neck. It attacks babies, children, and pregnant women. However, the vampire is the antithesis of the angel, which represents love, light, and salvation and, in prescientific cultures, vampirism is usually attributed to demonology or witchcraft. In contrast, the modern, literary vampire is an erotic creation that has evolved from folklore, literature, and motion pictures.

Classic literature contains a number of stories with vampiric elements. Vampire-like monsters appear in sagas such as the *Epic of Gilgamesh*, *Beowulf*, and *Le Morte d'Arthur*, and there are many stories about undead lovers and demons who crave the pleasures of the flesh. In the seventeenth century, scholars, among them the noted French theologian Dom Augustin Calmet, investigated a series of vampiric assaults that had plagued Eastern Europe for the past hundred years. They collected hundreds of stories about peasants who had returned from their graves. Most of these revenants were harmless, but some of them assailed members of their family and drank their blood before turning on other members of the community. Finally, their tombs were opened and their bodies were staked, decapitated, or burned.

The popularity of these stories inspired a number of authors to transform the vampire from a moldering peasant wrapped in its burial shroud to a literary device for exploring the themes of blood, sex, and death in daring new ways. Heinrich August Ossenfelder's poem, "The Vampire," which concerns the nocturnal visitation of a vampire lover, caused a scandal when it was published in 1748. Casanova's *Icosameron* (1778) and some of the works of his contemporary, the Marquis de Sade, describe the ecstasies of drinking human blood. Bürger's poem "Lenore" (1773), which tells of an undead lover, and Goethe's ballad "The Bride of Corinth" (1797) are based on classical sources. The latter work is an adaptation of Philostratus' story of "Apolloneus of Tyana" (circa 225 A.D.), which tells how a young man was rescued from a lamia who planned to fatten him with pleasure before devouring his flesh. Keats' "Lamia," which relates how a bride reverts to her serpent form when discovered to be a vampire, and "La Belle Dame sans Merci" were influenced by Goethe's poems,

"Lamius" (Copyright © 1992 Robert Michael Place. Used with permission)

while many of the works of Byron, Shelley, and other Romantic poets reiterate the theme of "fatal men" and "femmes fatales" who attract and destroy those they love.

The anonymous "Wake Not the Dead" (circa 1800) may be the first story in which the modern vampire can be recognized as such. It tells of a nobleman named Walter who becomes obsessed by the memory of his deceased wife, Brunhilda. He finds a necromancer who brings her back to life. At first he is ecstatic, but Brunhilda soon develops a thirst for human blood. After destroying his household and murdering the children whom he had fathered with his second wife, she turns on him. Walter overcomes her but, finally, pays a horrible price for disturbing the natural order.

The first vampire story in the English language was written by Lord Byron's physician and companion, Dr. John George Polidori. "The Vampyre" appeared in *The New Monthly Magazine* of April 1, 1819, under the misleading byline: "a tale by Lord Byron." It is based on an unpublished fragment that Lord Byron had written at the famous literary gathering in Switzerland where Mary Shelley was inspired to write *Frankenstein*. This story relies on the ancient belief that a vampire will come back to life if its corpse is exposed to moonlight.

In "The Vampyre," Lord Ruthven (who bears an intentional resemblance to the notorious Lord Byron) is a handsome, charismatic, jaded nobleman. Young Aubrey, who is fascinated by him, agrees to accompany him on a tour of the Continent. However, they part company in Rome when Aubrey learns of his companion's immoral nature. In Greece, Aubrey falls in love with a peasant girl named Ianthe, who tells him legends about the "vampyre . . . forced every year, by feeding upon the life of a lovely female victim to prolong his existence for the ensuing months." She is murdered—her body is covered with blood and there are teeth marks on her throat. Ruthven reappears. He and Aubrey resume their travels, but Ruthven is soon shot by bandits. Before he dies, he makes Aubrey swear not to tell anyone about his misdeeds or his death for a year and a day. Ruthven revives after he is exposed to moonlight, and his corpse vanishes. When Aubrey returns to London, he is shocked to find that Lord Ruthven is not only alive but is now engaged to his sister. Aubrey is not able to convince anyone of what he knows until it is too late to save his sister from the terrible thirst of the vampire.

Although Polidori's creation has few of the dramatic strengths and weaknesses that we have come to associate with the vampire, his novella transformed the vampire from a moldering peasant to a foreign and sinister nobleman. Lord Ruthven's progeny include Bram Stoker's Count Dracula and Anne Rice's vampiric elite.

"The Vampyre" caused a sensation in Europe, where novels, stories, and plays about Lord Ruthven and other vampires flooded the marketplace. The vampire was so popular that one critic complained in *The New Monthly Magazine*, vol. 7, "the 'Broucolaca' (or vampire) has hitherto become a favourite in the English closet. But at Paris, he has been received with rapturous applause at almost all the spectacles, from the Odeon to the Porte St. Martin; all the presses of the Palais Royale have for the last two years been employed in celebrating, and describing, and speculating on him and his adventures." A novel by Charles Nodier, *Lord Ruthven ou les vampires* (1820), which was based on "The Vampyre," was, in turn, revised as a play titled *The Vampire; or, The Bride of the Isles*. The play was translated into several languages and toured Europe and North America for years. Adaptations of "The Vampyre" appeared on a regular basis until the middle of the century. The last noteworthy performance, Alexandre Dumas' play *Le Vampire*, opened at the Ambrigue-Comique in 1851.

The first vampire novel in the English language is attributed to James Malcolm Rymer. *Varney the Vampyre*, which was published in 1847 under the name Thomas Preskett Prest, was so popular that it was reissued as a 109-part penny dreadful in 1853. Unlike "The Vampyre," *Varney the Vampyre* was intended as cheap, working-class entertainment. The poor quality of the writing and the many inconsistencies in the plot are offset by its unrelenting action and its vivid portrait of the vampire. Varney is tall and gaunt, with a white, bloodless face, fierce eyes, long fangs, and long nails that appear to hang from the ends of his fingers. In a series of more or less repetitive adventures, he attacks various women and transforms some of them into vampires. Eventually, he comes to regret his actions. He commits suicide several times but is always revived by moonlight. Finally, he throws himself into the crater of Mount Vesuvius. Many incidents that originated in *Varney the Vampyre* appear in later works, but experts disagree about what influence it may have had on Stoker's *Dracula*.

The Vampire Poets

The first contemporary vampire story in English was created by a poet, Lord George Byron, and later plagiarized by his onetime companion and physician, Dr. John Polidori.

Although history records Polidori as dour and dull, filmmakers such as Ken Russell and films like *Haunted Summer* hint that his relationship with Byron deepened beyond friendship, due mostly to their mutual enjoyment of narcotics such as laudanum. Their alliance proved provident when Byron received inspiration for his short story, "The Vampyre," during a night of storm and ghost tales that also promoted the creation of Mary Shelley's *Frankenstein*.

That evening is already popular folklore, although its aftermath is not so generally known. Driven to seek safety from a lover's purported pregnancy, Byron set up home in Geneva at Villa Deodati with Polidori, Percy Bysshe Shelley, and Shelley's wife, Mary. The bonds of friendship between Byron and the Shelleys were freshly formed, and their conversations were long and animated. On one evening, at the height of a storm, the youthful lord disturbed the company with stories of madness, death, and decaying corpses. His guests responded with horrors of their own, and the fun continued into debauched chaos until Byron started to recite lines from Coleridge's *Christabel*.

Percy Shelly, much the worse for red wine and soporific drugs, glanced nervously at his wife, shrieked, and ran from the room when he saw within her the image of an old crone whose nipples opened into clear blue eyes.

Byron used the incident to produce a short story called *The Vampyre*, which was published in the *New Monthly Magazine* during 1819. The narrative had been largely rewritten by Polidori, although it contained many plagiarized plot elements. Polidori's vampire is a young aristocrat named Lord Ruthven who drinks the blood of young women. His exploits could have been the subject of a libel case had the real Lord Grey de Ruthyn chosen to prosecute. When Byron was young, de Ruthyn had tried to seduce the boy into a homosexual relationship. The young lordling told his mother of the fumbled attempt not through homophobic disgust but because Byron was used to being the hunter of younger school boys rather than the hunted. The affair does, however, point to one of the reasons why *The Vampyre* never found the publicity afforded to Bram Stoker's *Dracula*.

The original story continued its lineage of adaptation with the 1847 publication of *Varney the Vampyre*, an 800-page penny dreadful attributed to the authorship of Thomas Preskett Press (later established as written by Scotsman James Malcom Rymer). Although the aristocratic bloodsucker has been named Varney, many of his adventures are similar to those in Byron's tale. If both characters are compared with the blue-blooded Romanian count Dracula of the early twentieth century, it is clear that Lord Ruthven is still very much alive in the works of other authors.

Byron's predilection for death, blood, and the supernatural also found light outside poetry and prose. His ancestral home is situated near Nottingham, Robin Hood country, and boasts a stunning chronology of weird goings-on. One wild part of its garden is called the "Devil's Woods" because many of the Evil One's minions are said to have taken vacant possession, while within the manor house the small gray-bearded figure of Sir John Byron is said to haunt one of the rooms.

A large portrait of Sir John used to hang over the fireplace in the dining room, and on one occasion a young lady entered to find the picture gone and the specter of Sir John sitting in front of the blazing fireplace.

While his ancestors continued their raucous behavior from beyond the grave, Lord Byron displayed certain vampiric instincts. The crypt beneath the manor included several large stone coffins, one of which he ordered to be excavated. Its artifacts were used to decorate the house while the empty coffin was placed in the great hall, to the mortification of servants who refused to enter the place at night and so could not tell whether their lord slept the sleep of the undead.

If Byron's sensual and pallid demeanor gave rise to rumors that he might have sold soul and body to a blood-hungry demon during his time in Switzerland, then the stories of Aleister Crowley's infernal immortality pacts and his use of psychic vampirism surely earned him the title of the "World's Wickedest Man."

Crowley became Britain's best known occultist but also excited popularity as a novelist and metaphysical poet. It was as a writer that Crowley flattered himself during ineffectual and drug-bloated old age, although many of his contemporaries, including the authors Bram Stoker, Bulwer Lytton, and William Butler Yeats, were in awe of his magical prowess. Yeats loathed the man but often commented on Crowley's magnetic character, while occult scholars Kenneth Grant and Israel Regardie (who was for a time Crowley's personal secretary) have hinted that the magician practiced some form of psychic vampirism, drawing body magnetism or life energy from those around them.

Crowley's writings also hint that he drew sexual energies from young male and female prostitutes and that he also sacrificed a black cat during a Paris magical working to drink its blood. The incident may well be true, but Crowley was a supreme joker and it should be viewed in much the same way as the story that Byron drank cat's blood from the pallet of an upturned skull.

Psychic vampirism such as that claimed by Crowley has long been associated with the likes of Shelley, Keats, Coleridge, Blake, and other visionary poets, although they are more likely to have been victims than perpetrators.

Periods of anemic lethargy that link the lives and temperaments of these writers could be blamed on illness, but occultists Crowley, Regardie, and the English mystic Dion Fortune have all indicated that these men might have been feasts for succubi. These demons may have infested the dreams of the poets, siphoned their sexual and life energies, and as consolation induced visions from which the highest poetry could be written.

There is, of course, little hard evidence of supernatural ingress past the theories of a few occultists, but if the supposed signs are examined a case for possession can be made. Each poet demonstrates a firm conviction in the supernatural, each extended his lifestyle beyond the bounds of society—through either debauchery or saintliness—and each had a receptive mind, which was impressionable to the lure of the vampire.

Whether the trade was fair—energy for inspiration—only the poets could say.

JOHN GILBERT

Title page of *Varney the Vampire*

Most early vampire tales concerned fatal men, but the Romantic poets inspired a profusion of stories about femmes fatales. Théophile Gautier was the founder of the French decadence movement. His masterpiece, "La Morte Amoureuse" (1836), was first translated by Lafcadio Hearn as "Clarimonde." It has been retranslated and reprinted as "The Beautiful Vampire," "Clarimonda," "Clarimonde, Vampire and Harlot," "The Dead Leman," "The Dead Lover," "The Dreamland Bride," and "The Vampire." The power of this tale lies in its dreamlike eroticism and ambiguity. Father Romuald is a pious young priest who is troubled by dreams of wild, erotic liaisons with a voluptuous courtesan named Clarimonde, whom he had met shortly before her death. These dreams take over his life, and he becomes weaker and weaker. When Romuald finally tells his superior about his dreams, he is told that he is under the spell of a succubus. They dig up Clarimonde's body and sprinkle it with holy water, whereupon it turns to dust. Clarimonde enters Romuald's dreams once more to berate him for betraying the love and happiness that she has given him. It is impossible to tell if Romuald was the victim of a succubus or if his dreams were a manifestation of his lust for his beautiful neighbor.

Joseph Sheridan Le Fanu's elegant presentation of "Carmilla" (1872) concentrates on the erotic relationship between a vampiress and her prey. It is narrated by the victim, a beautiful and lonely nineteen-year-old girl named Laura. Following a coach accident Carmilla takes refuge at Laura's castle in Styria. Laura's initial fear of her pretty visitor is soon overcome by a sensual attraction. Carmilla visits her every night and caresses and kisses her until she falls asleep. When Laura's health declines, an old friend of the family realizes that she is the victim of a vampire. Carmilla vanishes, but Laura and her family discover that Carmilla is Countess Mircalla von Karnstein, who had died more than one hundred and fifty years before. They search the ruins of the Karnstein estate, where they find the vampiress sleeping in a coffin that is lined with blood. When they drive a wooden stake through her heart, she emits a terrible scream.

Other notable stories about female vampires include "The Last Lords of Gardonal" (1867) by William Gilbert, "A Mystery of the Campagna" (1887) by Anne Crawford (von Rabe), and "Ken's Mystery" by Julian Hawthorne (1888). In Mary E. Braddon's "Good Lady Ducayne" (1896), a physician injects his employer with blood he has drained from her unfortunate servants. This story was inspired by the sixteenth-century Hungarian countess, Elizabeth Bathory, who murdered hundreds of young girls and bathed in their blood in an attempt to restore her youth and beauty.

The literary vampire began to assume a number of distinct, but often overlapping, forms as different authors defined vampirism in different ways according to their beliefs and the demands of particular stories. Some writers adapted stories from folklore. "Wake Not the Dead" and E. T. A. Hoffman's "Serapion's Story" (which is taken from a tale in *The Arabian Nights*) were translated into English in 1823. In addition, Nicolai Gogol's "Viy" (1835) and stories by Alexis Tolstoy and Ivan Turgenev retold the colorful folktales of their native Russia. Other adaptations of traditional sources include Sir Richard F. Burton's translation of the humorous Sanskrit collection, *Vikram and the Vampire*, which was published in 1870, and Po Sung Ling's anthology of horror stories, *Liao-Chai chih i* (1679), which includes several tales about Oriental vampires.

Others writers created an array of energy-draining vampires. According to Christopher Frayling (*The Vampyre*, 1992), Charles Wilkins Webber's *Spiritual Vampirism* (1853) is the first novel to feature a "psychic sponge." Like Sir Arthur Conan Doyle's well known novella, *The Parasite* (1894), it equates vampirism with hypnosis. Energy-draining vampires can be men, women, or things. They can also feed on various types of energy. For instance, in W. L. Alden's story, "The Vampire" (1894), a student absorbs her teacher's talents and ideas. The ways in which energy-draining vampires obtain the sustenance they need to survive are limited only by the authors' imaginations. Two of the most bizarre examples are J. Meade Faulkner's *The Lost Stradivarius* (1892), in which an undead sorcerer drains the energy of anyone who plays a certain violin, and H. J. Chaytor's *The Light of the Eye* (1897), where a man's eyes draw the lifeforce from his victims.

Two important novels about energy-draining vampires were published in the 1890s, before Bram Stoker's *Dracula* set the standard by which all other vampires would be measured. In James Maclaren Cobban's *Master of His Fate* (1890), Julius Courtney's friends deem him a brilliant and talented young man. However, he is older than he appears to be, for he has discovered a formula that enables him to renew his youth by absorbing energy from the people he touches. As the years pass, he needs to take more and more energy until his "donors" almost die. When Julius falls in love with his friend's sister, he declares himself unworthy of her and, finally, commits suicide rather than risk harming her. Florence Marryat's *The Blood of the Vampire* (1897) is a rare book about an energy-draining femme fatale. Many of the people who befriend the young heiress, Harriet Brandt, sicken and die. The explanation for these mysterious deaths lies in the fact that, just as some people are born to give of themselves and to nourish others, "Hally" is destined to take from and, ultimately, destroy the people she cares for.

Vampiric possession is an extreme form of psychic vampirism in which a being perpetuates its existence by taking over the body, mind, or soul of its host. In Guy de Maupassant's classic story "The Horla" (1886), the narrator becomes convinced that an invisible alien presence is attacking him in his sleep and is taking over his body and his soul. The tension builds gradually as he degenerates, and when he finds that he cannot destroy the Horla (or "stranger"), he commits suicide.

Edgar Allan Poe's tales of obsession and necrophilia influenced many of the writers of his day. In two of his fantasies, femmes fatales cheat death by taking possession of another person's body. In "Morella" (1835), the title character, who is wasting away from tuberculosis, vows that she will not die. On her death bed, she gives birth to a daughter who, to her husband's horror, grows to resemble her mother in face, form, and manner. The daughter remains unnamed until she is a young woman but, when her father baptizes her "Morella," she responds, "I am here!" She falls down dead and is buried in her mother's grave—which is found to be empty. Another of Poe's stories, "Ligeia" (1838), tells of a dead woman who reanimates the corpse of her faithless husband's second wife.

Another form of vampiric possession occurs in some versions of the Faustian legend, where youth or immortality is purchased through periodic human sacrifices. Smyth Upton's *The Last of the Vampires* (1845) and G. M. W. Reynolds' *Faust* (1847) contend that vampirism is a special form of magic in which the vampire obtains life, pleasure, and power by sacrificial means. In W. Harrison Ainsworth's "Auriol" (1850), the title character obtains an elixir of life in exchange for making a human sacrifice every ten years. A similar compact is implied in "The Vampyre," and Bram Stoker said that Dracula was a "sorcerer" and a "necromancer" who had studied with the devil at the "Scholomance."

The term *pseudo-vampirism* may be applied to novels and stories that do not contain vampires per se, but revolve around some aspect of vampirism. This category includes mysteries in which a murder or murders appear to have been committed by a vampire, but ultimately have a mundane solution; villains or femmes fatales who are characterized as vampires; and miscellaneous blood-drinking creatures. Clement Robbins' *The Vampires of New York* (circa 1831) is the first detective novel with a pseudo-vampiric theme, while *Vampires* by Julien Gordon (1891) uses vampirism as a metaphor to describe the destructive relationship between a femme fatale and her suitor.

Bram Stoker's opus *Dracula* (1897) combines mystery, romance, and horror in a way that has never been duplicated. It can be read as a horror story about the primordial battle between good and evil or interpreted in terms of sexual repression and alienation or the decline of Victorian England. The most important

events in this novel—Jonathan Harker's trip to the mysterious land of Transylvania, his discovery that his host is a vampire, his encounter with Dracula's "wives," his imprisonment and death-defying escape, and how, with the help of his teacher Professor Van Helsing, he and his friends band together to avenge a murder and save his fiancée (Mina Murray) and finally slay "The King of the Vampires"—have been retold many times in many ways.

However, many of the most common assumptions about Count Dracula do not come from the novel. For example, Bram Stoker describes him as a man of advanced age, with receding hair, massive eyebrows, a thick mustache, and pointed ears. He is the epitome of evil, and his actions are inevitably self-serving and cruel. When Hamilton Deane adapted *Dracula* for the stage in 1924, he simplified the plot and transformed the count into a tragic, romantic figure who resembles Polidori's Lord Ruthven as much as Stoker's creation. To this end, he dressed the count in the formal attire and full-length cape that have become the vampire's calling card. In the finale, one of the vampire hunters drives a wooden stake into Dracula's heart. This departs from the novel, which avers "But, on that instant, came the sweep and flash of Jonathan's great knife. I shrieked as I saw it shear through the throat; whilst at the same moment Mr. Morris's bowie knife plunged into the heart. It was like a miracle; but before our very eyes, and almost in the drawing of a breath, the whole body crumbled into dust and passed from our sight."

Bram Stoker's *The Jewel of the Seven Stars* (1903) and *The Lair of the White Worm* (1911) contain vampire-like creatures, while *The Lady of the Shroud* (1909) is a romance in which a princess poses as a vampiress. "Dracula's Guest" was published posthumously in 1914, two years after Stoker's death. This story was intended as the opening chapter of *Dracula*, but the publisher deleted it due to the length of the novel.

Three vampire novels that were written

during the following years are virtually unknown today. Thaddeus Williams' *In Quest of Life* (1898), C. Bryson Taylor's *In the Dwellings of the Wilderness* (1904), and Maurice Urquhart's *The Island of Lost Souls* (1910) place vampire-like beings among various lost races. *In the Dwellings of the Wilderness* takes place in Egypt, where archaeologists unearth the mummified body of a princess who is possessed by a demon. Her body disappears during the night and, shortly thereafter, a woman as beautiful as any creature created by God or the devil appears to the workers and beckons to them to follow her into the desert. Those who do so are never seen again. Deane, the leader of the expedition, goes searching for one of the missing men. He becomes lost in the desert and is blinded by the sun, but miraculously finds his way back to camp. As he nears the excavation something bites him on the shoulder and tries to drink his blood. Somehow, he fights it off . . . Deane and the remaining members of the expedition depart the next morning, leaving the desert to its secrets.

Many of the novels of this period involve energy-draining vampires (George Sylvester Viereck's *The House of the Vampire* [1907], Reginald Hodder's *The Vampire* [1913], and Dion Fortune's *The Demon Lover* [1927]) or, like Hans Heinz Ewers' *Vampir* (1921), use vampirism as a metaphor.

The next classic vampire novel, Sydney Horler's *The Vampire*, was not published until 1935. However, such illustrious British authors as Sabine Baring-Gould, Sir Arthur Conan Doyle, Edward Heron-Allen, M. R. James, and Vernon Lee composed a number of stories with vampiric themes. F. Marion Crawford's "For the Blood Is the Life" first appeared in his collection, *Uncanny Tales* (1935). A gypsy girl named Christina is murdered by thieves, but returns to life as a vampiress. Every night, she courts a young man who had rejected her in life, draining his energy and drinking his blood. Finally, he digs up her body and drives a stake through her heart. Years later, her ghost can be seen hovering above her grave on moonlit nights. "The Transfer" (1912) by Algernon Blackwood builds to a unique confrontation between two types of energy-draining vampires—Mr. Frene, a psychic sponge who absorbs people's energy and ideas, and an arid patch of land known as the "Forbidden Corner." E. F. Benson wrote two popular stories about vampiresses. In "The Room in the Tower" (1912), a spectral hag preys upon people who sleep in a certain room, while the vampiress in "Mrs. Amworth" (1923) appears to be a respectable, middle-age woman who has recently arrived in a quiet English town.

During the 1920s, the continuing success of Bram Stoker's *Dracula* inspired many of the contributors to the new American pulp magazines to write stories about vampires. Although they were not always of the highest literary quality, these stories thrilled and entertained millions of readers. The first and most famous pulp magazine, *Weird Tales*, was initially published from 1923 to 1954. It presented such classic stories as "Four Wooden Stakes" by Victor Rowan (1925), "The Canal" by Everil Worrell (1927), "Revelations in Black" by Carl Jacobi (1933), "Doom of the House of Duryea" by Earl Peirce, Jr. (1936), "Yours Truly—Jack the Ripper" by Robert Bloch (1943), and "The Traveller" by Ray Bradbury (1943). Vampires also appeared in several of the most popular series in the "unique magazine." C. L. Moore's Northwest Smith series includes some of the most memorable vampire stories in pulp fiction. In "Shambleau" (1933), Smith falls under the spell of a Medusa-like vampiress whose victims are held in her thrall by an irresistible but obscene pleasure. Many of Clark Ashton Smith's stories about "Averoigne" and "Zothique" contain exotic lamia-like beings, while Seabury Quinn's occult detective, Jules de Grandin, confronts many different types of vampires.

Weird Tales' most famous contributor, H. P. Lovecraft, created the "Cthulu Mythos" in which vampiric, extradimensional entities who once ruled the Earth attempt to return to power. Vampirism plays an explicit part in his stories "The Hound" (1924), "The Tomb" (1926), and "The Case of Charles Dexter Ward" (1941). Many of his students, including Robert Bloch, August W. Derleth, Robert E. Howard, and Frank Belknap Long contributed new stories to the "Cthulu Mythos," and his work has continued to inspire writers such as Ramsey J. Campbell, Brian Lumley, and Colin Wilson. *Horror Stories, Strange Tales,* and other magazines published some noteworthy vampire stories during the 1930s, but no other magazine attracted the quality (or quantity) of stories that appeared in *Weird Tales.*

August Derleth and Donald Wandrei founded Arkham House in 1939 to promote the work of H. P. Lovecraft. They eventually published anthologies that featured many of the above-mentioned writers. In the 1970s, Carcosa published four collections by contributors to *Weird Tales.* Manly Wade Wellman's *Worse Things Waiting* and Hugh B. Cave's *Murgunstrumm* reprint most of their vampire stories. The latter collection, which includes the title story, "The Purr of the Cat," and "Stragella," includes macabre illustrations by Lee Brown Coye.

Most of the vampire stories that appeared in the detective pulps are mysteries about bloodless corpses with two mysterious puncture marks in their necks. In contrast, the science fiction magazines of this period contained a variety of original, rational explanations for vampirism. As Margaret L. Carter points out in *The Vampire in Literature* (1989), many of these stories portray "vampires as members of a separate species" or treat "vampirism as disease." Eric Frank Russell's novella, "Sinister Barrier" (*Unknown,* 1939) is based on the Fortean theory that the human race serves as cattle for a superior race of beings, and in A. E. Van Vogt's "Asylum" (*Astounding,* 1942), alien species at different stages of evolution fight for control of our solar system. Vampirism is portrayed as a (mis)step in our evolution toward godhood.

This story was expanded as "The Proxy Intelligence" (*If,* 1968) and reworked as a novel in 1977. It also inspired Colin Wilson's novel, *The Space Vampires,* which was filmed as *Lifeforce* in 1985.

Richard Matheson's *I Am Legend* (1954) is an outstanding example of the theme of vampirism as a disease. It is set in 1970, after a mysterious plague has decimated humankind and transformed the survivors into zombie-like vampires. Robert Neville, who is immune to this disease, is the last human being. He sleeps during the night and emerges from his hiding place each day to destroy as many of his enemies as he can. Eventually, he finds a group of people who have learned how to neutralize the worst effects of the plague. To his dismay, their new society has no place for him and, when he learns that they see him as a monster, he commits suicide. *I Am Legend* was filmed as both *The Last Man on Earth* and *The Omega Man.* It is also the basis for George A. Romero's *Night of the Living Dead* trilogy.

During the 1950s, a new generation of fans was introduced to Dracula, Frankenstein, and the Wolfman when Universal's monster movies were revived for television. Their popularity inspired Hammer Films to create a new series of vampire movies, beginning with *The Horror of Dracula* (1958), which starred Christopher Lee. *Countess Dracula, Dracula—Prince of Darkness, Dracula's Daughter,* and *The Scars of Dracula* were subsequently adapted as novels.

The world's first monster movie magazine, *Famous Monsters of Filmland,* debuted the same year. It was edited by Forrest J Ackerman who contributed stories, articles, and puns under pseudonyms such as "Dr. Acula." In addition to his diverse accomplishments (which include the creation of the comic book character "Vampirella"), "4E" has inspired many writers and befriended legions of fans. The fact that he is cast as the world's leading authority on vampires in David McDaniel's Man from U.N.C.L.E. novel, *The Vampire Affair* (1966), and in Philip José Farmer's erotic underground classic, *The Image of the Beast* (1968), is an indication of his stature and his influence on vampire fiction.

In the early 1960s, Simon Raven and Theodore Sturgeon created memorable, literate novels about human blood drinkers. Sturgeon's masterpiece, *Some of Your Blood* (1961), broke new ground by discussing the drinking of menstrual blood. Leslie H. Whitten's *Progeny of the Adder* (1965) is set in Washington, D.C., where a detective who is attempting to solve a series of murders fails to realize that they are the work of a vampire. In the later part of the 1960s, Dan Ross began a series of novels based on the ABC television series "Dark Shadows." *Barnabas Collins* (1968) tells how Barnabas became a vampire as the result of a curse and how he arrived at Collinwood.

The copyright on *Dracula* expired in 1968. Thus, the 1970s saw a deluge of novels about Count Dracula. One of the earliest books, *The Adult Version of Dracula*, is a pornographic adaptation of Stoker's opus. Other novels, such as Gail Kimberly's *Dracula Began* and Asa Drake's *Crimson Kisses* (which was written by C. Dean Andersson and Nina Romberg in 1981 and revised as *I Dracula* [1993]), answer the question of how Dracula became a vampire. The events in Raymond Rudorff's *The Dracula Archives* (1971) take place before those narrated by Stoker and link Dracula with Vlad the Impaler and Countess Elizabeth Bathory, while Donald F. Glut's *Frankenstein Meets Dracula* (1977) is a continuation of both *Frankenstein and Dracula*. In John Shirley's bizarre offering, *Dracula in Love* (1979), Dracula's son, who is an executive in San Francisco, is called upon by God (Lucifer/Bill/Marg) to help overcome Dracula and his followers to prepare him for a new incarnation.

The 1970s saw the emergence of three series of novels about the the King of the Undead. Robert Lory's series and Peter Tremayne's series bring the count into the modern world. The first book in Fred Saberhagen's series (*The Dracula Tape* [1975]) retells the story of Dracula from a unique, satiric point of view that, nevertheless, remains true to Stoker's creation. The much-maligned count provides alternative explanations for most of the important events in Stoker's novel in an attempt to convince us that he has been unjustly portrayed as a monster by hordes of superstitious peasants and stake-wielding idiots. In the following book, *The Holmes-Dracula File* (1978), Dracula encounters Sherlock Holmes. The eighth book in this series, *Seance for a Vampire* (1994) brings them together again.

Many subsequent books rework the basic elements of *Dracula* in original ways. Stephen King's second novel, *'Salem's Lot* (1975), and John Skipp and Craig Spector's splatter punk opus *The Light at the End* (1986)—in which the vampires begin their conquest by taking over the subways of New York—are outstanding examples of this practice. In *Danse Macabre*, the master of modern horror says, "When I conceived of the vampire novel which became *'Salem's Lot*, I decided [to] use the book partially as a form of literary homage. . . . So my novel bears an intentional similarity to Bram Stoker's *Dracula*." *'Salem's Lot* speculates on what might happen if a vampire descended on a small town in modern America. The first part of the book describes 'Salem's Lot and the mundane hopes and fears of its inhabitants in detail. Thus, when a horde of vampires begins to take over the town, we participate in the suspense and terror that overwhelm the survivors. Finally, the vampire hunters are forced to overcome their fears and confront Barlow, the Master Vampire, in his lair.

Although classic vampire novels, such as Les Daniels' Don Sebastian de Villanueva series (1978 to 1991), Robert R. McCammon's *They Thirst* (1981), and George R. R. Martin's *Fevre Dream* (1982) continued to appear on a regular basis, the writers of the 1970s started to move away from the three Vs of vampire, victim, and vampire hunter to concentrate on the

The first in Les Daniels's Sebastian de Villanueva
vampire novels

vampire's motivations and emotions. This transition is evident in Robert Aickman's elegant novella, *Pages from a Young Girl's Journal* (which debuted in *The Magazine of Fantasy & Science Fiction* in February 1973). A young girl who is vacationing in Europe is alienated from her family and the stifling conventions of nineteenth-century society. It is easy to sympathize with her—until it becomes evident that she is awaiting the coming of her vampire lover who will transform her into one of the undead elite.

The concept of vampirism as a desirable state was brought to the attention of the public by the first book in Anne Rice's series, *Interview with the Vampire* (1976). This novel captures the magic, romance, and sensuality of the vampire myth and shows the reader what it is like to *be* a vampire. Louis, who is one of the oldest living vampires, examines his life from eighteenth-century New Orleans to the present day. He revels in the heightened powers and sensuality which life as a vampire affords him, while struggling to justify his existence as an immortal predator. *The Vampire Lestat* (1985) and *The Queen of the Damned* (1988) focus on the adventures of Lestat, the vampire who created Louis, and his attempt to trace the origins of the vampire to ancient Egypt. In *The Tale of the Body Thief* (1992), Lestat seizes a chance to regain his humanity.

Chelsea Quinn Yarbro's Count de Saint-Germain series was inspired by the mysterious eighteenth-century alchemist of the same name. Unlike many other members of the undead, Saint-Germain (and his faithful servant, Roger) have grown in wisdom over the years. He is more learned, sophisticated, and compassionate than his human adversaries, and we come to admire this count, not for any powers he possesses, but because he embodies the noblest qualities of the human race. The novels in this series are rich in historical detail. The first book, *Hotel Transylvania* (1978), is set in Revolutionary France where the count rescues his love, Madelaine de Montalia, from a Satanic cult. Subsequent novels are set in such exotic times and places as Nero's Rome and de-Medici's Florence. In *Out of the House of Life* (1990), Madelaine travels to Egypt in an attempt to discover the origin of the man who had given her eternal life.

Suzy McKee Charnas' episodic novel *The Vampire Tapestry* (1980) concentrates on the relationship between a predator and its prey. Dr. Edward Lewis Weyland is a member of an ancient race of predators that can escape detection by hibernating for long periods of time. When he emerges from his "grave," he forgets the details of his previous incarnations and the pain and suffering he has caused his victims. This enables him to assume a new identity in keeping with social and technological changes that have taken place. Part Four, *Unicorn Tapestry*, won a Nebula Award for best novella.

Early vampire literature often revolved around the "discovery" that vampires actually exist but, by the 1980s, it was evident that most readers took their existence for granted. This freed authors to construct original explanations about the origin of vampires and the nature of their powers. In Whitley Strieber's *The Hunger*, Miriam Blaylock is a member of a species of predators that has evolved separately from *homo sapiens*. Jan Jenning's *Vampyr* provides many well-thought-out explanations for vampires' strengths and weaknesses, while Garfield Reeves-Stevens' medical thriller, *Bloodshift*, portrays vampirism as the next step in our evolution. S. P. Somtow's haunting novel, *Vampire Junction*, revolves around Timmy Valentine, a fourteen-year-old vampire rock star who has emerged from the collective unconscious and can assume the form of people's deepest fears. The second novel in this series, *Valentine*, appeared in 1992. In Brian Lumley's *Necroscope* (1986), Harry Keogh of the British Secret Service is a psychic who can communicate with the dead. He and his Russian counterpart, Boris Dragosini, make contact with a vampire who has been buried in Romania and who lusts for freedom and revenge. In *Necroscope III: The Source*, Soviet scientists accidentally open a portal to the realm of the Wamphyri. The Vampire World series, which began with the publication of *Blood Brothers* (1992) is set on the hostile the planet of the ferocious Vamphyr warriors. In Nancy A. Collins' *Sunglasses After Dark* (1989), Sonja Blue is a debutante, a prostitute, and a vampiress who hunts the world of "changelings"—vampires, werewolves, etc., who live and hunt among us—to find the vampire who created her.

Many of the previously mentioned works are still in print, and many recent vampire novels reflect the influence of these books but develop the myth of the vampire in new and original directions. Dan Simmons' critically acclaimed *Carrion Comfort* (1989) concerns a society of energy-draining vampires, while his *Children of the Night* (1992) links Dracula and the vampire legends of Eastern Europe with a terrifying modern killer—AIDS. Kim Newman's *Bad Dreams* (1990) depicts highly evolved energy-draining vampires, while Bentley Little's *The Summoning* (1993) is a rare jewel about Oriental folk vampires. Two recent works deserve special mention. Poppy Z. Brite's first novel, *Lost Souls* (1992), is a classic vampire novel that combines the power and horror of Bram Stoker's *Dracula* with the desire to transcend the constraints of daily life. In contrast, Kim Newman's homage to vampiriana, *Anno Dracula* (1992), defies classification. It might be described as a horror/fantasy/satire novel that plays with what might have happened had Dracula succeeded in taking over England.

Although most vampire literature contains elements of horror, an increasing number of works also fall into other genres. Some of the best recent vampire novels may be classified as science fiction or fantasy. Brian W. Aldiss' *Dracula Unbound* (1991) portrays Dracula as a pterodactyl-like predator who threatens the future of humankind, while Christopher Pike's elegant *The Season of Passage* (1992) takes place on Mars. Kay Reynold's *American Vampire* (1994), which centers around a young vampire's struggle to meet the challenges of his new-found powers, portrays vampires as the link between our world and the realm of fantasy.

Mystery or suspense is an important element in a large number of vampire books. In Barbara Hambly's *Those Who Hunt the Night* (1988), a diplomat is pressed into service to discover who is killing the vampires of Victorian London. Richard Laymon's *The Stake* (1991) involves a group of friends who find the body of a young girl whose heart has been pierced by a wooden stake. The story revolves around what might happen if they pull out the stake. In Sherri Gottlieb's erotic thriller *Love Bite* (1994), a detective in Los Angeles comes to the conclusion a recent series of murders could only have been committed by a vampiress. Sharon Bainbridge's *Blood and Roses* (1993) challenges the reader to guess who the vampire is. Lucius Shepard's *The Golden* (1993) places a vampire detective in a surrealistic castle, and two new series feature vampire detectives. Patricia N. Elrod's Vampire Files series takes place in Chicago during the 1920s, while Tanya Huff's Blood Price series is set in Toronto.

Other vampire novels emphasize action and adventure. In Patrick Whalen's Monastery series, vampires who threaten to take over Seattle are destroyed by a nuclear explosion. Lois Tilton's novel *Vampire Winter* speculates on how a vampire might survive a nuclear winter, while her *Darkness on the Ice* places a Nazi vampire at the North Pole. John Steakley's *Vampire$* revolves around a group of professional vampire hunters, while Scott Ciencin's Vampire Odyssey series features a series of confrontations between a female police officer and the vampires who have claimed her daughter.

Recent years have also seen the appearance of an increasing amount of sexually explicit vampire material. Ray Garton's novels *Live Girls* (1987) and *Lot Lizards* involve vampire prostitutes, while Ron Dee's vampire novels combine violence and eroticism. Karen Minns' *Virago* (1990) and Jewelle Gomez's *The Gilda Stories* (1991) are explicit lesbian vampire novels, while John Peyton Cooke, Scott Edelman, and Jeffrey N. McMahan have written books about homosexual vampires.

The best vampire literature entertains us with suspense, horror, romance, and sensuality, while providing an outlet for our aggressive instincts and antisocial behavior. It is impossible to predict what form it will take in the future, for the vampire has transcended horror literature to become a powerful and fascinating metaphor for exploring our concerns about mortality and life after death. However, we can be sure that Dracula and his descendants will continue to entertain generations of new fans in whatever shape they assume.

ROBERT EIGHTEEN-BISANG

From Villain
to Hero

Everybody knows what a vampire is—a corpse reanimated by demonic forces, sustaining its unnatural life by consuming the blood of the living. According to popular myth, the vampire sleeps in a coffin by day, flits around in bat form by night, and suffers from a fatal allergy to sunlight. Garlic and religious symbols terrify him; a stake through the heart kills him. Moreover, the vampire projects an irresistible aura of sexual magnetism. The male vampire wears a tuxedo and a black cape, and often speaks with a heavy Eastern European accent. The female frequently wears a shroud like a white gown, talks like Eva Gabor, and has huge come-hither eyes and waist-length hair, usually black.

But this vampire that everybody knows is not universally typical, especially in contemporary science fiction and fantasy. When Bram Stoker created Count Dracula in his 1897 classic gothic novel, he was building upon an es-

tablished literary tradition that had grown throughout the nineteenth century. Although Stoker did extensive research into the vampire legend and superstition, his Dracula differs in important ways from the vampire of European folklore. In turn, the popular image of the vampire, drawn from motion pictures rather than directly from Stoker's novel, is far from identical to the Dracula Stoker envisioned. Furthermore, the various images of vampirism in the fiction of the last few decades depart still more radically from both Stoker's novel and the pop culture stereotype.

The magnetic fascination of the vampire began as a literary construct, with little or no basis in folklore. The typical Eastern European vampire was a filthy, shambling peasant, who returned from the grave to terrorize and prey upon his family.

Yet when the vampire entered English literature, during the Romantic period, he was transmuted into an elegant, aristocratic seducer. The earliest prose vampire tale in English ("The Vampyre," 1819, by John Polidori) was loosely based on an unfinished story by Byron, with the poet modeling the vampire after himself. This character began to shape the pattern for the nineteenth-century male vampire as Byronic villain-hero, a hypnotically compelling creature possessed by satanic pride or secret sorrows. We meet his nonsupernatural counterpart, of course, in heroes such as Heathcliff in Emily Brontë's *Wuthering Heights* and Mr. Rochester in Charlotte Bronte's *Jane Eyre*. The female vampire of nineteenth-century fiction is patterned after the fatal woman of the Romantic sensibility, such as Keats's Lamia and *La Bella Dame Sans Merci*.

Vampires appearing in Victorian prose sometimes appeal to the reader's sympathies. *Varney The Vampyre or the Feast of Blood* (1847), an 800-page-plus penny dreadful, is a tale expressing Sir Francis Varney's sorrow for the havoc he wreaks as a vampire. Finally, in a fit of remorse, he commits suicide in the crater of Vesuvius. Carmilla, in Sheridan Le Fanu's tale of the same name (1871), seems desperate for her victim's love. It was always taken for granted that vampirism itself was inherently evil. If the vampire aroused sympathy, it was in spite of its diabolic nature. The last two decades, on the other hand, have produced novels in which the vampire is not necessarily evil and may be the hero, or heroine.

Stoker's Dracula stands firmly in the Byronic tradition. Nonetheless, there are hints of deeper sorrow and an alienation from the place and time in which he finds himself. Dracula is far less overtly (as opposed to subliminally) erotic than his film counterparts. Stoker, in keeping with the folklore sources, gives him animalistic features—bushy eyebrows, blunt-fingered, coarse hands, hairy palms, and foul breath. When the heroine, Mina, describes her inability to resist him as he drinks her blood, she implies rape rather than seduction.

Stoker's Van Helsing continually asserts that the vampire is evil, the emissary of Satan on Earth. Stoker would have been appalled at the image of Dracula portrayed by actor Frank Langella, in both his stage and screen roles.

The shift in emphasis seems traceable to the Bela Lugosi film (1931), from which we get our cultural stereotype of the vampire. This movie picked up and magnified the subliminal eroticism of the novel, as well as the very slight hints of Count Dracula's sorrow over his isolation from humanity. For example, Lugosi's Dracula quotes from Algernon Swinburne, "There are worse things waiting for man than death," a line that does not appear in the book. Later films expand upon this erotic and sympathetic approach. Evidence for the dominance of this model can be seen in the Langella *Dracula*—not only the lush eroticism of its imagery but the very fact that this sensuality is what we remember it for. Audiences tend to overlook this Dracula's ruthless acts of violence, such as the murder of Renfield.

It is intriguing that the vampire becomes a hero in our culture for many of the same traits that made his nature threatening and repellent to the Victorians—for example, the vampire's sexual aggressiveness, which seemed to authors such as Stoker especially horrifying when displayed by women. Carol A. Senf, author of *The Vampire in 19th Century English Literature* (1988) remarks that in twentieth-century fiction, "There has been increasing emphasis on the positive aspects of the vampire's eroticism and on its right to rebel against the stultifying constraints of society." As Senf puts it, we tend to admire the vampire's "romantic independence" and "refusal to conform to arbitrary social standards," which to the average Victorian would have seemed simply dangerous—again, especially when expressed by a female character.

Leonard Wolf says, in *A Dream of Dracula* (1972), "The vampire fascinates a century that is as much frightened as it is exhilarated by its rush towards sexual freedom." Wolf calls Drac-

ula "the willing representative of the tempta-
tions, and crimes, of the Age of Energy. He is
huge and we admire size; strong, and we admire strength. . . . He has collected on the
devil's bargain, the infinitely stopped moment." After all, we are afraid of aging and
death and addicted to instant gratification. The
vampire offers us a chance at eternal life and
youth.

In a predominately secular society, we
seem to accept the vampire's powers as an as-
set without worrying about whether those
powers come from the devil. For example, two
novels by Lee Killough, *Blood Hunt* (1987) and
Blood Links (1988), feature a police officer who,
after his involuntary transformation into a
vampire, uses his hypnotic talent and superhuman strength in his law enforcement duties.
In Carol Page's study of contemporary blood
drinkers, *Blood Lust* (1991), she attributes the
vampire's allure for modern Americans to
power, sexuality, immortality, and the romantic aura that surrounds most cinematic vampires as well as those created by authors such
as Anne Rice. A typical real-life "vampire" (i.e.,
an individual who literally believes herself to
be a vampire) interviewed by Page "has created an elaborate belief system around her
blood drinking to romanticize and justify it,
seemingly borrowing most of her beliefs from
the vampire movies."

Not that the "vampire-as-the-offspring-of-
Satan" figure has completely died out. It is
masterfully developed in Stephen King's
'Salem's Lot (1975). King says that in writing
'Salem's Lot he "decided to largely jettison the
sexual angle, feeling that in a society where
homosexuality, group sex, oral sex . . . have
become matters of public discussion . . . the
sexual engine that powered Stoker's book
might have run out of gas." King modified this
view by the time he wrote his multimedia
study of horror, *Danse Macabre*. However blasé
society as a whole may have become about
sex, to each new generation discovering its
wonders it is still a fascinating and terrifying

phenomenon, perhaps even more terrifying
nowadays, when society seems to expect such
sophistication of its teenagers. For young boys,
says King, the vampire film confirms the belief
that "sex is scary; sex is dangerous." The sad
truth that sex is more frightening today than
when King wrote these words is reflected in
the fact that AIDS has already been featured in
several vampire tales.

King is not the only critic to assume that the
popular image of vampirism is mainly an adolescent male fantasy, a theory that neglects the
powerful appeal of vampire fiction to female
readers. In fact, writers of sympathetic, erotic
vampire fiction tend to be predominately female. Writers and fans alike find inspiration in
Count Saint-Germain, the 4,000-year-old hero
of Chelsea Quinn Yarbro's distinguished series
of historical novels. Saint-Germain's eroticism
is a whole-body phenomenon, not narrowly
focused on the genitals. Furthermore, it is an
experience of profound mutuality. Saint-
Germain can get full nourishment from blood
only if the donor—the word *victim* doesn't fit
here—gives herself willingly and shares in his
rapture. P. N. Elrod, female author of the *Vampire Files* series, has her vampire detective's
mistress tell him, "I really prefer it your
way. . . . When you do it this way, it just goes
on and on." The implied contrast with the limitations of mortal men is obvious.

The vampires in these novels are, of course,
not demonic. In fact, Yarbro shows her vampire count, in *Hotel Transylvania*, holding a coven of Satanists at bay with a consecrated
communion wafer, a stunning reversal of the
motif in *Dracula*. In another vampire detective
story, *Blood Price* (1991) by Tanya Huff, the
vampire is also pitted against a Satanist. When
an apparent divine manifestation banishes a
demon, Henry the vampire immediately
kneels and says a Hail Mary, just to be on the
safe side. Anne Rice's vampires, far more violent than Yarbro's, are not diabolical. They are
simply intent on surviving and coming to
terms with their altered condition. They in-

habit a nihilistic universe. In the original book, *Interview with the Vampire* (1976), the narrator, Louis, doesn't know where his kind come from, but it certainly isn't from the devil. "That is," he says, "how would you say today—bullshit."

Another way of creating a vampire who is not demonic, and making him or her attractive to the reader, is to take him out of the supernatural realm altogether. Numerous science fiction authors have presented vampires either as suffering from nonsupernatural illness or as a member of another species sharing the Earth with us. If the vampire is a creature of the natural world, it cannot be innately evil, any more than a tiger or a shark. In fact, portraying the vampire as an endangered species is one way of generating sympathy for him or her.

Miriam, the heroine of Whitley Strieber's *The Hunger* (1981), frequently kills, yet she remains an appealing and sympathetic character. She is also an erotic figure, thanks to her telepathic power of sharing her victim's emotions—naturalistic vampire fiction need not jettison the traditional sexual appeal. In her liaisons, direct mind-to-mind communion heightens the human partner's passion. Because she is the last survivor of her species, Miriam's isolation dominates the novel. The author explains, "She was lonely, and human beings gave her the love pets give." Moreover, she attributes her kind's extinction partly to the dangerous allure of humanity: "If one loved human beings, how could one also kill them and still be happy enough with oneself to love one's own kind, and bear young?"

Very different in tone is another portrayal of a solitary vampire as a species of one. In *The Vampire Tapestry* (1980), by Suzy McKee Charnas, the vampire anthropologist Dr. Weyland is the ultimate in isolation; he cannot remember any others of his kind, not even his own parents. He has survived for thousands of years by withdrawing into suspended animation, whenever life in the current place and time becomes too hazardous. Throughout the novel Weyland is referred to, and refers to himself, as an animal—a lynx, a tiger, a hawk. In the opening episode, "The Ancient Mind at Work," Weyland delivers a lecture in which he explores how nature would design a vampire, toying with his audience by detailing his own characteristics as the perfect predator. Charnas's stated objective in writing the story was to deromanticize the vampire, to present the nonsupernatural vampire as a superbly adapted beast of prey, equal or superior to us in intelligence, but with "the inner emotional life of the average house cat."

Yet, strangely, Charnas's work does not escape the sexual fascination of the vampire. Female readers, she found, consider Weyland as attractive as certain female characters within the novel do, despite Weyland's own contempt for pop culture vampires who "mix up dinner with sex," and his scornful remark, "Would you mate with your livestock?" The vampire engages in sex, though, to maintain his human facade, and in one case, with the psychologist Floria Landauer, who discovers his secret, he shares genuine communion. But Weyland's sexual appeal is understated. Central to Charnas's strategy in making Weyland attractive is the way she contrasts his predation to the far worse things people do to each other.

This device is frequently used in vampire stories. Rice's Lestat preys on human predators, the thieves and rapists who roam the streets. In Elrod's *Vampire Files*, the hero Jack's enemies are often brutal gangsters who inflict cruel deaths on their fellow men—more horrible than a peace-loving vampire who lives on cattle blood and takes an occasional sip from his very willing girlfriend. *Blood Alone* (1990), the second book in Elaine Bergstrom's alien vampire series, contrasts her noble, creative vampires, artists in stained glass, with the human horrors of World War II. In *The Vampire Tapestry*, Weyland seldom kills, except when driven to the act in self-defense. Most of his victims are none the worse for the small amount of blood he takes. In contrast to the destructive ambitions of human predators, Weyland says, "I wish only to satisfy my appetite in peace." Floria, the psychologist, reflects on the contrast between Weyland and some of her human patients, who have done far more damage to their fellow beings.

Another of Charnas's strategies is to show the vampire as vulnerable, helpless, and the object of persecution. In the novel's second episode, "The Land of Lost Content," Weyland has been shot by a would-be vampire killer. Near death, he becomes the prisoner of an opportunistic New Yorker who cooperates with a fanatical Satanist cult leader in putting the vampire on exhibition to a select audience of paying customers. The cultist plans to use Weyland as the centerpiece in a May Eve ceremony, with the vampire's death as the climax. Confined, humiliated, and finally starved in preparation for the rite, Weyland is clearly both less dangerous and less evil than the Satanist who wants to exploit him.

In *The Vampire Tapestry*, the vampire interacts with one person whom he treats as an exception to his general rule of considering everyone his prey—Floria Landauer, the psychologist whom he originally plans to use as a tool for keeping his professorship, but to whom he eventually reveals his true nature. Part of the appeal of Weyland's vulnerability is connected with his (at first reluctant) act of reaching out to a human being. Against his will, he finds that the more he reveals himself to Floria, the more real she becomes to him, no longer simply a potential food source. When she begins to know him, she perceives that, "Beneath your various facades your true self . . . wants, needs to be honored as real and valuable through acceptance by another. I try to be that other." She wishes neither to destroy, use, nor reform him, but simply to understand him. The allure of the vampire as alien is the allure of the Other. We are fasci-

nated with getting to know a mind that is almost human, yet not human, a mind that gives us a fresh, skewed viewpoint on our life and its limitations.

A similar human-vampire interaction dominates *Fevre Dream* (1982) by George R. R. Martin, set in the Mississippi riverboat era. Joshua, the vampire protagonist of Martin's novel, belongs to an alien race living secretly among us. Orphaned in childhood, Joshua grows up thinking himself an aberrant human being, possessed by an uncontrollable craving for blood at monthly intervals. By the time he rediscovers his own people, he has developed a sympathy for mortals that inspires him to spend his years searching for a blood substitute that will free his kind from the need to kill. Joshua has perfected this potion and has gathered a band of followers who share his dream of living without the slaughter of human prey. Joshua befriends a steamboat captain, Abner Marsh, to whom he tells the story of his childhood and his quest. This self-disclosure is a daring innovation. Joshua says, "I have never told the truth to one of you before." Captain Marsh retorts, "To one of the cattle. . . . Well, I never listened to no vampire before, so we're even."

A major theme of Anne Rice's *Vampire Chronicles* is self-revelation, as indicated by the very title *Interview with the Vampire*. In *The Vampire Lestat* (1985), the second book in the *Vampire Chronicles*, Lestat is targeted by the more conservative vampires because he dares to reveal the truth about his kind to the mortal world, while veiled in the glamour of a rock band.

J. R. R. Tolkien, in *On Fairy-Stories*, maintains that the desire to "hold communion with other living things" is a perennial human wish. Hence the talking animals so common in fairy tales. In real life, says Tolkien, "other creatures are like other realms with which man has broken relations, and sees now only from the outside at a distance." This kind of vampire satisfies the same needs addressed by the character of Commander Spock in *Star Trek*. A character like Spock, the alien who is also partly human, feeds the longing to understand a being that is both like and unlike humanity. Alien vampires of contemporary popular fiction feed this same desire.

These stories thrust into the foreground the question of how we should behave when we meet our first nonhuman intelligence. Ecological awareness dictates that if vampires exist and are an endangered species, they ought to be treated with as much care as dolphins, whales, and mountain gorillas. However, other ethical issues arise when dealing with a creature that is not quite so harmless as a gorilla. Can a vampire be blamed for preying on us any more than most people in our society can be blamed for eating cattle? Is a vampire any more guilty than a man-eating tiger? Each is only following the dictates of survival. But we do protect ourselves by shooting man-eating tigers if necessary, and few people seem to mind the slaughter of sharks in the *Jaws* films. We protect wolves in some locations, but pay bounties for shooting them in other regions. On the other hand, some creatures once considered dangerous beasts to be exterminated are now seen as worthy of protection, such as killer whales.

Both ecological responsibility and our cultural ideal of respect for the rights of the Outsider give vampires a claim on our sympathy. Anne Rice has compared her vampire subculture with the gay subculture and has noted that her novels have a strong appeal for homosexual readers. Also, she made Lestat a rock musician because they "are expected to be completely wild, completely unpredictable and completely themselves, and they are rewarded for that"—the glorification of the Outsider. Many science fiction and fantasy authors use vampirism to explore these issues, and the problem is even confronted in at least one series for children.

Danny, the protagonist of Mel Gilden's *Fifth Grade Monsters* novels, has a group of peculiar friends, among them a vampire boy, C. D. Bitesky. C. D. wears a tuxedo and cape (black most of the year but white for summer), turns into a bat at will, and carries around a thermos filled with a red liquid called Fluid of Life. He is not a supernatural, undead creature; he was born a vampire, and his parents and all their relatives are vampires. C. D. and the other little monsters are treated like members of an intriguing minority group.

In the third novel of the series, *There's a Batwing in My Lunchbox*, by Ann Hodgman, the only one not written by Gilden though it shares the "different is okay" theme that dominates the series, the fifth-grade teacher plans a traditional Thanksgiving feast. C. D. Bitesky is the only child with the courage to speak up and point out that a turkey and cranberry sauce do not carry much cultural resonance for him. Other students, emboldened by C.D.'s example, agree that immigrants who arrived after the Pilgrims should receive equal consideration. So the teacher changes the plan, asking each child to bring traditional recipes from his or her own family background, for a multicultural Thanksgiving party. We could hardly find a clearer example of the equation between vampires and real-life persecuted minorities.

In adult vampire fiction, as we have seen, often the difference is the attraction. The lure of the Other, the Outsider, speaks to our fascination, both intellectual and emotional, with exploring the unknown, nourishes our desire to communicate with a mind like and yet unlike our own, and also carries a large measure of sexual resonance. The erotic power of Otherness is seldom better expressed than in the scene in *The Vampire Tapestry* where Weyland and Floria share sexual intimacy. Lying with her vampire, Floria, as our representative within the story, experiences "unlike closing with unlike across whatever likeness may be found."

MARGARET L. CARTER

Bram Stoker: The Lifeblood of Dracula

Unlike many other authors of celebrated novels, Bram Stoker lived a fairly simple, conventional life. In his own time he was better known for his work as actor Henry Irving's theater manager than for his literary efforts. And by the latter half of the twentieth century, few people could even say who created the evil Count Dracula. The vampire has a life of its own, but the man who gave birth to the literary vampire had been nearly forgotten.

Bram, or Abraham, was the third child of Abraham and Charlotte Stoker, born November 8, 1947, in Dublin. The elder Stoker was a civil servant; his mother was an ambitious promoter for her five sons, though neglectful of Bram's two sisters. Bram came into the world quite sickly and was not expected to live. He did not walk until age eight. He survived, however, and grew to be the largest member of the family: a hearty, red-haired giant over six feet tall.

By the age of sixteen Bram already had begun "scribbling." He entered Trinity College at Dublin University in November 1864, throwing himself into athletics and philosophical debate. He loved theater and literature, particularly Walt Whitman's controversial *Leaves of Grass*. Bram's tastes ran to the macabre early on, perhaps fostered by his mother's harrowing tales of the Irish cholera epidemic of 1832.

Upon graduation in 1870, he followed his father into civil service at Dublin Castle, a dearly monotonous career. Nights were spent at the theater. Incensed at the lack of quality of dramatic criticism in the Dublin papers, he began writing the dramatic reviews for the *Dublin Mail* in November 1871. He was so confident of his opinions and the need for such a column that he wrote without pay.

Stoker's first book was the dry *Duties of Clerks of Petty Sessions in Ireland* (1879). His fa-

Like Mother, Like Son

Bram Stoker probably got his first taste of horror listening to Charlotte's stories of the Irish cholera epidemic of 1832. Various passages in his stories mirror her description of the terror her townspeople faced, as in this account, which she wrote in 1832, when she was twenty-four (in *A Biography of Dracula: The Life Story of Bram Stoker*, by Harry Ludlam, 1962, p. 26):

One action I vividly remember. A poor traveler was taken ill on the roadside some miles from the town, and how did those samaritans tend him? They dug a pit and with long poles pushed him living into it, and covered him up quick, alive. . . .

In a very few days the town became a place of the dead. No vehicles moved except the cholera carts or doctors' carriages. Many people fled, and many of these were overtaken by the plague and died by the way. . . .

There was a remarkable character in the town, a man of great stature who had been a soldier, and was usually known as "long Sergeant Callen." He took the cholera, was thought dead, and a coffin was brought. As the coffin maker had always a stack of coffins ready on hand, with the burials following immediately on the deaths, they were much of a uniform size and, of course, too short for long Sergeant Callen. The men who were putting him in, when they found he would not fit, took a big hammer to break his legs and "make" him fit. The first blow roused the sergeant from his stupor, and he started up and recovered. I often saw the man afterwards.

JOANNE P. AUSTIN

ther encouraged young Bram's career at Dublin Castle, warning him that the theater could be dangerous to his pension.

But he persisted. In 1876, the English actor Henry Irving returned to Dublin in *Hamlet*. Stoker had been thrilled with Irving's realistic portrayals years earlier, and flattered him in his theater reviews. Irving invited Stoker to dinner, and the two men discovered they shared many views. After dinner, Irving's recitation of the *The Dream of Eugene Aram* left Stoker profoundly moved, and Irving, also overcome with emotion, presented him with a signed photograph.

For the next two years, the men corresponded regularly and saw each other whenever their work permitted. By September 1878, Irving had purchased the Lyceum Theater in London and asked Stoker to be his acting manager. Stoker immediately resigned his position at Dublin Castle.

The other major event in 1878 was Stoker's marriage to Florence Anne Lemon Balcombe. She was a great beauty and eleven years Stoker's junior. Florence's other major suitor was Oscar Wilde, who was a homosexual and probably pursued her out of convention. The two men remained rivals only a short time; Florence and Bram were married on December 4 and left five days later to join Henry Irving in Birmingham. The Stokers' only child, son Noel, was born a year later on December 29, 1879.

Joining Irving was like a second marriage. Stoker threw himself into the management of Irving's Theater and affairs. So many details had to be acknowledged: the remodeling of the building, hiring of the actors, establishing the repertory, covering the enormous debts already accumulating. Stoker rarely wrote fewer than fifty letters a day. The theater's grand reopening on December 30, 1878, was a great success, and even critics gave Stoker credit. From that first night onward, Stoker always stood in evening dress in the vestibule, greeting theatergoers and watching the wings. He

This portrait of Bram Stoker anchors a Stoker memorabilia exhibit at the Count Dracula Fan Club (Courtesy Count Dracula Fan Club)

worshiped Irving as a god, and everything was done to make the actor's endeavors triumphant and effortless.

Playing Ophelia to Irving's Hamlet in that opening production was the famous actress Ellen Terry. She appeared with Irving's company for over twenty years, and Stoker found her radiant, beautiful, and full of life. She referred to Stoker as her "mama" and to herself as his "dutiful daughter." The three of them—Irving, Stoker, and Terry—*were* the Lyceum in the late nineteenth century.

As Irving's star ascended, so did the Stokers' place in society; Florence reigned over dinner with all of London's elite from their home at 27 Cheyne Walk along the river in Chelsea. They entertained Alfred, Lord Tennyson, J. McNeill Whistler, Sir Edward Burne-Jones, Mark Twain, author Hall Caine, and W. S. Gilbert. Oscar Wilde also frequented Florence's salon.

The Stokers sold 27 Cheyne Walk three

years later. On September 14, 1882, Stoker dived into the river to save a man trying to commit suicide. After a five-minute struggle, Stoker and the unidentified man were brought aboard the riverboat *Twilight*, and Stoker took him to his home. Stoker's brother, Dr. George Stoker, was unable to revive him, and Florence never got over finding a corpse in the dining room. Stoker received the Bronze Medal of the Royal Humane Society for his heroism, but Florence would not stay in the house. She may also have been rebelling against Stoker's overwhelming devotion to Irving at her expense.

In the fall of 1883, Irving began his first American tour, carefully orchestrated and promoted by the faithful Stoker. He was received enthusiastically and continued to tour America until his retirement in 1904. Stoker lovingly attended to every detail, and immersed himself in Americana while touring with the company. He was particularly taken with the contrasts of beautiful homes, tramps, inexpensive real estate, America's lack of class consciousness and airs, the comfort of the middle classes, crime and punishment, the exaltation of American women, and the ease of the upper-class club life.

In addition to serving Irving, Stoker studied for the bar and passed his exams in 1890. He wrote several books and magazine articles, including a children's book entitled *Under the Sunset* (1882), a strange collection of stories probably unsuitable for small listeners. Stoker traveled with the company, often without Florence or Noel, and maintained a schedule that few could endure. Stoker also arranged opening-night galas and banquets, late-night intimate suppers, and all-night discussions over brandy about drama and the arts.

The year 1890 proved to be very important in the evolution of *Dracula*. In April, Stoker met Professor Arminius Vambery, a professor of Oriental languages in Budapest. Vambery was quite knowledgeable about Eastern European folklore, including vampires, and probably served as the model for the vampire hunter

The Whitby Influence

Of all the settings Bram Stoker used in *Dracula*, few are more vivid and memorable than the three chapters set in Whitby, England. Perched at the mouth of the river Esk on a bend in the coastline in northern Yorkshire, Whitby faces the North Sea. It is an ancient Anglo-Saxon fishing port that still retains some of the mysterious aura that appealed to Stoker in the late nineteenth century.

Stoker visited Whitby in 1890, the year he started jotting notes for the novel that was to become *Dracula*. He was looking for a good place for a family holiday with his wife and son, and a friend had recommended Whitby. Stoker was enchanted, and he and his family spent three weeks there, enjoying the sea air. They took apartments at Mrs. Veazey's house at 6 Royal Crescent, a row of elegant houses on the West Cliff. Three women from Hertford, Isabel and Marjorie Smith and their friend Miss Stokes, also stayed at the crescent. Two became models for the characters Lucy Westenra and Mina Harker.

Chapters six through eight take place in Whitby, where Mina joins Lucy and her family for a holiday. She is concerned about her fiancé, Jonathan Harker, who had gone to do business in Transylvania, but who's ominously silent. Mina manages to enjoy outings with Lucy. They meet an old seaman, Mr. Swales (Stoker took the last name from a Whitby tombstone), who regales them with tales of the supernatural while they sit in the churchyard of the ruins of Whitby Abbey on the East Cliff. Lucy's favorite seat there, she learns, sits at the grave of a suicide victim—an unlucky spot.

Their holiday is soon marred. The ill-fated ship *Demeter*, bearing the caskets of the Count and his three vampire brides, crashes into Whitby's harbor. The captain is dead, lashed to the wheel with a crucifix clutched in his hands. A huge dog is seen leaping from the wreckage. Lucy begins to suffer restless nights. Two days later, Mr. Swales is found dead of a broken neck at the "suicide's seat."

Whitby as it was in 1889
(Courtesy Whitby Archives)

Lucy seems under a mysterious spell. She begins sleepwalking, and her energy diminishes. One night, Mina awakens to find Lucy gone. Looking out from the West Cliff to the ruins of Whitby Abbey and the churchyard of St. Mary's across the harbor, Mina spies the white-dressed figure of Lucy half-reclining on the suicide's seat. She dashes—quite a marathon dash—and as she gets nearer, sees a sinister, dark figure bending over her friend. She cannot tell if it is man or beast. She cries out for Lucy, and the figure looks up. Mina sees red eyes. She momentarily loses sight of them, and when she sees again, only Lucy is present. The rescue comes too late—Dracula's destruction of Lucy has already been set irrevocably in motion.

The *Demeter* was inspired by a genuine tragedy that occurred the summer that Stoker was in Whitby. A northbound ship smashed into a fishing coble, a type of boat descended from the Vikings' long ship and unique to England's northeast coast. The men on the coble shouted frantically to ward off the oncoming ship, but strangely no one was on watch and the decks were deserted. The ship sailed on as though oblivious to the damage it had done to the coble. Several of the coble's crew were rescued, but two drowned.

Many of the landmarks Stoker put in his book can be visited and seen today, and one can retrace the steps of Mina's heroic dash to the abbey ruins by following the Dracula Trail. The visitor's center at Whitby sells a small guidebook and map to the trail.

The starting point, and perhaps the best vantage point on the West Cliff, is the Bram Stoker Memorial Seat. This small, Victorian-style seat was erected by the Scarborough Borough Council and the Dracula Society of London in April 1980 to commemorate the link between Stoker and Whitby, and the inspiration he received there. The seat looks out to the East Cliff, and from it, one can see all the major landmarks in *Dracula*.

Right behind the seat is the famous Crescent, now called the East Crescent, a neighborhood built in the 1850s, where Stoker stayed. In *Dracula*, this is where Mina and Lucy stay, and also where lives the count's lawyer, who arranges for his importing to England his cargo of boxes of earth.

From this viewpoint, one can visualize Mina and Lucy as they admire evening sunsets. Far across on the East Cliff is the graveyard of St. Mary's Church and the abbey ruins, where Mina spies the sinister form bending over Lucy (she must have had unusually keen eyesight to see that in the dark, even aided by moonlight). And, on a later occasion, Lucy and Mina see a dark figure sitting on their favorite churchyard seat, and two glowing points of light that Lucy comments are "his red eyes again."

It is possible to run—or preferable to walk—the exact route taken by Mina on her mission of rescue that fateful night. It goes down the West Cliff, follows the river along a market pier, goes across an old wooden drawbridge, cuts through the cobblestoned and quaint Old Town, and leads to the worn 199 church stairs. In the book, Mina covers the ground in what seems like moments, yet the path is not that easy to negotiate, and the stairs alone require stamina.

From the graveyard atop the East Cliff, the town of Whitby spreads out below in glory. Rows and rows of weathered tombstones jut at crazy angles. Coupled with the old church and the ancient ruins, they create a spooky atmosphere. The "suicide's seat" favored by Mina and Lucy cannot be found today, but there is no lack of interest. One can rest on seats scattered among the graves and spend hours contemplating the classic tale of horror that unfolded here.

ROSEMARY ELLEN GUILEY

Abbey ruins (Photo by Rosemary Ellen Guiley)

character, Van Helsing. Also in 1890, Stoker visited Whitby, England, for a holiday, and later used the village as the setting for three chapters in *Dracula*. Finally, Irving had a stage production, *Lucy of Lammermoor*, the same year—perhaps giving the first name to Dracula's tragic victim, Lucy Westenra.

Other travels served the evolution of the novel and Stoker's craft in general. On holiday in 1892, Stoker came upon the small fishing village of Boscastle on the west coast of Cornwall. The sea squeezed through the rocks there with incredible power, and the locale became "Pencastle" in Stoker's short story *The Coming of Abel Behenna*. Exhibiting Stoker's interest in the macabre, the story tells of two fishermen in love with the same girl. One of the suitors dies and his corpse washes ashore on the day of the other's wedding during a wild storm. Corpses and violent storms also figure in *The Watter's Mou* (1895), a gothic tale of a coastguardsman in love with a fisherman's daughter, whose father's debts have pushed him into smuggling. Her father is lost at sea, and when the daughter drowns trying to save him, the young guard jumps in after her. Their corpses are washed ashore, joined together in an embrace. *The Watter's Mou* appeared as a companion volume to Sir Arthur Conan Doyle's book *The Parasite*.

As a setting for Stoker's works, Boscastle was surpassed by the town of Cruden Bay, a tiny fishing village below a castle's ruins in Scotland that Stoker discovered in 1893. He used Cruden Bay in *The Watter's Mou* and again in a story called *Crooken Sands* (1897). More importantly, Cruden Bay was the place where Stoker felt most at ease, spending his holidays there yearly. During the summers of 1895 and 1896, Stoker strode the beaches, developing the plot for his vampire novel.

Stoker's horror stories played upon the reader's every fear. One of his best is *The Squaw* (1894), in which a young couple travels to Nuremberg Castle and is joined by an American eager to see the torture chamber, specifically the Iron Virgin. From high on a parapet, the American idly drops a pebble down and inadvertently hits a kitten playing with its mother, killing it. The tourists proceed to the torture chamber, where the American insists on standing inside the Iron Virgin to imagine the full effect. The custodian, holding the torture machine's rope, is attacked by the vengeful mother cat. He drops the rope, and the American is impaled.

A vampire story had been simmering in Stoker's imagination for years. He had read with relish Joseph Sheridan Le Fanu's *Carmilla* (1872) about a langorous countess who is discovered to be a vampire and is killed when a stake is thrust through her heart. In 1819, John Polidori published *The Vampyre*, which he based on an unfinished story by his friend, Lord Byron. Critics credit Polidori for establishing the image of a modern vampire: cool, aloof, elegant, very attractive to women, and thoroughly evil. Even Mary Shelley's *Frankenstein* (1818) had an effect on Stoker, as a classic in English horror fiction.

Varnery the Vampyre, or *Feast of Blood* (1847), by James Malcolm Rymer (the book is often erroneously credited to Thomas Preskett Prest) established the look of Dracula: white, bloodless skin, glassy eyes, and fanglike teeth.

Of course, vampire lore had been around for centuries, particularly in Eastern Europe. In 1890, Irving entertained Vambery at one of the actor's famous all-night dinners in the Beefsteak Room at the Lyceum. Stoker listened in fascination as Vambery regaled the guests with stories of his adventures and cour-

age. Most likely, Vambery first introduced Stoker to the Wallachian prince Vlad Dracula, a real historical figure used as the model for Stoker's fictional vampire, Dracula.

Vlad Dracula V lived from 1431 to 1476, ruling Wallachia, now part of Romania, from 1455 to 1462. *Dracula* has come to mean "son of the devil," but "son of a dragon" is the more likely translation because his father was a member of the Order Draconis, established by Holy Roman Emperor Sigismund, the king of Hungary. Most simply, *dracula* is "son of Dracul." Vlad's reputation for bloodthirsty ferocity against the Turks, and his penchant for execution by impalement, earned him the nickname Vlad Tepeş (*tzepa* means "spike"). He did not save his wrath for his enemies alone,

Rumanian postage stamp commemorating Vlad Tepes
(Courtesy Count Dracula Fan Club)

Live from Transylvania

In researching *Dracula*, Bram Stoker borrowed from Transylvanian superstitions. He was greatly influenced by an article titled "Transylvanian Superstitions," written by Mme. Emily de Laszowska Gerard, who was married to a cavalry commander in the Austro-Hungarian forces posted to Transylvania, and published in 1885 in *XIX Century*, Vol. XVIII. Stoker used a number of items from this article, such as the superstitions surrounding St. George's day (April 23, or May 6 by the modern Western calendar). On this night, witches hold their sabbaths, and all the buried treasures in the earth begin to burn and give off a bluish flame, thus making auspicious conditions for treasure hunting. Other superstitions Stoker made use of can be found in the following excerpts from Mme. Gerard's article:

> Transylvania might well be termed the land of superstition, for nowhere else does this curious crooked plant of delusion flourish as persistently and in such bewildering variety. It would almost seem as though the whole species of demons, pixies, witches, and hobgoblins, driven from the rest of Europe by the wand of science, had taken refuge within this mountain rampart, well aware that here they would find secure lurking places. . . .
>
> The spirit of evil (or, not to put too fine a point upon it, the devil) plays a conspicuous part in the Roumenian [sic] code of superstition, and such designations as the Gregynia Drakuluj (devil's garden), the Gania Drakuluj (devil's mountain), Yadu Drakuluj (devil's hell or abyss), & c. & c., which we frequently find attached to rocks, caverns, or heights, attest the fact that these people believe themselves to be surrounded on all sides by a whole legion of evil spirits. . . .
>
> I may as well here mention the *Scholomance*, or school supposed to exist somewhere in the heart of the mountains, and where all the secrets of nature, the language of animals, and all imaginable magic spells and charms are taught by the devil in person. Only ten scholars are admitted at a time, and when the course of

ordering his mistress's stomach be split open to prove her pregnancy. He had the turbans of visiting ambassadors nailed to their heads when they did not remove them in his presence and burned a whole group of beggars alive at a sumptuous feast, justifying his actions as eliminating a source of pestilence. When a boyar complained of the screams and stench from the impaled Turks, Dracula had him impaled also—on a higher stake, above the scene.

This nobleman, a Romanian national hero today, was responsible for building the citadel of Bucharest in 1458 and for making Wallachia so safe that, allegedly, no crime ever occurred. Romanians justify his sadistic cruelty as necessary for political and military success. There is just enough resemblance between Vlad Dracula and Stoker's fictional count to cause confusion about the two. But no matter how bloody Vlad was, he was no vampire.

To add authentic detail to his vampire novel, Stoker researched Transylvania at the British Museum, and may have contacted Vambery for further information. He placed the count's castle in the Carpathian Mountains learning has expired and nine of them are released to return to their homes, the tenth scholar is detained by the devil as payment, and mounted upon an *Ismeju* (dragon) he becomes henceforth the devil's aide-de-camp, and assists him in "making the weather," that is to say, preparing the thunderbolts. . . .

Ravaging diseases, like the pest, cholera, etc., are attributed to a spirit called the *dschuma*, to whom is sometimes given the shape of a fierce virgin, sometimes that of a toothless old hag. . . .

Pomanas, or funeral feasts, are repeated after a fortnight, six weeks, and on each anniversary for the next seven years; also whenever the defunct has appeared in dream to any member of the family, this likewise calls for another *Pomana*; and when these conditions are not exactly complied with, the soul thus neglected is apt to wander complaining about the earth, and cannot find rest. These restless spirits, called *Strigoi*, are not malicious, but their appearance bodes no good, and may be regarded as omens of sickness or misfortune.

More decidedly evil, however, is the vampire, or *nosferatu*, in whom every Roumenian (sic) peasant believes as firmly as he does in heaven or hell. There are two sorts of vampires—living and dead. The living vampire is in general the illegitimate offspring of two illegitimate persons, but even a flawless pedigree will not ensure anyone against the intrusion of a vampire into his family vault, since every person killed by a *nosferatu* becomes likewise a vampire after death, and will continue to suck the blood of other innocent people till the spirit has been exorcised, either by opening the grave of the person suspected and driving a stake through the corpse, or firing a pistol shot into the coffin. In very obstinate cases it is further recommended to cut off the head and replace it in the coffin with the mouth filled with garlic, or to extract the heart and burn it, strewing ashes over the grave. . . .

First cousin to the vampire, the long-exploded were-wolf of the Germans is here to be found, lingering yet under the name of the *Prikolitsch*. Sometimes it is a dog instead of a wolf, whose form a man has taken either voluntarily or as penance for his sins.

ROSEMARY ELLEN GUILEY

near the borders of Transylvania, Moldavia (now Moldava), and Bukovina, and was congratulated by many on his accurate picture of the Transylvanian setting—quite a feat considering he'd never been there. English scenes were set at Whitby, in Yorkshire. Dracula comes ashore there and makes his first conquest, of Lucy, in the churchyard. Stoker knew the place well, and it has not changed much in the intervening years.

For story structure, Stoker used the style of author Wilkie Collins: telling the tale in the first person from the mouths of several characters. This method was effective in showing the different perspectives of Jonathan Harker, Mina Harker, Lucy Westenra, and Dr. John Seward.

The count was a tall, old man with white hair and a long, white mustache. He had an aquiline nose, hard mouth, and sharp white teeth surrounded by red lips. His pallid complexion contrasted with his black clothing. He had pointed ears and squat fingers with pointed nails. There was some resemblance to an engraving of Vlad Dracula made in 1458.

Dracula appeared in May 1897. Critical re-

Wie facht sich an gar ein graussem

liche erschröckenliche hystorien. von dem wilden wü-
trich Dracole weyde Wie er die leüt gespist hat vnd
gepraten vn mit den haüptern yn einen kessel gesotten

Woodcut depicting the impaling of victims on the order
of Vlad Tepes

views were mixed, but many saw it as the best
and most graphic of English horror fiction.
Stoker's mother Charlotte found the book to
be his finest work, though it was not a great
financial success. There were so many interesting characters: beautiful Lucy, the victim; Jonathan Harker, the brave protector of Mina;
Renfield, the lunatic who eats birds and small
animals; and Professor Abraham Van Helsing,
perhaps modeled after Vambery.

Stoker relished the literary attention, but
matters with Irving and the Lyceum eclipsed
all other concerns. The theater company was
falling on hard times. In December 1896, Irving fell on a dark stairway at the theater and
was unable to perform for ten weeks, precipi-
tating financial losses for the company. Even
worse, in February 1898, the storage warehouse for the theater burned down, destroying
over £30,000 worth of equipment, props, and
costumes. Just that year, Irving had instructed
Stoker to drop insurance coverage from
£10,000 to £6,000 to cut expenses.

Irving withdrew completely, leaving Stoker
to handle the business and the actors. The actor bitterly resented the loss, as well as the
failure of his most recent production and competition from other theaters. Struggling to go
on, he became ill with pneumonia and
pleurisy, losing another seven weeks. Overcome with the worry of it all, Irving agreed to
an offer from a syndicate called the Lyceum
Theater Company to buy the Lyceum, much to
Stoker's dismay.

By 1902, the syndicate was in arrears and
Irving was without a theater in which to perform. He made tours at home and abroad, including a farewell to America tour in 1904, but
his health was severely weakened. Nevertheless, lack of funds necessitated his constant
working. By October 1905, Irving was near
collapse, and on the thirteenth, he died.

Irving's death left Stoker completely bereft.
His own financial difficulties had caused him
to continue writing furiously, and he published ten books after *Dracula*. The stories emphasized either horror or romance, with the
heroines good and pure beyond belief. Yet
Stoker's supposedly chaste love scenes were
loaded with sexual imagery. The descriptions
of vampires licking their lips and writhing in
their coffins are nearly pornographic. Despite
his own use of sexual imagery, Stoker wrote
scathing reviews in magazines against sex in
literature, even advocating censorship.

Daniel Farson, a Stoker biographer and a
great-nephew, wonders if Stoker's search for
the ideal woman comes from his sexual frus-
tration with Florence. It has been speculated
that she avoided sex after the birth of Noel.

Stoker, consumed by guilt turned to prostitutes.

His last novel, *The Lair of the White Worm* (1911), is so strange that it could have been written under the influence of drugs. Stoker was under treatment for Bright's disease, a kidney disorder, and it may have influenced his thinking. The plot concerns a wealthy young Australian, Adam Salton, who returns to his ancestral home to meet Lady Arabella March, an odd woman dressed in white who repels snakes. In truth, Lady Arabella is the dreaded great white worm, an antediluvian leftover that feeds on innocents, similar to the vampires, in order to survive. She tries to lure Salton's fiancée down her hole, but is destroyed in a dynamite explosion that yields shreds of Lady Arabella, worms, and horrible stinking vermin for days. Although not as well known as *Dracula*, the book is a cult favorite and has been made into a film by Ken Russell.

With all his output, Stoker received little fame and even less money in his lifetime. By the end of his life, friends tried to ease his increasing penury and overlook his mental instability. When he died on April 20, 1912, at age sixty-four, he had only £4,723 to his name. The doctor ruled the official cause of death as exhaustion, but Farson speculates that he died from tertiary syphilis, probably contracted from a prostitute. The obituary that appeared in the *London Times* noted his devotion to Irving and briefly commented that Stoker was the master of lurid and creepy fiction. *Dracula*, the book that failed to earn him riches in life, went on to spawn one of the most commercially successful subgenres of horror in fiction and film.

JOANNE P. AUSTIN

Anne Rice:
Giving the Vampire a
Conscience

ovelist Anne Rice doesn't write about the supernatural because it sells—although that helps, of course. She sees her books as serious examinations of good and evil through the eyes and experiences of the ultimate outsiders: vampires, witches, mummies, and even castrati. For her, writing is a means of achieving the deepest core of meaning and acceptance, of "it," and using the supernatural is the fastest, most thrilling way to get there. Looking for "it" has been a lifelong search and series of reinventions.

Born Howard Allen Frances O'Brien on October 4, 1941, the little girl's first change was her name. She called herself Anne when she started first grade, and it stuck. The second of four girls of Howard and Katherine O'Brien, Anne was the one who made up stories, loved looking for ghosts, and was afraid of the dark.

Young Anne also loved the Catholic faith of her parents and growing up in New Orleans. "The Big Easy" is unlike any other city in the United States: a place with a European flavor that languidly drifts through the heat and humidity; the home of jazz, voodoo, and Mardi Gras, and redolent with the cadences and rituals of established Catholicism. The air hangs heavy with fragrance and the feeling that spirits could be hiding in the old Southern mansions or the aboveground cemeteries. For someone as impressionable as Anne, New Orleans was ideal.

Anne's earliest, and perhaps strongest, influence was her mother Katherine. Katherine's Irish father had died an alcoholic, and Katherine had resolved to be good and pure to compensate. She was very devout and expected the children to be good Catholics. On the other hand, Katherine had very modern ideas about child rearing, allowing the children great freedom. She encouraged their specialness whenever she could, allowing them to dress the way they wanted or to skip school. She also expected them to be perfect geniuses.

Although such a background was liberating for a female, Anne often felt that she and her sisters were different, when what she wanted was to fit in. Unfortunately, Katherine could not cope with her husband's long absence during World War II nor his long workday when he returned. She hated being alone, especially in the dark. Katherine began drinking, finally dying from alcoholism when Anne was fifteen. After Katherine's death, Howard moved his family to Richardson, Texas, a suburb of Dallas. Anne met Stan Rice, her future husband, in a high school journalism class. It was love at first sight for her, but not for Stan.

Anne rebelled at the double standards for women in the 1950s, and by her first year at Texas Women's University she had completely lost faith in Catholicism. She transferred to North Texas State University in Denton her sophomore year, but at the end of six weeks left with her roommate for San Francisco. Meanwhile, by the time Stan realized he missed Anne, she had already left for California. They corresponded for a year and then married on October 14, 1961, when Anne was twenty. They returned to San Francisco in 1962, where they lived in Haight Ashbury and took their bachelor's degrees from San Francisco State University. His was in creative writing; hers was in political science.

Living in San Francisco's Haight Ashbury district in the 1960s was a heady experience. Both Anne and Stan were naturally attracted to poets and artists, and they rubbed elbows with nearly everyone who passed through. They gave huge parties, at which drugs were sometimes used. Despite their popularity, Anne found drugs scary.

On September 21, 1966, Anne gave birth to their first child, Michele. Family was very important to both Anne and Stan, and they adored their beautiful blond little girl. Like her mother before her, Anne included Michele in all their activities, exposing her to adult ideas and situations. Their lives seemed to be going very well; Stan's poetry was receiving recognition, and Anne's short stories and books were starting to generate some interest. She began a master's program in creative writing at San Francisco State.

But by late 1970, their world shattered. Michele was diagnosed with leukemia. Both tried to maintain normalcy—Anne finished her master's—yet argued over whether to fight the disease to the last minute or let Michele enjoy life while she had it. Anne began drinking more heavily. On August 5, 1972, Michele died. Now Anne had lost both mother and daughter.

Those who have never experienced the loss of a child cannot begin to comprehend the effect of the tragedy on the parents. Besides grief, there is overwhelming guilt over all the things that might have been done and why, as the child's parents, they couldn't make things right. Anne and Stan grew apart, either arguing or not talking at all. She spoke of her early Catholic training with bitter longing and began exploring theories of the afterlife. Anne's drinking grew worse.

After a three-week stay alone with Stan's parents, Anne returned to San Francisco and took a job. But she hated it, and asked Stan whether she should try writing full-time. He encouraged her, and she began typing at night while Stan slept. During this period Anne suffered from Guillain-Barré syndrome, which gave her polio-like symptoms in her hands, feet, face, legs, and respiratory system.

In 1969, Anne had written a short story called "Interview with the Vampire," and she resurrected it as the basis for her first book. The main character, Louis, a reluctant vampire, comes from southern Louisiana and New Orleans and suffers tremendous guilt over his now-evil nature. Yet Louis is no Count Dracula; instead, he is an androgynous character, smooth and white-skinned, who succumbs to the desire for immortality yet finds it hard to bear. Unlike traditional vampires, Rice's immortals are beautiful, do not live in graves, do not avoid garlic, and can see their reflections in mirrors. According to Anne, in Catholic theology, the inability to see one's reflection means the soul is in hell, and she did not want her vampires to have any better assurance of God than mortals.

In a radio interview, Louis explains how he dealt with being a vampire, how he finally surrendered to his bloodthirstiness by attacking a five-year-old girl, and how his mentor Lestat saved her by making her a vampire as well. Young Claudia resembled Michele; Anne and Stan had even called her that once. In the first manuscript, Claudia joins a band of children terrorizing Paris, but lives forever, giving Michele immortality.

Anne finished the book in a feverish five weeks. Publishers rejected it initially, and overcome with a backlash of grief from Michele's death, Anne decided that she was poisoning the book and everything she touched. Obsessive-compulsive behavior caused her to constantly check locks and doors and wash her hands incessantly.

Anne underwent therapy, but didn't completely lose her compulsions until after attending a writers' conference at Squaw Valley in August 1974. There she met agent Phyllis Seidel, who offered to show the book to Victoria Wilson, an editor at Alfred A. Knopf. In October, Phyllis awakened Anne with the news that Knopf loved the book and was willing to give her a $12,000 advance for hardcover rights; $2,000 was standard. They wanted some minor changes, but Anne was delighted.

Ten weeks later, Anne's minor changes had completely revised the story. This time Claudia is killed in the end, which psychologically buries Michele as well. And instead of the young radio interviewer escaping with his life and the tapes, he begs Louis to grant him immortality. Vicky Wilson loved the new version, and *Interview with the Vampire* appeared in 1976. The book generated seventy-five mixed reviews—far more than a usual

first novel—and earned the Rices $750,000 for paperback rights and $150,000 for movie rights.

In 1977, only a year after *Interview with the Vampire*, Anne discovered she was pregnant. Both she and Stan worried about the birth, but it had been five years since Michele's death. Anne stopped drinking during the pregnancy, and Christopher Travis was born March 11, 1978. Anne and Stan realized that they wanted to eliminate alcohol from their lives altogether, so on May 31, 1979, they quit drinking completely.

Eager to try something besides vampires, Rice's second novel was a historical look at the free people of color- (blacks who were not slaves) in New Orleans during the 1840s. Like the vampires, they were outsiders of both the black and white races and had their own community with its own set of rules. She called the book *The Feast of All Saints*, named for the Catholic holy day on November 1 when the faithful go to the cemeteries and place flowers on the graves of their loved ones. The book garnered a $150,000 advance and appeared in 1979. But reviews were mixed and sales were fewer— only 20,000 hardback—yielding $35,000 for the paperback rights. Chief complaints about the book were that it was too heavy and dense to read easily.

Anne then turned to an historical novel, *Cry to Heaven*, about two *castrati* in eighteenth-century Italy. Published in October 1982, that book also received mixed reviews.

Stung by the criticism, Anne then tried contemporary fiction. Writing under the pseudonym A. N. Roquelaure (*roquelaure* means "cloak"), she produced a series of pornographic novels about the further adventures of Sleeping Beauty after her awakening by the prince: *The Claiming of Sleeping Beauty* (1983), *Beauty's Punishment* (1984), and *Beauty's Release* (1985). Using yet another pseudonym, that of Anne Rampling, Anne wrote *Exit to Eden* (1985), which deals with sexual pleasure and sadomasochism.

Anne's second vampire novel, *The Vampire Lestat*, was published in October 1985. The book landed on the the *New York Times* best-seller list within two weeks and stayed there for seven. Knopf sent Anne on a thirteen-week promotional tour, an event that both excited and terrified her.

The Vampire Lestat opens in 1985 with Lestat awakened by a rock band after lying in the ground since 1929. He adapts to the mid-1980s immediately, becoming a rock star himself. Anne found rock musicians outrageous, independent, and, again, outsiders. Lestat rides a Harley motorcycle, listens to his Walkman radio, and discovers movies on video. He is appalled with the evils around him and decides that he must try to rationalize his basically evil nature by trying to show evil to others. He uses rock music to repudiate evil through art.

Lestat also finds Louis's interview tapes and resolves to set the record straight with his own autobiography. He tells of his young manhood in prerevolutionary France and of his search for goodness and purity. Then he tells of receiving the Dark Gift. In further adventures, Lestat goes to Greece with the vampire Marius where he finds Enkil and Akasha, the Adam and Eve of all vampires. They are so old and powerful they are like the stone statues of gods, yet Lestat wakens Akasha and she lets him drink her blood.

The novel ends with Lestat's rock concert, in which he sings that mythic evils like vampires are irrelevant for the late twentieth century; war and hunger are the demons to eradicate. His aim is to goad all the evil vampires into appearing against him so that he can fight them and truly bring goodness into the world. The final scene is a cliffhanger, paving the way for the third book in the *Vampire Chronicles, The Queen of the Damned*, which was published in 1988 with an advance of $500,000.

In *The Queen of the Damned*, Anne pursues Lestat's theme of doing evil to accomplish ultimate good to its logical conclusion. Akasha destroys Enkil, proving herself the real source of vampirism, and abducts Lestat to help her carry out her plans for a new world order: to rectify all the cruelty and injustice perpetrated by men over the centuries, particularly against women, Lestat will help her kill 99 percent of the men on earth. The surviving women will then exact peace and worship Akasha as their goddess of salvation.

Seduced by Akasha's beauty, Lestat begins the work on the island of Lykanos. He loves the bloodletting; he is, after all, a male vampire. Akasha justifies her actions by her power alone, claiming she is the Queen of Heaven. After meeting with his vampire friends, however, Lestat comes to realize that saving one percent of the men was Akasha's acknowledgment that women cannot perpetuate humankind alone, and that possession of his male soul is her weak link. He sides with those morally opposed to Akasha's new order, and humanity is saved.

Before finishing *The Queen of the Damned*, Anne finally gave into her homesickness for New Orleans. The Rices bought a second house there in 1988 and moved permanently in 1989 to a Greek Revival mansion in the city's Garden District. Anne used the house as the setting for her next novel, *The Witching Hour*.

The Witching Hour may be the most autobiographical of Anne's novels, although she claims no witches in her background. But the hero, Michael Curry, carries her great-grandfather's family name, and the large Mayfair family mirrors Anne's love of family and connectedness. Through Michael's impressions and memories of New Orleans, Anne relates lovingly her New Orleans girlhood and the effect the city had on her.

The fourth book in the *Vampire Chronicles, The Tale of the Body Thief*, was published in 1992 and enjoyed a long stay on best-seller lists. The story is told by Lestat, who describes his attempt to commit suicide in the sun, followed by his fascination with a mortal who has perfected the art of stealing bodies, and offers Lestat the chance to once again enjoy life in a mortal body.

At home in New Orleans, Anne now describes herself as a Southern writer in the tradition of William Faulkner and Carson McCullers, writing about great families and generational sagas. In the end, however, she always returns to the struggle of good and evil: nothing abstract, but the alleviation of human suffering.

JOANNE P. AUSTIN

Wamphyri: Vampires for Modern Times

The mental picture of a vampire most often conjured is that of a middle-age man with a chalky face, a beak-sharp widow's peak cutting a swathe down over his forehead, and long pale hands that jet from a voluminous cloak.

The image of Dracula.

Since his fictional inception during 1897, this Romanian blood prince has become the seminal role model for all vampires, although his rapid ascendancy has been due more to the attention of American cinema than Bram Stoker's novel. Indeed, Stoker has been criticized by some as a weak, stylistically inept author who had one brilliant idea, and even that evolved from a sexual drive that eventually led to his death.

Dracula created the mold for the literary vampire, but the mold has become a stereotype in need of a good shake-up. Several authors and filmmakers have tried to reheat the embers—Anne Rice, Nancy Collins, John Skipp, and Craig Spector among them. After Rice, the contemporary horror-buying public seem inclined to go for author Brian Lumley's creations: the monstrous Wamphyri.

The reasons for this popularity are complex, but the overriding factor is that Lumley has ripped the monster from its failing European romantic roots, made it strong and attractive despite its physical ugliness, and, most importantly, provided it with a reason for existence. According to Lumley:

The way I saw the Wamphyri was that vampirism had started on a parallel world. By means of a gate, certain of them had come through to Earth and started vampirism—this could be 2,000, 3,000 years ago. On the other side of the gate they are all-powerful. They come from a world which is split by the Barrier Mountains: on one side is Starside, their night side, and the other, Sunside. When the sun goes down, the vam-

Brian Lumley: A Portrait

"It's possible that a good many writers, contemporaries in the (horror) field, have their own splashes of real horror in their backgrounds, but some of them don't come face to face with too much horror. It's not written in their faces."

Brian Lumley's grounding in real horror was garnered from twenty-two years in the British army. Born in 1937 within a colliery village in northeast England, he began his working life in his mid-teens as a woodcutting machinist, but left after a major disagreement with the foreman. He joined the army where he served as a military policeman and as the quartermaster of Edinburgh Castle.

His writing career sparked in Berlin while doing a tedious tour of duty on the night desk at a checkpoint control center in the midst of the Cold War. After completing his first two of three short stories, he contacted Arkham House publisher August Derleth, whose main interest was to keep alive the works of H.P. Lovecraft. Within a year Lumley was putting together a horror collection for Arkham House.

The Arkham House connection, and his own predilections, gave rise to many short stories with a clearly defined Lovecraftian lilt: his early tales of psychic detective Titus Crowe—which include the novel *The Burrowers Beneath*—contain monsters that would be at home in Lovecraft's Cthulhu Mythos, and even his Wamphyri vampire books hold truer to Lovecraft's unspeakable creations than to Bram Stoker's suave Count Dracula.

Lumley left the army to become a full-time writer in the early 1980s. His works have included such series as the *Psychomech!* trilogy, a fantasy/science fiction combination that begins when a wealthy industrialist wants a new body for his immortal and immoral mind, as well as hero books in which the victim of a road accident goes adventuring in the land of dreams.

His apocalyptic novel, *Demogorgon, The House of Doors*, follows the fortunes of a group of humans trapped in a machine that contains many worlds. *Fruiting Bodies*, a short story collection, was a 1988 British Fantasy Award winner.

Lumley likes to travel around the world, particularly to the Greek islands, where he spends most summers. He and his wife Dorothy, a literary agent, reside in Devon—suitably spooky countryside for an author of horror, fantasy, and science fiction.

JOHN GILBERT

---

pires come across the mountains. They can't during sun-up because it would have the same effect our sun has on them—a chemical effect. The fact is that some people, albinos for example, have a hard time in sunlight. But, there is that in the vampire make-up which deepens the effect: they will literally evaporate. Their fats steam away, they become less coherent, they fall to pieces, they turn black, they char. Anybody who doubts that sort of effect only has to hold a magnifying glass over a piece of paper in the sunlight and see what happens. That effect on the Wamphyri is magnified.

Lumley discloses the existence of the parallel world in part three of the five-book Wamphyri series, *The Source*, but he does build a host of hints toward the central revelation. The gypsy races of our world are, for instance, forever traveling because of survival instincts their ancestors picked up in the home world of the Wamphyri:

> There, a day is a week in our terms: the night lasts three days. It restricts the Wamphyri's moves: they can't go into Sunside for four of our days at a stretch, which gives the Sunsider humans plenty of time to move on. They daren't stay in one spot too long, lest the vampires find them too easily come nightfall. That's why the humans have become Travellers.

At first sight, the Wamphyri have little in common with Dracula. They may share a feudal instinct, but their powers appear to be greater than those exhibited by Stoker's Count, and their capacity for evil is more evident:

> A human being is to a vampire as a coconut is to a South Sea islander, useful in many ways: on their world, they refashion people to provide their fliers (their main mode of transport), refashion men for their warriors; in their eyries on Starside, the stairways are made of bone or cartilage. The awnings which carry their sigils are flayed skin, vampirised first to give it strength.

Lumley does, however, hint at why Dracula may be such a softy when compared with his Wamphyri elite, and it has to do with their crossover from their world to ours:

> The vampires, used to these long nights in which they were masters, have now come to a world where the nights are so much shorter. Also, there are far more human beings than there were Travellers, and we're years more advanced. We have atomic weapons, shot guns, we can use silver; sciences that the Travellers lost after a holocaust in their world. So the vampire is very much more susceptible to death in this world.

Apart from varying levels of strength and evil, the major difference between Lumley's creatures and those described by Stoker is in the milieu. They are still the vampire monster we know and recognize, except we now know more about them:

> I don't see my vampires as being different from the ones we all know. I see mine as having a reason for being which they didn't have before. We've always known what they do, but there's been no reason for these damn things. And, one thing that's always puzzled me: we've known there were quite a few of these guys, so why hasn't the plague proliferated, spread abroad? I've tried to supply an answer; because anonymity guarantees longevity, they can't become too apparent. Unlike on Starside, here on Earth people are going to come looking for them during the daylight.

Lumley's vampire is also that much more frightening than Stoker's pale parasite because it is seductive to both men and women who want apparent immortality, until they learn the dreadful price—more dreadful than any fanciful fear of losing your soul or of having to dig your way out of a coffin:

> We all wish we had these powers. We all know what we would do and what we would be. Alas, we're wrong. That's us thinking as human beings, but once we become a vampire, he's the one that takes over. My Wamphyri are two creatures: the human and the vampire within him. While the human thinks it's guiding its own destiny, the vampire is really guiding its destiny and causing it to do the things it wants. The horror of it is that we aren't in control.

The lack of control and the feelings of what it is like to be a vampire are explored to only a small extent in Stoker's novel. Lumley breaks down the barriers and individualizes his monster by narrating huge parts of the story through its eyes. Those set pieces also show the slow process of vampiric metamorphosis and expose our fascination to it and our repulsion from it:

> Mankind has already worked out its greatest fears. We already know the things which frighten us. We are frightened of diseases: like vampirism and lycanthropy. These are serious, hurting, diseases. And we also hate having something in us which has a grip on us. We can't bear to think that somebody else is in control. We like something of the old tradition in our books because they are the basic fears we've all held ever since the caveman woke up in the morning and gave a sigh of relief that nothing had ventured into his cave the night before.

While Dracula lacks complexity of motivation, the Wamphyri revel in it. Stoker may have created a Western stereotype for vampirism, but Lumley has produced a foundry of vampiric lore and devices: his is a chronicle, a series of books that reshapes and augments the legend, makes it new, and most definitely makes it his own.

Lumley and Stoker are as comparable as are their creations. Both men have produced good pulp fiction for their times and both have contributed powerful new ideas to their genres. But all else is dissimilar. Stoker's novel is a short story when compared with Lumley's chronicle, a seductive but monstrous cliché that has been turned on its head by the Wamphyri in the name of logic and realism.

Dracula is a supernatural being, child of a romantic yet sexually repressed historical period, whereas the Wamphyri are paranormal, fully grown for an age of science, unashamedly coarse, with their sexuality dangling gloriously between their legs.

And, whereas Stoker could only manage a few thousand words for his sequel—a short story called *Dracula's Guest* in which the Count doesn't make an appearance—Lumley has produced yet another series of novels called *Vampires' World*, which continues the parallel world where vampirism is the norm and subjugation by vampires is part of life.

Although Lumley may have done more as an individual for vampire fiction than did Stoker, the author of *Dracula* cannot be dismissed as the incidental initiator of a popular trend. Even Lumley admits:

> Given all the flowery passages, given all the waffle, take them away from the basic idea of *Dracula* and you've got a story which is hard to beat. I didn't set out to beat it when I wrote *Necroscope* [the first in the Wamphyri series]. I felt that Stoker had a good idea here, he made his characters very, very, real indeed, and I wanted my characters in *Necroscope* to be real with unreal powers and yet come across with believability.

Vampire's World is a long way from the romantic grotesquerie of *Dracula*. But Lumley's vision of vampirism may be the dominant modern vampire fiction. He has a message for all those critics who assert that the vampire has lost its fangs and can no longer frighten audiences. And that message is: the species survives.

JOHN GILBERT

Giving Voice to the Undead: Or, Vampire Authors

What do some of the world's leading authors of vampire novels have to say about their craft, their inspiration, their characters, themselves, the future of vampires in fiction—and more? Here, in selected "bites and pieces," the authors reveal themselves. Lists of their works appear in the appendices.

ANNE RICE

What was your original inspiration for the first vampire novel?

I was sitting at my typewriter wondering what it would be like to interview a vampire. I started to write the story and got into the vampire's point of view. Everything I was struggling to do as a fiction writer suddenly happened.

What is it about vampires that keeps bringing you back to these characters?

There has always been magnificent potential in this theme. The most shallow treatments of the vampire will have some echo or resonance that you do not necessarily find with other horror material. When a serious writer picks it up, it's a gold mine. I did what Stoker did—I took the material, selected what I wanted, and discarded the rest. I came up with my own "fang gang."

Did you feel the shadow of "The Vampire Chronicles" as you were writing *Interview*?

I knew that I was not finished with vampires when I completed the first book [*Interview with the Vampire*]. I did not foresee The Chronicles. If it continues to be this incredibly intense experience for me, I'll keep doing it.

Lestat has come a long way since *Interview with a Vampire*. How did he develop into the main figure of The Chronicles?

He developed by himself! In *Interview* I focused on the tragic Hamlet-like hero of Louis. In the background there was Lestat. I knew when I finished *Interview* that I wanted Lestat to tell his side of the story. As I began to write about him, he came alive and I knew everything he was going to do. I don't have to manipulate it; he goes and takes over.It seems that the vampires of your mythology have adapted well to the twenty-first century and even have acquired some of our habits, like becoming video junkies.Armand in particular has discovered the joys of watching videotapes. I think vampires would be that way. Imagine what it would be like to be a 7,500-year-old vampire and be able to watch sunlight at all different degrees on the screen. It must be a fantastic experience.

With the material you've written on the vampire, do you ever consider yourself a myth maker?

I see myself going back to myths as a source for vampires, reading a lot of Joseph Campbell, and Sir James Frazer's *The Golden Bough*, and the whole process in which myths develop and what they say about us. As far as being a creator of modern mythology, I don't know. I have an irresistible need to make stories, plots, and characters, and if it takes on a mythical quality, that is wonderful.

What scares Anne Rice?

Everything! I'm scared of the dark and of being in the house alone. I have lots of pets in the house.

Does the public's response to The Vampire Chronicles ever amaze you?

I was surprised by the public response. I hope The Chronicles will always be popular. I'm al-ways astonished by how many people come forward to buy my vampire books—they don't wait for the paperbacks. What destroys writers is indifference—not being read. To me the greatest aspect of success—the only real aspect that counts—is the fact that those people are reading the books and telling other people about it. It's wonderful. I never thought they'd be number one on the *New York Times* best-seller list. I just thought it was too weird.

CHELSEA QUINN YARBRO

What was the original inspiration behind your vampire series?

It started out some twenty years ago with what I intended to be a novella. It was a story about a sympathetic vampire, without the "Byronic" or "fifties" sympathetic trappings. I wanted to sustain the folklore, but demystify it without breaking those roles and at the same time changing the dogma. There was also the challenge of writing about a historic figure.

How did you come across Saint Germain?

I've been interested in occult studies because of their ties to essentially political organizations, such as the Freemasons. I was vaguely aware of Saint Germain, and did not intend to make him the vampire. I just threw the character in for authenticity and color. The deeper I researched, I found that he only wore black and white, he was never seen eating in public, and it was reported that he retained his youth by drinking the "elixir of life." Here was a historical character that had everything I was looking for. Why should I make up a vampire?

As you begin to write each new novel, who is telling the story—you or Saint Germain?

Saint Germain is separate from me, and is strong. He never demanded the last word, although in my latest novel he did. You learn after a while to trust these guys. Suzy Charnas says that they tap into very deep emotions—which is quite right—and you must be willing to let them do it their way. If it happens to be distressing to you—too bad!

What do you feel is the audience's attraction for the character?

It is his integrity and prospective—which are not mine, because I don't have the four-thousand-year retrospective hindsight he does—and he's good in bed. When you live this close with a character, nearly almost two decades now, you have to find a new slant. Four thousand years is handy that way. To make the character and period come together, in such a way that it pulls him and the audience in, there must be something about the context of that period in history that forces certain ethical, social, moral, psychological, or religious dilemmas. It has to be in terms of that period, and not as the twentieth century sees it. There are certain periods of his life I will never be able to write about simply because there is no way to make those criteria work on the page.

PATRICK WHALEN

What was the driving force that inspired your tale?

My idea was to pit a powerful, deadly human against a supernatural foe, and set it on an island so that they'd be unable to avoid each other. I had a human, a martial arts hitman, who literally died in a Vietnam torture camp—alive but dead inside. I put him up against a 900-year-old and powerful vampire—dead but alive inside. I came up with this theory that the black plague of fourteenth-century Europe was a story constructed by the Catholic Church to mask an outbreak of vampirism. It was easy for the church to suppress what really happened because they controlled all the printing. I did not rely on classic vampire mythology. My vampires can cross water, are not frightened by crucifixes, and don't need to be invited into someone's home. In *Monastery*, Gregory and his woman actually make their home in a church.

With such powerful characters, who has been in charge of telling each story?

The characters dictate their tales and carry the stories for me. If I think I'm going to kill one off, they let me know if they're not ready to die yet. In fact, I can hear Gregory whispering in my ear that he has an evil brother entombed in a church somewhere in Europe. If you think Gregory was bad, his brother is nastier and has plans to conquer Europe. It's just a matter of transporting Gregory and Braille to Europe, and then figuring out what countries they can demolish.

In your novels you combine numerous elements. What is the balance for you between humor, vampires, and horror?

I feel if a vampire can be humorous it makes him that much more endearing—you can make him more human. Gregory and Braille kill people and take blood. They don't like it, but then again they don't have a choice. You need humor to offset horror, just like you need romance in a horror novel. I find relentless horror boring. Elements of humor often make the horror that much more intense.

DEAN ANDERSSON

When did the vampire first inspire you to tell his tale?

When I was a child I can remember going to see the movie *Dracula* all on my own. At the time I didn't really know anything about him. The movie scared me bad and it left me with nightmares. It also sparked my curiosity. I bought a copy of Stoker's novel and read it. I began to devour anything I could find on the subject, both fiction and nonfiction. Eventually I stopped being afraid. By gaining this knowledge it gives you this power over it and it becomes your friend.

Do you ever worry about your works being obscured by the vampire boom?

I'm concerned about it, especially with Coppola's *Dracula* movie and all the tie-ins. It could create a glut of vampires, but I hope I've done a good enough job and my work will stand out on its own.

Being a writer of fiction, do you ever try to write in other areas and get out from under the fang?

It seems that everything I've written features some type of vampire. It might very well be a result of the fright I received as a child. Vampirism does not just involve blood drinkers, there are also energy- and life-force-draining vampires. Vampires are very potent symbols. There have been times in my own life when I've experienced negative people and places that have had a draining effect on me. Vampires are serial killers who can create other serial killers. Werewolves are serial killers; however, they are controlled by the full moon. When I got past the image of the corpse, bats, and blood drinking, it was the vampire's ability to get into your house at night, [when you're] asleep and not in control, that scared me the most. It's like when a hurricane comes along and turns your world upside-down. Vampires represent that random element that allows chaos into an ordered environment. I believe vampires serve a useful purpose.

FRED SABERHAGEN

How did you come upon your association with the vampire?

I reread Stoker's novel and realized his main character is hardly ever on stage. The other characters are running around discussing him, pondering his next move, and only catch glimpses of him. I wanted to latch onto him and see what Dracula was thinking.

What do you feel sets apart your vampire from others?

I go inside Dracula's mind and try to show things from his point of view. As I started to write, it felt like he was there just waiting for me to slip into his skin and explore.

How did the other books develop from the original idea?

They are a result of a small amount of success and that they were fun to do. Another favorite character of mine, Sherlock Holmes, was running around London at about the same time. I thought it would be interesting to have them run into each other—*The Holmes-Dracula File*. In much the same way, the other novels crept into my head and I thought they would be interesting.

Being that you've been associated with your vampire for so long, who writes the stories?

I suppose the character is some part of myself. It's like I've developed multiple personalities and felt natural. The voice seemed to pop up in my mind.

What is the hardest part of creating each new tale?

I'm inclined to research people, places, and events that interest me. If you have a good library you can get things like the *London Times* on microfilm. It's like a small time-machine.

With all the novels you've written, how did you find it trying to novelize James Hart's screenplay for Coppola's *Dracula*?

It is very different from writing a book. In some respects it is hard; in other respects easier. It was easier because I not only had Stoker's novel, there were also several drafts of the screenplay and production photographs. And, I could always talk to the screenwriter, James Hart. My character of Dracula and the film's Dracula are not the same, though they both have their interesting points. I was committed to staying with the film's characterization.

You've amassed such a body of work, do you feel that you've established yourself amongst the major vampire authors of history?

I believe I've established myself. I know that I have my own slant at looking at the theme, and especially at the character. I now read very little vampire fiction so that I am not influenced by it. I will go back and read Stoker, several other early works on the subject, and a few contemporary works.

Suzay McKee Charnas

Where did you find your vampire?

I was trying to get into the mood to write something else. So I went to New York for a break. There I saw both the original theatrical version of *Dracula* and *The Passion of Dracula*. Shortly thereafter I found myself in Grand Central Station with a copy of *Omni* magazine reading an article on artificial blood. The thought came to me—what if a vampire became involved with artificial blood research. About the same time I did a lecture at Skidmore College and was housed on the grounds in an old mansion that served as the faculty club. I like the place and it really got under my skin. To my thoughts of the vampire and artifi-cial blood I add this setting. The place you'd find artificial blood research is in a teaching hospital setting with a university. I knew that I didn't want to bog down the story with heavy medical material. So I made him a professor at the university where they were conducting synthetic blood research. I was bothered by all the romantic vampires running around and I began to think more of my vampire as predator. I began to write my story, and when I was done I knew that there was more to come because there were a lot of unanswered questions.

Being that you have such a good relationship with your vampire, who is in charge of writing the stories?

I began by trying to make a road for the vampire to come to the machine so that he might tell his story. For the first two chapters I asked it who it was, and it replied, "Okay, here is what I am and here is how I feel." After that the story took on a shape and momentum of its own. I don't bend the characters and I have no choice. It dawned on me that each chapter accomplished what it had to in order to bring the vampire to a certain point. It was amazing how it constructed itself without me really being aware of it.

You've cut your vampire from a different bolt of cloth. So, what exactly is your vampire?

He is not supernatural or a physical being. He is an animal. As far as I'm aware, he is the only parallel species vampire. What I'm interested in is the limits of humanity, the limits of animality. My story is a very long discussion of what makes us different from the animals. All monster stories deal with creatures with few choices or no choices at all. Man defeats it by learning the rules that govern it and using them to defeat the monster. The vampire has its roots in a typical devil story with religious overtones. As religion has become less important to society, it has become less important to the vampire mythology. It has transmuted into the scientific laws of how vampires are supposed to live, and we then find the reasons to justify all these laws.

F. Paul Wilson

It's true that you've employed vampire images in several of your works.

I used the classic image of the vampire in my novella *Midnight Mass*. I worked in all the Christian, Catholic, and vampire myths and used them at face value. I enjoyed bringing together a priest and a rabbi, and having the rabbi come to terms with the fact that only the Christian images worked. As a result, my vampires go into the Jewish section of town first because they know they'll be less likely to encounter a cross. That story was the only time I used vampires in their traditional form. In my novel *The Keep* I used all the trappings of the classic vampire story, like the Gothic elements. However, I employed these traditional elements such as a red herring to set the reader up for something that I hoped was much worse. In *Sibs*, I tried to come up with a sexual type of vampire. Here the character is psychically able to push a person's consciousness out of their body and take over. He then uses it to fulfill his own deviant sexual desires. It is a vampire in the sense that the character is taking something from these other people.

Why do you feel the vampire is so popular?

I've often wondered myself. I believe vampires appeal more to women then men, which may have something to do with the sensuous and liberating qualities of the fiction. It's not an easy answer.

In all the cases where you've drawn upon the vampire image it has remained true to its evil nature. Do you believe a vampire can be a hero?

The vampire is the lowest form of creatures—a parasite. By definition a parasite takes and does not give. I can't buy trying to romanticize that type of creature. I've tried to read Anne Rice's "Vampire Chronicles" and I could not get through it. I don't relate to her point of view or sympathize with her creatures. It was actually Chelsea Quinn Yarbro's *Hotel Transylvania* that inspired me to write *The Keep*. She just employed too many moral acrobatics to make Saint-Germain acceptable. I sent her a copy of *The Keep* and mentioned this to her. It seems to be a popular attitude to say that the ugly is beautiful, the perverse is acceptable. I am a realist. What is ugly is ugly, what is beautiful is beautiful, and a parasite is a parasite. I can understand the artistic impulse, but it is a trend and will eventually pass. It may be part of our universal proclivity for immortality, and the vampire is that proof. The question is, what are you willing to sacrifice for it?

Since so many modern day writers have humanized the vampire, do you think we've lost the romantic vampire villain?

We have lost the vampire; we've trivialized the vampire. I think it happened about the time "Count Chocula" found its way to cereal boxes. My mother saw the film *Dracula* when she was thirteen. She and her girlfriend ran home and slept with holy water at their bedside and rosary beads under their pillows. My mother lived in rural Massachusetts and it was her first encounter with a vampire, or a horror movie. Now we have cute vampires selling cereal. The vampire has become part of pop culture, instead of a monster lurking in the dark. In a sense, we have lost our fear of the vampire. I've been a fan for forty-five years and there is just too much "vampire." By becoming a fad, this powerful image has been trivialized. I'm not happy about it—I'm sick of vampires.

How does this fad affect the writer?

The vampire can still hold one of the greatest threats, that of death. To do that the writer must turn to a classical approach. After all, what was *Dracula* about but good guys versus bad guys. Dracula was more than just a bad guy; he was a force of death, and also represented something worse than death. *Dracula* also personalized the horror; the vampire set a target. Vampires today drag people into a dark alley, like a victim of random violence. If you make the vampire operate on that level he is nothing more than a mugger. It's less likely that I'd use the vampire again. If Robert McCammon hadn't written me and asked for a story for the anthology *Under the Fang*, I would never have written *Midnight Mass*. I think we've gone too far with the vampire, and I can't see how people take it seriously anymore.

LES DANIELS

Your vampire is a very historic figure. What were the influences that inspired your character?

Like most people, I think I've grown up with vampires. I think my first encounter with them must have been a 1950s horror comic, when they were all the rage. Of course there were the films, from Universal to Hammer and everything in between, and television shows. I can remember being interested in all aspects of supernatural fiction at an early age, and I'd read anything I could get my hands on. I made my vampire an amalgamation of all the vampire powers. My impulse was to use the character as a central figure, rather then this impersonal monster. Almost simultaneously, Anne Rice, Chelsea Quinn Yarbro, and I came out with our books, which all three turned out

to be a series. One of the most interesting questions for me is that of a half-human, half-supernatural creature—what they do and what they know that we don't. I didn't want to be too explicit about the "great beyond" because it would have only led to arguments. I didn't want to domesticate my vampire, but make him more of an antihero. I placed him in settings where the humans were looking so poorly that the vampire looked like the only person of integrity. The challenge has been not to "whitewash" him and still elicit sympathy from the reader. The contrast between the appeal and repulsion is what makes him interesting. Relying on blood too much is not interesting. If we just end up with these wealthy immortal people, we lose the attraction and the horror of the story. The point is that there is this Faustian bargain: they are trading something for their immortality.

With one trilogy behind, will your next novel be the beginning of a new one?

I never really plan things out in advance. So, I never rule anything out until I've formally ruled it out. *The Black Castle*, *The Silver Skull*, and *Citizen Vampire*, while referred to as a trilogy, were really separate novels with the recurring character of Sebastian. The next three really are a trilogy, with a second recurring character. With the last book, *White Demon*, that will be the end of the trilogy.

Is Sebastian a counterbalance for the traditional vampire?

I like to think he is a happy medium. He may be somewhat more homogenized than the traditional vampire, but he retains that sense of remorse that most of the modern sympathetic vampires have lost. Also, I usually work it into one scene or another that he is in touch with the great beyond. Most of the books are tragedies. The humans and the vampires are flawed.

Are there other supernatural characters that interest you as much?

I guess there are not. The vampire is one of the rare characters where the half-human, half-monster can come together. I have written short fiction about other things, but my novel-length fiction has been about vampires.

What do you feel vampires offer readers?

There are so many different types of vampires that they must each serve a function. I think sexuality has always played a big factor. There is the idea of immortality that we all long for. The supernatural and the mysterious in relation to our existence holds the appeal for me. I like to hint at it and not lay out new dogma. History has not been pleasant, so maybe that means humanity has not been pleasant. The vampire is no more frightening than we are!

NANCY COLLINS

What is your attraction to the vampire?

The character of Sonja Blue has been with me since high school, and I really didn't know what to do with her. Over the course of fifteen years, I've tried to formulate my own theories of vampires as both a sociological disorder and a disease. I originally intended it to be a comic series, but was having trouble finding an artist so that I could pitch the idea to a comic company. So I decided to turn her into a prose character. It had never occurred to me that my mythology was that different from other fiction. At that point, I had to stop reading vampire fiction altogether. I tried not to be influenced.

What vampire fiction have you read?

I try to avoid novels with similar characters and situations. I think it's safer in the long run. I'm interested in the Gothic fiction, supernatural, and the contemporaries like Mathe-son's *I Am Legend* and *Some of Your Blood* by Theodore Sturgeon. I did read Anne Rice's *Interview*, about a year after it came out. My major influence was *Tomb of Dracula*, a comic from Marvel Comics, written by Mark Wolfman. If nothing else, Dracula was the main character, but not the hero.

Your vampires are different than what we've come to expect as traditional vampires. What are your theories of vampire sociological disorder and disease?

I haven't decided yet if these creatures are supernatural or "creature-natural." Their origins are as shrouded in mystery as are our own. Any race or culture that spends its time preying on other beings must be of a mindset where they believe what they are doing is not wrong. To a certain extent, my vampire society is modeled after an insect society. In an insect society there are usually just one or a few creatures that know what is going on while the larger masses serve as workers. While they are social animals, they are far from social among themselves. The vampires are very competitive. When you live so long you get bored. What they do to amuse themselves involves these very dangerous power plays. It's just a game as far as they're concerned. If the tables turn and they become the victim, their position changes. Even if they are supernatural, their method of replication should follow a natural order. If they kill a human in the process of biting them, and don't damage the corpse, in three to five days the body will revive. Basically, the body has vampire sperm in it. It is a dormant stage where the body's DNA is altered. If it takes longer than three to five days, you end up with a zombie, a brain-damaged vampire. They look like burned-out street people. At the other end of the vampire spectrum are the Kings. They have evolved to the point where they no longer require blood. They live off of negative psychic energy. It is not just eating; it is an art form.

Much of your violence takes place on a surreal plane of reality. Why do you choose to set it there?

I've always liked using dream imagery. The opening to *Sunglasses After Dark* is set in an asylum because perceptions of reality vary from patient to patient. We accept that anyone who believes in vampires must be crazy. So when we are confronted with what we believe can't be true, we ignore anything that proves it, or medicate it, place it in a straitjacket, and lock it away. Added to that is that fact that Sonja Blue is mentally ill. I wanted to show that vampires live on another plane. They are telepathic and can go into people's minds and tamper with their emotions. When you manipulate people's realities it opens up the tale to the possibility of potent imagery.

What do you feel is the future of vampirism versus romanticism?

It seems to swing both ways. There will always be the undercurrent of sexuality. When *Dracula* became popular during the Victorian era, there was a sexual revolution going on and venereal disease was rampant. At the same time, sex was not to be spoken of outside the bedroom. We can't even begin to imagine the social upheaval that gave rise to the success of the Gothic appeal. Vampires' new success is due to, yet again, a new sexual plague and the silicon revolution. Our society finds vampires an attractive monster. I really worry when I get letters from fans who are not happy being human. Vampires lost much of their edge in the twentieth century because of the real-life horrors that have risen and can be found in our daily newspapers and the nightly news. Personally, I couldn't take vampires seriously once I got past the age of twelve.

Can we reclaim the vampire?

Yes! I've tried to stress in my books that while the vampire may look and try to pass itself off as human, it is basically everything that is bad with humanity. Vampires take, take, take, and never give—they're parasites. They feed off of our fear, hate, and anger. They are the shadow of the human soul personified. They are a black mirror. Sonja is a rarity for vampires. What makes her heroic is that she refuses to surrender her humanity. It is "dog-eared" by now, but she realizes that it has to be better than these vampires. She knows she can never go back, and it angers her. Still, she tries to be human, and some times succeeds. She's human enough to want a companion, but she is dangerous to be around. She realizes that an act of kindness on her part can make things worse.

Seeing how you've written short fiction in the horror genre, do you have other supernatural interests?

American werewolves. Again, these are social creatures that can be more complex because wolves are more of a social animal. There is a lot of source material that has been published on the social behavior of wolves over the past few years. Also, maybe I'll get the chance to write a few stories about Orgs. We really don't need them at this point in time because we have serial killers.

While I know you happen to love the genre, I'm also aware that you don't particularly like overzealous fans.

People, dressed in black capes and plastic fangs, will walk up to me at conventions to shake my hand and tell me how *much* they enjoyed my book—I can tell. In my books I'm trying to put it across that vampires are not nice—you don't want to be one. I'm aware of the power fantasies, and why people would want to be one. Overall, I find it creepy. When I look at these people I don't see Count Dracula or Elvira; I see Renfield—regardless of sex, age, or race. For vampires, Renfield is a noun like paper clip. They are disposable and easily replaced. Most have a type of psychic power, which the vampires can help them control. The vampires act as dampers. The other character trait is that most of these people are paranoid schizophrenics. So like Renfield, they hear these voices in their heads. These people who dress up and want to be vampires often feel like they have no power in their lives. It enables them to fantasize and deal with it. It is no different from people who latch onto Superman.

J. B. MACABRE

The Stagestruck Vampire

The popularity of the vampire in fiction in the early nineteenth century was quick to translate to the stage. The first wave of vampire plays was sparked by the publication of "The Vampyre" in the *New Monthly Magazine* on April 1, 1819, a short story attributed to Lord Byron but authored by his onetime physician, Dr. John Polidori, who plagiarized Byron. The French led the way in dramatizing vampires.

On June 13, 1820, the Theatre de la Porte Saint-Martin, in Paris, brought to the stage "Le Vampire, melodrame en trois acts avec un prologue." Although initially not well received, subsequent productions received favorable reviews by the press, which added to the success of the play and brought all of Paris flocking to the theater nightly to see the exploits of the notorious Lord Ruthven as the vampire. Other theaters began to offer their own vampire productions as the undead became en vogue. Due to the diversity of theaters and the clientele that attended them, the works were from merely frightening to lurid and sexual. The excitement and blood lust spread from Paris to London, into central Europe, and across the Atlantic Ocean to the shores of America and the New York theater district.

However, for all the forms the productions took, and the various stages they played on, it was the Paris theaters that spawned the most vampire plays. Perhaps the prime reason was that Paris was the home of the most violent and graphic plays known as the Grand Guignol. This theater of sex, violence, and blood all came together beautifully in the tragedy of the vampire. Indeed, the vampire was what Paris craved. At the time, France was in a blood lust of revolution, which began with storming of the Bastille on July 14, 1789, and did not come to an end until June 18, 1815, but had reverberations in bloody revolutions in July 1830 and June 1848.

Just as this first wave of vampire plays was ebbing, a new interest came about with the publication in 1847 of *Varney the Vampyre*, credited to Thomas Preskett Prest (although the real author was James Malcolm Rymer). It was never produced as a dramatic production, perhaps because of its sheer size: 220 chapters and 868 pages. Due to its success, it was serialized and reprinted in 1853 as penny dreadfuls, making it available to a larger audience.

Bram Stoker's *Dracula* saw its first printing in 1897. Stoker was a man of the theater, working closely with the celebrated actor, Henry Irving. Stoker's friends took an interest in adapting his novel to the stage. *Dracula* was dramatized by Hamilton Deane, whose grandfather and Reverend Abraham Stoker, Bram's father, lived on adjoining estates in County Dublin. The production was first performed on March 9, 1925, at the Wimbledon Theatre, and then again on February 14, 1927, at the Little Theatre in London. Raymond Huntly took to the cape as Count Dracula, and Deane himself portrayed Van Helsing. While the play was in no way as strong as the novel, the public's fascination with the subject was enough to keep the play alive as it moved from theater to theater in London. On November 5, 1927, a new adaptation of Stoker's novel, by Charles Morrel, opened at the Court Theatre in Warrington, England.

Interestingly, it was Deane who dressed up the Count in elegant evening clothes, making him a dashing man-about-town in London—a look that was borrowed for Bela Lugosi in the first film of *Dracula*. This image of the sophisticated vampire became firmly entrenched in the vampire literary myth.

Across the Atlantic, Stoker's *Dracula* was produced at the Shubert in New Haven, Connecticut, premiering on September 19, 1927. On October 5, it opened at the Fulton Theater in New York. The cast included Edward Van Sloan as Van Helsing and Bela Lugosi as the Count. The producers of the play stated in their press materials, "Local theatergoers are warned in advance that it would be wise for them to visit a specialist and have their hearts examined before subjecting them to the fearful thrills and shocks that *Dracula* holds in store for them." Nurses were present, and at the end of the second and third acts, their services were required as women in the audience swooned.

Hamilton Deane's play, with adaptations for the American stage by John Balderston, was revived in the 1970s. Actor Frank Langella brought a new, modern sexuality to the Count in the starring role. The production was enhanced by remarkable set designs by the talented macabre artist Edward Gorey. There was little change in the original text; most of the innovations came in the form of new theater technology. Still, it was Langella's sensual performance that influenced the production in making the leap from the stage to the motion picture screen.

While Frank Langella was starring in *Dracula*, in another part of New York, at the Cherry Lane Theater, Christopher Bernau was starring as the Count in Bob Hall and David Richmond's *The Passion of Dracula*. This play appears to be a fusion of source material, drawing upon Stoker's novel, Deane and Balderston's play, and the screenplay used by director Tod Browning for the film *Dracula*, starring Lugosi.

Bernau's play is different from the novel. Lucy and Mina are merged into a single character named Wilhelmina Murray. There is a new character called Dr. Helga Van Zandt, a colleague of Dr. John Seward and Professor Van Helsing. Dr. Seward's first name becomes Cedric, and we are never presented with Van Helsing's first name. Dracula talks more about his ties to his past, his royal heritage, and his homeland.

Renfield is written to be more than just the vampire's stooge, and becomes more of a true henchman. At the end of the play Renfield is alive and well, while he mourns the death of the Count and is remorseful for his part in this tragedy. The play is well constructed. The plot dwells more on the Count's downfall as a result of his slavery to passion and not his pride. The set designs are sparse, but this adaptation does not draw on intricate sets and effects. Its richness comes from well-paced and finely tuned dialogue. It is a rare play—both an enjoyable production and an entertaining read.

The next vampire play of the 1970s was Ted Tiller's *Count Dracula*. It was first produced on December 10, 1971, at Stage West in Massachusetts. Tiller's adaptation is a more straightforward adaptation of Stoker's novel, although he altered several names of characters. Tiller tries an epic approach to the play, but the suspense of the large-scale chase that takes place in the novel does not translate to the stage. (Tiller's version is limited to two sets: Dr. Seward's office and the crypt where Lucy is buried.) Furthermore, Tiller's play, like the novel, is wordy. He takes some liberties with characters: for example, Lucy, called Sybil Seward, seems to be molded more after Shakespeare's Ophelia. Overall, it is an interesting adaptation that is slightly more substantial than the Deane-Balderston version.

On April 28, 1973, the Oval House in London premiered Snoo Wilson's *Vampires*. His play uses the vampire theme more as a metaphor, with no references to the Count. Wilson's production is a three-act play, with each act separated by fifty years. By doing this, the author tries to examine the changing face of oppression and its relativity to a given age. In his second act, he combines the elements of World War I, ghosts, and the psychologies of Sigmund Freud and his famous pupil, Carl Jung. The author's use of the vampire seems to be summed up in Freud's assertion that originally all the dead were vampires who had a grudge against the living and sought to rob them of their lives. Wilson's play is an engaging drama that uses the image of vampirism to stir up repressed emotions and draw the audience into the horrors of repression. It is a fine piece of theater, although not what vampire fans may crave.

In August 1973 the Royal Playhouse in New York became the home of Crane Johnson's *Dracula*, which ran until June 1974. It seems that Johnson simply turned to Stoker's novel for inspiration and characterizations. It is interesting to note that the two previous Dracula plays were "based on Bram Stoker's novel," while Johnson's play is "from the novel by Bram Stoker."

Johnson's play is unique because his Professor Van Helsing was played by a woman with very masculine traits, including cigar smoking. It is a very simplistic adaptation that takes its share of liberties with the original work. The set designs for this production were rather sparse. It is Renfield who enters into a battle of wits with Van Helsing, whose battle with the Count seems superficial. Dracula, for all his years and book knowledge, comes across as a braggart, and there is little mystery to his persona.

As the vampire material thinned, playwrights looked to other sources for material on the undead, as well as to fresh ways to shape the vampire theme and the image of the Count. In 1979 Neal Du Brock wrote *Countess Dracula!* Du Brock tries to create a play of mysteries, and cast members play more than one character. Once again we find ourselves in the Seward Asylum, or sanatorium, but a few years after the demise of the Count. The play becomes a game of double identities. The story attempts to give the audience a female vampire's point of view, and a new sexuality that comes with it. The Countess is not a true relation to Dracula, but is based on the historical figure of Elizabeth Bathory. The play takes itself too seriously, and as a result has less of an impact. In its effort to be creative, it allows several small, yet noticeable, plot holes.

In the 1980s, the stage image of the Count began to take a back seat to the theme of vampire as a metaphor. Following a premier in Seattle, *The Vampires* by Harry Kondoleon opened at the Astor Place Theater in New York on April 11, 1984. The play examines the lives of successful but discontented people. The main character, Ian, becomes a vampire because he is bored with life. He bites his wife to achieve his wish. While the rest of the characters try to deal with everyday life, Ian goes about living his fantasy. Ian's brother, Pat, presents him with a script, which he wants Ian to rewrite. Ian does so with a lot of secrecy. The cast prepares to do a bizarre production of Pat's script as they wait for guests to arrive. It's a "play-within-the-play," looking something like a weird Judy Garland–Micky Rooney film. Overall *The Vampires* is an interesting piece of strange theater. Vampire fans will probably be disappointed by the content of the play, but serious theatergoers may find it satisfying.

One of the most successful Off-Broadway productions of a vampire theme was Charles Busch's *Vampire Lesbians of Sodom and Sleeping Beauty or Coma.* The production opened on June 19, 1985, at the Providence Playhouse and ran for several years. *Vampire Lesbians* is a satire, and in the original production many of the female characters were played by men in drag. The play opens in Sodom, during the old days, as a virgin is about to be sacrificed to a succubus. The creature feeds on the girl but she does not die. The two meet again in Hollywood during the 1920s. The girl, having attained some stature in society, has come to take her revenge on the succubus. Both of them are stalked by a vampire killer. They barely escape. They next meet in present-day Las Vegas, on the back stage at Caesar's Palace. They are now able to reconcile as they realize their mutual need for each other.

Busch injects wit, satire, sexuality, and drama into the piece. His vampires become Hollywood vamps, who in the present day have given up their blood drinking for the chance to use their power to destroy mortal lives as parasites. These two parasites eventually come to the realization that their obsession to destroy each other is ruining their own lives. *Vampire Lesbians* is an interesting use of the vampire theme that may be disappointing to vampire purists, but is certainly good theater.

In 1988, playwright Tim Kelly made a straightforward adaptation of John Polidori's *"The Vampyre."* Kelly tries very hard to keep the Gothic nature of the piece and creates a very traditional Grand Guignol climax. *"The Vampyre"* has been performed by amateur productions. While there were many adaptations of the novella, there are few available for inspection.

With all the dramatic attention devoted to vampires, it was inevitable that someone would come along and write a vampire musical. *Possessed—The Dracula Musical*, with lyrics by Jason Darrow and music by Carter Cathcart, includes songs written for Melissa Manchester and Jane Oliver. Darrow has worked on various albums and produced stage shows from Carnegie Hall to the Olympia in Paris. Working with Cathcart on *Dracula*, Darrow created eighteen new songs for the musical. The team creates a sweeping drama with a dash of comedy thrown in for good measure. *Dracula*'s musical numbers are well written and not far from operatic. The recording features Thomas Young as Dracula. Young's voice has graced such productions as *Evita*, *Jesus Christ Superstar*, and *Pippin*. The musical was first produced for a limited run at the American Stage Company. It is an enjoyable and entertaining work that captures the Gothic tone of Stoker's novel.

Dracula, having found his rhythm in music, then found his dancing feet in ballet. Stuart Sebastian choreographed a ballet based on Stoker's novel, which premiered at the Dayton Ballet in 1990. While the choreography was original, Sebastian used the music of Verdi, Rossini, Rachmaninoff, and Debussy to create the climate for his dance numbers. The sweeping dance numbers are enhanced with some special effects, such as fog, thunder, lightning, and a few screams. The costumes are simple, but elegant. The most interesting costumes are those created for the three vampire brides. In dance, these creatures are almost as sensual as the vampire brides created in Francis Ford Coppola's 1992 film, *Bram Stoker's Dracula*. The ballet played at the Royal Ballet of Flanders in

Count Dracula (David Pittenger) dances with his three vampire wives (left to right, Melissa Taylor, Jeanette Hanley, and Patricia Fenkel) in the American Repertory Ballet Co. production of *Dracula: The Ballet* (Photo by W. Warner. Courtesy American Repertory Ballet Co.)

Belgium in January 1991, the same month Sebastian died of AIDS.

The final form of theater that adapted the vampire theme is performance art, which encompasses various theatrical elements, much in the way opera can have voice, music, singing, and dance, and may be further enhanced by various media elements, such as slides, film, and sound effects. Performance art may not create an overall story, but seeks to stimulate an audience's emotions or create an atmosphere. It is not bound by the limits of the traditional forms of theater.

Using F. W. Murnau's 1922 film as a source of inspiration, Ping Chong created *Nosferatu— A Symphony of Darkness*. The piece begins with a Kabuki dance number that depicts two angels caught in a mortal struggle. At the climax, the good angel removes the "heart of darkness" from the evil one. The heart ends up under the couch, in the home of Jonathan and Mina Harker, who are yuppies in a world where Chong equates chic to the plague of Bremen of 1838. Chong incorporates slides from Murnau's 1922 silent film, *Nosferatu*, with subtitles, special lighting effects, multitrack sound, vivid costumes, and modern dance. Death is everywhere, and as the players go about their numbed existence unaware, the legendary monster emerges in their materialistic lives. During one very disturbing moment in the performance, a digitally enhanced voice, with the words appearing on a haunting green background, asks, "Where did the darkness

Ping Chong's performance art creation, *Nosferatu—A Symphony of Darkness* (Photo by Carol Rosegg/Martha Swope)

come from?" It is a deeply disturbing production in a way that is similar to Murnau's film which, after all these years, is still able to frighten.

La MaMa E.T.C. in New York City was the birthplace of another vampire performance, *Carmilla*, based on Joseph Sheridan Le Fanu's novella of the same name. The piece was scripted by Wilford Leach, with music by Ben Johnston. Here again, the staging was a multi-media event. Styled after a chamber opera, the musical score features rock, jazz, and classical styles. The piece is remarkably faithful to the novella, with Laura and Carmilla being the only two characters on the stage for the majority of the play. While the piece draws upon many of the images in Le Fanu's novella, it does favor the more erotic lesbian overtones of the story.

In one scene of the play, Laura and Carmilla are seated on a couch where there are carved faces in the framework that come to life as a chorus. It is a wonderfully imaginative adaptation of Le Fanu's tale that employs a wide variety of theatrical elements to bring the story to life. This piece has been performed at the Berlin Festival, Spoleto Festival of Two Worlds, Vienna Festival, Dubronvik Festival, Holland Festival, and numerous other European festivals and theater houses, in addition to winning several awards. It was originally produced at La MaMa E.T.C. in 1971, with a revival in 1989. The vinyl recording is, unfortunately, out of print.

The ongoing interest in the vampire, which stimulates the publication of new novels every month and a continuing production of vampire films, undoubtedly will provide fuel for more vampire stage productions. If Shakespeare had known of the tragic Count, he would most likely have written a play about him, too.

J. B. MACABRE

Staked by Silver: Vampires and the Silver Screen

The tale of the vampire concerns blood, sex, violence immortality, and, more recently, rock music. The exploits of Count Dracula and his blood brothers and sisters once were for private consumption only behind the closed doors of people's homes, in the form of prose or radio dramas. With the invention of the motion picture, the vampire was offered for public display. What people could only imagine in their mind's eye was given shape and form, and then, color and voice, on the silver screen.

In the 1920s, filmmakers employed simple lighting tricks and shrewd manipulation of the camera, which we take for granted in this age of high-tech special effects, to shock and horrify movie audiences. Vampire films have always passionately embraced the taboos of society and laughed at the protection religion claims to offer against the supernatural. With the horrors of World War II and the paranoia of the atomic age still some twenty-five years away, it is no wonder that early vampire films shocked and horrified a very moral and timid movie audience. Vampire films, the most censored film genre prior to the rise of the slasher films, created a commotion.

The age of the silent film was a time of exploration into the miracle of motion pictures. While some filmmakers used movies to capture and document history, many, like Thomas Edison and George Melies, used the medium to create the fantastique. Just like the fictional vampire, early motion picture film stock was a volatile medium and was destroyed by exposure to air and harsh light. Only a handful of early films about the undead still exist. Who knows how many more there may have been?

Before Bela Lugosi took to the stage in the 1927 American version of the play *Dracula*, the silent film era captured several likenesses of

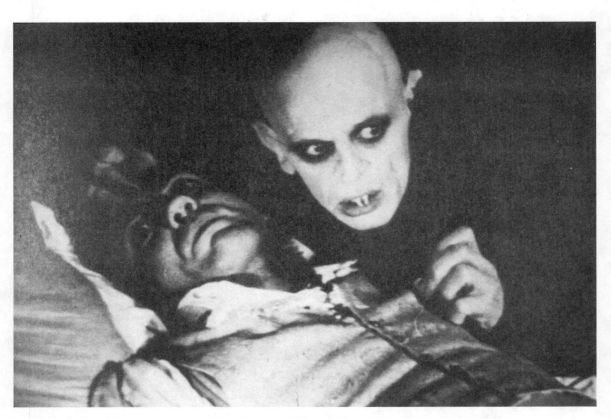
Klaus Kinski portrays a vampire closer to folklore in Werner Herzog's remake of *Nosferatu*

the count. Many film scholars believe that the earliest adaptation of Bram Stoker's novel was a 1921 Hungarian production titled *Drakula*, directed by Karoly Lajthay. Unfortunately, there are no surviving prints of the film, or photos, to provide us with clues as to the count's image.

In 1922, German filmmaker F. W. Murnau shot a film entitled *Nosferatu*, featuring the vampire Graf Orlock, played by actor Max Schreck. Murnau's production was ill-fated, for his screenwriter, Henrik Galeen, had freely adapted Stoker's novel without obtaining the rights. In turn, Florence Stoker, Bram's widow, sued the film company and won. The court ruled that the negative and all the prints be destroyed. Luckily, some of the prints survived. Murnau's film, while rather stiffly shot

and acted, is memorable for the director's use of light and shadow and the creepy appearance rendered by Schreck as the count. Decades later, director Francis Ford Coppola borrowed from Schreck's performance in his own adaptation of Stoker's tale, *Bram Stoker's Dracula*.

Another early film adaption of the literary undead was the 1913 production of *The Vampire of the Desert*. The film is based on Rudyard Kipling's poem "The Vampire," which recounts the tale of a female vampire and her hypnotic powers.

Prior to his 1931 production of *Dracula*, Tod Browning's first encounter with the undead was the 1927 film, *London After Midnight*. In it, actor and makeup artist Lon Chaney goes to great pains to create a menacing image of a vampire. However, the vampire is not "real," but is a device employed to catch a murderer. Once thought to be lost, the majority of the film's reels over the years have been unearthed.

Several other pieces produced during the silent era captured shadows of the vampire. Often, different aspects of the legend were exploited and combined with other supernatural creatures and villains. The legendary French filmmaker George Melies borrowed from the vampire in his film *The Haunted Castle*. The image of a bat flying around a castle is transformed into a devil, not a vampire.

The true vampire and horror boom began in the 1930s with the invention of "talkies"— the addition of sound to motion pictures. Vampire films produced during this era were still causing an up-roar among the censors, and swooning among faint-hearted audience members, largely due to their sexual overtones and antireligious themes. In hindsight, this seems strange because these films generally lacked fangs or blood-letting, and the "good guys" always won.

In 1930, there were two productions of Stoker's novel, produced simultaneously by Universal Studios. While Tod Browning was shooting his film, starring Lugosi, by day, director George Melford was filming a Spanish version, starring Carlos Villarias as the count, by night. Melford not only used the same sets as Browning, he also used the same script. Many film critics are of the opinion that Melford's film is a better paced and photographed film, and that the performance of Villarias is superior to that of Lugosi. Melford's film was believed lost for many years. Then a nearly complete print was discovered, and in 1990 it was restored and eventually released on video by MCA/Universal.

Browning's film was released on Valentine's Day, 1931. Although Lugosi was brought from the stage production to play the count on screen, he was not Browning's first choice. It was the untimely and tragic death of Lon Chaney that left the cape vacant for Lugosi to

fill. If Browning's *Dracula* feels "stagey," it may be a direct result of Lugosi's familiarity with the role and screenwriter Garret Fort's basing of the screenplay largely on Deane and Balderston's play adaptation of the novel. While the characters of Dracula and Renfield have weathered the test of time, the rest of the film is dated. Browning's *Dracula* is of importance because it signals the beginning of the horror boom and Universal Studio's place in film history as "the" monster movie studio.

Another important vampire film of the 1930s is director Carl Theodore Dreyer's loose

Max Schreck is an eerie, repulsive vampire in W.F. Murnau's *Nosferatu*

adaptation of Joseph Sheridan Le Fanu's 1872 tale *Carmilla*, titled *Vampyr*. Dreyer's film is often cited for its use of simple camera effects to create a sense of a dream-like state in the film. However, the film suffers from poor production values, such as misspelled title cards, and it is very hard to follow.

The 1940s were the era of the monster compilation films. Universal had the idea that if a single monster in a film was successful, then more monsters would be more successful. In 1943, Lugosi again took up the cape in Universal's *The Return of The Vampire*; however, he was not Dracula, but a resurrected vampire named Armand Tesla. On the other side of the studio lot, Lon Chaney, Jr., was playing Count Alucard, an anagram for Dracula, in the film *Son of Dracula*. Yet, in 1944 when Chaney was cast in the compilation film *House of Frankenstein*, he played a werewolf, and the vampire's cape was passed to actor John Carradine. In the sequel, 1945's *House of Dracula*, Carradine once again played the blood-thirsty count.

The tragedy of the compilation films and Universal's exploitation of the count was that this shocking figure, as well as other monsters, became caricatures of what they had been during the '20s and '30s. It is no wonder that the final sequel to these films was 1948's *Abbott and Costello Meet Frankenstein*. Not only did this mark Universal's last outing for the classic monsters, it was also the last, and only second time, that Lugosi officially played the count on screen.

It would not be until 1958, and across the ocean in Britain, that the count was returned to his royal status in the halls of horror, and Stoker's novel was taken seriously. Hammer Studios gave us Christopher Lee as Dracula. He was a presence to be reckoned with: an imposing bearing, bloodshot eyes, frightening fangs, and a sinister snarl. Lugosi's Dracula seemed tame and innocent by comparison. Vampire films gained a new respect. In his essay, "The Horrors of Hammer: The House that Blood Built," from *Cut! Horror Writers on Horror Film*,

T. Liam McDonald points out the true importance of Hammer Studio's *Horror of Dracula*:

> The grandeur of the film is evident right from the opening credits with the blaring theme music over the stark image of an eagle (Dracula's symbol), the camera panning over the castle and fading into a shot of Dracula's name emblazoned upon a coffin. Bright red blood drips upon the bronze nameplate, and we cut to the first scene of Jonathan Harker journeying to Dracula's castle. The shot of blood is symbolically important, not in the context of the film, but in the context of Fisher's (and Hammer's) approach: the shot is not part of the narrative, and figures no way in the story. It is merely as part of Hammer's opening statement of purpose, as it were. This is horror, and you will see blood and haunted castles and the living dead and all the elements you ask for. It sets the tone and grabs the viewer right from the beginning.

Hammer Studios quickly became king of the horror films. Its successful formula of blood and sex was copied by other filmmakers. In Europe, the vampire theme was used to make even more graphic and sexy films as noted by Bernhardt J. Hurwood in his book *Vampires*:

> Following Hammer's lead, especially where it involved the element of sex, a rash of erotic films began to appear. The Italians, commencing in the fifties and going well into the sixties, produced a string of steamy potboilers involving everything from extraterrestrial aliens to well-endowed panting femme fatales.

South of the American border, vampire films were churned out at an unbelievable rate. Taking their cue from the American films, they cast aside the classical myths and legends to reshape their films as they saw fit:

> In 1956, the Mexican film industry began production of a cycle of vampire films which carry on the eclectic and extravagant

expressionism of Universal studios. Beginning with *The Vampire* (*El Vampiro*, 1956), the films freely recruited elements from the catalogue of both sublime and ridiculous genre conventions. Dense ground fogs and manor houses flanked by spectral forests are the locations for the operations of such undead nobleman as Count Duval in *The Vampire* and Count Swobota in *World of the Vampires* (1960). While the former portrays the vampire as a blood-sucking gigolo who uses his erotic appeal to captivate and live off the maiden aunt of the heroine and who is easily reduced to smoldering remains by a semi-comic doctor, *World of the Vampires* imposes its particular lore on a revenge narrative—the vampire has come to the new world to annihilate the descendants of a family which persecuted his ancestors in Hungary—including a Transylvanian melody with "certain combinations of notes" which raise the dead and play as much havoc with a vampire's senses as the sight of a cross. . . .

The most detailed and consistent of the Mexican Dracula prototypes is Nostradamus, also featured in a series of motion pictures in 1960. Fully as arrogant as any American or European vampire, Nostradamus dresses with a continental flair.

The bottom line in all these films was still blood. If you craved it, coveted it, or just needed it to live, you had the basic premise for a vampire film.

In 1956 producer/director Roger Corman took the vampire into outer space with his "B" black-and-white movie *Not of This Earth*. Cosmic bloodsuckers, looking like mafia thugs, come to earth in order to replenish their blood supply. Instead of fangs, these vampires prefer the more scientific approach of transfusion. In 1988, Corman remade the film with director Jim Wynorski, featuring porn star Tracy Lords. The original version still carries weight, and some of the film's darker moments have

weathered the test of time. *Not of This Earth* is important because it signaled a departure of American filmmakers from classical/literary plots for films.

The sixties also saw increased productivity in the Italian film industry, including numerous vampire films. In 1960, the Italians made what may be the first satire on the subject, *Uncle Was a Vampire*, with Christopher Lee as Uncle. Lee's character tries to help out his improvised nobleman cousin by biting him on the neck. While the film tries to ride on the coattails of Lee's box office success in *The Horror of Dracula*, there is a definite decrease in the intensity of Lee's work.

In 1965, vampires began to crop up in all kinds of places. More were found in outer space, as in Mario Bava's *Planet of the Vampires* (also called *Terror in Outer Space* and *The Demon Planet*). The biblical character Goliath challenged the undead in the 1964 Italian film *Goliath and the Vampires*. Perhaps the most resourceful use of the vampire myth came with the 1964 film *The Last Man on Earth*, based on Richard Matheson's novel, *I Am Legend*, one of the most acclaimed pieces of vampire fiction of its time. David Pirie, in his book *The Vampire Cinema*, commented on how Hammer was the first studio to attempt to turn the novel into a film, with the guidance of the author:

In 1957, immediately after making *Dracula*, Hammer had bought the rights to Richard Matheson's classic modern vampire novel *I Am Legend*. They even flew the author over to London to write his own script, which was retitled *Night Creatures* and was described by everyone who read it as among the best work of one of America's most talented screenwriters (*Incredible Shrinking Man, Fall of the House of Usher*, etc.). But even as shooting was due to begin word came from the censor's office that, if Hammer went ahead with the film, they could expect an outright ban in Britain. Faced with this pressure, Michael Carreras, who had supervised the project since its inception, had no choice but to pull out.

And so the Hammer version died aborning. The project next became a joint venture between U.S. and Italian filmmakers as *The Last Man on Earth*. It was directed by Sidney Salkow and starred Vincent Price. In 1971, Matheson's novel was filmed starring Charlton Heston and was called *The Omega Man*. Salkow's film is more faithful to both the novel and literary vampire themes. Price employs traditional methods like garlic and stakes to dispatch the creatures he faces, while Heston finds that automatic weapons do a far better job. Both films have their terrifying moments.

In the history of films, no matter how filmmakers have manipulated the legend of the undead, vampire films usually have done well at the box office. After Hammer was able to persuade Christopher Lee to put the fangs back in his mouth, with the 1965 film *Dracula— Prince of Darkness*, a new era of vampire films began and lasted for several years.

Lee starred in various Hammer offerings, opposed by Peter Cushing as Van Helsing. The two next did battle with the undead in Hammer's *The Brides of Dracula*. The film is basically an attempt by Hammer to draw on the success of *The Horror of Dracula*. The project generated much in-house friction at Hammer Studios, but the film works as a result of Cushing's talent and Terence Fisher's direction. The most gripping and ingenious moments of the piece come in the climax when Cushing is bitten and improvises, with a rather masochistic method, to cleanse the wound.

Various directors, studios, and countries have made multiple contributions to vampire films, but Hammer is the only studio to leave a sincere legacy. The company brought to the silver screen such classics as *Countess Dracula, Dracula A.D. 1972, Dracula Has Risen from the Grave, Kiss of the Vampire, The Legend of the Seven Golden Vampires, Lust for a Vampire, Taste the Blood of Dracula*, and *Vampire Circus*, to name a few.

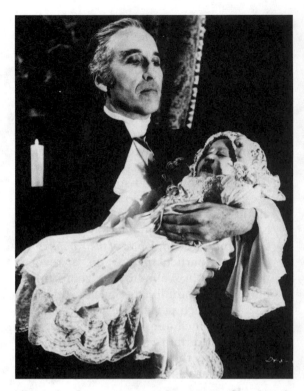

Christopher Lee creates a regal vampire in *Dracula and Son* (Quartet Films)

In America, Universal Studios was the definitive home of the monster movie, and produced cross-genre films such as *House of Dracula, House of Frankenstein*, and *Abbott and Costello Meet Frankenstein*. Interestingly, Universal distributed numerous Hammer films in the United States.

Filmmakers on both sides of the Atlantic began looking once again to literature and history for plot ideas. Hollywood found new blood in Le Fanu's *Carmilla*. Screenwriters took to their history books and unearthed the Countess Elizabeth Bathory, wife of Count Ferencz Nadasdy, who, in the late sixteenth century, developed a literal taste for blood baths to stay young. Some critics believe that Le Fanu used Bathory as his inspiration for Carmilla.

What the film industry found in both the fictional and historical tales was the foundation to develop a female vampire character that would give rise to a wave of lesbian vampire films.

There have been many attempts at adapting Le Fanu's story. *Blood and Roses* (1961), *Terror in the Crypt* (1963), *The Vampire Lovers* (1970), *Lust for a Vampire* (1971), and *Countess Dracula* (1971) all draw from Le Fanu's narrative with some intermixing with the historical figure of Bathory. *Blood and Roses* only uses small pieces of Le Fanu's tale, but contains some rather interesting moments, great locations, and a mixture of black-and-white and color to create atmosphere in the film. The film's Carmilla character is presented more as a psychic vampire and not a literal bloodsucker. *Terror in the Crypt* tries to be a truer adaptation of Le Fanu's tale. The film's Gothic feel and ability to keep the audience off balance, by the mixture of fantasy, dread, and reality, as seen from Laura's point of view, bestows a classic sensitivity to the picture.

Hammer's *Countess Dracula* stands alone in its attempt at telling the tale of the historical Elizabeth Bathory. What Lee did for Dracula, Ingrid Pitt accomplishes in her portrayal of Bathory. However, Pitt's vampire does not directly draw blood from her victims, but consumes blood more like the waters from the fountain of youth. The film uses a different cinematic style than that employed in *The Horror of Dracula* and tries to capture a feel for the period in which the historic horrors transpired.

A film that credits itself as being based on Le Fanu's *In a Glass Darkly*, a collection of tales featuring *Carmilla*, is the 1932 black-and-white West German film by director Carl Dreyer, *Vampyr*. Dreyer's plot does not resemble Le Fanu's narrative, but certainly captures the mode of *Carmilla* in its highly stylized production values—such factors as lighting, art direction, settings, and costume design—and use of the vampire myth. Dreyer was a visionary, a filmmaker ahead of his time. Using a gauzelike material to film through, he creates a dream-like world of illusion and fantasy. One of the most memorable scenes comes as Dreyer conjures up strange images for the character Gray's nightmare. It is through Dreyer's manipulation of the fantastique that he breeds a kind of terror that remains unique to the cinematic vampire myth and lingers with the viewer for quite some time afterward. Only in the late 1980s did the film received critical acclaim.

With a glut of vampire films, the American public began to grow tired of the vampire. People were still going to the movies, but they were also staying at home more and watching

Peter Cushing as the vampire hunter Dr. Van Helsing

television. As a result, the motion picture industry tried to lure audiences back into theaters by making films based on popular television programs.

Beginning in the late seventies, horror films began to take on more weight as the art of special effects improved. The work of special effects artists like Dick Smith, Tom Savini, Rick Baker, and Stan Winston were adding to the box office draw of films. Film projects that were once impossible because of the special effects needed began to get a second look from filmmakers as techniques like blue-screen and go-motion animation became more refined.

In 1979 two important films emerged as theatrical productions. One was John Badham's *Dracula*, which brought actor Frank Langella from his Broadway role to the silver screen. The second was the adaptation of Martin Cruz's vampire novel *Nightwing*, released by Columbia Pictures. Major studios were taking seriously the amount of money coming into the box office from ticket sales generated by horror films. As a result, they were willing to spend money on large-scale productions. It seemed to them a sure bet if their source material was a proven success, as was the case with Langella's popularity on Broadway and Cruz's best-selling novel.

However, good source material and talent did not guarantee a true adaptation, a well-run project, or the support of ticket buyers. Badham's direction creates a fast-paced intense film. He employs several interesting effects sequences, but unfortunately he rushes the final confrontation, kills off Van Helsing (played by Sir Laurence Olivier), and brings the film to an abrupt end, disregarding Stoker's novel and the successful stage adaptations done by Hamilton Deane and John Balderston. On the other hand, *Nightwing*, a wonderful piece of fiction, was not well-served by Steve Shagan's screenplay or direction of Arthur Hiller. Even the bat effects, for a major studio, are poor.

In 1983, two films were released that tried to use literary source material and remain

Frank Langella and Kate Nelligan made perhaps the sultriest Count Dracula and Mina Harker in John Badham's *Dracula*

faithful in their adaptations. Whitley Strieber's novel *The Hunger* was turned into a major motion picture under the direction of Tony Scott. The film stars Catherine Deneuve and rock star David Bowie as the central vampire figures of Strieber's novel. Some of the most fascinating moments take place during Bowie's character's accelerated aging process, accomplished by effects artist Dick Smith. While the film takes occasional liberties with the novel's plot, it remains a highly stylized, gripping, and tolerable adaptation.

Also in 1983, F. Paul Wilson's novel, *The Keep*, made its way to theaters under the direction of Michael Mann. A major problem with

Count Dracula's castle in John Badham's *Dracula*

this film was that the script dropped all of the novel's references to vampirism, which is, at best, implied. The film offers some great special effects sequences as German officers are consumed by a mysterious creature. An especially eerie and sinister castle serves as the film's setting. Tangerine Dream provides a wonderful contemporary musical score.

The Hunger and *The Keep* are important because they show how filmmakers were able to start with good source material, yet end up with entirely different types of films, sometimes good, sometimes faulty. Also, the higher production values used in these motion pictures helped pave the way for future vampire films.

Two years passed before another serious attempt at a vampire film was released. In 1985 director Tom Holland presented audiences

with *Fright Night*, the tale of the vampire next-door. William Ragsdale plays Charlie, the kid next-door, who cannot get anyone to believe he has a vampire living across the way from him. His only hope lies in Peter Vincent "Vampire Slayer," played by Roddy McDowall, and host of late-night's *Creature Features*. The film offers some wonderful special effects, but it is the splendid performances by McDowall and Chris Sarandon, as the vampire, that make the film memorable. Some changes occur here in the vampire myth in relation to the Van Helsing subplot. McDowall's character must face the reality of the fictional monsters he introduces on the screen—in effect, he must face the reality of his nightmares. Presented with such a wonderful character, veteran actor Roddy McDowall turns in one of the most memorable performances of his career.

George Hamilton is a campy Count in *Love at First Bite*

Also in 1985, director Tobe (*Texas Chainsaw Massacre*) Hooper went to London to make the outer space vampire film *Lifeforce*, based on a novel by Colin Wilson. A group of astronauts uncover a strange space vessel and its survivors in the tail of the returning Halley's Comet. Brought back to earth, these humanoids awaken and begin to feed off the life force of humans. It is the film's Van Helsing–like character who deduces that these creatures are the basis for the legends of vampires and man's fear of comets. There are some stunning visual effects as victims have their life force drained and are reduced to withered corpses that return to life to feed, and explode when they cannot feed. There are also the images of strange batlike creatures that lie under the surface of their humanoid appearance, which

emerge when they are killed. The gripping images are enhanced by a great musical score by composer Henry Mancini. The film tends to come apart at the end, but remains satisfying, nonetheless.

Some of the best vampire movies played not in the giant multiplex cinemas but in smaller theaters, art houses, and museums. It was these types of theaters that were showing George Romero's *Martin*, Andy Warhol's *Dracula*, and the bizarre 1970 West German film, *Jonathan*. Hans W. Geissendorfer uses his film *Jonathan* as a political statement against fascism and not simply as entertainment. The film has some interesting moments as Jonathan journeys to the Count's castle. There are scenes that seem to be influenced more by the works of Kafka than the vampire of Stoker. The film offers a rather different climax as Jonathan, joined by the villagers, forces the Count and his fellow vampires into the sea, thereby destroying them.

An interesting mixture of the vampire myth and the children's classic *Peter Pan* came in the 1987 film *The Lost Boys*, directed by Joel Schumacher. A gang of teenage vampires roam the boardwalks of Santa Clara, California. Their "father" feels they need the guidance of a mother, so he comes up with a plan to bring the children of a single mother into their fold. Prior to jumping off a train platform and following his brothers into the mist, Kiefer Sutherland tells Jason Patric, one of the sons of the single mother, "Think about it. You can stay up all night, do whatever you want, and never grow old." *The Lost Boys* is an extraordinary film. Some of the best scenes come in the film's final confrontation as the two brothers come up with ingenious ways of defending themselves against the teenage bloodsuckers, such as the bathtub full of holy water and garlic that they use to fill their water guns.

In 1987 director Kathryn Bigelow gave us her tale of a vampire spawned during the Civil War and his band of undead followers in *Near Dark*. While the film was very traditional in its approach, there are some ingenious scenes where the band of roaming vampires don goggles and heavy clothing and tape aluminum foil over the windows of their vehicles to keep out the hazardous effects of the sun. For a while, they carom about in a recreational vehicle, which, as a gas hog, serves as a wonderful metaphor for vampirism.

Thanks to a new special effects technique, there are several graphic scenes where the vampires venture into the daylight and catch fire. The realistic-looking scenes are breathtaking. Actor Lance Henriksen's strong screen presence and depiction of the Civil War vampire figures significantly in the success of the film. The fine performances by the rest of the cast, including Bill Paxton and Jenette Goldstein, and Bigelow's nonstop action sequences

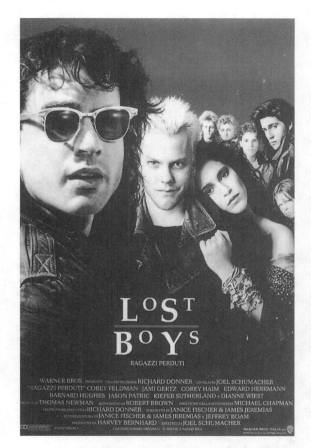

Vampire youths terrorize their mortal peers in *Lost Boys*, starring Kiefer Sutherland (center) and Jason Patric (left) (Courtesy Warner Bros., Inc.)

are intensified by the moody musical score of Tangerine Dream.

By 1987 the video industry had established a strong hold in the area of home entertainment. With rising costs to market, advertise, and distribute a film, not to mention the large fees some actors were demanding, many small films never saw theatrical release. In addition, major studios were suffering as a result of the decaying economy and therefore were less likely to pick up independent films to distribute. Ratings standards were changed, forcing more horror films to cut back on graphic violence to obtain an R rating. Independent filmmakers could not afford the costs of reediting.

Freddy Krueger a Vampire?

The vampire myth not only has spawned a mini-industry of vampire films but it has influenced other types of horror films as well. In the early 1980s, slasher films became popular. At the top of the crest was Wes Craven's creation, Freddy Krueger of *Nightmare on Elm Street* and its sequels. It would appear that Krueger, the "bastard son of a thousand maniacs," could very well be a modern vampiric hybrid.

Krueger uses a razored glove resembling the fangs of the vampire to dispatch his victims. The majority of his attacks take place at night, although he is able to haunt the daydreams of his victims. His attire may not be elegant; however, he is as arrogant, if not more witty, than Stoker's Dracula. As the sequels expanded on Craven's character, the films revealed that Krueger is not just out for revenge but actually consumes the souls of his victims to gain power. It is only when he is buried in hallowed ground and sprinkled with holy water, impaled by his own glove (offering the image of staking), or exposed to daylight, that he can be stopped—at least until the next film.

By the sixth feature film, *Freddy's Dead: The Final Nightmare*, Springfield, the town that gave birth to Krueger, has been reduced to a ghost town, much like the peasant villages of Transylvania, and those senior villagers still walk the streets there like the undead. We learn that as a troubled youth, Krueger was seduced by a greater evil, the dream demons, who gave him his power to cheat death. If Freddy Krueger is figuratively the bastard son of Count Dracula, and not a thousand maniacs, the screenwriters never give the audience a blunt clue as to their intentions. Still, the similarities of plot elements are mysteriously striking.

J. B. MACABRE

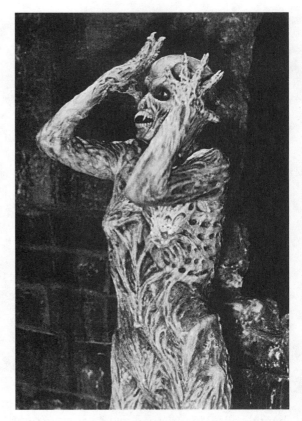

Vampire Regina Dandridge (Julie Carmen) begins to decompose after being exposed to sunlight in *Fright Night—Part 2*

Many films never made it to the big screen. After a long wait, they might—if they were lucky—surface on the shelves of video rental establishments, or on cable TV or pay-per-view TV. Other films were less fortunate, and mysteriously vanished into a void. Films like *Fright Night II, Dracula's Widow, Rockula, Graveyard Shift, Red Blooded American Girl, Subspecies,* and *Sundown: The Vampire Retreat* all went directly to video.

Although many of these vampire films would have been passable in theaters, some are so bad that it is refreshing not to pay the high cost of a movie ticket to see them. The major problem with these vampire films is that the writers and directors fail to seek inspiration

Jonathan Harker (Keanu Reeves) woos Mina Harker (Winona Ryder) in Bram Stoker's *Dracula: The Film and the Legend* (Copyright © 1992 Columbia Pictures Industries, Inc. Used with permission)

in places other than the film industry. Story lines are nothing more than rehashed plots of other films.

In 1991, a new interest in vampire films arose when Academy Award–winning director Francis Ford Coppola announced that he would make *Bram Stoker's Dracula*, derived from Stoker's novel. Coppola cast Anthony Hopkins in the role of Van Helsing, and Gary Oldman as Count Dracula. As a result of Columbia Pictures' commitment to Coppola's project, vampire film productions began to spring up all over the place. Pat Broeske, in the *New York Times*, noted that *Bram Stoker's Dracula* brought:

> Horror. Blood. Lust. Eroticism. The promise of eternal life. Welcome to the dark, alluring world of the vampire.... But vampires—a veritable staple of the horror genre—have historically materialized in B-movies and, more recently, direct-to-video quickies. Now the genre is getting a shot of fresh blood with some high-profile projects with major studios. Consider Columbia Pictures' $40 million *Bram Stoker's Dracula*, directed by Francis Ford Coppola.

The vampire King Lothos (Rutger Hauer) tempts cheerleader Buffy (Kristy Swanson) in *Buffy the Vampire Slayer* (Courtesy Twentieth Century Fox)

Mr. Coppola's film . . . is but one of more than a dozen vampire movies in production or active development.

Coppola's film is only one of the motion pictures responsible for yet another resurgence of Hollywood's interest in the vampire film and its potential as a major box office draw. Other significant factors were John Landis' major studio vampire film, *Innocent Blood*, and the announcement that the film based on Anne Rice's *Interview with the Vampire* was finally about to get a studio commitment. These three films, with major directors and backed by major studios, sent other Hollywood filmmakers hunting for vampire projects to produce so as not to be left out in the cold.

Hardly a year has passed without the appearance of a few small-production vampire titles appearing at local theaters or on video shop shelves. The market for vampire films has increased over the years largely due to the romantic nature of plots found in the vampire fiction being published. These romantic and glamorous plots, enhanced by advances in the art of special effects, have influenced the motion industry to produce these films.

James V. Hart's screenplay for *Bram Stoker's Dracula* draws largely upon the tragic love story of the historical figure of Vlad Tepes and develops this element as the main driving force behind the characters' motivations. Previous films have examined the parallel between the historic and fictional characters, but neglected the romantic themes in relation to the historic figures.

Bram Stoker's Dracula is overly adapted. Nonetheless, Coppola, an Academy Award–winning director, created a furor by attracting a major studio, Columbia Pictures, an Academy Award–winning actor, and a hot supporting cast. While there are many good things about Coppola's film, *Bram Stoker's Dracula* suffers from its share of problems. Even though the costumes are rather stunning, some seem awkward for the time period in which the story is set. Coppola did not want many special effects in the film and sought to employ old "in-camera" tricks to create what he was after, thereby saving on the budget of the film. However, Gary Oldman had problems with his motivations in two scenes of the film, so, Coppola relented on the effects issue and werewolf and bat suits were created. They look like rubber suits as Oldman moves in them, and Oldman's words are muffled by the bat suit.

Buffy the Vampire Slayer, released several months before Coppola's film, relied on many of the bad aspects of vampire films made during the B movie era, and was specifically geared to a teen audience. The film's plot focused on "the slayer" of the vampires, and the vast cast of the undead was there just so Buffy could strut her stuff. The head vampire remains in the background of the story, and other than in the final confrontation with Buffy, is never shown taking any blood. And speaking of blood, there is none. *Buffy the Vampire Slayer* is a bloodless vampire movie. The goriest aspect of the film is the pop sound track.

Meanwhile, the most-awaited vampire epic in recent years was continually put on hold. Anne Rice's Vampire Chronicles novels and her famous vampire, Lestat, were bounced around from studio to studio. Lorimar Pictures held the rights for several years, but let them expire unused, and they reverted back to Rice. Finally, Paramount took the rights. There were still more delays, but production got under way in 1993 for *Interview with the Vampire*, Rice's first novel in The Vampire Chronicles. The director is Neil Jordan, and the film, scheduled for release in the fall of 1994, stars Tom Cruise as Lestat and Brad Pitt as his sidekick, Louis.

In the end, it becomes apparent that no matter how filmmakers try to reshape, exploit, corrupt, or alter the vampire myth, the vampire seems not to suffer any ill effects on the silver screen.

While movie makers keep watch over their shoulders to make sure they don't miss out on the next "wave," the ticket-buying public appears to be sending studios and filmmakers a message: You keep staking them and we'll watch more!

J. B. MACABRE

Those Who Direct the Undead: Conversations with Vampire Filmmakers

The directors of some of the most popular and intriguing vampire films comment on working with the myth of the Undead.

ADAM FRIEDMAN
To Sleep with a Vampire

What attracts filmmakers to vampire films?

The vampire is a character that lives among us, almost indistinguishable from us. Certainly, he is gifted, or cursed, with immortality. It is a wonderful and interesting conceit to get involved with. Any genre picture, any creature or monster, offers the filmmaker a chance to do what we do best—to create our own universes. Any time you can deal with a fictional character, or a situation that does not exist as we really know it right now, there comes such an enjoyable experience at creating and exploring this new world.

I can't tell you how many times, while I was directing this movie, people would come up to me and say, "You can't do that, because a vampire wouldn't do that." My response was, "How do you know?" I don't care what's been written about vampires. I do care to the extent that there are some really wonderful films, like Murnau's *Nosferatu* and to a less extent Herzog's remake of it, but I don't care what has gone before. I do not feel that I'm beholden to anyone as a filmmaker. My vampire is different. I saw my vampire as a character in a Greek tragedy, more than some omnipresent, "never-can-die" beast. My vampire is going through a "mid-millennium life crisis" and is starting to feel lonely.

As you get into a film there are so many questions that beg to be answered. I could not answer them all in this film, but as a filmmaker, and working with my actors, they provide some very interesting moments. There are times when you ask yourself, "What if? Why is he like this? What's going on in his mind?" To try to figure that out and have it come across in the film is very interesting and satisfying.

What was it about the script that attracted you to the idea of doing the film?

Very good point, and very simple. As I've grown up, and I would not portray myself as being a grown-up (but in the process), I've always been upset by characters that are portrayed as either good or bad. In fact, I've never met anyone in my life who is either all good or all bad. I've read about some people who are close, but we all have bad within us. To get to a character like a vampire, who is very tormented, cursed, and evil, it is very compelling. To then bring in the character of the heroine it made me want to try and make these people believable. My goal in doing this film was to make a genre *Wuthering Heights*.

I don't know if Roger Corman agreed with that, and I had many arguments with Mike Eliott about whether this film was really a love story or a horror story. To me it was far and away a love story. By making it a love story, the elements of horror become more horrific. The analogy I drew for my actors was that of a dysfunctional relationship, my vampire being a drug addict male. I was surprised how well that worked in giving direction to my actors. The vampire is fine until he had these pangs, which are cravings for and sucking of blood. In a figurative sense this is what an addict does to those around him—he sucks the life out of those around him.

JOEL BENDER
Midnight's Kiss

What attracted you to direct this vampire film?

I've always liked horror movies, and a few years ago I directed a film called *The Immortalizer*. What attracted me to this particular script was that it has this character who loses control of her life. The main character, a police woman, must track down the vampire that bit her, as she is turning into a vampire herself.

Since there is a long literary tradition to the vampire myth, do you feel that makes it easier to tell their story on film, as opposed to, say, slasher films?

Definitely. There are more grounded elements in the vampire myth. You have the elements of romance, where this individual is able to sweep you off your feet and take your will away. The vampire myth lends itself to a strong story that has reverberations in everyday life.

Are there plot twists or elements new to the vampire myth in your film?

I think the point of view from which the story is told is unique. As the main character struggles to overcome the situation she has been placed in by the vampire, we see it all from her point of view, that of the victim. It is also a woman's story about trying to make it in a man's world, in this case the police department. In one respect she gets her wish—she gets these extraordinary powers where she becomes stronger than the men she works with, but things do not turn out the way she thought they might.

FRAN RUBEL KUZUI
Buffy the Vampire Slayer

What attracted you to direct the film?

Buffy the Vampire Slayer is really not a vampire movie. It's a love story and a comedy with vampires in it. If this film is about anything, it's about believing in and accepting oneself. A slayer is a person who believes in herself or himself. If you do that, you can do anything,

Fran Rubel Kuzui, director of *Buffy the Vampire Slayer* (Courtesy Twentieth Century Fox)

whether it is killing vampires, directing movies, or being a doctor, lawyer, spouse, or parent. A slayer is a person who's not afraid.

But vampires are still vampires! What images did you call upon to create the vampires in the film?

Vampires used to be kind of creepy, scary guys in pop movies. Recently, we've made them multifaceted characters with all kinds of emotions. My Buffy vampire's frame of reference is old movies. When kids get changed, they don't think of Anne Rice; they remember old movies and try to act like those vampires.

Considering that this film is aimed at a younger audience, what role do violence and blood play in the film?

I wanted to find some way for Buffy to slay vampires that had nothing to do with killing, since I was not interested in making a violent film. I am a great fan of Chinese martial arts films, which are for the most part pretty bloodless affairs. Since Buffy is a vampire slayer, not a killer, I had the idea that she would rely on the martial arts as much as possible to get the job done.

There aren't a lot of female film directors who have been given the chance to direct this much action. Usually, the only cars in our movies are station wagons filled with kids and dogs. Imagine an action movie with no blood, drugs, or guns!

How did you become involved with the film?
The instant I saw the title, I knew this was a film I had to make. Five pages into the script, I was hooked. The more I read, the more I was attracted to the world that writer Joss Whedon had created. The challenge in making this movie was to stay true to someone else's vision, yet make it my own at the same time.

FRANCIS FORD COPPOLA
Bram Stoker's Dracula

You've had a stellar career. Why did you decide to remake one of the most often filmed stories in film history?
Right away I knew that would be our biggest problem. People would wonder why someone would go through the trouble to make the same story again, with all the same stuff. My answer was, and still is, you've never seen it acted with this kind of emotional intensity, and we would do justice to the complex character of Dracula. He's been portrayed as a monster or as a seducer; his biography made me think of him more as a fallen angel, like Satan. The irony of the story is that he is a champion of the church, a hero who single-handedly stopped the invading Turks. He renounces God because his wife commits suicide and is denied holy burial.

What was it about Stoker's novel and the cinematic history of the story that drew you to the film?
To this day, I think that nobody could tell you the second half of the story of Dracula. Each film that has been produced, in its turn, has

Francis Ford Coppola, director of *Bram Stoker's Dracula: The Film and the Legend* (Photo by Ralph Nelson. Copyright © 1992 Columbia Pictures Industries, Inc. Used with permission)

picked and chosen how it would tell his story, while throwing out large portions of this epistolary novel. This film is very authentic to the book. It is unusual, and a little experimental. For me, fun. It's like giving unusual food to kids. Maybe they'll say, "I don't want to try that." And maybe years later those same kids will say, "Oh, I remember when I had that. I loved it."

With all the work you put into the project, why did you call it Bram Stoker's Dracula?
My father had a slogan he always used to tell us, and it's a good slogan: "Steal from the best." So I made this film with the guidance of cinema history.

What are some of your earliest memories of Dracula?
I remember as a kid, loving horror films, and in particular *Dracula*. I think the first Dracula film I saw was *The House of Dracula*, with John Car-

radine. I loved the way he would lift his cape and turn into a bat. I was a little older, about fourteen, when I saw Bela Lugosi in Tod Browning's film. I loved Lugosi, especially in the scene where Harker first meets Dracula in the castle. Those scenes are the greatest part of the film.

What do you think is the most impressive vampire film of all time to date?

Murnau's 1922 *Nosferatu*. It is a very powerful movie that probes the strange part of us that's obsessed with vampires. Murnau was very free handed in retelling the story, as in moving the setting to Bremen, Germany, but that was because it was an unauthorized version. Stoker's widow ended up seizing the film. Murnau's film is a masterpiece, and is probably the greatest film ever made on the Dracula story.

How familiar were you with Stoker's novel?

The first time I read the book I was young. What excited me the most were the early scenes in the book where the Count tells Jonathan Harker about the old days and the battles. I remember being a kid and going to the *Encyclopedia Britannica*, which we had in our home, to look up Dracula and found in there "Dracula—Vlad the Impaler." I was thrilled to think that he really was a guy; there really was a Dracula. The next time I can remember coming across the book was as a teenager. During the summers of my youth I worked as a drama counselor at a camp in upstate New York. I was responsible for a bunk of eight- and nine-year-old boys. Almost every night I would read to the group, and one summer I read this particular group *Dracula*. I remember when I came to the scene in the book where Harker looks out the window and sees Dracula crawling along the castle wall like a bug, and the look in those kids' faces told me that they knew this was going to be a great book.

What do you feel is the central message of Stoker's novel?

I feel that *Dracula* is about our blood tie to the creation. We are bound sacredly to God, and that is a two-sided affair. Man can renounce God if he wishes to. Yet, how many of us can renounce our blood tie to the creative spirit and become Draculas, and become "soulless?" Man's relationship with God is sacramental and is expressed through the symbol of blood—Christ hanging on the cross. When Dracula rejects God it is blood that becomes the basis for all kinds of unholy sacraments in the story. Blood is the primary metaphor. In *Nosferatu*, Murnau saw the connection between the vampire's diseased blood and plague; people today may see, as we did, the connection with AIDS. Even if people today don't feel a sacramental relationship with God, I think they can understand how many people renounce their blood ties to the creation—to the creative spirit, or whatever it is—and become like living dead. The vampire has lost his soul, and that can happen to anyone.

Having mentioned AIDS, how do you feel the film addresses that issue?

The question is whether you are infected or not—that is the issue we have to deal with in this film. Blood is the symbol of everything—of passion, of life. It is the main metaphor in this film; it is the sauce that makes the characters potent. Jonathan Harker as the hero is like a man frightening AIDS. Blood is also the symbol of human passion, the source of all passion. I think that is the main subtext of our story. We tried to depict feelings so strong they can survive across centuries, like Dracula's love for Mina. To live in love is a great thing. Dracula sees that as a great thing. It is only love that brings the sweet and pure thoughts. Love conquers everything, ultimately even death. And it is that idea that love can conquer death, or worse than death, that Mina can actually give back to the vampire his lost soul. Gary Oldman was clearly capable of expressing this depth of passion in his acting.

JOHN LANDIS
Innocent Blood

What attracted you to this film—because vampire films are en vogue?

I don't think that vampire films are necessarily en vogue—there have always been vampire films. You have to remember I wrote *An American Werewolf in London* back in 1969 and made it in 1981. It took a long time to make—for one reason, it was considered too bizarre. People did not get that it was scary and funny. I received a lot of negative response because the story was tragic: both characters die. It was only after my commercial success that I was able to make it.

The other thing I faced was the attitude, "Who cares about wolfmen?" I finally got to make it, and that year there was *The Howling*, *Wolfen*, *Full Moon High*, and *My Stepfather Was a Werewolf*. Why was that? Did everyone think, "Hey, let's make werewolf movies." I don't think so, I think it just happened. There was a whole wave of movies where adults switch souls with kids, or was that where women became men?

Dracula is one of the most filmed literary properties. The reason why I did *Innocent Blood* was because I was involved with another vampire movie. Mick Garris and Richard Matheson Jr. had pitched me an idea called *Red Sleep*, about a vampire in Las Vegas—who is basically Elvis as a vampire. Mick and Richard wrote a script, which I did not like, but I like the idea and Mick's original concept. Then Joel Silver paid me money to rewrite it, and I did. I was very pleased with it. It was wild, and it had musical numbers. Essentially it was about show business and blood sucking, which are

often the same. It was a Warner Brothers project, but Warner thought it was just too outrageous after they read it. It was too scary for them. They said, "John we love the script and think you did a great job, but how about doing this other script instead?" They gave me *Innocent Blood*.

I had been offered *Innocent Blood* a few times in the past. I thought it was a very good script, but ultimately not what I wanted to do. I had my blood lust up to do this other film. However, I took *Innocent Blood* and met with its writer, Michael Wolk. I said to him, "Listen, I would like these changes." The studio told me to go ahead and do them myself, but I said, "No, its his script." He did the changes, and did a wonderful job.

By the way, I wanted to make *Dracula* in 1978. *Animal House* had come out, and it was an enormous success—you are never hotter than you are after your first big hit. At that time the *Dracula* revival, which had been designed by Edward Gorey, was on Broadway, and was a big hit. I saw it, and loved it. Walter Merish bought the film rights. I said that I would kill to do this movie. Walter signed Frank Langella, and I said, "Look, I like him, but he's completely wrong. He's a matinee idol and he will not translate right." Walter said, and I think incorrectly, "The only reason *Dracula* is a hit on stage is Frank Langella." I didn't want to say to him, "Look, the two reasons *Dracula* is a hit on stage is one, Bram Stoker, and the other is Edward Gorey." In fact, that part was acted equally well by the other stage actors who played the part after Langella. I really disagreed so I didn't get to make *Dracula*. They made a very different movie than I would have made.

What do you think is the attraction of vampires?

It's sexual. More than any other character in the genre the vampire is essentially a real creature of the subconscious. All monsters are, but vampires really are monsters of the id. Also, you have to remember that the image of the vampire as all powerful and a satanic figure comes from Bram Stoker. The whole concept of blood sucking, bloodletting, and AIDS, and the idea of vampirism as a communicable disease, are all part of the mystery and the attraction. There is that wonderful line that Bela Lugosi utters, "There are far worse things awaiting man than death." I actually have that scene from the film in *Innocent Blood*. It's fascinating that vampires are bisexual—they bite men and women. I'm fascinated by vampires as another fantasy to make real. If I can convince the audience that the woman in the film that they are watching is really a vampire, then I think I did a good job.

The Bat Takes Flight: Vampires on Air

The motion picture industry went through its birth pangs in the 1880s, but it was not until 1906 that the age of radio began. On December 24, 1906, Reginald Fessenden of Massachusetts made the first radio broadcast by sending a radio transmission to a nearby ship. A new era in communications dawned.

The early pioneers of radio were nothing more than experimenters filling the airwaves with whatever they could think of. Radio reached its full potential when it began to enter the common man's domain in September 1920, and took off with a bang as people swarmed to local appliance stores to purchase radios. Families came together in the evenings to sit around the radio and listen to stories from the rest of the world.

In the early days, radio was an information medium. Then, in August 1922, a small group of musicians and singers took to the airwaves on WGY in Schenectady, New York, giving birth to radio drama.

By the end of the 1920s, major radio networks incorporated this type of entertainment into their regular programming. It quickly developed into a variety of forms, from full-scale productions in front of live audiences to simple readings of classic works in small studios. Radio celebrities became as popular as motion picture stars, and the years from the late 1920s to 1952 came to be known as the Golden Age of Radio.

Among the most popular shows were those that had a mystery or suspense format such as *Light's Out*, *Suspense*, *I Love a Mystery*, and *The Inner Sanctum*. In 1937, a young, up-and-coming actor by the name of Orson Welles put together a theatrical company that produced *The Mercury Theater Company on the Air*, and on July 11, 1938, they gave their first production, *Bram Stoker's Dracula*. Using several voices, live music, and sound effects, Welles was able to take the listener's imagination to the cold, dark nights on the Carpathian mountains, and walk with the cast along the streets of London at the turn of the nineteenth century. Most of all, Welles brought to life the mysterious and ghastly Count Dracula. By mixing just the right amount of each of the elements, Welles allowed the listener's imagination room to create the full effect in the mind's eye. Most gripping of all is the unparalleled talent of Welles' sonorous voice as he became the voice of Dracula.

While Stoker's tale, as well as other classic pieces of vampire literature, would seem likely candidates as source material for other radio dramas, there are only a minimal number of productions compared with all the stage adaptations. Stoker's tale was not performed again until 1974, in the twilight days of radio. At the time, radio drama as an art form was being kept alive by Himan Brown's *CBS Radio Mystery Theater*, which featured E. G. Marshall as the host and the sound of a squeaking door, most likely borrowed from *The Inner Sanctum*. With a very limited production budget, actors were required to take on several voice parts, and music and sound effects were used sparingly. However, the technology was such that, unlike Welles' dramas, where everything was done live at the time of the performance, Brown was able to record the separate elements and mix them together later. Brown aired his version of *Dracula* on January 6, 1974. It was a weak adaptation that severely abridged Stoker's novel.

The vampire theme found its way into two stories on the show *I Love a Mystery*. A young actor by the name of Tony Randall was featured in an episode called "Temple of the Vampire," which aired on January 24, 1950. The story dealt with a group of treasure hunters who invade a mysterious cave full of large vampire bats. While the sound effects employed to bring the giant bats to life were gripping, the overall plot was more of an *Indiana Jones* adventure story. The second episode was a multi-episode piece called "The Vampire."

The plot involved a series of crimes where the main character was finally believed to be a vampire, but during the climax of the final episode, was revealed not to be a vampire at all.

With the passing of the Golden Age of Radio, there still were those who tried to keep the art form alive. The majority worked in public radio on very limited resources. *J. B. Macabre's Macabreotorium* took to the airwaves of New York City on March 1, 1988, on radio station WBAI. It took advantage of the new digital technology, the binaural recording process, and a glut of aspiring actors living in the Big Apple to offer up tales of the weird and macabre. The program aired for three and a half years. Among the many episodes was a tale of a modern-day vampire, "Bad Blood." The plot placed an aspiring young black doctor, who had developed a vaccine that could arrest the course of AIDS but not cure it, up against a rich and powerful vampire who was being destroyed by the disease. While the plot employed traditional vampire themes in relation to the myth, the characters were motivated by modern convictions, all taken to extremes in a climax that became a paradox. Reaction to the program was so great that the station manager rebroadcast the program the next day. For the next year and a half, *J. B. Macabre's Macabreotorium* was aired twice a month.

In 1990, WBAI aired a program called *Avenue X*, which was produced by Brenda Black and written by Nate Torres. It was an episodic program that followed the lives of a group of vampires that lived along Avenue X in Brooklyn, New York. The show featured the radio voices of many of the station's local talent, including the mysterious Fred Geobold. The program borrowed many of its plot elements from several literary works on vampires, but Nate Torres helped to make the show successful by adding other unique elements to the plot and capturing a feel for that part of the New York area. The program lasted two years and went off the air not due to lack of audience support but as a result of problems within the cast and production team.

There were many other programs during the Golden Age of Radio that featured horror/suspense/mystery themes. Many programs were short-lived and produced for local audiences; others were produced by affiliate stations and picked up for national broadcast.

However, even the few shows that offered occult tales concerned themselves primarily with mystery, murder, and revenge themes. Vampires continue to make occasional appearances on the airwaves, but the vampire myth is perhaps best suited to the imaginings of the inner eye made possible by the novel and to the visual potential offered by film and television.

J. B. MACABRE

Don't Touch That Dial: Vampires on the Tube

In the 1950s, television was the new sensation. The popularity of TV gave Hollywood a run for its money, borrowing the tried-and-true from the big screen and adapting it to the small screen. The made-for-TV movie was rather a bastard child of a Hollywood film, shortened by the addition of commercials. Later, television tackled large projects under the format of the mini-series. Soap operas and sitcoms (situation comedies) are the true children of the television format, but even these shows can trace their roots back to the Golden Age of Radio.

The vampire readily made the transition to the little screen and served as excellent fodder for virtually all TV formats, from TV movies to soap operas to sitcoms to mini-series.

The first vampire welcomed into American homes via television was none other than the illustrious actor, John Carradine. NBC fea-

tured a program called Matinee Theater, performed live before an audience in New York City. Carradine starred in the title role of *Dracula* on November 23, 1956.

Also in the 1950s, former coat-check girl Malia Nurmi, dressed like Charles Addams's Morticia character, became Vampira, KABC-TV's late-night master of ceremonies of old horror movies. Her mix of the macabre and sexuality, enhanced by her comic timing and wit, were as compelling and hypnotic as Dracula's gaze. America's eyes were fixed to their sets as this macabre image in an amazing package offered motion pictures that had shocked the censors of their days. Vampira was a huge hit. While many local stations tried to come up with their own macabre hosts, none of the latecomers was able to capture the same level of audience attention as Vampira.

In 1964, CBS debuted *The Munsters*, a response to the popular *The Addams Family* running on ABC. Both were sitcoms. *The Addams Family* was based on the Charles Addams cartoons, and featured the vampiric Morticia as the lady of a most strange household. Of the two, *The Munsters* played the vampire theme more.

The Munsters were an immigrant family from Transylvania: They included Herman (played by Fred Gwynne), a Frankenstein-type guy; Lilly (played by Yvonne DeCarlo), a vampire; Grandpa (played by Al Lewis), the actual Count Dracula; Eddie, a werewolf boy; and Marilyn, a "horribly normal" niece. The plots usually stemmed from the family's eccentric habits and strange relatives. Grandpa drank steamy brews while trying to deal with his temperamental bat, Igor. The series ran for seventy episodes and was so popular that two feature film spin-offs were produced.

In 1988, MCA tried to resurrect the series with a new, updated show based on the characters, called *The Munsters Today*. The premise was that Grandpa had brewed a potion that put the family to sleep for a while. Howard Morton played Grandpa, and Lilly was played by Lee Meriwether. Unfortunately, the show was poorly written and plots often seemed contrived. It also suffered from poor production values. Nevertheless, it lasted seventy-two episodes.

Comedy was king in the early days of television, and vampires became a source of comic relief as they turned up in early sitcoms. In 1966, Vincent Price, wielding a mock Lugosi accent, showed up as a blood drinker at Fort Courage on the show *F Troop*. On *The Phil Silvers Show*, Silvers' character, Sgt. Bilko, tried to pass off one of his privates as a vampire in one of his many get-rich-quick schemes. The episode was titled "Bilko's Vampire."

In June 1966, the vampire myth entered daytime television, injecting new life into the medium and setting new standards in the industry. On June 27 of that year, TV history was made when producer Dan Curtis presented us

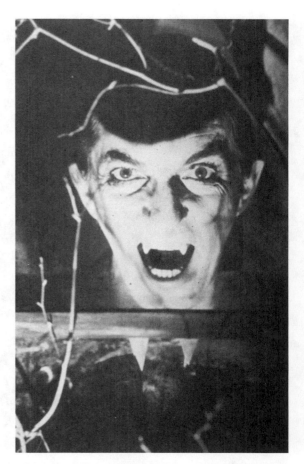

Barnabas Collins (Jonathan Frid), television's favorite vampire, seen on "Dark Shadows"

with a small-time crook, Willie Loomis, whose grave-robbing escapades set free a vampire who had been chained in his coffin for more than 150 years. The soap opera, *Dark Shadows*, chronicled the tragic story of Barnabas Collins, the cursed Collins family, and the Gothic town of Collinsport.

Jonathan Frid, a Shakespearean actor, gave us a traditional vampire figure with a twist to his abilities and his history. The show's writers reshaped the traditional myth by working in flashbacks to 1795, which gave the audience a firsthand glimpse of the vampire's tragic past, the vampire's origins, and the ramifications of those events on the present.

Collinwood, the spooky setting for NBC's "Dark Shadows" (Photo by Fred Sabine. Copyright © 1991 MGM-Pathe Communications Co. Used with permission)

By November 1969, Barnabas had relived his past trials and tribulations, and was again confined to his coffin. This time he was freed by a gypsy named Sandor, and his motivations took on a mission for good. The vampire became a time traveler in an effort to remove the curse that plagued the Collins family. During this quest, Barnabas learned that he was the pawn of a greater power, collectively known as the Leviathans.

But Barnabas's usefulness to the show began to wane, and by the summer of 1970, he had diminished blood lust. By January 1971, he was reduced to a shadow of his former self, and the status of his battle with his curse became ambiguous. As the series came to an end in April 1971, the vampire was a fleeting memory. Frid then portrayed Bramwell Collins, the

son of Barnabas, in a plot the writers borrowed from *Wuthering Heights* and Shirley Jackson's *The Lottery*. The show ended and quietly slipped into syndication.

Dark Shadows gave rise to two successful feature films, *House of Dark Shadows* and *Night of Dark Shadows*, as well as a thriving merchandising campaign. There were *Dark Shadows* models, paperback books, records, games, lunch boxes, and more. The program developed a cult following that is still strong, supporting annual conventions, numerous fan publications, and lots of fan merchandise. In addition, *Dark Shadows* expanded upon the vampire myth by treating vampirism as a disease that could be cured and by giving the vampire the ability to travel through time.

The ongoing cult following, and the in

creasing popularity of vampires in general, encouraged a reprise of *Dark Shadows* in January 1991 on NBC, with Curtis as producer. Actor Ben Cross wore the fangs, and actress Jean Simmons reprised her role as Dr. Lang. NBC pushed the new series with a publicity campaign equal to that of a major motion picture. A four-hour mini-series debut went well, but the one-hour series premier was delayed due to the Persian Gulf conflict and the preempting of the news programs. The series was jockeyed around date and time slots, and the show began to lose its audience. NBC aired only thirteen episodes, the network's commitment for one season and then canceled the show.

There were many excuses why the show failed. Even with its strong production values, it could not hold the interest of modern audiences. The new show attempted to cover the same ground as the old show, but what worked in the 1960s did not work in the 1990s. In the twenty years since the show had gone off the air, the world had changed, and our expectations of entertainment had changed. The horror genre, in both its literary and film forms, had exceeded many of the limits set in 1966. Also, one of the elements that gave the original series its edge was its crude video look. The new series lacked the look and the edge of its predecessor.

One has to wonder about producer Dan Curtis's fascination with the macabre. On January 11, 1972, ABC aired his TV movie, *The Night Stalker*. Darren McGavin plays Carl Kolchak, a die-hard reporter, who finds himself face-to-face with a modern vampire, Janos Skorzeny, played by Barry Atwater. When Kolchak finds that no one will believe him about the vampire, he must personally do battle alone with the undead. The story was based on a novel by Jeff Rice called *The Kolchak Papers*, was scripted by Richard Matheson of *I Am Legend* fame, and was directed by John Llewellyn Moxey. *The Night Stalker* was one of the highest-rated TV movies of its time.

In 1973 Curtis produced and directed a sequel called *The Night Strangler*, again scripted

Vampire Barnabas Collins ("Dark Shadows," played by Ben Cross) goes for blood with Carolyn Stoddard (Barbara Blackburn) on the grounds of the Collinwood estate (Copyright © 1991 MGM-Pathe Communications Co. Used with permission)

by Richard Matheson. This story, although not a vampire tale, has a vampiric element. It deals with a doctor who stumbles upon an elixir that is a fountain of youth. The only hitch is that the elixir requires blood from a woman's brain, removed within thirty seconds of death.

On September 13, 1974, McGavin got a regular paying job when *Kolchak: The Night Stalker* became a weekly series for ABC television. For twenty episodes Kolchak did battle with a vari-

Louis Jourdan creates an elegant Count Dracula for Public Broadcasting System's made-for-TV version of Stoker's novel

ety of supernatural foes. Only one episode, the fourth, features a vampire. In it, Kolchak hears about a series of murders from Las Vegas to Los Angeles and leaves Chicago, his hometown base, to investigate. Actress Catherine Rawlines plays a vampire posing as a prostitute.

A major force in bringing the macabre into our homes was a writer discovered through an amateur writer's contest. Rod Serling, the creator of the successful CBS television series, *The Twilight Zone*, took us on a journey into a new realm of horrors. In the twilight zone, anything could happen, and anything, no matter how bizarre or macabre, was real.

So successful was the show that an anthology-type spin-off, *Night Gallery*, was launched. The debut of *Night Gallery* featured an outstanding cast, including Ossie Davis, Joan Crawford, and Roddy McDowell, and an episode directed by a young, up-and-coming but unknown director, Steven Spielberg. Like *The Twilight Zone* before it, Serling's new creation broke new ground in television history.

Whereas *The Twilight Zone* concentrated more on the surreal and uncanny, often having a science fiction edge to the plot, *Night Gallery* looked at the world of dark fantasy and horror, a place where the vampire could dwell. Serling turned to one of the hardest-working men in the horror genre for source material: Richard Matheson, who used his vampire tales *The Big Surprise* and *The Funeral* to create scripts for the show. *The Funeral* is one of Matheson's darkest and funniest tales. A vampire plans his own funeral, arranging the proper send-off he never had. Among the mourners is a witch, a hunchback, a werewolf, ghouls, and a cast of other unruly guests.

Night Gallery vampires also included an adaptation of a short story by eminent horror author Fritz Leiber, *The Girl with Hungry Eyes*, about a succubus/vampire. Actor Leonard Nimoy, famous for his role as Mr. Spock on *Star Trek*, took on an early directing challenge for the episode "Death on a Barge," about the terrorization of a vampire. Each of these tales relied on traditional vampire mythology, but placed the undead in modern settings and situations. Serling's two television series were imitated often, but the imitators were never as successful.

In 1986 Serling's *The Twilight Zone* was resurrected as *The New Twilight Zone*, with a new musical introduction composed by the classic rock group, The Greatful Dead. The creators sought to blur the guidelines set for *The Twilight Zone* and *Night Gallery* and thus created a hybrid. The hour time format varied, consisting of one full story, two tales, or several small vignettes. The piece "Monsters!" presented the viewer with the tale of a young horror fan who befriends a 147-year-old vampire, played by Ralph Bellamy, who has come home to die. It is a sentimental tale in which the vampire warns the boy that there are more things than vampires to be afraid of when midnight strikes.

Another vampire piece, "Red Snow," is set in a Siberian village, near the Arctic Circle, where a KGB agent investigates the unusual deaths of two party members. What he uncovers in this small town, which remains in darkness for most of the year, is that among its population are a group of vampires dating back to Stalin's reign. *The New Twilight Zone* aired Friday night at 8:00 P.M., did fairly well, and lasted a season and a half. The show did much better in the overseas market and was picked up by a British company, which produced several more episodes that were aired in the United States in syndication.

Nineteen eighty-six seems to have been a revival year for the anthology genre series. In addition to *The New Twilight Zone*, Steven Spielberg gave us *Amazing Stories* on Sunday nights, aired on NBC. Insomniacs who were running the dial in the wee hours of the morning could find *Tales from the Darkside*, produced by the horror team of George Romero and Richard Rubenstein, who founded Laurel Entertainment. They turned out numerous episodes based on tales penned by some of the modern masters of horror, such as Stephen King. "The Circus," scripted by George Romero and based on Sydney J. Bounds' story by the same title, deals with a strange carnival that boasts a variety of dark attractions, such as a vampire, a werewolf, a living mummy, and a man-thing. The mysterious proprietor, Dr. Nis, is confronted by a broken-down reporter. The vampire remains an image seen in the shadows through the entire tale.

In another episode, "My Ghostwriter—The Vampire," a vampire offers his life story to a struggling horror writer. While audiotaping his interviews with the Count, the writer decides to kill the vampire, and succeeds. The vampire is resurrected when the author's blood mixes with the vampire's remains and the vampire has his revenge. A final vampire story produced for *Tales from the Darkside* was titled "Strange Love." Set in the 1930s, the tale deals with a young doctor who is called to treat a vampire's wife, who is also a vampire, and ends up becoming a player in a macabre love triangle. *Tales from the Darkside* ran for three seasons, went into syndication, and had several episodes released for the home video market.

The show was successful enough to spawn a new series from Laurel Entertainment, sans Romero, titled *Monsters*. Executive producer Richard Rubenstein enlisted Dick Smith, a master of modern special effects, as creative makeup consultant. The focus of the tales in this series was the "monsters," and emphasized vampires more than did *Tales from the Darkside*. Again, the producers called on the modern masters of horror to lend their stories as source material for teleplays. "The Legacy," based on the short story by Robert Bloch, has a vampire figure making a cameo appearance when a biographer of a horror movie idol opens the deceased actor's makeup kit and the horrors unfold. Bloch's original tale had the case belonging to screen legend Lon Chaney.

"The Offering" is the tale of a boy in a car accident, which gives him the strange ability to see a cancerous, vampirelike creature that is draining his mother's life away as she lays dying in a hospital bed. The teleplay, based on the original short story of the same name, was scripted by horror author Dan Simmons. Simmons recounts his experience with the process of scripting his story, and offers both the short story and the teleplay, in a collection of his short fiction called *Prayers to Broken Stones*, published by Dark Harvest. Both the story and teleplay offer a refreshing twist on the vampire theme with the cancerous creature.

"Pool Sharks," another vampire episode, was written, scripted, and directed by Alan Kingsberg. This tale considers two pool sharks in the middle of hustling a game. It becomes apparent that one of them, Natasha, may be other than what she appears. Another story created and scripted by Simmons is "Shave and a Haircut, Two Bites." Tom and Kevin, high school students, suspect that the local barbers are actually vampires. They break in and uncover an odd assortment of ancient instruments and jars of leeches. However, their bloodsucker turns out to be the granddaddy of all leeches that the local barbers tend to. "The Vampire Hunter" is a typical tale of the hunter becoming the hunted, with an *Indiana Jones* type of plot.

The last in the list of vampire tales produced for the *Monsters* was "The Waiting Game." The plot is more of a science fiction tale with a horror twist. Two launch officers are trapped in an underground base after a missile battle. They are locked in due to radiation. They finally establish contact with two other survivors at another base. When they finally are able to venture into the mist, they observe figures that appear to be human but are not.

Although the story lines were often weak, the premier season of *Monsters* was well received, but the show proved to be a hard sell to the local networks and was slowly moved from its prime-time slot to a late-night schedule. Episodes were collected in groups of three and released on video. The show's demise was aided by weak production values and stringent story guidelines, such as the requirements that the monsters be the heroes, and that there were more than two settings per episode.

Trying to ride on the success of the Laurel Entertainment programs and anthology format shows, Paramount television teamed up with director and producer Frank Mancuso, Jr., who made famous the *Friday the 13th* slasher films, to create *Friday the 13th, The Series* for television. It aired for several seasons in syndication in various time slots. The creators hoped to rely on the success of the films by the same title, which concern a deformed, supernatural serial killer named Jason in a hockey mask. The TV program bore no resemblance to the films, but used their title. The premise for the show was that an antique dealer sold his soul to the devil, and as a result all the items in his shop became cursed. Characters Ryan Dallio, Micki Foster, and Jack Marshak spent each episode cataloging the cursed objects, trying to locate others and get them back so they could lock them safely away from humanity.

In "The Baron's Bride," Micki and Ryan uncover the whereabouts of a mysterious cape. When they come upon the person wearing it, they find a snarling vampire. In the struggle to retrieve the cape, Micki's and Ryan's blood fall on the cape's clasp, causing them to be transported back to nineteenth-century London. Micki comes under the vampire's influence and is sent back to the present, leaving Ryan to defeat the vampire, reclaim the cape, and get himself back to the twentieth century. In the final episode of the first season, "Bottle of Dreams," Uncle Lewis's ghost, the cursed owner of the shop, appears to inform Marshak that Ryan and Micki have been exposed to a gas that will cause them to relive their worst nightmares, this time killing them. Micki is thrust back into nineteenth-century London and must now face the vampire alone. Marshak is aided by his friend and psychic, Rashid, in hopes of saving them before it is to late. Of course, they all survived to return the following season.

Taking some license with the vampire myth, the writers came up with an episode called "The Sweetest Sting." The cursed object here is an antique beehive. The bees that live in it kill people by draining their blood. The honey the bees create from this blood becomes a fountain of youth. The person in possession of the hive must have a steady diet of the honey or he will lose his youth and die a painful death. There were a few other plot points to the episode, a small amount of tension, and

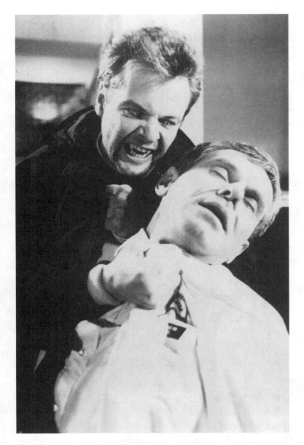

Nick Knight (Geraint Wyn Davies) is a good-guy vampire-turned-cop in Paragon Entertainment's TV spin-off series, "Forever Knight" (Courtesy CBS)

Its legend holds that following a human sacrifice, the cross is empowered to destroy vampires with fire. When Kurt finally tracks down the vampire, he discovers his wife, Michelle, transformed into one of the undead. Blinded by his love for her, Kurt takes her to a warehouse, where he tries to lure in a prostitute to provide the blood Michelle desperately craves.

Sometimes a good vampire is hard to keep down. In 1989 rock star Rick Springfield starred in the made-for-TV movie *Nick Knight*. The plot centered on a vampire-turned-cop who made amends for the sins of his vampirism. The response to the movie was so positive that a spin-off series was created. On May 5, 1992, the premier, two-part episode aired on the CBS late-night series *Crimetime After Primetime*. Geraint Wyn Davies replaced Springfield in the lead role of Nick Knight. The series, called *Forever Knight*, chronicled the life of Nick, a thirteenth-century vampire, who lives and works as a homicide detective for the Toronto police force on the night shift. Nick hopes that his efforts to atone for his 700 years of evil will result in his ability to regain his mortality.

The new series premier restated some of the plot elements of the film. It also revealed that the vampirelike murders Knight is investigating are a result of LaCroix, the vampire master that created Knight in Paris in 1228. The show features numerous flashbacks where we learn of the parallels between Nick's present and dark past. Originally budgeted for thirteen one-hour episodes, the show was so successful in its 11:30 P.M. Tuesday time slot that twenty-six more episodes were ordered.

To compete with the increase in cable and home video viewing, many of the major film studios began to purchase independent, local television stations and group them together under their banners. In the early nineties, Universal began to flood their newly acquired stations with programs produced at their Hollywood and Orlando facilities. One such program was the "all-family weekly action-adventure" program called *Dracula—The Se-*

the usual outcome—someone dies and the heroes get the cursed object back.

The other episode during the run of the series to feature a vampire theme was "Night Prey." While on their honeymoon, Kurt Bachman's wife is killed by a vampire. Even though time has passed, Kurt has become obsessed with avenging his wife's death. He loses control of one of his attempts to destroy a vampire and flees into a church, where he steals a silver crucifix. A priest sees him taking the cross and tries to stop him. As the priest struggles with him, a blade emerges from the cross and kills the priest. Our antique hunters learn that this cross is a cursed relic called "The Cross of Fire."

Geordie Johnson is the Count in "Dracula—The Series"
(Courtesy Universal Studios)

ries. At the core of each episode are two teenage American brothers, Max and Chris Townsend, who are on a long visit to Europe with their mother. Max has an unusual interest in vampires and discovers that the local entrepreneur, Lucard, not only has a sinister plot to rule the world but is actually Count Dracula. The boys team up with their Uncle Gustav Helsing, who is a descendant of the Van Helsing family, to try to defeat, or at least thwart, the vampire's scheme. Unfortunately, Dracula looked more like a spoiled Wall Street yuppie than a sinister vampire, the kids came off as spoiled brats, and Gustav was terrible and too old. The European street sets on the studio's backlot were overused, which detracted from the show. The producers were paid to deliver thirteen episodes, and that's what we got, and thankfully no more.

Cable networks also have expanded, and many of the premium channels (those you pay an extra fee to have), such as Showtime, HBO, and Cinemax, have produced their own original series. Joel Silver (whose Silver Productions was behind such action-adventure films as *Lethal Weapon*) teamed up with director Roger Zemeckis (*Back to the Future*, *Death Becomes Her*, and other films) and acquired the rights to fifty-two stories that had appeared in the E. C. Comic publications. Their show, *Tales from the Crypt*, featured slick production values, big-name stars, accomplished film directors, talented screenwriters, and state-of-the-art special effects, all freed from the restraints and censorship of commercial television. Effects artist Kevin Yager, who created the Cryptkeeper host, also directed each episode's opening and closing sequences. There were three vampire stories purchased and produced over the series' four seasons (a fifth and final season did not come about because they ran out of material).

"The Reluctant Vampire" is the tale of a queasy vampire who works the night shift as a guard in a blood bank. He falls in love, is discovered, does battle, and lives, that is, dies, happily ever after. "The Secret" deals with a young boy who is adopted by a vampire family where he is treated more like the family's Thanksgiving turkey, with a small—but you can see it coming—twist ending. The boy turns out to be a werewolf. Another episode, "Werewolf Concerto" is set in an old, dark hotel out in the middle of nowhere, where guests are being killed off. The showdown is between a vampire and a werewolf.

In general, *Tales from the Crypt* transcended anything that had been produced for television to date. The show's dark humor and wit added a nice touch to each piece. Each season debuted with a three-part special, a few of which were packaged for the home video market. Unfortunately, none of the vampire episodes made it into those collections.

Various cable channels cater to specific au-

A vampire (Malcolm McDowell) guards a bloodbank, but is under suspicion by a mortal (George Wendt) in "The Reluctant Vampire," an episode of "Tales from the Crypt"

diences. Nickelodeon is a station designed for and by kids. In the summer of 1992, Nickelodeon premiered *SNICK*, upscale programming for kids on Saturday nights. One of the new shows was a series called *Are You Afraid of the Dark?*, a well-written young adult dark fantasy. A group of kids, called The Midnight Society, gather around a campfire as they take turns spinning yarns of dark fantasy. "The Tale of the Nightly Neighbors" is the story of a brother and a sister who believe their new next-door neighbors are vampires. As the older sister becomes fanatical in her quest to prove she's right, it is revealed that the neighbors may be odd, but everything they do is explainable. In a second twist, we learn that the mother and father are the Renfields, and it is actually Junior who is the vampire, sleeping in a coffin, locked in a meat locker, by day. *Are You Afraid*

of the Dark? has the potential to scare younger audiences and older viewers might find it entertaining

Vampires have also found their way into the daylight as animated characters in Saturday morning cartoons. Most often their representations are similar to the images created in the classic *Abbott & Costello Meet Frankenstein*. While the vampires may be drawn in traditional attire and fangs, they simply serve as coloring to mask traditional plots. Even Count Duckula, who was born on the *Danger Mouse* series, has his origins as a comic henchman. The series *Duckula* explains that once every thousand years these Counts can be revived, but this time something went wrong. The new Count does not drink blood and likes vegetables. Bugs Bunny, the Pink Panther, and other cartoon characters have come in contact with traditional vampire images who haunt dark and dreary castles. The vampires become straight men, with special powers, to the slapstick physical humor of these cartoon leading "men."

The witch character of Sabrina was developed as a character in the *Archie* comics and was a teenage answer to the success of the television series *Bewitched*, about a good witch who marries a "normal" man. The Archie gang was translated to TV cartoons. Sabrina's relatives are the Groovie Ghoulies, and they often cross over into the realm of the Archies. The vampire, Cousin Drac, and his fellow monsters typically are reduced to a collection of bumbling misfits.

As long as vampires attract audiences and generate high Nielsen ratings, they will have easy access to our homes via the small screen. With the popular emphasis on sexuality, which gives the undead a soap opera quality and attracts a large female following, vampires do seem to have a unique commercial value.

Television standards began to change significantly in 1993, with programming that challenged the censorship standards for language and violence. If standards become substantially more liberal, who knows what may lie in store for the vampire and television.

J. B. MACABRE

It Seems to Be Our Vampire Friend Again: The Undead in Comic Books

The comic book, still perhaps the least respectable art form in the United States, has played a key role in the care and feeding of vampires. During certain periods in the development of our popular culture, this neglected medium has provided a haven for the undead, keeping them at least approximately alive when they were in danger of expiring from neglect in fiction and films. Comic books have also helped to expand and elaborate this ancient myth, moving the traditional figure into the modern world and transforming a classic villain into a sympathetic protagonist. In fact, comics paved the way for many of the innovations later introduced elsewhere and had a powerful influence on an audience of predominantly young readers, some of whom grew up to perpetuate these variations in other venues.

For many members of the baby boom generation, which helped to bring horror into the mainstream of American entertainment, comic books were the only place where the living dead still lurked, the one sinister fortress where they still held sway.

If the decade following World War II was the dominant era in the relationship between this medium and this monster, the symbiosis between them is almost as old as the comic book itself. Comic books began as vehicles for reprinting newspaper strips, but really began to come into their own when original material was created for them. With the debut of *New Fun Comics* (later called *More Fun Comics*) in 1935, one company, National Comics, inaugurated the concept of recurring characters in an anthology format. They followed it up with *Action Comics* (which introduced Superman in 1938) and *Detective Comics* (which introduced Batman in 1939), thus inaugurating the idea of the costumed superhero. Both Superman and Batman quickly acquired their own titles, the company took the name DC (from *Detective*

Comics), and a new form of entertainment was born.

With superheroes all the rage during what has been called the Golden Age of Comic Books, there was soon a crying need for villains who also possessed extraordinary powers, and vampires answered the call. In what might be considered the first significant manifestation of the undead in comics, Batman battled vampires in his fifth appearance (*Detective Comics* 31, September 1939) and finished them off in the following issue. The pairing seemed appropriate, especially since Batman's creator Bob Kane admits that one of the influences on the development of his hero was the 1931 film version of *Dracula*. The untitled, twenty-page story, written by Gardner Fox and drawn by Kane, may have been intended as a tribute to Bram Stoker's character, but Kane's early art is more functional than atmospheric, and Fox's story takes so many twists and turns that it's possible he didn't decide on the vampire gimmick until well into the second part of the story.

At first the villain appears to be merely a hypnotist, who casts his spell on Batman's fiancée, Julie Madison (soon dropped from the series). Julie is lured into a cruise to Europe, where the menace is revealed as "the arch-criminal known as The Monk." He sends an ape to attack Julie in Paris (shades of Poe), tries to drop Batman into a snake pit, and then flees for Hungary uttering threats about werewolves. At this point The Monk's actual job description would be tough to guess, but his behavior is no less baffling than that of Batman, who starts the second half of has adventure by inexplicably dragging poor Julie along with him to Hungary, where she is promptly bitten in the throat by The Monk's slinky female companion, Dala. Eventually, both couples end up at The Monk's castle "in the lost mountains of Cathala by the turbulent River Dess." By now the evildoers have definitely been established as vampires, but nonetheless The Monk transforms himself into a wolf briefly, as Bob Kane had seen Bela Lugosi do in the movies. Finally, to complete the confusion between lycanthropy and blood sucking, a disgruntled Batman trails the vampires to their coffins and shoots them with silver bullets.

A fascinating example of comic book primitivism, Batman's battle with The Monk and his mate is top-heavy with gimmicks as if to compensate for its static technique. The creators of the first comic books were generally young amateurs with few developed talents except an instinct for what even younger readers might enjoy. Individuals like Kane and Fox increased in sophistication along with the medium, and before long their work improved. Batman changed, too. Reportedly, the editors at DC were not happy with a hero who killed people (even the undead), and Batman was forbidden to engage in such grim behavior for decades to come. Only in the in the 1980s would writers return to the vengeful figure of 1939, and in the intervening decades there would be much concern about the content of comic books.

Another major hero of the Golden Age of Comics to encounter a vampire was Captain America. Created in 1941 by the team of Joe Simon and Jack Kirby, Captain America was wrapped in a costume based on the flag, and immediately became a best-seller and the most popular character produced by the company that would later be known as Marvel Comics. A product of World War II, this superhero specialized in battling Axis antagonists, and the comics in which he appeared were noted for unusual page layout, exaggerated action poses, and grotesque villains.

In the 1942 story *The Vampire Strikes*, Cap and his kid assistant Bucky took on a crazed Japanese scientist, Dr. Togu, who had "delved into the realm of black pseudo-science" and created a formula that could transform him into a vampire. Ugly enough without chemical assistance, Togu after downing his drug became a humanoid monster with leathery wings, huge pointed ears, and fangs several inches long. This image of the vampire, hardly traditional, would gain wide exposure four decades later in makeup-heavy movies like *Fright Night* (1985). Nothing dismayed Captain America, however, and he greeted the fiend with breezy remarks like, "I think you're a vampire and I'm gonna play rough," or, "Good grief! It seems to be our vampire friend again!" Artist Al Avison's view of the vampire, juxtaposed with the hero's wisecracks, gives the story a surprisingly modern touch despite its dated plot and racial attitudes.

The vampire stories featuring classic characters like Batman and Captain America were only the tip of the iceberg. Innumerable comic book heroes battled the undead during the medium's early days, but these were not exactly horror comics as we know them today. The stories that came closest concerned heroes who were less super than supernatural. Many comic book anthologies featured stories about magicians; perhaps the most successful was Ibis the Invincible, who made his debut in the first issue of the anthology *Whiz Comics* (February 1940) from Fawcett Publications. Two years later Ibis got his own comic book, *Ibis the Invincible* (February 1943), and because his foes were almost invariably supernatural, it can be argued that its appearance marks the genre's official inauguration. And in its concluding story, the resurrected Egyptian prince battles the ancient Mayan bad god, Zoltil, in a tale with clear vampiric overtones.

By the mid-forties, with the end of the war, public interest in superheroes was on the wane, and a new era dawned in which overall sales rose to new heights as publishers tried every conceivable genre, from humor to crime to western to romance. In this environment, experiments with horror became increasingly commonplace. Artist Dick Briefer mixed humor with horror beginning with the first issue of *Frankenstein* in 1945, depicting the monster, which he had previously portrayed seriously, as a lovable dimwit whose nose had been inadvertently placed in the middle of his forehead. A forerunner of the 1964 television series *The Munsters*, Briefer's comic book featured a variety of genial ghouls. In the eleventh issue (January 1948), actor "Boris Karload" meets the monsters and is frightened into retiring after an affectionate female vampire plants a harmless kiss on his neck.

Considerably less innocent was the lurid "jungle" genre, often no more than an excuse to show scantily clad people engaging in acts of nasty mayhem. In Fox Feature's *Rulah, Jungle Goddess* (17, August 1948), the title character, clad in what looked like a giraffe-skin bikini, battled "The Wolf Doctor." The writer seems to be confusing werewolves and vampires, as most of the tribe of werewolves on view here are women who are not noticeably furry, drink blood, and must be killed with wooden stakes through their hearts. Rulah spends most of the tale's ten pages shoving spears bloodily into their torsos while offering helpful remarks like, "Sorry, but you were a doomed creature of evil." Comics like these, along with comparably gruesome offerings in titles like *Crime Does Not Pay*, were beginning to make the whole medium controversial, especially because it was widely (if not completely accurately) believed to appeal only to children. Yet readers hadn't seen anything yet. The full-fledged, no-holds-barred horror comic book was just around the corner.

In January 1947, Avon Periodicals published one issue of a comic book called *Eerie* and then promptly forgot about it. Yet *Eerie* is remembered today and sometimes cited as the first horror comic, despite such predecessors as *Ibis the Invincible* and *Frankenstein*. *Eerie* did introduce the format that would characterize the genre during its heyday: a collection of short terror tales with no recurring characters. *Eerie* would be revived four years later, when horror comics were finally taking the country by storm, and its twelfth issue would include a twenty-five-page adaptation of Stoker's *Dracula*. However, the first regularly published horror anthology was American Comics Group's *Adventures into the Unknown* (Fall, 1948).

Adventures into the Unknown, which lasted for 168 issues over nineteen years, may have been a pioneer as far as format was concerned, but the contents were tiresomely traditional, with stiff drawing and rigid writing. Vampire stories were commonplace, but so were their plots: boy meets girl, girl meets vampire, and boy saves girl. The only personal characteristic the vampires seemed to display was a fondness for evening wear. It was going to take more than this to create a horror comics craze.

What came along was *Tales from the Crypt*. This most infamous of horror comics, along with its companions *The Vault of Horror* and *The Haunt of Fear*, created a sensation upon its debut in April 1950 and is still making its presence felt more than forty years later. EC produced these comics, and the publisher was William M. Gaines.

Bill Gaines had two unique qualifications for presiding over the creation of what turned out to be the classic line of horror comics: he was a lifelong horror fan and he had inherited a comic book company. His father, M. C. Gaines (who is credited with inventing the comic book as a commercial commodity), had been a major force in the pioneering DC Comics before leaving to start Educational Comics. This was not a very successful enterprise, and when Bill took over he turned it into Entertaining Comics. He dropped high-minded mags like *Picture Stories from American History* and went with the current trend toward crime comics, but before long, horror stories were appearing in their back pages. Gaines plotted these with his editor Al Feldstein, who when wrote the scripts, and they enjoyed the experience so much that they turned the crime comics into *The Vault of Horror*, *The Haunt of Fear*, and *Tales from the Crypt* (which was called *The Crypt of Terror* for its first three issues).

In lieu of continuing characters, EC provided three hosts to introduce the stories: the Vault Keeper, the Old Witch, and the Crypt Keeper. Based on the narrators of radio horror shows like *Inner Sanctum* and *The Witch's Tale*, the hosts specialized in graveyard humor and monstrous puns, thus creating a certain aesthetic distance between the reader and visual displays more gruesome than anything seen previously in the mass media. A typical EC story might show a murderer who ends up the victim of supernatural revenge, and such retribution was terribly messy. In one notorious instance, the parts of a dismembered killer's body were used for baseball equipment. Most of these short narratives were constructed like jokes, with a grim punchline at the end. The writing was unusually literate, and the artists were encouraged to develop their own techniques rather than conform to a house style. The result created a sensation.

EC did not neglect vampires, nor did the dozens and dozens of imitators that followed. During the early 1950s, when novels or films with supernatural themes were in a state of hibernation, the boom in horror comics kept vampires in the public eye.

EC's first vampire story, entitled simply "Vampire," appeared in the second issue of *Haunt of Fear* (July 1950). It concerns an isolated Louisiana community where a young doctor concludes that mysterious deaths must be the work of a vampire. His suspicions center on a wealthy neighbor, a dignified gentleman who wears a tuxedo and resides in a neglected mansion with his invalid daughter. When the hero finds two wounds on her neck, he concludes that her father is one of the undead and promptly kills him with a stake. This seems to be the same old stuff, and the reader can be forgiven for expecting the story to end with the usual embrace, but instead the demure young daughter suddenly admits that she was the vampire and proceeds to sink her fangs into the brave but not exactly brilliant medical man. In its modest way, "Vampire" is EC's manifesto on the subject. The most common theme was that anybody might be a bloodsucker, and tales frequently climaxed with an apparently innocent party suddenly lunging for a throat. In this early effort, readers were clearly expected to believe what the hero did: people who wore tuxedos were fiends in human form. In EC's pages, vampires were democratized.

Some EC vampires even were in show business. Johnny Craig, who had drawn "Vampire," soon became the company's only artist to regularly write his own stories, and in his best work involving the undead he depicted them as entertainers. Craig drew in a clean, elegant style, and his characters looked as if they belonged in the era's advertisements; the contrast between their appearance and their activities was dramatically effective. In "One Last Fling" (*Vault of Horror*, October 1951), Harry and Olga are performers who have a knife-throwing act. Olga is bitten while they tour Europe, and after her death returns as a vampire. Harry, who sill loves her, is delighted to have her back again and arranges to protect her as they travel across America in their trailer, leaving corpses in every city where they put on their act. Eventually the strain begins to take its toll on Harry, and the marriage disintegrates. When he demands that she control her addiction and locks her in by sealing their door with a cross, Olga can't help herself and takes a sip of Harry while he sleeps. "I just took . . . a little!" In despair, her husband solves their problem in a professional manner. On stage, dying from lack of blood, he announces a show-biz first and deftly dispatches his wife with a well-flung stake. What makes the story remarkable is not the gimmick but rather the emphasis on personalities. It would be years before novelists would follow the lead and begin to treat vampires as complex characters instead of sinister stereotypes.

Craig's sweetest, sickest vampire love story was "Two of a Kind" (*Vault of Horror*, August 1952). An actor and an actress, both stage stars reeking of glamour, fall in love and run off for a ski weekend. "Sounds like a lot of goofy mush, eh?" leers the Vault Keeper. "Well, don't be impatient! The good part is just beginning!" It turns out that he's a ghoul and she's a vampire, and they end up snowbound in an isolated cabin. Trapped, starving, but committed to the concept that love is strong as death, they romantically refrain from destroying each other. Instead, she secretly drinks her own blood while he furtively devours his own flesh, and neither survives.

Bill Gaines and Al Feldstein, who wrote almost all the EC horror stories except Craig's, were not so sentimental about relationships. In their typical stories, marriage was little more than a motive for murder. In "Bats in My Belfry," illustrated by Jack Davis (*Tales from the Crypt*, June 1951), an actor becomes unemployable when he loses his hearing and is nagged by his mercenary wife into seeking treatment from a quack. He is cured by a transplant from a bat's "auditory system," but side effects transform him into a vampire. He makes a nice adjustment, however, putting the bite on his wife and her lover and then retiring to a coffin and a new career as a supernatural menace. Employment remained a problem for many EC vampires, however; they weren't aristocrats with ancestral castles, and many of them had to scramble for survival.

Jack Davis, the most prolific of EC's horror artists, was an especially appropriate choice for tales about the undead on the job. A fast worker who used a slightly cartoonish style in even his grimmest work, Davis made a specialty of rumpled, seedy, slack-jawed characters. He eventually became one of the country's most popular illustrators, appearing in magazines from *Time* to *TV Guide*, but in 1951 he was knocking out EC's funniest and funkiest vampire yarn, "The Reluctant Vampire" (*Vault of Horror*, August 1951). The premise, which in lesser hands might have been the punchline, is that a vampire has taken a job as a night watchman in a blood bank. This idea had been kicked around for years (the *New Yorker*'s macabre cartoonist, Charles Addams, reported that people were constantly suggesting it to him), but EC picked it up and ran.

Mr. Drink, a pathetic derelict, sleeps by day in the trash-filled basement of an abandoned building and maintains his existence by pilfering supplies from the office. His modest aspirations are achieved, but only until it is announced that the blood bank may close because its quota for donations has not been met. In desperation and disgust, Drink takes to the street for the first time in years, forced to kill and then contribute the blood so he won't lose his job. He works so hard that his boss wins a medal "for patriotic and unselfish effort," but Drink's deeds are discovered and the medal goes to him—pinned to his chest with a stake.

Another Jack Davis offering, about a moonlighting taxi driver who consumes his passengers, was entitled "Fare Tonight, Followed by Increasing Clottiness . . ." (*Tales from the Crypt*, June 1953). In tales like this one, which expended most of their energy inventing something new for a vampire to do, the trademarked EC violence was notably restrained. The shock lay not in gruesome visuals but in increasingly outrageous variations on a theme.

The apotheosis of EC's audacity may have been achieved in "A Little Stranger" (*Haunt of Fear*, July 1952). It was drawn by Graham Ingels, the third in EC's triumvirate of top horror artists, who often signed his work "Ghastly." A master at delineating shadowy decay, Ingels used ink to suggest the essence of putrescence, often in a Gothic setting like this tale's. In old Bavaria, a male werewolf and a female vampire fall in love, but angry villagers see to it that he is shot with a silver bullet while she is transfixed by the traditional shaft. Undaunted by such impediments to desire, the lovers rise from their graves and are wed amid a throng of rotting corpses. Months later, the dead gather once more, this time to celebrate a birth. The vampire lies in her coffin, a baby cradled in her arms, and that infant is the narrator of the story—the Old Witch herself. In this unexpected bit of meta-fiction, the vampire has become the mother of the very comic book in which she and her daughter appear.

EC used the werewolf and vampire combination with surprising frequency, usually in stories with a jack-in-the-box structure characterized by the climactic revelation that the least likely person was a vampire. In Craig's "Werewolf Concerto" (*Vault of Horror*, December 1950), a hotel is haunted by a werewolf, and suspicion falls on a glamorous guest. Actually, the manager is the guilty party, but in the end he is killed by the woman who, although not what she seemed to be, is nonetheless definitely a vampire. In "The Secret," written by Carl Wessler and drawn by George Evans (*Haunt of Fear*, March 1954), an orphan is adopted by parents who have undead designs on his blood, but he turns out to have lycanthropic tendencies and ends up eating them instead. Readers were left to wonder which sort of monster was actually tougher (the element of surprise seemed crucial), but by then EC had bigger problems: "The Secret" was one of the stories that publisher William Gaines was summoned to defend before the U.S. Senate Subcommittee to Investigate Juvenile Delinquency.

By 1954, EC's success had inspired a host of inferior imitators, and dozens of different horror comics were on sale each month. Comic book circulation was at an all-time high; close to 70 million issues of all types (not just horror) were published monthly. It was almost inevitable that someone would declare the medium a menace. A New York psychiatrist, Dr. Fredric Wertham, declared in his book *Seduction of the Innocent* (1954) that the lurid images in comic books were corrupting the youth of the nation, causing everything from mental illness to juvenile delinquency. Wertham spearheaded a successful campaign, working up the public to the point where humble newsprint pamphlets became the subject of congressional consideration. The hearings included such enigmatic exchanges as this one between Gaines and subcommittee investigator Herbert Hannoch, who asked the publisher, "Do you know any place where there are such things?"

"As vampires?" asked Gaines in turn.

"Yes."

"No sir," answered Gaines. "This is just fantasy."

Ultimately the government did nothing about comic books, but the industry did. Unnerved by Dr. Wertham, the Senate, and the public, publishers capitulated to an attack on a mass medium that set the pattern for many more to come but remains the most devastating to date. A self-censorship body, the Comics Code Authority, was established by leading comic book companies to regulate content and placate an unduly inflamed nation. Restraints included a ban on almost all horror themes, including vampires and vampirism. Despite these efforts, if not because of them, comics went into a slump that lasted for years. Most publishers went out of business. EC survived and finally flourished by turning its humor comic book, *Mad*, into a black-and-white magazine that was not subject to the Comics Code. The horror comics, however, were stone dead.

Most of the horror comics that flourished between 1950 and 1955 were blatant attempts to cash in on EC's success, and thus not much of a loss. Take the case of a comic book called *Mysterious Adventures*, published by Story Comics. In April 1953, EC's *Tales from the Crypt* presented "Midnight Mess," in which artist Joe Orlando depicted an entire town full of vampires. An innocent traveler, dropping into a restaurant for a late meal, is marked for death when he inadvertently reveals himself as an interloper by failing to digest such dishes as french-fried scabs. This bit of sick humor, which became EC's most renowned vampire tale when it appeared as a segment of the 1973 movie *The Vault of Horror*, was also popular with the editors of *Mysterious Adventures*. They condensed it to four pages, retitled it "Ghost Town," and printed it in their February 1954 issue.

Rival publishers didn't always sink to pure plagiarism, however, and occasionally came up with a cute idea in the EC vein. In the first issue of Farrell Comics' *Strange Fantasy* (August 1953), anonymous creators had a nice gimmick for the story "Nightmare Merchant": wearing a black uniform and driving a black van, a "milkman" for the undead makes nightly deliveries of bottled blood to selected customers on his route. The dark inversion of a wholesome ritual makes the story sound far better than it is, however; the art is stiff and the plot makes so many pointless turns that its impact is lost. Only EC had the knack for introducing modern twists into an ancient theme.

A traditional approach was likely to be even less rewarding. "Partners in Blood," a story from Superior Comics' *Journey into Fear* (March 1952), seems almost wholly dependent on Hollywood cliches. A professor and his niece visit a European castle, complete with a hunchbacked caretaker, and soon encounter its owner, the beautiful Baroness von Erich. The professor discovers she is a vampire through time-tested means like family records and mysterious portraits, and on the story's last page he hammers a stake into her. With only a few panels left for this trivial tale, the writer attempts an EC-style surprise: the professor's niece has been recruited to the ranks of the undead. There is still a third of a page left, however, and possibly some qualms about letting villainy triumph, so at the last moment the new vampire and the hunchback accidentally fall off the castle's battlements to their apparent deaths, complete with cries of "Agggggg" and "Eeeeeee!"

A look at the competition, in short, only shows how much EC gave to the undead. Bill Gaines and company defined the horror comic and the vampire's place in it. They used vampirism as a metaphor for everything from drug addiction to a dead-end job and also presented the condition as a desirable opportunity to fight injustice, to create a viable subculture, or even to experience undying love. All in all, the three EC horror comics published thirty-one vampire stories, and in the process they changed this legendary figure from an abstract embodiment of evil into a complex, contemporary figure. It would take the other media decades to catch up.

The suppression of the horror comics proved, if nothing else, that it's hard to keep a good vampire down. EC's contribution to popular culture would gradually be validated by film adaptations, a television series, and countless reprints, but the undead came crawling back even faster. By 1957, America was caught up in a new horror boom that has continued to the present day. A package of horror films, including entries in the classic *Dracula* series from Universal Pictures, was released to television and attracted huge audiences. At the same time, small studios like American-International and England's Hammer Films began producing new movies with traditional supernatural themes.

Within a year, the United States was enjoying a widespread "monster" fad, and in 1958 it spawned a magazine called *Famous Monsters of Filmland*. Published by James Warren and edited by Forrest J Ackerman, *Famous Monsters* was a celebration of fright films geared to a juvenile audience; its success encouraged other magazines of the same ilk, including Warren's own *Monster World*. With its first issue in 1964, *Monster World* introduced film adaptations in comic book form; Warren was testing the waters.

In 1964, Warren Publications released the premiere issue of *Creepy*, an event marking the return of the horror comic after a decade spent in an unmarked grave. *Creepy* used a format similar to *Famous Monsters* and *Mad*: larger than a traditional comic book and printed in black and white, it was technically a magazine for a mature audience and thus not under the jurisdiction of the Comics Code. Still, it might have

had trouble getting distribution if anyone had still believed the once compelling contention that comics were capable of corrupting the nation.

With its first issue, edited by Russ Jones, *Creepy* presented two vampire tales, both written by Archie Goodwin. A dedicated EC fan, Goodwin became editor with *Creepy*'s fourth issue and wrote virtually all the stories during its most fruitful period. However, it was the artists who most firmly established *Creepy* as a direct descendant of *Tales from the Crypt*. The cover of the first issue was drawn by Jack Davis, who also designed a host called Uncle Creepy. Davis was only one of the EC alumni to come on board, and their artwork was shown to good advantage by large, clear, monochrome reproductions that emphasized detail.

Inevitably, many of the handsome if horrific images in *Creepy* involved vampires; as noted, the undead were on view in two of the first issue's seven stories. "Pursuit of the Vampire," illustrated by Angelo Torres, concerns a visitor to an Austrian village who helpfully rids the region of bloodsuckers, but is ultimately revealed to be a werewolf who wants exclusive grazing privileges for himself. In "Vampires Fly at Dusk," the new bride of a Sicilian Count finds evidence that someone in her villa is drinking blood. Convinced that her husband is guilty, she draws back a window's velvet curtains to destroy him with sunlight. She dies instead, an amnesiac whose mind blotted out memories of her own transgressions. With these two tales, writer Goodwin demonstrated his facility with gimmick stories and also with a more psychological approach and showed a distinct fondness for period pieces that was enhanced by Reed Crandall's drawing for "Vampires Fly at Dusk." Crandall, who had worked at EC and soon became a mainstay for *Creepy*, had developed an elegant style based on fine-line work; it suggested Victorian engravings.

Vampires began popping up in almost every issue, and so did former EC artists: Joe

Orlando, George Evans, Al Williamson, John Severin, and Wallace Wood. Johnny Craig made a comeback, initially working under the alias "Jay Taycee," and contributed a piece about a maritime vampire, "Midnight Sail," for the tenth issue. Other artists arrived of equal talent, including Steve Ditko, Alex Toth, Neal Adams, and Gene Colan, and although contributors came and went, overall they represented an impressive collection of talent. Younger artists like Berni Wrightson and Richard Corben would later make their mark as well. A few opportunities were missed, however. A long adaptation of J. Sheridan Le Fanu's vampire classic *Carmilla*, in the nineteenth issue, was faithful to the author but fatally weakened as a result of mediocre artwork by Robert Jenney.

Warren Publications soon followed *Creepy* with an identical twin called *Eerie*. Using the same approach and the same contributors, it flourished as well, and was joined in 1969 by *Vampirella*. This sister publication, which constituted a distinct departure, was the first regularly scheduled comic book to include vampires in its title.

Publisher James Warren took credit for the idea of *Vampirella*, which was inspired by Jean-Claude Forest's *Barbarella*, a sexy French comic strip with a science fiction theme (a young Jane Fonda played the title role in the 1967 film version). Warren wanted an attractive female character to star in a horror comic, and ended up with a totally sympathetic vampire years before such characters became commonplace in fiction. She was presented to the public, wearing a scanty red costume that was stronger on form than function, on the cover of *Vampirella* (issue 1). The striking cover illustration was the work of Frank Frazetta, whose powerful paintings had been one of the chief attractions of the earlier Warren comic books.

Inside the first issue, Vampirella's debut was scripted by Forrest J Ackerman, editor of *Famous Monsters of Filmland* and an inveterate punster who coined the term "sci-fi." Thus it was perhaps inevitable that her initial adventure, drawn by Tom Sutton, would be a humorous space opera. She was depicted as a denizen of a world whose ecology was based on hemoglobin rather than water, just a healthy young woman who bathed in blood and cracked bad jokes. She arrived on earth after her planet suffered a drought, and within a few issues her story had taken on a much more serious tone. Sutton toned down the more cartoonish aspects of his artwork, Archie Goodwin took over the writing, and Vampirella became a heroic figure, fighting off the forces of uncanny evil while fleeing from human enemies who failed to comprehend her basically virtuous character. She may have lived on blood, but somehow she never seemed to kill anyone who didn't deserve it. In short, with her magical powers, skintight costume, and endless battles against oppression, Vampirella became some sort of supernatural superhero. As such, she enjoyed an extraordinary run. Along with other "Illustrated Tales to Bewitch and Bedevil You," her adventures appeared in 112 issues of *Vampirella* from 1969 to 1983, making her the champion of comic book vampires as far as longevity is concerned.

Vampirella underwent many metamorphoses over the years, thanks to writers including T. Casey Brennan, Steve Engelhart, and Bill DuBay. Perhaps the most notable of later artists was Spaniard Jose Gonzalez, whose European style suggested fashion illustration as much as comic book technique. A supporting cast evolved, including the father-and-son team of Conrad and Adam Van Helsing, who were descendants of the vampire hunter created by Bram Stoker for *Dracula*.

Count Dracula has never been far from the minds of people working on horror comics, and in fact he became a character in some of Vampirella's adventures. Later, the Count was given his own series in the pages of *Vampirella*, with scripts by Gerry Boudreau and drawings by Esteban Maroto. With Stoker's creation free from the clutches of copyright, he was popping out of his coffin with increasing frequency. As early as 1966, Ballantine Books had published a 150-page adaptation of Stoker's novel in paperback form. The script by comic book veterans Otto Binder and Johnny Craig (under the alias Craig Tennis) was an unusually accurate version of a book frequently subject to change, but the artwork by Alden McWilliams, although capable, was lacking in panache.

Another version, more condensed at fifty-five pages, was published in 1973 by Pendulum Press. The art by Nestor Redondo was effectively atmospheric, but perhaps the most remarkable aspect of this version was that it was conceived and marketed as an educational tool for use in schoolrooms. Part of the Now Age Illustrated Series, this *Dracula* was intended to encourage students to develop reading skills. Things had changed quite a bit since the days when horror comics were being condemned as a menace to American youth. The supervisor of Now Age, Vince Fago, had been one of the first editors at Marvel Comics, and it was Marvel that would bring vampires back into the mainstream of color comic books.

In 1971, Marvel took on the Comics Code. Stan Lee, Marvel's editor-in-chief, was determined to do a story in which the popular hero Spider-Man could warn readers about the dangers of drug addiction, but this was a topic strictly forbidden by the code. Convinced that the code was outdated and that he was working in a good cause, Lee went ahead with the story and the sky did not fall. In fact, it was widely praised, and as a result the Comics Code was revised and modernized. The new guidelines permitted the use of such "traditional" horror figures as vampires, and although the ruling was not exactly a license to splatter the page with gore, the undead were unleashed. Almost immediately, Spider-Man ran into a menace called Morbius, the Living Vampire, whose condition was the result of a scientific experiment gone awry. Marvel's real move, however, came when it took on the mass media's number one nosferatu, the bloodsucker

with the biggest brand name of all.

The Tomb of Dracula made its debut in April 1972 and ran until 1979 for a total of seventy issues (there were also six issues of a black-and-white magazine version). Billed during the peak of its popularity as "Comicdom's Number 1 Fear Magazine," *Tomb of Dracula* enjoyed sales that were anything but anemic and, in fact, enjoyed a longer run than any other comic book centered around the career of a villain. The artist for each and every issue was Gene Colan, a veteran who had already demonstrated a considerable talent for terror in *Creepy*. Colan had developed a moody, dramatic style with a strong emphasis on lighting and shadows, which he realized would find a perfect vehicle in a vampire epic. He lobbied for the job, which proved to be a highlight of his career.

The earliest issues of *Tomb of Dracula* were written by Gerry Conway and the ubiquitous Archie Goodwin, but after a few issues the series fell into the hands of the suitably named Marv Wolfman, who carried it to the end. Wolfman, who claimed to be unfamiliar with any version of Dracula except the one in the original novel, employed a strategy rather similar to the one Bram Stoker had originally used. Dracula was a powerful presence brooding over the narrative, and his entrances were impressive, but his appearances were cleverly rationed, and in some issues he barely bothered to drop in.

Wolfman's story, which continued from month to month, gained much of its momentum from the human characters who interacted in the course of their battle against a bloodthirsty antagonist. Almost inevitably, Wolfman's heroes included descendants of Stoker's creations, notably Quincy Harker. Stoker spelled the name "Quincey," but either way, this was the baby born at the end of the novel, surviving into the late twentieth century as an elderly vampire hunter confined to a wheelchair. He was killed fighting Dracula, and so was the beautiful young Rachel Van

Helsing, who was transformed into a vampire and then demanded her own destruction. Each of them had the satisfaction of believing that their sacrifices had laid Dracula to rest at last, but his apparently infinite ability to resurrect himself gave him the last laugh. *Tomb of Dracula* was not always reassuring.

What finally killed Marvel's Dracula (although presumably a slump in sales had something to do with it) was a conspiracy of characters, armed with a magic spell. Series regulars like Blade (an African-American armed with wooden knives) and Hannibal King (a private eye resisting the infection of vampirism by sheer willpower) showed up in the pages of *Dr. Strange*, a Marvel comic book that featured the exploits of the world's most powerful wizard. Dr. Strange, using an incantation called the Montesi Formula, eradicated all the vampires in the known universe, or at least Marvel's universe. This cosmic cancellation lasted for years, although there are recent signs that the spell is something less than permanent.

By the time Dr. Strange was casting his spell, dramatic changes were taking place in the comic book business as well. Once available on virtually every newsstand in the country, comics had gradually become a specialty item, with customers including collectors and connoisseurs as well as kids. Comic book shops by the thousands sprang up all over the country and soon accounted for a substantial majority of sales. These changes did not necessarily mean a reduction in the impact of the medium; in fact, certain popular heroes continued to set sales records. Yet publishing programs became more focused, and a number of new independent companies were started to share at least a small portion of the market with giants like Marvel and DC. Theoretically, the independents provided a forum for individualistic projects that were not geared toward huge sales, but in practice, economic considerations encouraged comics that were spin-offs from popular films or books. As a result, creativity was not really at a premium.

Fright Night, a Columbia film about a teenager battling a vampire, proved to be quite successful on its release in 1985, and a sequel was being prepared for 1989 when Now Comics introduced its *Fright Night* comic book in 1988. *To Die For*, a considerably less impressive movie, nonetheless inspired a one-issue adaptation from Blackthorne Publishing; its only distinguishing characteristic was the fact that it was produced in 3-D, complete with red-and-blue glasses. When the old supernatural soap opera *Dark Shadows* (1966–1971) made a prime-time television comeback in 1991, a comic book from Innovation Publishing was close behind (there had also been a comic book spin-off from Gold Key of the original series). Innovation Publishing has also capitalized on today's most popular vampire fiction by producing versions of Anne Rice's best-selling novels *Interview with the Vampire*, *The Vampire Lestat*, and *Queen of the Damned*. In her own interviews, Rice has expressed some doubt about the degree to which the comics capture the mood of her work, but they are handsomely produced, employing full-color paintings instead of line drawings.

Reprints of classics from the Warren and EC lines are a welcome feature of today's comic book scene, but most publishers have gone straight for the main vein by producing endless variations on the theme of Dracula. Warp Graphics published *Blood of the Innocent* (Dracula vs. Jack the Ripper). Malibu Graphics released *Scarlet in Gaslight* (Dracula vs. Sherlock Holmes) and *Ghosts of Dracula* (Dracula vs. Houdini). Warp Graphics bounced back with *Blood of Dracula*, which in turn produced four separate spin-offs: *Dracula in Hell, Death Dreams of Dracula, The Vampiric Jihad*, and even *Big Bad Blood of Dracula*. Malibu is retaliating with *Dracula: The Suicide Club*, mixing Stoker's character into a story by Robert Louis Stevenson.

Meanwhile, Marvel revived its old *Tomb of Dracula* for at least a four-issue limited series, complete with the writer–artist team of Marv

Panels from *Night Children* by Wendy Snow-Lang (Courtesy Wendy Snow-Lang)

Wolfman and Gene Colan. And, in what must now be seen as an inevitable move, DC teamed Batman with Dracula in a book-length graphic novel, written by Doug Moench and illustrated by Kelly Jones. The title is *Red Rain*. With Batman battling the undead again, just as he did in the earliest days of the medium more than half a century ago, the story of vampires in comic books has come full circle.

In the early 1950s, comic books were the only place on the cultural landscape where vampires still flourished. In the 1990s, comics serve mainly to remind us that vampires are available just about everywhere else. Yet talented artists and imaginative writers can still bring these uncanny creatures to life.

LES DANIELS

The Music of the Vampire

If music be the blood of life . . .

Shakespeare, of course, never wrote this phrase. At least, not exactly: his concerns were food and love, not blood and life. But in the world of the vampire, the two sets are synonymous. The vampire's only food is blood; the love it knows is a consuming one for life itself, which blood alone provides. For the vampire, there is no blood *of* life. "The blood *is* the life," to quote the Bible. This equation underlines the intensity of the vampire's existence, which is reflected in the music inspired by the lore of the vampire. But how does music itself fit into this equation?

Music, by definition, is a succession of tones over some range of time combining to form a continuous composition. So says the dictionary. But music, by experience, has always been, and will always be, far more than a succession of tones. We are drawn to music for the emotional substance it provides. We are perhaps a bit vampiric if we are music lovers. We feel compelled to purchase recordings by Miles Davis or Peter Murphy or Sting or any of a thousand other artists, composers, or performers because we want to feel something we would not otherwise feel—we want to imbibe the essence of their creations. And listening to a piece of music, we "feed" on its capacity to generate our desire to continue listening—every mouthful tastes like more, or rather, every earful feels like more.

More is what the vampire always needs, always craves. More blood. More victims. More feeding. The music lover, too, always needs more—not only more of one specific song or piece or composition until it reaches its end but more songs, more pieces, more compositions, even more versions of the same work. More sensory experience. Ultimately, we want to feel the deepest sadness, the most exultant joy, the greatest thrills, even the long-

(Courtesy Sally Howard)

est and loudest laughter—all from the act of turning on the radio or stereo or attending a concert.

Music is also more than the experience we have as individuals. It is, like literature, art, and film, a component of the society's culture. Like other cultural components, it reflects the nature or temper of the society in its makeup. When the society intensifies, culture follows suit and may even go one or more steps further. In this context, a more intense society is one whose members have a hunger to have their needs met as quickly as possible. When those needs are not quickly gratified, the people become frustrated and resort to violence. A more intense society is characterized by more noticeable violence, especially more random violence. Culture begins to reflect that hunger, and that violence.

The vampire, as an icon of personal violence, cannot arise as a cultural symbol/literary figure until a social boiling point is reached. Even then, the culture must subsequently absorb the meaning of it, fully integrate it, and reflect it in cultural icons. Once the vampire begins to show up in earnest in various cultural formats—literature, art, and

especially music, it is clear that the society recognizes its own intensity.

We say especially music because music is strictly an auditory medium. Keep in mind that while 75 percent of the stimuli we respond to are visual, only 10 to 15 percent of those stimuli are auditory. But the vampire, more than any other supernatural or monstrous creature, is a particularly graphic representation of personal violence—a most emphatically visual cultural icon. One does not hear a vampire—one sees him. While as far back as the eighteenth century, British and Continental society produced literary and (occasionally) artistic vampires, no musical vampire had emerged, aside from that in an obscure opera. In fact, it was not until the twentieth century that the vampire began to play a part in the musical arena. If the vampire emerges in music, there is no doubt that the culture has acknowledged society's intensity.

There is another essential feature of the vampire that should be noted in this context—the explicit romanticism he embodies. The vampire is a powerful loner, an isolated figure who, through sheer will, through the ferocity of his own individual emotionality, can effect dramatic changes in the lives of those he encounters. The power of his influence alone makes him a romantic figure. The original meaning of the term *romance* was a story whose characters were, in essence, larger than life and who could effect miraculous good or damnable evil. The vampire's romantic nature has strengthened his existence all the more and has meant that his appearance in cultural works has even been melodramatic. This is as much true in music as it is in other cultural formats. The romantic nature of the vampire's existence has had a potent influence on the music in which he makes his appearance.

Once music inspired by the lore of the vampire arose, it could not help but be characterized by unusual or striking changes in tempo or chords or just by out-and-out volume. There are basically two modes of music with the vampire as inspiration: rock and film soundtrack music—some of which is, in fact, rock.

Vampire Rock

We listen to rock because we want to feel a strong emotion within a short space of time—in essence, we want a "life bite." It's not mere coincidence, given the nature of the vampire's life and that of rock itself, that Anne Rice, in *The Vampire Lestat*, gave the title character the role of a rock star for his contemporary existence.

In the early rock era, known for such greats as "Monster Mash," "The Purple People Eater," and "I Put a Spell on You" by the inimitable Screamin' Jay Hawkins, no well-known song of vampiric nature seems to have been recorded. There are a few minor exceptions: "Dinner with Drac," the B-side of "Monster Mash," and "I Want to Bite Your Hand," an obvious spoof on the Beatles' "I Want to Hold Your Hand." None of these satirical songs were popular. The vampire in American popular music in the late 1950s and early 1960s was as much an object of ridicule as a political figure skewered by Mort Sahl or a popular movie star lampooned by *Mad* magazine.

Early rock songs, from the 1950s and 1960s, were spoofs of the vampire—as if to say, "Nothing's really that scary and violent, right?" It was not until the 1980s that songs inspired by the vampire really started to make their mark. Or should we say leave their marks?

The emotion shared by the lore of the vampire and the world of rock is what has led bands with many differing styles to explore vampiric themes. As time went on, rock diversified considerably, spawning many subgenres. Each subgenre expresses emotions in a different way.

As the 1960s progressed, changes in American and (particularly) British society occurred, that led to dramatic changes in the nature of rock. In the United States, violent events—political assassinations, on-campus murders, rioting, and the country's involvement in the Vietnam War—began demonstrating that the society was blatantly self-destructive. In the United Kingdom, society had maintained its repressive nature even as the twentieth century rolled into its second half. As the British economy began to worsen, unmet needs were addressed by the same social mechanisms that had been in place for decades—increasingly inappropriate responses for increasingly severe problems.

Strangely enough, it took American pop music a few years to reflect society's drive for self-destruction. In England, by the late 1960s, rock had started changing dramatically; heavy metal was born with the emergence of bands like Led Zeppelin, the prototypical metal band, and Black Sabbath, perhaps the first real heavy metal band. Heavy metal was rock that made no bones about the dark side of life, about how deeply you could feel pain or hurt or longing—even to the point of the experience bordering on or embracing the supernatural.

Yet Black Sabbath's material did not refer to the vampire's world; the band was more concerned with satanic matters. Led Zeppelin was not a band that involved itself with the supernatural at all. Still, England was the first society to break through the conventions of bubblegum and "Britpop" like the Beatles, the Animals, and the Dave Clark Five, with music that surprised the followers of rock. The United States followed the United Kingdom's lead, not so much with heavy metal but with bands like New York Dolls and Alice Cooper. The lone American rock song even remotely connected to the lore of the vampire from this period (actually 1971) is Alice Cooper's "The Ballad of Dwight Fry," which pays homage to the actor who portrayed Renfield in the 1931 production of the film *Dracula*.

The United Kingdom was also the source for punk rock, a sure signal that British culture

Bauhaus (now disbanded), with lead singer Peter Murphy (second from right), rose to fame with "Bela Lugosi's Dead," used as the title track for the film *The Hunger*, based on the novel of the same name by Whitley Streiber

had intensified. Punk was rock that arose in the mid- to late 1970s, and was characterized by lyrics deriding social convention more blatantly than any rock had ever done; by faster, harder tempos; and by sharp, abrupt guitar chord patterns and changes. It was a far cry from acid/psychedelic rock, its most famous immediate subgenre precursor (barring heavy metal). But even the harsh format of punk did not pay attention to the vampire. It couldn't, really; punk dealt with the real-life issues of society like the queen and sex and unemployment and anarchy, and the vampire was something altogether different. Punk was reality; the vampire was fantasy. Punk was razors and safety pins; the vampire was fangs and stakes.

Punk died a relatively quick death because it was not iconic enough; it lacked the symbolic tone and temper that must characterize any art form for its survival. It was too immediate, which may be an odd thing to say, because rock is known for its immediacy. However, the immediacy of the best rock thrills us just because it can convey something more than a quick impression in its few minutes—it reverberates within us. It does that by providing sonic images that mean more than what they superficially say. This is the romance of rock, and this is where another connection exists between the vampire and the rock world. The larger-than-life nature of romance is nothing if not symbolic and mythic; the lyrics from the best rock songs express that emotional mythic quality of life.

The power of rock to sway us based on this symbolic communication was not lost in England because of punk's death. From the ashes of punk arose a more romantic, iconic rock form—Goth. Here was rock that kept punk's contempt for social convention, but modified it to embrace symbolic themes. It transcended punk's "immediate immediacy" for a more mythic approach. In 1982, Bauhaus, one of the first of the Goth bands, released the single "Bela Lugosi's Dead." Peter Murphy, Bauhaus's leader and chief songwriter, pays homage to the first famous portrayer of the consummate vampire, Dracula. (Murphy sings this song in the opening sequence of the 1983 vampire film, *The Hunger*.) "Bela Lugosi's Dead" was probably the first popular rock song to explicitly cite the vampire. Murphy added to the mystique by occasionally dressing and making himself up to resemble one of the undead, or at least to emphasize the darkness of his concerns—black clothing, whiteface accentuated by bright red lips, and blackened eyes.

Also in 1982, a lesser-known, postpunk band, the Birthday Party, fronted by Nick Cave, released the song "Release the Bats" on its first album, a sharp sardonic jab at social convention. The time of the vampire in pop music had begun in earnest.

Bauhaus set the tone for the springing forth of the Gothic (or Goth) rock subgenre, which not only took hold in the music arena but in fashion and in print—a cultural test of any subgenre's staying power. At least two magazines emerged devoted exclusively to the ethos of Goth rock: *Gothic* and *Propaganda*. The latter, a U.S. publication still alive today, especially revels in the glorifying of death (in fact, Goth in the United States is commonly called "death rock"), as typified not only by the music itself but also by a fashion statement comprised of predominantly black clothing (including Nazi insignia), whiteface/black lip-nails makeup,

John Koviak, lead singer of the former London after Midnight, strikes a vampire-like pose for *Propaganda* magazine (Copyright © Fred S. Berger. Used with permission)

and "whiteman's dreadlocks," an unusual combination of slicked back hair (top) and shaved head (sides and back).

The 1980s altered American and world society dramatically, with a marked increase in random personal violence, that is, violence that can be done by or visited upon individuals at any time, in any place, without warning. This contrasted sharply with the social violence of the 1960s, which was somewhat predictable, impersonal, controllable, and "safe" (i.e., if it wasn't happening near you, you didn't have to worry about it). The "new" violence was brought about principally from excessive or reckless involvement in two of the three modes of pleasure mentioned in a popular 1960s catchphrase—"sex, drugs, and rock 'n' roll." Sexual violence—rape and child molestation—mushroomed through the 1980s. So did addiction and drug-related violence: theft and murder.

Within a relatively short time, culture in the 1980s began to reflect this heightened level of personal violence. The vampire emerged as an icon of this in all cultural formats including music.

At the same time, rock became so diversified and eclectic that it was almost impossible to tell what the subgenres were any more. Yet rock's emotionality was always sustained, if not heightened. Vampire songs emerged from such varied artists as Siouxsie and the Banshees ("We Hunger"), Sting ("Moon Over Bourbon Street"), Non ("Theme from Dark Shadows"), Blue Oyster Cult ("Veins," "Tattoo Vampire"), Oingo Boingo ("Help Me"), Wire ("Feed Me"), J. Geils Band ("Fright Night"), and Grace Jones ("Vamp"). These few songs alone represent Goth, mainstream rock, post-punk, heavy metal, new wave, and jazz pop, among others. The last two tracks mentioned were written especially for films of the same name.

In some cases, as in Sting's "Moon Over Bourbon Street," the artist acknowledged a specific source of inspiration—here, Anne

Katrina (singer Grace Jones) performs a mysterious and erotic dance at the After Dark Club in *Vamp* (New World Pictures)

Rice's *Interview with the Vampire*. The United Kingdom heavy metal band Warfare paid homage to the now defunct British film organization Hammer with their album "Hammer Horror," which features the song "Screams of the Vampire." In 1991, the California band L.A. Guns released their album "Hollywood Vampires," also inspired by and dedicated to Anne Rice.

The stage makeup of London after Midnight (now disbanded) appealed to vampire fans (Copyright © Fred S. Berger. Used with permission)

But by far, the subgenre most overtly—even maniacally—dedicated to the vampire song remains heavy metal. Aside from the tracks by Blue Oyster Cult and Warfare mentioned above, songs have come from metal bands on both sides of the Atlantic (U.S./U.K.): "Nosferatu" by Coroner, "Transylvania" by Iron Maiden, "Waltz of the Vampire" by Motorhead, and "Fiend for Blood" by Autopsy, to name a few. There was even a short-lived heavy metal band called Nosferatu.

Why heavy metal? Heavy metal identifies with the extremes of human emotion—sexual desire, the capacity to terrorize, blinding hatred, lust for power—which are linked to the vampire. The emphasis is on what the song's narrator can do to the listener, or can do in the story of the song to other characters. Heavy metal has been the most violent rock—certainly the loudest. Metal revels in the power of human emotion. If we acknowledge the vampire as a creature of romance, whose mere presence powerfully affects the lives of those he encounters, then it's not hard to understand the connection.

By contrast, there has never been, and never will be, any track written about the vampire by an industrial band. Industrial rock—as typified by bands like Skinny Puppy, Front Line Assembly, Klinik, and Front 242—is the antithesis of heavy metal. It is rock that either plays down human emotion in favor of developing technology or else deals with the raw human emotions caused by others or by outside forces. As creatures of romance, vampires are not affected by others or by outside forces—sunlight, fire, and wooden stakes destroy them, but our view here of the vampire as a mythic being temporarily puts asides its weaknesses.

Industrial music has made extensive use of "samples," that is, outside sources, which heavy metal never will. Heavy metal is rock that screams at the listener to wake up, drop what you're doing, and feel how much power you really have. Industrial is rock that screams at the listener to wake up, drop what you're doing, and realize how much is really being done to you. Vampires don't pay attention to what is being done to them—they're too busy doing things to others.

As the 1990s have progressed, subgenres have blended and merged with each other like never before. Faith No More's "Surprise! You're Dead!" from their 1990 album, *The Real Thing*, is about a vampire—but is the song heavy metal? Power pop? Thrash? Similarly, Concrete Blonde's "Bloodletting (The Vampire Song)" from their 1990 album of the same name is not really garage rock, nor is it post-punk, but something very different indeed. And "I Bleed" by The Pixies is a "metavampire" song—one that, while citing the vampire as its impetus, depicts the despair in which extreme personal violence may culminate. Although it was released in 1989, this song is a clear, fierce example of where the best rock in the 1990s is going—toward a domain where no other art form can go, a musical/lyrical language characterized by subtlety and intensity, by violent tenderness, mythic reality, wild mockery, and gentle torment.

The level of random personal violence throughout the world has continued to increase, which means the vampire will no doubt continue to appear in rock, albeit in different forms and guises. If and when personal violence ever abates, we should expect the vampire's presence in cultural works to fade. But that likelihood seems a long way off.

SANGUINARY SOUNDTRACKS

Whereas rock has been an art form that reflects social and cultural changes, film music has been almost wholly dependent for its genesis and development on the film industry. The joint concerns of what the director wants and what the composer hears when he or she sees the film footage converge to produce the music we hear when watching a movie. Film can also be responsive to the issues and events that confront us, but its music is subsidiary to its visual component (here we are referring to original soundtrack music within the last ten to fifteen years).

There have probably been more vampire movies than any other subgenre of horror film—with the possible exception of the ghost story—since Georges Melies' short, *The Haunted Castle*, first graced the screen in 1896. It would be impossible to comment on music created for even most of these films, so the aim here is to highlight those scores that are either innovative or uniquely creative or those that are representative of their time, illustrating stylistic techniques common to a specific period.

Although the short by Melies was the first vampire film, it was only two minutes long. The first full-length vampire film, a masterpiece, was F. W. Murnau's 1922 *Nosferatu*, produced during the silent era. Several soundtracks have since been created for it by contemporary musicians. Among the more interesting scores is one played by the Caution Dog Orchestra, a collection of upstate New York musicians (including horror novelist Thom Metzger) who tootled, slapped, bowed, strummed, beat, and blew kazoos, cello, whistles, guitars, and drums in a wholly improvised plethora of sounds. Unfortunately, it was never recorded. A second score was recorded in 1989 by Art Zoyd, a French-Belgian art rock group that created what must be one of the most distinctive, gripping scores in the entire horror film soundtrack repertory.

Art Zoyd makes use of chimes, sax, koto, cello, piano, bass drum, organ, vocals, harmonium, a whole host of unusual percussive and tonal synthesized sounds, and samples of lapping water, ghostly Japanese voices, rushing winds, creams, and singing birds. This polyrhythmic, multitimbral work can easily stand on its own as a masterpiece of horrific music.

In 1931, talkies were just beginning, and for directors the advent of sound had different implications. For Tod Browning, an American, it meant a strict emphasis on dialogue in *Dracula*, starring Bela Lugosi. The only music heard in the entire film is during the opening credits, and that was lifted from the classical repertory. But for Carl Dreyer, a Dane, sound in film meant the addition of a full-blown soundtrack to *Vampyr*—the first historically created for a feature-length vampire film. The composer, Wolfgang Zeller, wrote a somber, brooding score, carried primarily by strings. In some scenes, the strings convey more of a quality of impending mystery, with a plucked bass line underlying tentative, ascending lines cried by a solo violin or a single clarinet. The dialogue in *Vampyr* is sparse; for Dreyer, the soundtrack was a key contributor to the rich oneiric mood of the film.

Dreyer was lucky to have found Zeller; other directors did not fare so well with their films' soundtrack composers. In 1943, *The Return of the Vampire* included a score by Mario Tedesco that was standard American movie music for an undistinguished feature of that period in which studios dictated everything. Here, clarinet, bass clarinet, and oboe create what was thought at that time to be a "haunting melody," but sounds significantly more melodramatic than its visual material warrants. However, in spite of the clichéd material, there are a few brief passages of interesting, original work, most notably the scene when a young woman finds the account of the vampire written by her father. Unfortunately, this is subsumed by trite phrasing characterizing the score in general, including sanctimonious organ music.

The 1940s and early to mid-1950s were not a fertile period for the vampire, or horror, film music. In the late 1950s came the first major breakthrough in the development of vampire film music. For a period of just over ten years, until the early 1970s, the vampire film was dominated by the British film studio Hammer. The studio matched its dramatic use of Technicolor with startling musical enhancement of the films' imagery. Chief among their composers was James Bernard.

In 1958, Hammer released Terence Fisher's *Dracula* (retitled *Horror of Dracula* in the United States), and it became obvious that James Bernard was a soundtrack composer to be reckoned with. Although his work shows the influence of the greatest film composer of all time, Bernard Herrmann, it possesses tremendous power and originality. Never before had vampire film music—in fact, horror film music—been envisioned and composed with such dramatic ferocity. Bernard added significantly to the success of Hammer's *Dracula* film series, as well as the other horror films for which he wrote music.

The composer uses tympani—enhanced by crashing cymbals, gongs, and occasional tom-tom—underneath a strings motif that veers wildly from high to low registers to underline the intensity of a vampire's presence in an ordered, nineteenth-century British world: Dracula's motif. This underscoring of violent, screaming strings with pounding tympani and gongs or with chimes is pure, characteristic James Bernard—terror made palpable. Bernard influenced the soundtracks of other Hammer composers—David Whitaker, Harry Robinson, and Christopher Gunning—but also the work of Americans, primarily Robert Cobert.

Bernard's Dracula motif was used throughout much of the entire series of seven films (eight if the non–Christopher Lee *Brides of Dracula* is included). In 1969's brilliant *Taste the*

Blood of Dracula, Bernard was asked to modify his style to embrace a more overtly romantic sound. He complies with a theme whose strings provide a sweet complement to the oboe's lilting melody. In spite of this, much of the soundtrack carries forth his characteristic dramatic style, including the unique use of the gong.

Bernard scored six Hammer vampire films; one was *Kiss of the Vampire*, a non-Dracula work. In Hammer's 1972 *Vampire Circus*, another non-Dracula film, with music written by David Whitaker, Bernard's stamp of drama is clear. Yet it is made more insidious, more tentative, underlining the vampires' inveigling positions among their human prey, rather than standing so completely apart from them as Dracula does. What Bernard brought to vampire and horror film music was a direct emphasis on the use of the motif to boldly underline the character of the monster. Certainly motifs had been used in film music prior to Bernard, but no composer for a horror film before *Horror of Dracula* had ever created as dramatic and romantic a motif as he did.

Although Hammer Studios dominated the vampire film during this period, they certainly had no monopoly on it. Perhaps the most striking non-Hammer vampire film from this period was Roman Polanski's *Fearless Vampire Killers* (British title, *Dance of the Vampires*), notable not only for its cinematic originality but for its soundtrack. Whereas Polanski had worked with the American jazz musician Chico Hamilton for his previous horror film, *Repulsion*, he turned to a fellow Pole and frequent collaborator, Krzysztof Komeda, for *Fearless Vampire Killers*.

Komeda provided a markedly original score, which opens the film with a goofy combination of Gregorian chantlike choral voices and cabaret music. The choral voices are used throughout the film as the vampires' motif, but the eeriness of their effect is often thrown out of whack by a Swingle Singers–sounding melody pattern. Komeda pokes fun at the horror film sonically much as Polanski does visually: a jazzy bass line underscores a minor-keyed folk melody; a string bass ostinato plays against a droning tambura and echoing marimba; and the dance scene minuet endlessly repeats the same simple melody on a harpsichord just a bit too loudly for the expected balance of sound and picture. The overall effect somehow manages to be witty and creepy at the same time.

As mentioned before, James Bernard's influence extended across the Atlantic. For 1970's *House of Dark Shadows*, Robert Cobert composed a score that rises above the quality of the film itself. After the opening trademark *Dark Shadows* theme (Cobert was the composer for the TV series as well), the music occasionally emulates Bernard in its frenzied, scherzo strings passages when visual violence strikes. For the most part, there is a slower, spookier pace with Cobert's own trademark musical signature—a descending echoing solo flute figure, often coupled with strings glissandi. The glissando, from that point on, was a staple in American horror film music until the widespread use of the synthesizer (though glissandi continued to be used).

In 1971's *The Night Stalker* (the most popular TV film up to that time), Cobert takes a jazzier approach to the soundtrack; the story, after all, is more in line with the Ray Bradbury/Stephen King style of horror, occurring in everyday life. Yet the same descending echoing flute is here, as are the strings glissandi. Cobert also adds suspended xylophone tones and short, staccato motifs played by electric guitar and bass to enhance the suspense elements of the film. The influence of James Bernard is not in evidence here, although Cobert certainly showed it three years later in the 1974 Dan Curtis production of *Dracula* starring Jack Palance.

Even before Hammer's reign of horror had come to its close, some noble independent efforts were made in the arena of vampire films.

In fact, the 1970s was a boom era for the vampire film—certainly in the United States. There was a spate of non–United Kingdom foreign vampire films as well. One of the best of these was 1972's *Daughters of Darkness*.

This Belgian film is known for its sensuous visual feel, which is well complemented by François De Roubaux's score. By turns, it is jittery, tenuous, stately, seductive, and brooding. The composer moves from rock instrumentation (electric guitar, bass, and piano) to moody use of unusual instruments (harp, zither, and organ with Leslie), to more traditional scoring (cello and double bass). The alternating of various styles and sounds creates a noticeable degree of tension; we move back and forth in the film, not always clear on what will happen, but always compelled to find out.

De Roubaux's scoring of *Daughters of Darkness* and Cobert's scoring of *The Night Stalker* are good examples of a developing trend at the time in soundtrack composing for horror films. This was a rebellion of sorts from Bernard's voluminous scoring in favor of simpler instrumentation. Another highly original vampire film soundtrack in this sparser style is the one by Carl Zittrer for Bob Clark's 1972 work, *Death Dream*. Here Zittrer takes a more musically experimental approach. He uses electronically modified whispering voices and echoing plucked piano strings to give the film an effectively eerie atmosphere in certain scenes. Elsewhere, sparse strings play a muted, somber, Bartok-like motif, underlining the tragedy of a lone member of the undead among the living, and in other scenes, the strings evoke jumpy, skittery figures. Zittrer is probably one of the more original composers in American film.

This sparser, simpler style of scoring seems to have been associated for the most part with independent horror films, both domestic and foreign. Another fine example of this style is Donald Rubinstein's soundtrack for George Romero's 1977 film *Martin*, considered by some to be Romero's best work. As was Clark's *Death Dream*, Romero's film is the story of a loner. Rubinstein evokes Bartok in some of his minor key strings passages. The main theme, a slow folk melody sung by a wordless female voice over drifting piano chords and sustained strings, echoes throughout the film, sometimes by a solo violin, sometimes by solo flute, sometimes by the female voice over suspended cymbal and steady tom-tom, emphasizing a dirgelike quality. Rubinstein makes extensive use of solo instruments—sax, oboe, violin, and flute—to underline Martin's isolation. In contrast to the Hammer Dracula character, the vampire is a decidedly unromantic figure who is too confused much of the time to influence anyone's behavior—even his own.

The simpler scoring of these mid-1970s films gave way to an eclectic orientation. Soundtrack composers (at least for vampire films) used whatever instrumentation they and their directors felt appropriate for films being produced. This is illustrated in three vampire films from 1979.

For the Australian *Thirst*, Brian May is nothing if not eclectic. The score is a screwy mix of church choir, tinkling piano, TV cop show theme music, Bernard Herrmann steals, 1970s style soft rock, and melodramatic brass and strings that segue crazily from one "suspenseful" sequence to another in an effort to generate some degree of nail-biting terror, including string glissandi. So fraught with musical styles and figures is this soundtrack that one can only sit back and try to take it all in. The plan of attack here seems to be, "if eclectic is in, let's do it in spades." Considering the over-the-top nature of the film, the soundtrack just may be appropriate.

Charles Bernstein's score for *Love at First Bite* is also eclectic, but the material here is radically different. The film is a broad spoof, and Bernstein has a lot of fun with the music. Although not as witty as Komeda's work for *Fearless Vampire Killers*, the music nevertheless strikes the right chord at the right time. There are grand Hungarian-style strings, complete with a sobbing gypsy solo violin. There is flamboyant organ music. There are short rock passages, an overly lush love theme, and an "American madcap movie chase" sequence at the end. And, of course, there is the famous disco scene with spoofs on *Saturday Night Fever*.

Love at First Bite is also noteworthy because it introduced dance-oriented rock into the vampire film. Dance has been a part of vampire film since the minuet scene in *Fearless Vampire Killers*, but in *Love at First Bite* the erotic/romantic aspect of dance is heightened by heavily rhythmic music.

The film is additionally of interest because it marks a return to the vampire as a romantic figure, after a decade or so of mostly antiromantic vampires. The return of romance is clearly emphasized by the vision of a closely entwined couple, spinning in each other's arms on the dance floor.

John Badham's *Dracula* (1980), starring Frank Langella and Kate Nelligan, is one of the most telling examples of a vampire film whose music bests its visual imagery. It is a film of pure romance—in both the grand and lesser sense of the word. The figure of Dracula is one of great personal magnetism and influence. More than one love story unfolds here. John Williams' score does a considerable amount to express that romanticism. In fact, nowhere in the soundtrack repertoire is the romance of the vampire better described than in this score. It is one of the true masterpieces of music for the horror film.

The music is purely orchestral, relying primarily on strings to carry the nonverbal emotional impact of the film. Comparison to James Bernard may be made in instrumentation (though Williams eschews the gong and cymbal as primary instruments), but the composer here does not have Bernard's characteristic ferocity. Yet Williams certainly does utilize the staples of the symphony orchestra, as Bernard did, to portray a nineteenth-century world so substantially thrown off balance by such an intense series of events. This is revealed in the scherzoid "To Scarborough," the tense "Abduc-

tion of Lucy," and "The Bat Attack," which segues from a jittery opening to a somber end section. And Williams frequently juxtaposes ostinato bass with shrieking strings, also reminiscent of Bernard.

But like Bernard before him, Williams is a true original. It is interesting to note, as an aside, that with the notable exception of this film, none of the top three American fantasy film composers—Bernard Herrmann, Jerry Goldsmith, and John Williams—have ever scored a vampire film. Whatever the reason, there can be no doubt that Williams' music here, in much grander fashion than that written for *Love at First Bite*, marked a definite return to the romance of the vampire.

Just as was true for rock, the 1980s were a time of significant change for film music in a number of ways. While electronics had certainly been used in soundtracks before (as far back as Kendall Schmidt's score for 1965's *Planet of the Vampires* for a vampire film, and to 1956's *Forbidden Planet* for any film), no score for a vampire film had yet made extensive use of the synthesizer, first available courtesy of Robert Moog in the early 1970s. This was to change.

For 1983's *The Hunger*, director Tony Scott called on the talents of two synthesists, Michel Rubini and Denny Jaeger, to create an electronic complement for the classical music (Ravel, Schubert, and Lalo) that graces the film. The two radically different types of music are used to emphasize the initially disparate but ultimately fused aspects of the vampires' lives. The intervals of classical music underline their isolated, seductive, upper-class lifestyles, while the echoing, dissonant, otherworldly electronics accent the violence, corruption, and decay of their existence. In more than one scene, the two types of music are juxtaposed, creating a strongly unsettling feeling. As the film progresses, the two types of music take each other's places more and more until we realize that seduction is total corruption, that isolation is complete decay.

The 1980s also saw both the replacement of at least some of the soundtrack's instrumental music by rock, started in *Love at First Bite*, and the growing prevalence of teenagers as protagonists in vampire films. These two trends are closely related. As long ago as 1957, teens were the featured players in Herbert Strock's *Blood of Dracula*, but that was the lone teen vampire film for quite a while.

The convergence of teen protagonists and a rock/synthesizer soundtrack was perfectly melded in 1985's *Fright Night*. Here, Brad Feidel provided the electronics while the rock was performed by Devo, April Wine, Sparks, Ian Hunter, Autograph, and others.

Feidel, a talented composer, developed two strong motifs for this film: a seductive, slowed-down Philip Glass–like sequence of guitar, growling bass, and wailing synthesizer that simultaneously cries passion and fear as well as a four-note snarling bass synth riff that tells the listener danger is imminent. Evil Ed's death scene in particular shows off Feidel's skill; it's an eerie, experimental synthesizer sequence complete with strings glissandi.

The rock is all dance rock, which is mostly heard in the dance club seduction scene, although the title track by the J. Geils Band is used for the end credits. In fact, *Fright Night* was one of the first two commercial movies to successfully explore the rock/vampire connection; the other, *Once Bitten*, was released the same year but proved a minor effort.

Near Dark from 1987 is one of the best vampire films from the 1980s, and arguably one of the best in the last twenty years. Although there is no rock song in the soundtrack, the music by Tangerine Dream is an impressive mix of the atmospheric electronics and propulsive rhythmic—sometimes pure rock—sequences for which the band is known. The group apparently wanted to capture the desolation of always-hungry wanderers—the Texas road vampires that form the nucleus of the film's story—in a wide-open, burning country. They succeeded. Even the soft "Mae's

Theme," with its repeating descending chords and folk melody, manages to give a feeling of loneliness tempered only by the chance meeting that sets off the action of the film.

And in the 1987 *Graveyard Shift*, a vampire film written and directed by Gerard Ciccoritti (not to be confused with the Stephen King *Graveyard Shift* of 1990), Nicholas Pike uses a high-end musical computer capable of generating an enormous array of sounds for the entire soundtrack. And that capability is amply in evidence here. There are Tangerine Dream–like propulsive rhythms, warped arpeggios, sustained tones, percussive effects, and even traditional-sounding rock riffs.

However, soundtrack composers for vampire films have not flocked to synthesizers and samplers in large numbers. Rock seems a bigger attraction; 1990's *Def by Temptation* (the fourth American black vampire film) relies on a who's who of black music performers—Freddie Jackson, Najee, Melba Moore, and others. And 1992's teen-oriented *Buffy the Vampire Slayer* likewise enlists rock from various bands to supply the music. Films have been increasingly marketed as a combination package of visual and aural entertainment—see the film, buy the album. And rock sells. As is true for several types of genre films, such as mysteries and westerns, vampire films arrive in packs, like wolves hungry for the consumers' dollars. And once in a while, when they sound off, the listener can truly say, "Ah, the children of the night. What beautiful music they make."

MUSIC IN A DIFFERENT VEIN: OTHER VENUES

Once we leave the realms of rock and film soundtracks, the land of vampire music is rough going—not much to hold on to. Jazz? Only Sting's "Moon Over Bourbon Street," and with a vocal that's pop. Folk? Perhaps. But nothing readily comes to mind. Country and western? Never.

In the entire classical music repertory, there seems not to be a single piece of instrumental music inspired by the lore of the vampire. Even in the realm of opera—the live, dramatic fusion of sonic and visual arts—only one work appears to have been written: *Der Vampyr* by Heinrich Marschner in 1828. This piece was obscure enough never to have been produced or recorded after the era of its creation.

Although many horrific works of classical music do exist, the vampire appears not to have been the focus of any of them. Those composers drawn to horrific themes—Liszt, Prokofiev, Mahler, Penderecki, Ligeti, and others—seem to have as their concerns the more somber issues of death, the devil, and religious heresy. The vampire is too trivial a subject, no doubt, for the "grave" concerns of classical composers.

Musical theater, however, a step or two down from classical music's solemnity and part popular culture, has embraced the vampire theme, albeit somewhat minimally. The most well-known pieces date from the 1970s or so.

Carmilla was originally produced in 1970 by the New York–based experimental theater company La Mama and has seen a number of revivals. The script comes from the story by Joseph Sheridan Le Fanu about a seductive vampiress. For this piece, the American composer Ben Johnston wrote the music. Johnston, better known for his orchestral and computer-based compositions, was an unusual choice. Here he approaches the score as he would a pop chamber piece. With essentially six pieces (flute, clarinet, cello, electric bass, keyboard, and percussion), the composer fashions his songs and incidental music in a style far removed from that of Broadway theater. The quirky, sometimes decidedly odd phrasings and passages accent the unusual cultural milieu for the work—an Off-Off-Broadway musical that, nevertheless, was recorded (now out of print).

Possessed is something completely different. Subtitled *The Dracula Musical*, it was created in 1989 by the composer Carter Cathcart and writers Jason Darrow and Robert Marasco, the latter a horror novelist. Cathcart has a background in TV and radio commercials, TV film music, rock, jazz, and fusion. Here he tackles musical theater very differently from Ben Johnston, as though he were writing a big production Broadway show, which is reflected in much of the phrasing and melody structure of his musical pieces. The overture opens the work with musical drama, incorporating an entire spectrum of instruments: organ, harpsichord, piano, bells, strings, tympani, brass, woodwinds, and synthesized-type sounds as well.

For the body of the musical, the composer uses many different musical forms to express the differing moods, circumstances, and temperaments of the characters: pop/soft rock, hard rock, pseudo-Latin rock, the show tune format, near-operatic recitative, and the bouncy equivalent in music of a penny dreadful. The power of the music of the vampire is softened by the composer's awareness of the Broadway musical theater genre which, to be successful, must present even the most intense themes with enough sentimentality, tonality, and occasional humor to border on drawing room melodrama.

Television is a younger medium than film, and original works about the vampire for the small screen are practically brand new. With the exception of the original *Dark Shadows* series (1966), its spin-off film *House of Dark Shadows*, and the TV film *The Night Stalker*, there were only four or five TV films of variable quality within the last ten to fifteen years. *Dracula: The Series* was laughable enough to not even make one think twice about the accompanying music. There was the ill-fated remake of the *Dark Shadows* series in 1991.

And there was *Forever Knight*. Based on a late 1980s American TV film, this Canadian-produced series details the exploits of a vampire police detective. While it does have its faults, it boasts some excellent music by Fred Mollin. Mollin is known as the composer for the on-again, off-again TV series *Friday the 13th*, which included an episode entitled "Baron's Bride," concerning the seduction of the female lead by a nineteenth-century vampire. The composer again uses a Kurzweil, a high-end computer music system, to create a entire panoply of sounds—strings, woodwinds, keyboards, and varied percussion. In a number of scenes, Mollin seems to be a latter-day electronic version of James Bernard. One of his trademark techniques is pounding tympani underlying screaming strings. He can also be quite lyrical, and takes advantage of the Kurzweil's sophistication to generate a whole barrage of eerie atonal and polytonal sequences. Mollin has scored feature and TV films and is also a songwriter.

As the vampire continues to haunt us in these violent times, so too will its music. From the songs of Cronos and Creepy Rick to soundtracks by Jonathan Elias (*Vamp*) and Henry Mancini (*Lifeforce*), from heavy metal for full orchestra to weird electronics, millions of notes have arisen from a thousand different imaginations to form entire works, each with its own character, its own temper. Each of these works gives us something of the lore of the vampire—the romance, the violence, the intense drama, the hunger, and the dark passion—that, to one degree of another, resonates within us. If the music stays with us a little longer, then we have recognized something more of ourselves by virtue of listening to that particular combination of notes.

As the wolves cease their howling and day finally breaks, as the violence of the night comes at last to an end with the rising of the sun, we all know that night must fall again. And someone somewhere will always be creating the music of the vampire.

LAWRENCE GREENBERG

In memory of
Mrs. SARAH WHEELER
wife of
Mr. Elisha Wheeler
who died
Dec. 6. 1775. Aged 21.

Within the confines of the tomb
Death lays my body low,
Snatch'd from my friends in early bloom.

Fans and
Fang Gangs:
Vampires in
Real Life

The Magic of
Blood

Blood is the focus of the vampire cult: the vampire steals it from others, either literally or symbolically, thus robbing the living of life. Because blood is the "river of life," carrying the vital energy of the cosmos through the body, human beings have throughout history conferred upon it great mystical and magical powers. Blood is soul, strength, and the rejuvenating force. Blood sacrifices of humans and animals are performed to unleash those powers and propitiate the gods with the greatest of all gifts. The blood of gods and monarchs shed upon the fields ensures the fertility and abundance of crops. The drinking of the blood of one's enemies—a widespread and ancient practice—enables one to acquire the strength of the enemy.

The Koreans have an ancient belief that the blood of a faithful son serves as an elixir. According to this tradition, when a parent is near death, a son cuts himself, for example, on the

thigh, and uses his blood to prepare the magic elixir.

The strongest oath is the blood oath, in which the parties mingle their blood. The blood oath is meant to be unbreakable and transcends all other duties and obligations. He who betrays it commits a grievous sin. Thus the vampire, by consuming the blood of a victim, wields not only the power of life and death but magical power as well and establishes a connection to the victim that is difficult to break.

Blood is a potent ingredient in magical charms and spells: a drop of a person's blood can be used in ritual to bring a victim under the magician's power. In many cases, the blood of an evil person is believed to have the greatest magical power. For example, the blood of executed criminals is said to be a powerful protector against disease and bad luck because of the energy of resentment and fury released upon

Count Dracula in his mortal incarnation as Vlad the Impaler, the story given in *Bram Stoker's Dracula: The Film and the Legend* (Copyright 1992 Columbia Pictures Industries, Inc. Used with permission)

Unholy Communion

The Old Testament strictly prohibits the drinking of blood "for the blood is the life of the flesh" (Genesis 6:10; Deuteronomy 12:23). In contrast to this ancient warning, shortly before his death on the cross Jesus told his disciples "Unless you eat the flesh of the Son of Man, and drink his blood, you shall have no life in you. Whoever eats my flesh and drinks my blood has eternal life, and I will raise him up on the last day" (John 6:53-54). This saying is repeated in all four Gospels, and the events of the Last Supper are reenacted in the sacrament of Holy Communion. This affirmation of a relationship between the drinking of blood and immortality allowed Christians to interpret the vampire's thirst for blood as a form of "unholy communion" and to see the vampire's return from the grave as a parody of Christ's resurrection.

ROBERT EIGHTEEN-BISANG

execution. In East Prussian lore, the blood of executed criminals should be drunk for good luck. In Pomerania, a merchant who catches drops of the blood of a beheaded murderer on his handkerchief will be guaranteed an increase in business.

Similarly, the blood consumed by vampires, or the vampire's own blood, has great magical potency, according to Eastern European folklore. It is always dangerous, but can be a charm or a curse. When vampire corpses are disinterred and staked or cut up, the living must take care not to be sprayed by the corpse's blood, for they will either go mad instantly or die instantly. These beliefs are not surprising, for vampire hunters several centuries ago found that the violated corpses invariably exploded with sprays of gases, blood, and decomposing flesh. These explosions were caused by the sudden release of the pressure inside the corpse caused by the buildup of gases. Thus, vampire corpses were carefully covered before mutilation, and most onlookers stood well away from the body. In Romanian lore, the staked vampire is believed to always send a geyser of blood high into the air. The blood, it is said, issues from a second heart that enables the vampire to stay alive.

Contrary to beliefs about the destructive power of the vampire's blood are beliefs that the blood has great healing properties. Consequently, victims of vampires should either smear themselves with the vampire's blood or drink it to secure release from the vampire's curse. A variation of this was reported in the Mercy Brown vampire case in Rhode Island in the nineteenth century. Her ailing brother was given a medicine made with the ashes of her burned heart and liver. The brother died despite the medicine. In other cases, equally dismal results have been recorded.

The famous vampire case of Arnod (Arnold) Paole of Medvegia, Serbia, in 1727, involves two instances of the use of vampire's blood as an antidote. Paole had been a soldier stationed in Greece, where he learned about the local beliefs concerning vampires. He also discovered that his company was staying near a site haunted by vampires. One night he was attacked by a vampire, and he went the next day to its grave and dispatched it. To prevent further trouble, he ate some of the earth of the grave and smeared himself with the vampire's blood. His troubles did not end, however, and after he returned home he continued to feel weakened and depressed. He fell off a hay wagon, broke his neck, and died.

About twenty to thirty days later, people complained that he had turned into a vampire and was attacking them. Four people died. Paole was soon dug up and found to be in the vampire condition, complete with bloody lips that gave away his nocturnal prowlings. A stake was driven through his heart, and he bled copiously. He also groaned or shrieked, which further convinced the peasants that he was a true vampire. In fact, these noises were caused by gases being forced up the throat by the violent compression of the chest cavity.

During the same period, other people in the village were falling victim to vampire attacks. One of these was a twenty-year-old woman named Stana, whose child died immediately after being born. Stana herself then fell seriously ill. (In many folklore traditions, such events are blamed on vampiric birth demons and viscera suckers.) She smeared herself with the blood of a vampire, but died anyway, after a three-day illness. She, too, became a vampire. When her corpse was disinterred two months later, it was found to be undecayed, with a large quantity of fresh blood in the chest

cavity. She was dispatched in the customary manner with a stake.

The purported magical properties of blood continue to be the primary element of appeal in modern-day fascination with the vampire. Sometimes, obsessions with blood lead people to the vampire myth; they either become absorbed by it or to want to become some sort of living vampire who consumes blood. Others want the association with blood but do not wish to drink it themselves. The mere association with blood conjures up magic and power, what the want-to-be vampire desires most.

ROSEMARY ELLEN GUILEY

Blood Substitute

For all those vampires who eschew blood but want to keep up appearances, Damien Vanian, London's most famous living vampire, offers this recipe for a blood substitute. According to Damien, it delivers the taste and consistency of clotting blood without the risks of illness associated with blood drinking.

Take a liter container and fill it half and half with tomato juice and orange juice. Stir well, let the mixture sit for a while, and then serve warm, preferably at body temperature (98.6 degrees Fahrenheit). For adventure, replace the plain tomato juice with Bloody Mary mix, clam and tomato juice, or spicy tomato juice.

ROSEMARY ELLEN GUILEY

The "I Wanna Be a Vampire" Syndrome

Our collective fascination with the vampire does not end with our interest in vampire entertainment. The vampire myth is so powerful, alluring, and mysterious, that it compels numerous people to want to become vampires and seek out ways to accomplish that.

The vampire of folklore is so repulsive it is hard to imagine anyone wishing to become one: a mouldering corpse who stalks the living. Alas, this vampire—the real vampire—has been thoroughly staked and then resurrected in arts and entertainment as a tragic hero. The vampire has evolved from an evil villain to a romantic idol: Bram Stoker, Anne Rice, Chelsea Quin Yarbro, and a host of other artists have polished the vampire to an irresistible shine. For example, Anne Rice's vampires are "made" through an exchange of blood; they live immortal lives in their own bodies, frozen in time at the moment of their "making"; and they are incredibly beautiful.

No ugly demons or ghoulish revenants, but creatures so exquisite and perfect they could pass for angels.

Rice's books, plus the similar emphasis of numerous other artists, have led many vampire fans to think of vampires as exotic beings to be admired and emulated. Who wouldn't want to live forever in a young body, be resistant to disease, have fantastic powers, and be wealthy to boot? The price is only your soul and a little blood!

Anyone who researches vampire fandom soon receives a substantial pile of mail from sincere wanna-be vampires and vampireophiles. "I never believed in vampires until I read [Anne Rice's] *Interview with the Vampire*," wrote a young woman from the Midwest. "Now I believe in them. Please tell me they're real, and where I can find them." And a young man from Long Island wrote to say he had been made into a vampire and was part of a

Some aspiring vampires like to adopt a forbidding appearance (Model: Eunice Tavolacci. Copyright © Fred S. Berger. Used with permission)

lives. They don't want other people to know they're vampires. Most of them are between the ages of seventeen and twenty-eight, which is not surprising considering these are years when people are unsettled, still experimenting, and often rebellious. There are also, however, self-described living vampires in their mid-forties.

Many of these living vampires feel they did not fit into mainstream society for any number of reasons. From early in childhood, they considered themselves to be outsiders. Many express feelings of being misunderstood or underestimated by others. The ficitional vampire seemed to offer a way to escape to an exotic life or build self-image. Most immersed themselves in vampire fiction and films.

Many of them say that they came from unhappy home environments where they had suffered psychological abuse, sometimes sexual abuse, and sometimes physical abuse that may have made them taste their own blood at a very young age. It is possible that dissociation is a factor in at least some vampire escape fantasies.

After someone decides he wants to be a vampire, he seeks out other living vampires, perhaps in a nightclub or at school. He is then made into a vampire in rituals involving a small exchange of blood and sometimes sex.

After he is convinced he has become a vampire, the initiate undergoes some changes, which probably are really induced by auto-suggestion. Such changes include a preference for nocturnal hours; aversion and sensitivity to sunlight; allergy to garlic; and—last but not least—an acquired taste for blood. Some believe they actually change physically—they know they acquired supernormal strength or abilities, or the physical nature of their bodies was no longer entirely human. Not surprisingly, they do not seek out or agree to medical exams for proof. Most likely, they don't want their fantasy to burst, but they tend to explain their reluctance by saying that they don't need medical proof to know they are vampires.

vampire coven. A Texas man wrote about how he was a full vampire and was 500 years old. He was part of an elaborate hierarchy of vampires, run by females, and populated by full and half vampires.

It's one thing to fantastize about being a vampire, and it's another to really consider yourself a vampire. Yet, there are people who believe they either were born vampires or were transformed into vampires by other living vampires. These living vampires are rather hard to find because they like having secret

On the Perils of Running The Vampyre Society

'It's a strange and fascinating business, running The Vampyre Society, one of England's leading vampire fan organizations. Based in Chippenham, Wiltshire, The Vampyre Society publishes a quarterly journal, *For the Blood Is the Life*.

Beginning The Vampyre Society seemed quite a good idea at the time . . . I'd seen all kinds of nonsense written about vampires by people whose knowledge of the genre seemed limited to watching Hammer horror films on television. Having read most of the classic literature and having a reasonable working knowledge of the legends, I thought I could do better and decided to put my typewriter where my mouth was. To my pleasant surprise my articles got published, not just in vampire-related magazines but in fanzines devoted to Gothic rock bands. It was one of the latter that provided the trigger—people began to write to me asking for advice and more information. It seemed fairly logical to put the articles and the advice together and start a newsletter. So, in October 1987 The Vampyre Society was born in my home in Chippenham, Wiltshire, and its newsletter, pretentiously referred to as a "journal," was given the name *For the Blood Is the Life* after a quote from *Dracula*.

Right from the beginning, things got weird. Even before the society was properly off the ground, I received a letter telling me that my articles were "nice" but "a little misinformed." And who else to put me right but a mysterious correspondent, Ilona? After all, she was a vampire herself—or so she claimed. It was a story she stuck to, although it was fairly obvious that she was getting most of her information from Anne Rice's books, even going so far as to claim that one of Rice's characters was her boyfriend. She kept it up for the duration of our correspondence, but I was never convinced that it was anything other than an in-joke. Several people have tried the same thing: "Let's write to The Vampyre Society and pretend that we're genuine vampires," but it's never been done better than the first time.

Once the society had been launched, the next step was some publicity and the inevitable requests for interviews. I was asked to participate in a television show based on eccentric obsessions. I declined, naturally. Some interviewers came along with the intention of sending me up; others just didn't listen to a word I said. I spent an hour talking into one journalist's portable cassette recorder, patiently explaining that people who dress in black cloaks and hang around in graveyards aren't really vampires, and I thought I'd done a good job of making my point. Then the journalist's photographer asked if I'd just slip into a black cloak and put in some plastic fangs for a photo session, preferably in the local graveyard. I said no, pointing out that I don't even *own* a black cloak. When the article was published, it started off by complaining that the vampire expert wouldn't make a fool of himself for the photographer and then went on to discuss death-obsessed people with blood addictions while pointing out that I wasn't actually like that myself, of course.

Even favorable publicity can have its drawbacks. Most of the correspondence I deal with from day to day tends to be requests for information and membership details, but I'm occasionally asked to send "all the information on vampires that you have" for some student's college paper or thesis. Such requests are seldom accompanied by so much as a self-addressed envelope, obviously assuming that I'd be only too happy to pay for the privilege of handing over the product of my researches to date without so much as the promise of a researcher's credit. What these folks actually receive is a membership information leaflet, a recommended reading list, and a note quoting the price of a sample copy of *For the Blood Is the Life*. They seldom respond. There is also an occasional letter from impressionable, Anne Rice vampire–obsessed young women who take it into their heads that I'm a genuine, supernatural, blood-sucking vampire and offer to rush to my side to share my coffin if I'd only bestow the Dark Gift upon them. I have to disappoint them by pointing out that in fact I'm an extremely mortal vegetarian who turns queasy at the sight of blood. The reality is never as much fun as the fantasy, I'm afraid.

I regularly have to deal with people who confuse vampires with blood fetishists. I do my best to point out that The Vampyre Society confines its interests to the legendary, literary, and cinematic representations of vampirism and is in no way involved in its practice. Indeed, in twelve issues of *For the Blood Is the Life* human vampirism had never been covered. However, because a number of members had expressed an interest in the subject, I decided to research it. Part of the process involved sending out questionnaires to self-declared practicing blood drinkers with follow-up interviews. One of my subjects, with eye-teeth capped into fangs, offered to guide me around the vampire scene. Wondering what I'd let myself in for, I agreed and found myself—at midnight, naturally—in a small dark club in the heart of London. Around the room, in obscure dark corners cloaked in smoke made from dry ice, sat small knots of people dressed in black and wearing sunglasses. A cluster of young ladies on the dance floor wearing little more than fluorescent wigs and stiletto-heeled leather thigh boots obviously belonged to a different social group than myself.

As the night wore into the early hours, I was introduced to some people who said they were, or had been, blood drinkers. Most of them chose not to discuss the statement, and all of them declined to be interviewed. One young male told me that he drank only menstrual blood. Although I didn't really get any useful material for my article, it proved to be a most interesting night. A few weeks later, the club was raided by the vice squad and closed down.

Running The Vampyre Society may be strange. It can be hard work at times, but it's seldom dull!

ALLEN J. GITTENS,
Founder and President of The Vampyre Society

Some would-be vampires like to sleep in coffins, which might prove distressing to others (From *Curse of the Vampires*, a Philippine film)

Most living vampires are ambivalent about blood. Some may say they like it, but they drink it only rarely or occasionally. Those who try to drink blood in substantial quantities get ill. Most consume small amounts—a few drops licked from a cut or perhaps a little wine glass full—at periodic intervals. Numerous living vampires claim that vampires really do not need to subsist on blood. Understandably, fear of AIDS and other diseases has put a damper on frequent or indiscriminate blood drinking.

What the fantasy of vampirism really offers people is control in a world perceived as rapidly going out of control because of global politics, war, crime, economic downturn,

environmental crises, and more. Instant communications and media have created a global village, and individually we feel too overwhelmed to cope with everything we know is happening around us. The fantasy vampire is untouched by the ravages of the world and is always in control.

Thus, in its own way, the fantasy vampire provides a needed social function. The vampire of yore was a means to explain untimely or unfortunate death, lack of respect for the dead, and misfortune for the living. The fantasy of vampirism provides a way for at least some people today to feel in control of their lives and destinies.

ROSEMARY ELLEN GUILEY

Living Vampires, Magic, and Psychic Attack

Vampires are horrific supernatural beings, and in folklore are associated with various dark magical and occult practices. Bram Stoker linked his Count Dracula to black magic and a pact with the Devil, yet these associations have, for the most part, not carried into modern popular portrayals of the vampire. Notable exceptions are the 1973 Hammer film, *The Satanic Rites of Dracula*, in which the Count is connected to rituals of black magic, and the 1988 film *Dracula's Widow*, in which the female vampire intrudes on a gathering of satanists and massacres the lot of them. Generally, the image of the vampire in popular culture tends to have no direct links to the occult arts.

This is certainly not the case when it comes to the old legends regarding the undead. Vampire chronicler Montague Summers wrote, in *The Vampire: His Kith and Kin* (1928), "The vampire is believed to be one who has devoted himself during his life to the practice of Black Magic, and it is hardly to be supposed that such persons would rest undisturbed, while it is easy to believe that their malevolence had set in action forces which might prove powerful for terror and destruction even when they were in their graves." Even beyond the idea of sinister magic leading to vampirism after death, there are modern students of the occult who feel that some human beings may be able to master vampiric powers without having to experience death first.

One occult method of attaining vampiric power is in the magical creation of an astral entity that can psychically attack and drain energy. This entity is in essence a vampiric thought form. While this might sound farfetched, occult authorities have long considered it to be a workable practice for those who engage in the darker sorceries.

Writing in *Aurora*, a British occult periodical, in July 1973, David Edwards, an authority on magical operations, observes, "The vampire of occult attack is a deliberately created ghoul. In essence this is a thought form vitalized as an artificial elemental. But it is charged with one direction, Destroy!" Edwards states that the victim often does not realize what is going on; he might just feel a bit run-down. In the end however, sudden death may be the result. Similarly, the modern magical theorist Kenneth Grant has remarked on the dark astral entity he refers to as the "shadow." In his book, *Cults of the Shadow* (1976), he notes, "If the shadow is strongly developed and is under the control of a black magician, it can be projected into the aura of sleeping people and obsess them with sexual fantasies that can drive them to madness and suicide. It is then withdrawn by the vampire who dispatched it and he nourishes himself on the energy which the shadow has 'collected.' " Grant adds that the magician who collects energy in this way may greatly extend his normal life span.

One particular case of a vampire thought form is related in an article that appeared in a theosophical magazine, *The Word*, in 1905. "The Voodoo Vampire" by James H. Connelly tells the story of an African-American musician named Alonzo from New Orleans who was performing at clubs in New York. One night in the city he saw a man he believed had stolen the woman he loved. Seeking revenge, Alonzo went to a well-known voodoo priestess by the name of Mama Mokele. In appearance, she looked to be less than thirty years old, but people in their eighties claimed she looked the same when they were young.

Taking a tablespoon of blood from the little finger of Alonzo's left hand, she muttered something over the cut, which quickly healed. She told him to come back the following night at midnight. When he did, she gave him a very small box that she said contained a spirit form (or astral elemental) in the image of a bat. His own blood had helped to create it. He was to slip the box into the coat pocket of the man he hated. Once that man opened it, the "bat of

death" would crave fresh blood and eventually kill him.

The man who was targeted, John Alden, found the box in his coat pocket and opened it. In it he could see what looked like a stain of blood. He didn't think much of it, but that night he had dreams of drowning. In the morning he found a bleeding wound by his right jugular vein and felt so weak he had to return to bed. That night, wounds appeared on his hands, and he saw a bat darting away from one of them.

On the third night, the man's doctor and servant saw the materialized bat flying in his bedroom. The creature was promptly beaten to the ground and stomped on, at which point it burst like "a huge capsule of blood." Alonzo, the vengeful musician, was found dead the next morning, apparently having burst a blood vessel.

When it comes to the mastery of dark, unearthly forces, one name that often crops up is that of the notorious occultist Aleister Crowley (1875–1947). A supreme egotist, opportunist, hedonist, sensationalist, and heroin addict, he was the first to adopt the word *magick* with a *k* to signify the use of ritual and mental focus to effect some level of reality. Magick is, in his own words, "the Science and Art of causing change to occur in conformity with the will."

One aspect of Crowley's proficiency in magick was his alleged ability to generate vampiric entities that could be sent out to vex his enemies. Such magick was characteristic of Crowley's nature, especially because one of Crowley's most persistent traits was his penchant for turning close friends into bitter enemies. One former friend and mentor was Samuel Liddell MacGregor Mathers, the head and a key founder of the prominent magical organization, the Hermetic Order of the Golden Dawn, which officially started in England in 1888. Under Mather's support and patronage, Crowley was brought into the organization in 1898. Even at that time, Crowley had such a widespread reputation as a disreputable character that his admission into the order created major disruptions within the Golden Dawn.

Several years later, Crowley decided he was the rightful head of the order, as he described in his autobiography *The Confessions of Aleister Crowley* (1960). He wrote a formal letter to Mathers notifying him and then declared war on him. Thus began a grand magical feud between the two renowned adepts. Crowley claimed that Mathers magically killed most of his bloodhounds and made his servants ill. A strange plague of horned beetles seemed to come out of nowhere, infesting Crowley's house and property. Even a workman on the property inexplicably went berserk and started attacking Crowley's wife.

Crowley, in turn, evoked "Beelzebub and his forty-nine servitors" to attack Mathers. The creatures sent out in this magical assault were said to be hideous in appearance. Crowley's wife described one as having lips that were "greeny bronze and slobbery." Another was "a large red spongy jellyfish."

Mathers himself described one of the vampiric creatures attacking him as having a flat head, blubbery shoulders, and glowing coral-colored eyes. Especially repulsive to Mathers was the creature's long tongue—a gray, tubular, hollow thing that rapidly moved in and out of its mouth like a snake's tongue. When he was caught off guard, the tongue, he said, "would suddenly strike at me, like a greedy missile, attempting to suck out my auric vitality." He described a painful sensation when the tongue reached his skin, and this, he added, "was followed by a total enervation of my body and spirit for a week or more. A listless dread experience." According to one account, when Mathers died in 1918, his widow declared that Crowley was responsible, having committed murder by "vampiric attack."

Besides this connection with vampiric thought forms, Crowley was said to have at least one encounter with a human vampire, a living person of flesh and blood. The account is given by one of Crowley's early biographers, J. F. C. Fuller, and is quoted by Crowley in his own autobiography. In that account, the person in question is referred to as "Mrs. M." Crowley was warned that she was a vampiress and sorceress and was asked to help free a woman who was caught in her clutches.

On the day Crowley met Mrs. M, he was at one point alone in a room with her. He was sitting near the fireplace and gazing at a bronze head of the novelist Balzac. A "strange dreamy feeling" came over him, and he looked up to see Mrs. M bending over him, the soft erotic touch of her fingertips having just glided over his hand. However, she was not the middle-age woman to whom he had just been speaking. She had transformed into "a young woman of bewitching beauty."

Crowley calmly rose from his seat, talking to her in a way that would imitate small talk. She sensed now that by engaging him in this way she had entered into a life and death struggle; her efforts were "no longer for the blood of another victim." Recognizing that Crowley was a true match for her, she appeared to be even more beautiful and irresistible than before as she approached him.

With catlike agility, she sprang toward him with the clear intention of giving him a fatal kiss. Crowley stopped her, held her away from him, and then "smote the sorceress with her own current of evil." With that, he could see a blue-green light appearing around her head. What had been an exquisitely beautiful young woman rapidly turned into a wrinkled, decrepit old woman, cursing as she left the room.

Crowley himself admitted this story has been told rather "floridly," but he still presented it as a true experience. We might consider it just another exaggerated legend spawned from the many bizarre adventures in his life. Yet, surprisingly, there have been other reports of living female vampires that bear some striking similarities to Crowley's experience. These accounts are all the more remarkable in that they do not fit the stereotype of the

Draculesque undead vampire commonly found in fiction and film.

One such case was brought to the attention of Elliott O'Donnell (1872–1965), a researcher who in his day was considered one of Britain's leading ghost investigators. A friend of his, Mrs. South, gave him information about a man named Jack who had recently married. He lived with his new wife in a rather isolated house in the English county of Devonshire. When one of his old friends came by to visit with him for a few days, Jack looked terrible, having wasted away to a shadow of his former self. In contrast, Jack's wife literally dazzled the visitor with her beauty. At the same time, some things about her appearance were quite unusual. She had bright red fingernails, fingers that were long and pointed, and skin that was extremely white. At dinner she seemed reticent to eat anything.

After dinner the visiting friend found it quite an effort to stay awake and so retired early. The next morning he discovered a strange red mark on the lower part of his neck. By that evening he again felt an irresistible sensation of sleepiness after dinner. Once in bed, he thought he had a dream of a woman entering his room and putting her lips on his neck wound. That morning he woke to find the mark on his neck even more inflamed.

On his last night there, he deliberately laid awake in bed. At midnight he saw Jack's wife enter the room and move toward him, "gliding as stealthily and noiselessly as a snake." He waited until he could feel her breath, then quickly threw his arms around her. This attempt to capture her failed as she easily slipped out of his arms like an eel and escaped. He chose to leave the house early that morning. Some time after that he heard Jack had died.

Montague Summers heard a report in 1905 of a living female vampire in Lithuania and described the case in his book *The Vampire in Europe* (1929). The man who related the account was known as Captain Pokrovsky, an officer in what was then called the Russian-Lithuanian Guards. While on his uncle's estate in Lithuania, Pokrovsky learned of a rich farmer who began to sicken and waste away after his marriage to his second wife. The man's sister remarked, "Since he has remarried, he cries out in the night." Pokrovsky saw that the man looked pale and listless, even though he was a hearty eater.

When a doctor was brought in to examine the man, it was determined that he had lost a large amount of blood, yet there was no wound large enough to explain such a loss. The only thing the doctor could find was "a small puncture in the neck with inflamed edges." When Pokrovsky asked his own cousin, who lived in the area, what the problem was, she replied, "I do not know, but the villagers all declared that a vampire is getting at him." The villagers in fact suspected that his wife was the vampire, and when the man eventually died of his illness, his widow felt compelled to move out of the district. His neck wound had grown much larger by the time he died.

Stories of living female vampires seem to be even more prevalent in the regions of Eastern Asia and the surrounding islands. There are even texts of tantric magic that speak of methods whereby young women may become immortal through the absorption of male energy. A number of reports of living vampires in the Orient have been noted by Western researchers.

Warren Smith reported a case from Hong Kong in his book *Strange Monsters and Madmen* (1969). Lem Chee was on his way out of mainland China in 1949 to escape the communist takeover when he met a pretty young peasant woman. Instantly infatuated, he married her in a small village en route before they finished their trek to Hong Kong. After they settled in the sanctuary of the city, Lem Chee became a prosperous merchant. By 1963, something became quite obvious to him. He had aged normally to his true age of sixty-two. His wife, however, did not look any older than the day he married her.

When he sought the advice of an old wise woman in the hills, she told him of another vampire she knew of, a farmer's wife who had not aged at all in fifty years. If Lem Chee wanted to know for sure if his wife was this kind of unaging vampire, he should put her someplace where she could not sneak out at night to satisfy any peculiar needs. Against his wife's wishes, he placed her in a special clinic for medical observations.

She was there for less than a week when one night an orderly entered the room where blood was stored. To his horror, he saw the woman gorging herself on the pints of blood. She had ingested more than three quarts of it before she was stopped. On another occasion she attacked a nurse and almost succeeded in biting her on the neck. At night the woman kept repeating the word *blood* as she lay strapped to her bed. Staff Dr. A. Chiang is quoted as saying, "She insisted she needed blood to live."

It was noticed that Lem Chee's wife aged rapidly during her confinement. In the clinic less than three weeks, she died there looking like an old woman. Warren Smith quoted an unnamed professor as saying, "The old woman claimed there are about two hundred vampire girls in all of Asia. They must drink blood to remain forever young."

Another researcher, Mervyn Pereira, has come across similar beliefs in Malaysia. Many people there believe that vampires are commonly women who appear to be young and beautiful and lead normal lives, but simply never age. The witch doctors he interviewed told him that there are a hundred of them in Malaysia alone. One witch doctor admitted to knowing one of these women personally. He said she is happily married to a shopkeeper, but she hasn't aged in half a century.

It isn't always the case that vampire women in the East leave their husbands unharmed. The French news service, Agence France-Press, reported the following story for March 19, 1975:

> Djakarta, Indonesia—A vampire has been blamed for the deaths of the five successive husbands of an attractive 25-year-old woman living in South Sumatra. All five husbands died of acute anemia. The woman's parents finally consulted a local medicine man who concluded that she was possessed by a *nagnagasjatingarong*, a sort of vampire, which had sucked all the blood from the bodies of the five unfortunate husbands.

If we give any credence to these tales of living human vampires, the question remains: How does one become a living, rather than an undead, vampire in the first place? Beij Beltrisi, a young man who started his own vampire society by the same name in Richmond, Indiana, has stated he has always known he was a vampire. A number of other self-proclaimed vampires have expressed similar sentiments. The idea that true vampires are born that way is expressed in an article titled "Real Vampires," which appeared in the Fall 1988 issue of *Fireheart: A Journal of Magick & Spiritual Transformation*. Written by Daile Nicholson, a practitioner of magick herself, the article defines a vampire as "a person born with an extraordinary capacity to absorb, channel, transform and manipulate 'pranic energy' or life force." She says the physical biochemistry of these individuals usually makes them literally night people who have difficulty functioning in the daytime and who generally avoid the sun.

Nicholson explains that only real vampires, who inherently have the power, can actually absorb the pranic energy they need from fresh blood. However, it is also her claim that most vampires can absorb energy from others in less direct ways. Many are unconscious of their true nature and may be psychic sponges that take energy from any available source around them. On an extreme level, a vampire might become a psychic vortex, absorbing all energy within its range.

This notion of a psychic vampire, someone who saps vital energy from others just by being in their presence, has long been known in occult circles. Theosophist Dr. Franz Hartman wrote on the subject in the July 1986 issue of *Borderland*:

> They unconsciously vampirize every sensitive person with whom they come in contact, and they instinctively seek out such persons and invite them to stay at their houses. I know of an old lady, a vampire, who thus ruined the health of a lot of robust servant girls, whom she took into her service and made them sleep in her room. They were all in good health when they entered, but soon they began to sicken, they became emaciated and consumptive and had to leave the service.

Henry S. Olcott, a Theosophist, wrote in a pamphlet titled "The Vampire" in 1920, "This magnetic vampirism is practiced every day and hour in social, most especially in conjugal, intercourse: the weak absorb strength from the strong, the sickly from the robust, the aged from the young." A woman claiming to be a psychic vampire described her abilities in the fourth issue of *Crimson*, a modern British publication for vampire aficionados. She mentions that she feels slow and groggy during the daytime, is sensitive to bright light, and avoids the sun on hot days. She claims she can actually feel the need to feed, that is, the need to drain energy from someone. Her three main methods for feeding are the embrace, the kiss (or love bite), and sex. She states, "Sexual energy is by far the best form as the contact is relatively prolonged and the donor gives out huge amounts of energy that need only be sucked in." Nicholson has observed that many people will feel creepy or weird when they are in the presence of a vampire because they are actually feeling energy being drawn out of them. She also notes that vampires often have uncontrolled magickal and psychic experiences and that many of them are attracted to magickal paths.

Those who have studied vampirism have sometimes wondered if there are actual techniques of magick that can transform a person into a living vampire. While there are medieval manuscripts that describe the rites for transformation into a werewolf, there is nothing of that age that does the same for vampires. However, in the last few decades of the twentieth century some modern occultists have succeeded in filling that gap.

The Temple of the Vampire in Lacey, Washington, claims to provide just such a ritual. It is a pronouncement of the Temple that, "A Vampire is made, not born." Headed by Lucas Martel, the temple seeks recruits for its ancient "religion of Vampirism."

Like other magical orders, the temple offers a series of teachings to members as they progress through various levels. In the temple's letter of basic information it is stated, "At the lower levels of development, the Living Vampire draws out the life force, while in simple physical contact with his victim . . . at the highest level, advanced Living Vampires directly and consciously alter the structure of reality through the practice of true magic." The letter also states, "The Vampire sits atop the food chain of this world as the predator of humans." However, the temple does not allow the damage or destruction of any living creature, human or otherwise; and there is no physical drinking of human blood.

The temple's ritual that is said to transform a mortal human into the vampiric condition is called the rite of vampiric communion. In this rite the ancient vampire gods, who have transcended beyond the need for a physical body, feed off the life force of those who make the ritual contact with them. These gods are known by various names, including the Undead, the Ancient Ones, and the Elder Gods.

Apart from the Temple of Vampire, there is an obscure occult document that also speaks of Elder Gods as ancient otherworldly beings who have guided receptive humans into a vampiric state. Published in 1983 out of West Danby, New York, it is titled *The Alchemy of Immortality: Vampires and the Aristocracy of Blood* (1983). The author, identified as Frater PVN, has a strong background in magick derived from the writings of Aleister Crowley. In this document, Frater PVN contends that a commitment to sexual ecstasy in combination with certain magickal practices can trigger multidimensional linkages beyond the normal human limitations of the space-time continuum. In other words, what he calls the vampiric alchemist has the means to bypass the laws of nature in this reality, even to transcend the need for physical death. To Frater PVN, the life essence is inherently sexual in nature. While specifics are not given, he indicates that sexual fluids (including menstrual blood) are charged with energy and can be used to nourish such vampires.

Frater PVN clearly states that his writings are not designed to be a "cookbook for the novice." In 1985, just a couple years after his treatise came out, a booklet was released that does resemble a recipe book for those aspiring to be vampires. It is titled *How to Become a Vampire in 6 Easy Lessons*, and the author's name is given as Madeline X. The necessary ingredients are listed at the beginning, which include three raw white eggs, vinegar, and a raw chicken liver. The six-day formula described is similar to the kind of thing found in popular spell books, with specific actions and chants to be performed. How seriously it is meant to be taken is left up to each person who reads it. Printed by the Count Dracula Fan Club in New York, it is their best-selling publication. Those who are serious in their intent should be pleased with the booklet's final assertion that if the instructions have been followed exactly, "you will awaken the following night . . . AS A VAMPIRE!"

Those with a desire to become vampires have usually been influenced by popular culture, which tends to portray the vampire as a romantic and sensuous creature. Some individuals may also be enticed by the vampiric powers they think they might gain. Yet, many who claim to know do not paint a bright picture for the life of an occult vampire. It can be an isolated existence on the dark side, in which the vampire endlessly seeks to feed from and drain out the life energies of others. There is one main conclusion for anyone considering joining the ranks of living vampires: in the long run, it probably isn't worth sticking your neck out!

MARTIN V. RICCARDO

Vampire Crime Gallery

ere is a sampling of famous blood drinkers—and a blood bather—from past to present.

Elizabeth Bathory

The best-known living female vampire in history is Elizabeth Bathory, called the Blood Countess. It is not known if she drank blood, but she was obsessed with bathing in it, certainly a novel form of vampirism. Bathory was born in 1560 to a noble family who dominated Transylvania in the southeast of Hungary, in what is now Romania. She was a great beauty, and was married at age fifteen to Count Ferencz Nadasdy, a wealthy man who was many years her senior. Bathory took many lovers.

She was an accomplished hostess, but also sadistic to servants and peasants. The Magyar nobles had virtual free reign to do whatever they pleased, and the slightest whims and grossest of perversions had to be obeyed. Bathory seemed to enjoy tormenting pretty girls. A cousin of her husband's was accused of stealing fruit, and in punishment Bathory had her tied naked to a tree and smeared with honey to attract insects. Her husband also taught her to discipline servant girls by putting oiled paper between their toes and setting the paper afire. The girls' wild attempts to get rid of the paper were called "star-kicking," to the amusement of the nobles.

By age twenty-five, Bathory was terrified of losing her beauty, a fear that grew worse with each passing year. After her husband's sudden death—possibly of appendicitis—in 1604, she began to lead a twisted double life. She had already dabbled in sorcery, attending secret sacrifices of white horses and encouraging the company of a sorceress named Anna Darvulia who brought out her worst.

Elizabeth Bathory

The story goes that Bathory was introduced to the benefits of blood by accident. To punish a clumsy maid, she took a pair of scissors and struck the girl in the face, cutting her and causing blood to splash upon Bathory's hand. Bathory seemed to think the blood restored the youthful appearance of her skin (she was perhaps by now in middle age past menopause). Her sorceress concurred with her that bathing in virgin's blood would indeed help her to regain and retain her youth. Bathory began bathing in blood as often as possible, as a ritual at four in the morning, a mysterious time specified by the Darvulia.

The ritual quickly degenerated into the vilest practices. Serving girls were fattened up, tortured, bled, and killed. Bathory had them tied up tightly so that their blood would spray out when they were cut with scissors or pricked with pins. She also had hot pokers stuck into their mouths, and when she was done bleeding them, she had them beaten to death with a whip. Bathory also visited other abominations upon the hapless girls, such as ironing their feet with a hot iron, pouring cold water over them as they stood naked in the snow, and forcing them to eat the cooked flesh of other murdered serving girls.

One of Bathory's favorite activities was to sit beneath a cage full of servant girls that was hoisted up off the floor. The cage was lined with sharp spikes, and the girls were prodded into the spikes with burning irons. This way, Bathory had her own blood shower.

And so the atrocities went. Young girls were lured to her castles—her husbands had owned several—with offers of fine jobs. Once inside, they were imprisoned, never to see the outside again.

By 1609, Darvulia was dead and Bathory was convinced that the blood baths were no longer holding back the march of time. She consulted another sorceress, and was told that her victims should be virgins of nobility. Securing these victims was a bit trickier, but Bathory used the ruse of offering them jobs as maids of honor. Still, there weren't enough noble young ladies to fill the blood bowls, and Bathory's accomplices were forced to dress up peasant girls in fine clothing to pass them off as nobility.

Rumors about Bathory, which had been circulating, finally could no longer be ignored (perhaps it was of no official concern if only peasant girls were meeting their deaths, but the murders of gentry were another matter). One of Bathory's cousins, Lord Palatine, Count Thurzo, inspected her castle at Csejthe in 1610 and was horrified at what he found—the bodies of tortured girls, and living girls who'd been "milked" and were penned up like animals. Lord Palatine immediately arrested Bathory's accomplice servants. Exhumations revealed the remains of more than fifty bodies. No one knew just how many girls had been killed, but estimates placed the number at 600 or more.

The accomplices were tried and convicted. One was beheaded and burned, and two had their fingers torn off one by one with hot pincers and then were burned alive.

Bathory was not arrested or tried, probably because of her nobility. Nonetheless, she was punished. Her cousin believed her to be insane and had her walled up in her bedroom in her castle at Csejthe. Slits let in air, but very little light. Food was sent in through a slot. There she lived in isolation and misery until August 21, 1614, when she died suddenly.

FRITZ HAARMAN, "VAMPIRE BUTCHER" OF HANOVER, GERMANY

Fritz Haarman was born in Germany on October 24, 1879, to a stern household. He particularly disliked his authoritarian father. Haarman was a poor student and joined the military, where he fared better. After the service, he returned home to Hanover, where he was accused of molesting children and was placed in a mental institution. He escaped and attempted to resume living with his father, but the relationship soon degenerated into physical violence.

Haarman then took up a violent, crime-ridden life on the streets, spending much of his time in jail. After release in 1918, he found a job as a butcher and then as a police informant. He began to molest boys. His modus operandi was to wake up boys sleeping at the Hanover railway station and demand to see their ticket. If they had none, he would offer them a place to stay for the night. The boys mysteriously disappeared after that.

In 1919, Haarman met Hans Grans, a twenty-four-year-old male prostitute, whom he recruited as a lover and as an accomplice to his sex and murder schemes. They selected their victims based upon Grans' taste for their clothes. In killing the boys, Haarman would bite into their throat and drink their blood.

Haarman and Grans went about their grisly business until 1924, when police discovered human remains in the Seine River and along the mud banks. At about the same time, Haarman was jailed on indecency charges. While he sat in jail, police searched his rented room and found bloodstains. The blood was determined to be human, which set police off on a more careful search outside. They found the remains of twenty-two corpses.

The evidence, however, was circumstantial, and no charges could be brought against Haarman, until a mother of one missing boy identified a scrap of clothing worn by her son, which was traced to Haarman. Questioned by police, he confessed to murder and named Grans as accomplice.

All the victims were between the ages of twelve and eighteen. Grans would often select the victims. Haarman would take them to his meat shop, where he also kept his room. He would feed them a generous meal, lavish praise upon them for their beauty, and then turn into a vampire killer, sexually assaulting them and inflicting a fatal bite upon their necks. (If Haarman failed to kill the victims, Grans would beat him.) Grans got some of the victims' clothes, and the rest were sold through Haarman's butcher shop. It appears that some of the victims were sold as meat and sausages as well. A third man, Charles, who was also a butcher, assisted Haarman in grinding and cutting up the bodies. After one such episode, an unwitting shop patron helped Haarman with the making of the human sausages in the kitchen, which they both cooked and ate on the spot.

In court, Haarman claimed that he was sane, but that when he committed the murders, he was always in a trance and not aware of what he was doing. The court rejected that argument, based on Haarman's quite specific description of the manner in which he would have to bite the victims to kill them.

In all, Haarman was accused of twenty-four murders. Some estimated that his actual number of victims was much higher. Haarman himself opined that he had killed thirty or forty boys. Haarman was judged sane and was beheaded in 1925. He asked that his tombstone read, "Here lies Mass-Murderer Haarman," and that Grans should lay a wreath on his grave every year on his birthday.

Charles disappeared, and Grans was sentenced to life in prison.

John George Haigh

Born in England in 1910, Haigh was raised in a strict Pilgrim Brethren family. He seemed to have a normal childhood and remained affectionate toward his parents throughout his life. He was intelligent and made friends easily. Briefly married at age twenty-five, he expressed no further interest in sex after the mar-riage ended. In the following ten years he served three prison sentences for dishonesty and fraud.

During his childhood, from about the age of six, Haigh enjoyed blood and would wound himself so that he could suck his own blood. He was also fascinated by the Holy Communion and the Crucifixion. He frequently dreamed about railway accidents with injured and bleeding people. These symptoms went into remission until 1944, when at age thirty-five, blood dripped into his mouth from an accidental head wound. He began again having dreams about blood. In a typical dream he would see a forest of crucifixes change into green trees that were dripping blood, which he would drink, and then awake with the desire for blood. The dreams tended to follow a weekly cycle of increasing intensity from Monday through Friday.

With a growing compulsion for blood, Haigh rented a storeroom and bought some drums of acid. In the next five years he killed nine of his acquaintances, drank their blood, and dissolved their bodies in the acid. He was arrested, tried, and executed in London in 1949.

ROSEMARY ELLEN GUILEY

Appendices

The Literate Vampire: A Bibliography

This bibliography provides an extensive guide to English-language vampire material. It concentrates on classic vampiriana, but includes some minor and obscure works that deserve attention.

The list is divided into three sections: novels, anthologies, and studies. Authors are listed in alphabetical order, but their works are listed chronologically to show the development of their work and the evolution of vampiric characters (such as Chelsea Quinn Yarbro's Count Saint-Germain) and series (such as Anne Rice's Vampire Chronicles and Brian Lumley's Necroscope series).

Due to the extensive number of vampire books, the bibliography is limited to works in which vampires play a major part. Therefore, many novels by authors such as Piers Anthony, Frank Aubrey, Clive Barker, Robert E. Howard, Stephen King, Dean Koontz, and Michael Moorcock, who often use vampires in a minor capacity, have been omitted. Juvenile novels, young adult novels, and books about vampire-like things such as plants, swords, and vampire bats have also been excluded. However, works that use the word *vampire* and its cognates in their titles have been included. This convention is necessary for completeness and to distinguish classic vampire novels from books that involve pseudo-vampirism or use vampirism as a metaphor for cruelty or various forms of parasitism.

Some of the most important vampire stories have been reviewed in the text, but there are so many stories in books, magazines, and fanzines that it is not possible to include a list of this material. Therefore, the second section is limited to a review of vampire anthologies and collections (i.e., anthologies that contain the work of only one author). Most of the books in this section include stories that are not easily available in their original formats. Alan Ryan's anthology *Vampires* (1987) provides an outstanding selection of classic vampire tales, while Richard Dalby's *Dracula's Brood* (1987) and Robert Weinberg's *Weird Vampire Tales* (1992) consist of rare, out-of-print stories. Byron Preiss's collection, *The Ultimate Dracula* (1991), and Martin H. Greenberg's *Dracula: Prince of Darkness* (1992) consist entirely of stories about Count Dracula.

Many of the anthologies edited by Ramsey J.

Campbell, Charles L. Grant, Peter Haining, Stephen Jones, Marvin Kaye, Hugh Lamb, Stuart David Schiff, Kurt Singer, and Robert Weinberg contain at least one vampire story, while certain annual anthologies such as *Best New Horror, The Pan Book of Horror Stories, The Year's Best Fantasy and Horror*, and *The Year's Best Horror Stories* usually contain vampire stories. Mass-market magazines such as Isaac Asimov's *Science Fiction Magazine, The Magazine of Fantasy & Science Fiction*, Marion Zimmer Bradley's *Fantasy Magazine*, and *Weird Tales* often carry vampire tales, while a variety of small-press magazines publish vampire stories by well-known authors and talented newcomers. *After Hours, Cemetary Dance, Dead of Night, Deathrealm, Eldritch Tales, Fantasy Macabre, Grue, Haunts, Iniquities, Midnight Zoo, The Silver Web, Space & Time, The Stake, The Tome, 2 A.M.*, and *Weirdbook* are included in this category. *Prisoners of the Night* and *The Vampire's Crypt* are dedicated to vampire fiction.

Up-to-date information about science fiction, fantasy, and horror can be found in non-fiction magazines such as *Locus, The New York Review of Science Fiction, Science Fiction Chronicle*, and *Science Fiction Eye. Horror, Draculina, Necrophile, Scarlet Street*, and *The Scream Factory* review horror fiction.

The studies presented in the third section of the bibliography discuss vampirism from various points of view. The vampire bibliographies by Margaret L. Carter, Greg Cox, Brian J. Frost, Donald F. Glut, Robert Eighteen-Bisang, and Martin V. Riccardo review many of the works that have been cited in *The Complete Vampire Companion* in more detail and provide invaluable guides to additional vampire material.

The accompanying alpha-numeric code provides a concise review by indicating what type of vampire is involved and the genre of each novel. For example, *Al* stands for alien life form, *Bl* for blood, etc., while *1* indicates horror, *2* science fiction, etc. In addition, novels with movie tie-ins and studies about vampire movies are designated by *M*, and books with comic-book tie-ins are followed by *C*. A complete key follows.

Vampire

D	Dracula, vampire named Dracula
V	Vampire, vampiress
Al	alien life form
Bl	Blood drinking, blood sacrifice
En	Energy-, essence-, or soul-draining
Fo	Folk vampire
Im	Immortality, longevity
In	Invisible, incorporal vampire
La	Lamia
Me	Metaphor
Po	Possession
Ps	Pseudo-vampirism
Su	Succubus
We	Weird/miscellaneous vampiric entity

Genre

1	Horror
2	Science fiction
3	Fantasy, sword, and sorcery
4	Magic, occult, supernatural
5	Literature, general fiction
6	Literature, based on fact, biography
7	Mystery, detective, spy
8	Action, adventure
9	Romance
10	Eroticism, pornography
11	Cruelty, sadism
12	Comedy, satire
C	Comic book tie-in
M	Movie tie-in

NOVELS

Acres, Mark. *Dark Divide.* New York: Ace, 1991. Pb. [V, 3]

Aldiss, Brian W. *Dracula Unbound.* New York: HarperCollins, 1991. Hb. London: Grafton, 1991. Hb. Rpt. 1992. Tr. Pb. New York: HarperPaperbacks, 1992. Pb. [D, 2]

Alexander, Jan (Victor John Banis). *Blood Moon.* New York: Lancer, 1970. Pb. [Ps, 9]

Alexander, Karl. *The Curse of the Vampire.* New York: Pinnacle Warner, 1982. Pb. [V, 1]

Andersson, Dean. *Raw Pain Max.* New York: Pinnacle, 1988. Pb. [En (Elizabeth Bathory), 1, 4, 11]

———*I Am Dracula.* New York: Zebra, 1993. Pb. Revised and expanded version of *Crimson Kisses.* See: Asa Drake, *Crimson Kisses* (1981). [D (Vlad Tepes), 1, 4]

Anthony, Patricia. *Cold Allies.* New York: Harcourt, Brace, Jovanovich, 1993. Hb. New York: Ace, 1994. Pb. [Al, En, 3]

Anthony, Piers (Piers Anthony Dillingham Jacob). *Pornucopia.* Houston, TX: Tafford, 1989. Hb. and Tr. Pb. [V (cameo), Su, 10, 12]

Armstrong, F. W. (T. M. Wright). *The Devouring.* New York: TOR, 1987. Pb. [V, 4, 7]

Ascher, Eugene (Harold Kelly). *There Were No Asper Ladies.* London: Mitre, 1946. Pb. Retitled: *To Kill a Corpse.* London: World Distributors, 1965. Pb. [V, 4, 7]

Atholl, Justin. *The Grey Beast.* London: Everybody's Books, n.d. (1944). Paper. Story. [V, 3]

Atkins, Peter. *Morningstar.* New York: HarperPaperbacks, 1992. Pb. London: HarperCollins, 1993. Hb. Rpt. 1994. Pb. [V, We, 1]

Aubin, Etienne. *Dracula and the Virgins of the Undead.* London: New English Library, 1974. Pb. [D, 1]

Baker, Nancy. *The Night Inside.* London: Penguin, 1993. Tr. Pb. Rpt. 1994. Pb. New York: Fawcett Columbine, 1994. Hb. [V, 1]

Baker, Scott. *Nightchild.* New York: Berkley, 1979. Hb. New York: Pocket Books, 1979. Pb. Revised edition. [Al, We, 2]

———*Dhampire.* New York: Pocket Books, 1982. Pb. [V, 4]

Ball, Brian. *The Venomous Serpent.* London: New English Library, 1974. Pb. Retitled: *The Night Creature.* Greenwich, CT: Fawcett, 1974. Pb. [En, 1]

Bainbridge, Sharon (Sharon N. Faber and Sharon Rose). *Blood and Roses.* New York: Diamond, 1993. Pb. [V, 1]

Barker, Sonny. *Vampire's Kiss.* San Diego, CA: Phenix, 1970. Pb. [D?, V?, Ps?, 1, 10]

Beath, Warren Newton. *Bloodletter.* New York: TOR, 1994. Hb. [V, 1]

Beatty, Elwood, and D. L. Crabtree. *Rebirth of the Undead.* Santa Clara, CA: Pentagram, 1984. Paper. [D (and Barnabas Collins)], 1]

Behm, Marc. *The Ice Maiden.* In: Marc Behm; *The Eye of the Bedholder (and) The Queen of the Night (and) The Ice Maiden.* London: Zomba, 1983. Hb. and Tr. Pb. Trans. from the French of 1983. [V, 1]

Bergstrom, Elaine. *Shattered Glass.* New York: Jove, 1989. Pb. New York: Ace, 1994. Pb. [Austra Family #1. V, 1]

———*Blood Alone.* New York: Jove, 1990. Pb. New York: Ace, 1994. Pb. [#2]

———*Blood Rites.* New York: Jove, 1991. Pb. New York: Ace, 1994. Pb. [#3]

———*Daughter of the Night.* New York: Jove, 1992. Pb. New York: Ace, 1994. Pb. [#4]

———*Tapestry of Dark Souls.* Lake Geneva, WI: TSR, 1993. Pb. [Ravenloft series. V, 3, 8]

Billson, Anne. *Suckers.* London: Pan, 1993. Tr. Pb. New York: Macmillan Atheneum, 1993. Hb. [V, 1]

Bischoff, David. *Vampires of Nightworld.* New York: Ballantine, 1981. Pb. [Nightworld series. We (cyborgs), 2]

Black, Campbell. *The Wanting.* New York: McGraw-Hill, 1986. Hb. New York: Jove, 1987. Pb. London: Severn House, 1993. Hb. [En, 1]

Blackburn, Thomas. *The Feast of the Wolf.* London: MacGibbon & Kee, 1971. Hb. [V, 1]

Blacque, Dovya (Pseud.) *South of Heaven.* Mkasheff: Poway, CA, 1991. Paper. [V, 3, 10]

Bloch, Robert. *Yours Truly, Jack the Ripper.* Eugene, OR: Pulphouse, 1991. Paper. Story. Originally published in 1943. [Im, 4]

Bok (Pseud.). *Vampires of the China Coast.* London: Jenkins, 1932. Hb. [Ps, 6]

Briery, Trace. *The Vampire Journals.* New York: Zebra, 1993. Pb. See also: Mara McCuniff and Traci Briery. [The Vampire Memoirs #2. V, 1]

Brite, Poppy Z. *Lost Souls.* New York: Delacorte, 1992. Hb. New York: Dell, 1993. Pb. London: Signet, 1994. Tr. Pb. [V, 1, 10]

Brett, Stephen (Stephen Mertz). *The Vampire Chase.* New York: Manor, 1979. Pb. [Ps, 7]

Brown, Carter (Alan Geoffery Yates). *So What Killed the Vampire?* Sydney, Australia: Horowitz, 1966. Pb. New York: Signet, 1966. Pb. London: New English Library, 1967. Pb. [Ps, 7, 12]

Brust, Stephen. *Agyar.* New York: TOR, 1993. Hb. Rpt. 1994. Pb. [V, 1]

Burke, John. *Dracula—The Prince of Darkness.* In: *The Second Hammer Horror Film Omnibus.* London: Pan, 1967. Pb. Rpt. n.d. [D, 1, C, M]

Burke, Norah. *The Scarlet Vampire.* London: Stanley Paul, 1936. Hb. [Me (dictator), 3]

Butler, Jack. *Nightshade.* New York: Atlantic Monthly Press, 1989. Hb. [V2]

Byers, Richard Lee. *The Vampire's Apprentice.* New York: Zebra, 1992. Pb. [V, 1]

Byron, Lord (Pseud.). *The Bride of the Isles.* Dublin, Ireland: J. Charles, n.d. (c. 1820). Rpt. in: Haining, Peter, ed. *The Shilling Shockers.* New York: St. Martin's, 1979. Hb. [V (Lord Ruthven), 1]

Caine, Geoffrey (Robert Walker). *Curse of the Vampire.* New York: Diamond 1991. Pb. [V, 1]

Carew, Henry. *The Vampires of the Andes.* London: Jarrolds, 1925. Hb. New York: Arno, 1978. Hb. [Bl, Ps, 3]

Carlisle, Robin. *Blood and Roses.* New York: Hillman, 1960. Pb. [V ("Carmilla" Karnstein), 1, M]

Carroll, Joy. *Satan's Bell.* Markham, Ont., Canada: Pocket Books, 1976. Pb. [Im, 4]

Carter, Nicholas (House Pseud. Written by Walter Bertram). *The Vampire's Trail.* New York: Street and Smith, 1912. Pb. [Ps, 7]

Casanova, Jacques [de Seingalt]. *Casanova's "Icosameron."* New York: Jenna, 1986. Hb. Rpt. n.d. Tr. Pb. Trans. from the French of 1778. [Bl, 3]

Caunitz, William J. *Exceptional Clearance.* New York: Crown, 1991. Hb. [Bl, Ps, 7]

Jacques Cazotte. *Biondetta, The Devil in Love,* and *The Enamoured Spirit.* See: Anon., *The Devil in Love* (1973).

Cecilione, Michael. *Domination.* New York: Zebra, 1993. Pb. [V, 1]

Charnas, Suzy, McKee. *The Vampire Tapestry.* New York: Simon & Schuster, 1980. Hb. New York: Pocket Books, 1981. Pb. London: Granada, 1983. Pb. New York: TOR, 1986. Pb. London: Women's Press, 1992. Tr. Pb. Albuquerque, NM: University of New Mexico Living Branch, 1993. Tr. Pb. [V, 1]

Chaytor, N. J. *The Light of the Eye.* London: Digby, Long, n.d. (1897). Hb. [En, We, 1]

Cherryh, C. J. (Caroline Janice Cherry). *Rusalka.* New York: Ballantine, 1989. Hb. Rpt. Pb. [Rusalka #1 Fo (Russian, Rusalka), In, 3]

Chetwynd-Hayes, R. *The Monster Club.* London: New English Library, 1975. Pb. London: Severn House, 1992. Hb. [V, 12, C, M]

———*The Partaker.* London: Kimber, 1980. Hb. [V, 3]

Ciencin, Scott, *The Vampire Odyssey.* New York: Zebra, 1992. Pb. [Danielle Walthers #1. V, 1]

———*The Wildings.* New York: Zebra, 1992. Pb. [#2]

———*Parliament of Blood.* New York: Zebra, 1992. Pb. [#3]

Cilescu, Valentine. *Kiss of Death.* London: Headline, 1992. Pb. [The Master #1. V, 4, 10]

———*The Phallus of Osiris.* London: Headline, 1993. Pb. [#2]

Clayton, Jo. *Drinker of Souls.* New York: DAW, 1986. Pb. [Brann series #1. Al, En, 3]

Cobban, J. Maclearan. *Master of His Fate.* Edinburgh, U.K.: Blackwood, 1890. Hb. New York: F. F. Lovell, 1890. Hb. Elstree, Herts., U.K.: Greenhill, 1987. Hb. [En, 1]

Coffman, Virginia. *The Vampyre of Moura.* New York: Ace, 1970. Pb. Rpt. n.d. [V, 9]

Collins, Nancy A. *Sunglasses After Dark.* New York: Onyx, 1989. Pb. London: Kinnell, 1990. Hb. [Sonja Blue #1. V, 1, 10]

———*Tempter.* New York: Onyx, 1990. Pb. [V, 4]

———*In the Blood.* New York: ROC, 1992. Pb. [#2]

———*Cold Turkey.* Holyoke, MA: Crossroads, 1992. Paper. Story. [#3]

Condé, Philip. *Skyway Vampire.* London: Wright and Brown, 1938. Hb. London: Mellifont, 1940. Hb. Abridged. [Ps, 8]

Constantine, Storm. *Burying the Shadow.* London: Headline, 1992. Pb. [Al, 3]

Cooke, John Peyton. *Out for Blood.* New York: Avon, 1991. Pb. [V, 1]

Coolidge-Rask, Marie. *London After Midnight.* New York: Grosset & Dunlap, 1928. Hb. [Ps, 7, M]

Cooper, Louise, *Blood Summer.* London: New English Library, 1976. Pb. [Sarah Bailey #1. V, 1]

———*In Memory of Sarah Bailey.* London: New English Library, 1977. Pb. [#2]

Corbett, James. *Vampire of the Skies.* London: Jenkins, 1932. Hb. [Ps, 7]

Courtney, Vincent. *Vampire Beat.* New York: Pinnacle, 1991. Pb. [Christopher Blaze #1. V, 1]

————*Harvest of Blood.* New York: Pinnacle, 1992. Pb. [#2]

Crozier, Ouida. *Shadows After Dark.* Huntington Station, NY: Rising Tide, 1993. Tr. Pb. [V, 3, 10]

Cullum, Ridgewell. *The Vampire of N'gobi.* London: Chapman & Hall, 1935. Hb. Philadelphia, PA: J. B. Lippincott, 1936. Hb. [Ps, 3]

Cusick, Richie Tankersly. *Buffy the Vampire Slayer.* New York: Archway, 1992. Pb. [V, 12, M]

Dalman, Max. *Vampire Abroad.* London: Ward, Lock, 1938. Hb. [Ps, 7]

Daniels, Les. *The Black Castle.* New York: Scribners, 1978. Hb. New York: Ace, 1979. Pb. London: Sphere, 1981. Pb. [Don Sebastian #1. V, 1]

————*The Silver Skull.* New York: Scribners, 1979. Hb. New York: Ace, 1983. Pb. London: Sphere, 1981. Pb. [#2]

————*Citizen Vampire.* New York: Scribners, 1981. Hb. New York: Ace, 1985. Pb. London: Sphere, 1981. Pb. [#3]

————*Yellow Fog.* West Kingston, RI: Donald M. Grant, 1986. Hb. New York: TOR, 1988. Pb. Revised edition. [#4]

————*No Blood Spilled.* New York: TOR, 1991. Pb. [#5]

Daniels, Philip. *The Dracula Murders.* London: Hale, 1983. Hb. New York: Lorevan, 1986. Pb. Guilford, CT: Ulversoft, 1988. Hb. [V?, Ps, 7]

Darke, David (Ron Dee). *Blind Hunger.* New York: Pinnacle, 1993. Pb. [V, 1]

Davies, David Stuart. *The Tangled Skein.* Wymouth, Dorset, U.K.: Theme, 1992. Hb. Aldeney, Channel Islands, U.K.: Island, 1993. Hb. [D (vs. Sherlock Holmes), 1, 7]

Davis, Andrew J. *The Diakka: and their earthly victims.* New York: Davis, 1873. Hb. New York: Colby & Rich, 1873. Hb. [En, Fo (diakka), 4]

Davis, Jay & Don Davis. *Bring on the Night.* New York: TOR, 1993. Pb. [V, 1]

Dear, Ian. *Village of Blood.* London: New English Library, 1975. Pb. [V, 1]

Dee, Ron. *Blood Lust.* New York: Dell, 1990. Pb. [Blood Lust #1. V, 1]

————*Dusk.* New York: Dell, 1991. Pb. [V, 1]

————*Blood.* New York: Pocket Books, 1993. Pb. [V, 1]

————*Sex and Blood.* Leesburg, VA: TAL, 1994. Paper. [V, 1]

————*Shade.* New York: Zebra, 1994. Pb. [Blood Lust #2]

————*Succumb.* New York: Pocket Books, 1994. Pb. [Su, 1]

de la Mare, Walter. *The Return.* London: Arnold, 1910. Hb. London: Collins, 1922. Hb. Revised edition. Rpt. in: Wagenknecht, Edward, ed. *Six Novels of the Supernatural.* New York: Viking, 1944. Hb. [Po, 4]

Delap, Richard, and Walt Lee. *Shapes.* New York: Charter, 1987. Pb. [Al, Po, 1]

Dempsey, Al, Joseph Van Winkle, and Sidney Levine. *Miss Finney Kills Now and Then.* New York: TOR, 1982. Pb. [En (youth), 1, M]

Dennis, K. C. *Blood Red!.* New York: Vantage, 1983. Hb. [V, 1]

The Devil in Love. London: Hookham and Carpenter, 1793. Hb. London: Heinemann, 1925. Hb. Sawtry, Cambs, U.K.: Dedalus, 1991. Tr. Pb. Retitled: *The Enamoured Spirit.* London: Lee and Hurst, 1798. Hb. Retitled: *Boindetta, or, the enamourd spirit.* London: J. Miller, 1810. Hb. Written anonymously by Jacques Cazotte. Trans. from the French of 1772. [Su, 4]

DeWeese, Gene. *The Wanting Factor.* New York: Playboy, 1980. Pb. [Bl, En, 1]

Dicks, Terrance. *Dr. Who and the State of Decay.* London: Target, 1982. Pb. [Dr. Who series. Al, 2]

Dillard, J. M. *Demons.* New York: Pocket Books, 1986. Pb. London: Titan, 1991. Pb. [Star Trek series. Al, Po, 2]

————*Bloodthirst.* New York: Pocket Books, 1987. Pb. London: Titan, 1987. Pb. [Star Trek series. Al, En, 2]

————*Covenant with the Vampire: the diaries of family Dracul.* New York: Dell Abyss, 1994. Tr. Pb. [D, 1]

Dille, Flint, and David Marconi. *Acolytes of Darkness.* Lake Geneva, RI: TSR, 1988. Pb. [V, 7]

Dobbin, Muriel. *A Taste for Power.* New York: Marek, 1980. Hb. [V, 1 2]

Doherty, P. C. *The Prince Drakulya.* London: Hale, 1986. Hb. [Drakulya vol. 1. D (Vlad Tepes), 6]

————*The Lord Count Drakulya.* London: Hale, 1986. Hb. [vol. 2]

Douglas, Gregory A. *The Unholy Smile.* New York: Panda, 1979. Pb. [Bl (Giles de Rais), Im, 4]

Douglas, Theo (Mrs. H. D. Everett). *Malevola.* London: Heath, Craton & Ouseley, 1914. [En, 1]

Doyle, [Sir] Arthur Conan. *The Parasite.* London: Constable, 1894. Pb. New York: Harper &

Brothers, 1895. Pb. Story. [En (will), Po, We (through hypnosis), 1]

The Dracula Collection. London: Octopus, 1981. Hb. London: Galley, 1984. Hb. [D, 1]

Drake, Asa (C. Dean Andersson and Nina Romberg). *Crimson Kisses.* New York: Avon, 1981. Pb. Revised and expanded as *I Am Dracula.* See: Dean Andersson, *I Am Dracula* (1993). [D (Vlad Tepes), 1, 4, 10]

Dreadstone, Carl (House Pseud. Written by Ramsey J. Campbell). *Dracula's Daughter.* New York: Berkley, 1977. Pb. London: Star, 1980. Pb. As by E. K. Lytton (House pseud.). [V, 1, M]

Duigon, Lee. *Lifeblood.* New York: Pinnacle, 1988. Pb. [V, 1]

Dunn, Gertrude C. (Gertrude C. Weaver). *The Mark of the Bat.* London: Butterworth, 1928. Hb. Retitled: *Vampires Living and Dead.* London: Butterworth, 1928. Hb. [V, 1]

Dvorkin, David. *Insatiable.* New York: Zebra, 1993. Pb. [V, 1]

Eadie, Arlton. *The Veiled Vampire.* London: Fiction House, n.d. (c. 1930). Pb. [V, 1]

Eccarius, J. G. (Pseud.). *The Last Days of Christ the Vampire.* San Diego, CA: III Publishing, CA, 1988. Tr. Pb. [Me (for society), 5]

Edelman, Scott. *The Gift.* New York: Space & Time, 1990. Tr. Pb. [V, 1]

Eliot, Marc. *How Dear the Dawn.* New York: Ballantine, 1987. Pb. [V, 1]

Elstow, T. Francis. *A Human Vampire.* London: Modern Publishing, n.d. (c. 1935). Hb. [Ps, 7]

Elrod, P. N. *Bloodlist.* New York: Ace, 1990. Pb. [The Vampire Files #1. V, 7, 12]

——*Lifeblood.* New York: Ace, 1990. Pb. [#2]

——*Bloodcircle.* New York: Ace, 1990. Pb. [#3]

——*Art in the Blood.* New York: Ace, 1991. Pb. [#4]

——*Fire in the Blood.* New York: Ace, 1991. Pb. [#5]

——*Blood on the Water.* New York: Ace, 1992. Pb. [#6]

——*I, Strahd.* Lake Geneva, WI: TSR, 1993. Hb. [Ravenloft series. V, 3, 8]

——*Red Death.* New York: Ace, 1993. Pb. [Johnathan Barrett #1. V, 1]

——*Death and the Maiden.* New York: Ace, 1994. Pb. [#2]

Enfield, Hugh (Gwilym Fielden Hughes). *Kronos.* London: Fontana, 1972. Pb. [V, 1, C, M]

Engstrom, Elizabeth. *Black Ambrosia.* New York: TOR, 1988. Pb. [V, 1]

Erwin, Alan. *Skeleton Dancer.* New York: Dell, 1989. Pb. [Fo, Po, 1]

Estleman, Loren D. *Sherlock Holmes vs. Dracula.* Garden City, NY: Doubleday, 1978. Hb. London: New English Library, 1978. Hb. Harmondsworth, Middlesex, U.K.: Penguin, 1979. Pb. [D (vs. Sherlock Holmes), 1, 7]

Eulo, Ken. *The House of Caine.* New York: TOR, 1988. Pb. [V, 1]

Ewers, Hanns Heinz (Hans Reimann). *The Sorcerer's Apprentice.* New York: John Day, 1927. Hb. Trans. from the German of 1907. [Bl, Me, 4, 11]

——*Alraune.* New York: John Day, 1929. Hb. Arno: New York, 1976. Trans. from the German of 1911. [Bl, We, 4, 11]

——*Vampire.* New York: John Day, 1934. Hb. Retitled: *Vampire's Prey.* London: Jarrolds, n.d. (1937). Hb. Trans. from the German of 1921. (Bl, Me, 4, 11]

Falk, Lee. *The Vampires and the Witch.* New York: Avon, 1974. Pb. The Phantom series. [V, 8]

Faulkner, J. Meade. *The Lost Stradivarius.* Edinburgh, U.K.: Blackwoods, 1895. Hb. New York: Appleton, 1896. Hb. New York: Dover, 1982. Tr. Pb. [Im, In, Po, 4]

Farmer, Phillip José. *The Image of the Beast.* North Hollywood: Essex House, CA, 1968. Pb. London: Quartet, 1975. Pb. London: Futura, 1975. Pb. London: Grafton, 1989. Pb. [The Image of the Beast #1. Al, En, 2, 10, 11, C]

——*Blown.* North Hollywood: Essex House, CA, 1968, CA, 1969. Pb. London: Quartet, 1975. Pb. London: Futura, 1976. Pb. London: Grafton, 1989. Pb. [#2]

——*Image of the Beast.* Chicago, IL: Playboy, 1979. Pb. Combines: *The Image of the Beast* (1968) and *Blown* (1968).

Farrar, Stewart. *The Dance of Blood.* London: Arrow, 1977. Pb. [Bl, Im, 4]

Farrare, Claude (Frédéric Charles Pierre Édourd Bargone). *The House of the Secret.* New York: Dutton, 1923. Hb. Trans. from the French of 1911. [En, Im (Saint-Germain), 4]

Farrington, Geoffery. *The Revenants.* London: Dedalus, 1983. Tr. Pb. [V, 1]

Farris, John. *All Heads Turn When the Hunt Goes By.* Chicago, IL: Playboy, 1977. Hb. New York:

TOR, 1988. Pb. Retitled: *Bad Blood*. London: Gollancz, 1989. Pb. [La, 1]

———*Fiends*. Arlington Hts., IL: Dark Harvest, 1990. Hb. New York: TOR, 1990. Pb. London: Grafton, 1992. Pb. [Fo (Icelandic huldufólk), 1]

Fearn, John Russell. *No Grave Need I*. Tyne and Ware, U.K.: Harbottle, 1984. Paper. Story. [V, 1]

Finney, Jack (Walter Braden Finney). *The Body Snatchers*. New York: Dell, 1955. Pb. London: Eyre and Spottiswoode, 1955. Hb. Beacon, 1956. Pb. Revised as: *Invasion of the Body Snatchers*. New York: Award, 1973. Pb. New York: Dell, 1978. Pb. New York: Fireside, 1990. Tr. Pb. Revised. Los Angeles, CA: Fotonovel, 1979. Pb. Fumette. [Al, Po, 2, M]

Firth, Wesley N. *Spawn of the Vampire*. London: Bear, Husdon, n.d. (c. 1945). Paper. Story. [V, 1]

Flanders, Jack. *Night Blood*. New York: Zebra, 1993. Pb. [V, 1]

Fleming, Nigel. *To Love A Vampire*. Encino, CA: World-Wide, 1980. Pb. [V, 1]

Ford, D. N. *Born Again*. Falmouth, MA: Succanesset Press, 1893. Hb. [Po, 4]

Ford, John M. *The Dragon Waiting*. New York: Simon & Schuster, 1983. Hb. New York: Pocket Books, 1983. Pb. New York: Avon, 1985. Pb. [V, 3]

Forest, Salambo (Tina Bellini). *Witch Power*. New York: Olympia, 1971. Pb. [V, 10]

Forestal, Sean. *Dark Angel*. New York: Dell, 1982. Pb. [Su, 1, 4]

Fortune, Dion (Violet Mary Firth). *The Demon Lover*. New York: Douglas, 1927. Hb. London: Aquarian, 1957. Pb. New York: Weiser, 1972. Pb. London: Star, 1976. Pb. [In, Bl, 4]

Foster, Prudence. *Blood Legacy*. New York: Pocket Books, 1989. Pb. [V (Elizabeth Bathory), 1]

Fowler, Karen Joy. *Sarah Canary*. New York: Holt, 1991. Hb. New York: Zebra, 1993. Pb. [V, We, 3]

Fredrick, Otto. *Count Dracula's Canadian Affair*. New York: Pageant, 1960. Hb. [D, 8]

Freed, L. A. *Blood Thirst*. New York: Pinnacle, 1989. Pb. [V, 1]

Frezza, Robert. *McLendon's Syndrome*. New York: Ballantine, 1993. Pb. [V, 3, 12]

Fuentes, Carlos. *Aura*. New York: Farrar, Straus and Giroux, 1975. Tr. Pb. Rpt. 1980. Hb. Trans. from the Spanish of 1962. [Bl, Im, 4]

Gallagher, Stephen. *Valley of Lights*. New English Library, 1987. Hb. Rpt. Pb. New York: TOR, 1988. Pb. [Al, Po, 2]

Gardine, Michael. *Lamia*. New York: Dell, 1981. Pb. [La, 1]

Gardner, Craig Shaw. *The Lost Boys*. New York: Berkley, 1987. Pb. [V, 1] [M]

Garton, Ray. *Seductions*. New York: Pinnacle, 1984. Pb. [Su, 1]

———*Live Girls*. New York: Pocket Books, 1987. Pb. London: Macdonald, 1989. Hb. [V, 1, 10]

———*The New Neighbor*. Lynbrook, NY: Charnel House, 1991. Hb. [Su, 1, 10]

———*Lot Lizards*. Shingletown, CA: Zeising, 1991. Hb. [V, 1]

Gaskell, Jane, *The Shiny Narrow Grin*. London: Hodder and Stoughton, 1964. Hb. [V, 1]

Gautier, Theophilé. *Clarimonde*. New York: Brentano's, 1899. Hb. Trans. by Lafcadio Hearn. Retitled: *Clarimonde, Vampire and Harlot*. Girard, KS: Haldeman-Julius, 1922?. Pb. Retitled: *The Beautiful Vampire*. London: A. M. Philpot, 1926. Hb. Trans. by Paul Hookham. New York: R. M. McBride, 1927. Hb. Story. Trans. from the French, "La Morte Amoreuse" of 1839. [Su, 1, 10]

Geare, Michael, & Michael Corby. *Dracula's Diary*. New York: Beaufort, 1982. Hb. [D (cameo), V, 12]

Gerrold, David. *Under the Eye of God*. New York: Bantam, 1993. Pb. [Al, Bl]

Gibbons, Cromwell. *The Bat Woman*. New York: World Press, 1938. Hb. [V, 3]

Gideon, John. *Golden Eyes*. New York: Berkley, 1994. Pb. [V, 1]

Giles, Raymond (John Robert Holt). *Night of the Vampire*. New York: Avon, 1969. Pb. London: New English Library, 1970. Pb. [V, 1]

Glut, Donald F. *Frankenstein Meets Dracula*. London: New English Library, 1977. Pb. [D, 1]

Golden, Christine. *Vampire of the Mists*. Lake Geneva, WI: TSR, 1991. Pb. [Ravenloft series. V, 3, 8]

———*The Enemy Within*. Lake Geneva, WI: TSR, 1994. Pb. [Ravenloft series. V, 3, 8]

Golden, Christopher. *Of Saints and Shadows*. New York: Jove, 1994. Pb. [V, 1]

Gomez, Jewelle. *The Gilda Stories*. Ithaca, NY: Firebrand, 1991. Tr. Pb. [Gilda series. V, 3, 10]

Gordon, Julien (Julie Grinnell [Storrow] Cruger). *Vampires*. In: *Vampires (and) Mademoiselle Reseda*. Philadelphia, PA, 1891: J. B. Lippincott. Hb. [En, Me (femme fatale), 5]

Gottlieb, Sherry. *Love Bite*. White Rock, B.C., Canada: Transylvania Press, 1994. Hb. New York: Warner, 1994. Pb. [V, 1, 7]

Goulart, Ron. *Bloodstalk*. New York: Warner, 1975. Pb. London: Sphere, 1975. Pb. [Vampirella series, based on the character created by Forrest J Ackerman. Vampirella #1. Al, 3, C]

————*On Alien Wings*. New York: Warner, 1975. Pb. London: Sphere, 1975. Pb. [#2]

————*Deadwalk*. New York: Warner, 1976. Pb. London: Sphere, 1976. Pb. [#3]

————*Blood Wedding*. New York: Warner, 1976. Pb. London: Sphere, 1976. Pb. [#4]

————*Deathgame*. New York: Warner, 1976. Pb. London: Sphere, 1976. Pb. [#5]

————*Snakegod*. New York: Warner, 1976. Pb. London: Sphere, 1976. Pb. [#6]

Grant, Charles L. *The Soft Whisper of the Dead*. West Kingston, RI: Donald M. Grant, 1982. Hb. New York: Berkley, 1987. Pb. Revised edition. [V, 1]

————*Night Songs*. New York: Pocket Books, 1984. Pb. [Fo (siren), 1]

Graverson, Pat. *Sweet Blood*. New York: Zebra, 1992. Pb. [Adragon Hart #1. V, 1]

————*Precious Blood*. New York: Zebra, 1993. Pb. [#2]

Gray, Linda Crockett. *Siren*. New York: Playboy, 1982. Pb. New York: TOR, 1989. Pb. [Fo (siren), 1]

Greenfield, Irving A. *Succubus*. New York: Dell, 1970. Pb. Rpt. as by Verdo, Campe. New York: Manor, n.d. Pb. [Su, 4]

Gresham, Stephen. *Bloodwings*. New York: Zebra, 1990. Pb. [V, 1]

Griffith, Kathryn Meyer. *Vampire Blood*. New York: Zebra, 1991. Pb. [V, 1]

————*The Last Vampire*. New York: Zebra, 1992. Pb. [V, 1]

H. M. P. *A Vampire of Souls*. Paisley, Scotland: Alexander Grant, 1904. Paper. [Not seen. Montague Summers describes it as "a semi-apocalyptic novel."]

Haley, Wendy, *This Dark Paradise*. New York: Diamond, 1994. Pb. [V, 1]

Halidom, M. Y. (Pseud.). *The Woman in Black*. London: Greening, 1906. Hb. [V, 1]

Hall, Angus. *The Scars of Dracula*. London: Sphere, 1971. Pb. New York: Beagle, 1971. Pb. London: Severn House, 1987. Hb. [D, 1, M]

Hambly, Barbara. *Those Who Hunt the Night*. New York: Ballantine, 1988. Hb. Rpt. 1989. Pb. Retitled: *Immortal Blood*. London: Unwin, 1988. Pb. [V, 1, 7]

Hamilton, Laurell K. *Guilty Pleasures*. London: New English Library, 1993. Pb. New York: Ace, 1993. Pb. [Guilty Pleasures #1, V, 1, 3]

————*The Laughing Corpse*. London: New English Library, 1994. Pb. New York: Ace, 1994. Pb. [#2]

Harmon, Jim. *The Man Who Made Maniacs*. Los Angeles: Epic, 1961. Pb. [Ps, 7]

Harris, A. L. *The Sin of Salome*. London: Greening, 1906. Hb. [En, We, 1]

Hawke, Simon (Nicholas Yermakov). *The Dracula Caper*. New York: Ace, 1988. Pb. [Ps, 2]

Hébert, Anne. *Héloïse*. Toronto, Ont., Canada: Stoddart, 1982. Hb. Trans. from the French of 1980. [V, We, 4]

Heinlein, Robert A. *The Puppet Masters*. New York: Doubleday, 1951. Hb. New York: Signet, 1953. Pb. New York: Ballantine, 1986. Pb. New York: Ballantine, 1990. Pb. Revised edition. [Al, Po, We, 2]

Hell's Bitch. New York: Star Distributors, 1979. Pb. [V, 10]

Henrick, Richard. *Vampire in Moscow*. Lake Geneva, WI: TSR, 1988. Pb. [V, 4, 7]

Heron-Allen, Edward. *The Princess Daphne*. London: H. J. Drane, 1888. Hb. Chicago, IL: Belford, Clarke, 1888. Hb. New York: National Book Co., n.d. (c. 1888). [En, Po, We, 4]

Herter, Lori. *Obsession*. New York: Berkley, 1991. Pb. [David de Morrisey #1. V, 1, 7]

————*Possession*. New York: Berkley, 1992. Pb. [#2]

————*Confession*. New York: Berkley, 1992. Pb. [#3]

————*Eternity*. New York: Berkley, 1993. Pb. [#4]

Heyse, Paul. *The Fair Abigail*. New York: Dodd, Mead, 1894. Hb. Trans. from the German of 1892. [V, 1]

Hichens, Robert S. *Flames*. London: Heinemann, 1897. Hb. [Po, 4]

————*The Dweller on the Threshold*. London: Methuen, 1911. Hb. [Po, 4]

Hill, William. *Dawn of the Vampire*. New York: Pinnacle, 1991. Pb. [V, 1]

————*Vampire's Kiss*. New York: Pinnacle, 1994. Pb. [V, 1]

Hocherman, Henry W. *The Gilgul*. New York: Pinnacle, 1990. Pb. [Fo, Po, 1]

Hodder, Reginald. *The Vampire*. London: Rider, 1913. Hb. [En, 4]

Hodge, Brian J. *Shrines and Desecrations*. Leesburg, VA: TAL, 1994. Paper. [V, 1]

Hogan, Robert J. *The Bat Staffel*. New York: Berkley, 1969. Pb. Rpt. from *G-8 and His Battle Aces* #1. Oct., 1933. [Ps (vampire bats), We, 8]

Home-Gall, Edward R. *The Human Bat*. London: Mark Goulden, n.d. (c. 1950). Pb. [The Human Bat #1. V, 8]

———*The Human Bat V. the Robot Gangster*. London: Mark Goulden, n.d. (c. 1950). Pb. [#2]

Horler, Sydney. *The Vampire*. London: Hutchinson, 1935. Hb. New York: Bookfinger, 1974. Hb. [V, 1]

Huff, Tanya. *Blood Price*. New York: DAW, 1991. Pb. [Henry Fitzroy #1. V, 1, 7, 12]

———*Blood Trail*. New York: DAW, 1992. Pb. [#2]

———*Blood Lines*. New York: DAW, 1993. Pb. [#3]

———*Blood Pact*. New York: DAW, 1993. Pb. [#4]

Hughes, William. *Lust for a Vampire*. London: Sphere, 1971. Pb. New York: Beagle, 1971. Pb. [V, 1, M]

Hume, Fergus. *A Creature of the Night*. London: R. E. King, n.d. (c. 1891). Hb. London: Sampson, Lowe, Marston, 1893. Hb. London: F. F. Lovell, n.d. (c. 1895). Hb. [Im, Po, 4]

———*A Son of Perdition*. London: Rider, 1912. [Im, Po, 4]

Hurwood, Bernhardt J. *By Blood Alone*. New York: Charter, 1979. Pb. [V, 1]

Hutson, Shawn. *Erebus*. London: Star, 1984. Pb. New York: Leisure, 1988. Pb. [Bl, We, Ps, 1]

Huysmans, J. K. *Down There*. London: Boni, 1924. Hb. London: Sphere, 1974. Pb. Retitled: *Làbas*. London: Fortune, 1946. Hb. New York: Dover, 1972. Sawtry, Cambs., U.K.: Dedalus, 1992. Tr. Pb. New York: Hippocrene, 1992. Tr. Pb. Trans. from the French of 1891. [Bl (Giles de Rais), 4, 6, 11]

Hyder, Alan. *Vampires Overhead*. London: Philip Allan, 1935. Hb. [Al, Ps, 2]

Irwin, Sarita. *To Love a Vampire*. North Hollywood, CA: Carousel Star, 1982. Pb. [V, 1]

Ivanhoe, Mark. *Virgintooth*. San Francisco, CA: III Publishing, 1991. Tr. Pb. [V, 1]

Jane, Fred. *The Incubated Girl*. London: Tower Publishing, 1896. Hb. [En, We, 2]

Jennings, Jan. *Vampyr*. New York: TOR Pinnacle, 1981. Pb. [V, 1]

Jensen, Ruby Jean. *Vampire Child*. New York: Zebra, 1990. Pb. [V, 1]

Jeter, K. W. *Soul Eater*. New York: TOR, 1983. Pb. [Po, 1]

Johnson, Ken. *Zoltan: hound of Dracula*. London: Everest, 1977. Pb. Retitled: *Hounds of Dracula*. New York: Signet, 1977. Pb. Retitled: *Dracula's Dog*. New York: Signet, 1977. Pb. [D (cameo), V, We (dog), 1, M]

Johnson, Kenneth Rayner. *The Succubus*. London: Blond & Briggs, 1979. Hb. New York: Dell, 1980. Pb [Su, 1]

Johnstone, William W. *The Nursery*. New York: Zebra, 1983. 351. Pb. [V, 1, 4]

Judd. A. M. *A Daughter of Lilith*. London: Simpkin, Marshall, Hamilton, Kent, 1899. Hb. London: J. Long. (c. 1914). Hb. [Im, Ps, 4]

———*The White Vampire*. London: J. Long, 1914. Hb. [Ps, 7]

Kahn, James. *World Enough, and Time*. New York: Ballantine, 1980. Pb. [Josh Green series. V, 3]

Kalogridis, Jeanne. *Covenant with the Vampire*. New York: Delacorte Abyss, 1994. Hb. [V, 1]

Kaminsky, Stuart. *Never Cross a Vampire*. New York: St. Martin's, 1980. Hb. New York: Mysterious Press, 1984. Pb. [Ps, 5 (with Bela Lugosi)]

Kantor, Hal. *The Adult Version of Dracula*. Los Angeles: Calga, 1970. Pb. [D, 10]

Kapralov, Yuri. *Castle Dubrava*. New York: Dutton, 1982. Hb. [V, Ps, 9]

Kast, Pierre. *The Vampires of Alfama*. London: W. H. Allen, 1976. Hb. Trans. from the French of 1975. [V, 1]

Kearny, Maxwell. *Dracula Sucks*. New York: Zebra, 1981. Pb. Note: Not published. A fumette titled: "DRACULA: a film revue magazine" was published by Dolphin in Los Angeles in 1979. [D, M]

Kells, Sabine. *A Deeper Hunger*. New York: Leisure, 1994. Pb. [V, 9]

Ketchum, Jack (Dallas Mayr). *She Wakes*. New York: Berkley, 1989. Pb. [V, 1]

Key, Samuel M. (Charles de Lint). *Angel of Darkness*. New York: Jove, 1990. Pb. [V, We, 1]

Killough, Lee. *Blood Hunt*. New York: TOR, 1986. Pb. [Blood Hunt #1. V, 1, 7]

———*Bloodlinks*. New York: TOR, 1988. Pb. [#2]

Kilpatrick, Nancy. *Near Death*. New York: Pocket Books, 1994. Pb. [V, 1]

———*Sex and the Single Vampire*. Leesburg, VA: TAL, 1994. Paper. [V, 1]

Kimberly, Gail. *Dracula Began*. New York: Pyramid, 1976. Pb. [D (Vlad Tepes), 1]

King, Stephen. *'Salem's Lot.* Garden City, NY: Doubleday, 1975. Hb. New York: Signet, 1976. Pb. London: New English Library, 1977. Hb. Rpt. Pb. New York: Plume, 1991. Tr. Pb. Rpt. in: *Stephen King: The Shining, 'Salem's Lot, (and) Carrie.* London: Peerage, 1983. Hb. Rpt. in: Anon., ed., *Great horror film stories: The Omen, David Seltzer; Rosemary's Baby, Ira Levin; (and) 'Salem's Lot.* London: Octopus, 1984. Hb. [V, 1, M]

King, T. Stanleyan. *Vampire City.* London: Mellifont, 1935. [Ps, 7]

Kiraly, Marie (Elaine Bergstrom). *Mina.* New York: Berkley, 1994. Pb. [D, 1]

Knaak, Richard J. *King of the Grey.* New York: Warner Questar, 1993. Pb. [V, We, 3]

Knight, Amarantha (Nancy Kilpatrick). *Darker Passions: Dracula.* New York: Masquerade, 1993. Pb. [D, 1, 10]

Knight, Mallory T. (Bernhardt J. Hurwood). *Dracutwig.* New York: Award (and) London: Tandem, 1976. Pb. [D (cameo), V, 12]

Knight, Robert J. *Carnival of Fear.* Lake Geneva, WI: TSR, 1993. Pb. [Ravenloft series. V, 3, 8]

Kolbe, John A. *Vampires of Vengence.* London: Fiction House, 1935. Pb. [Ps, 7]

Lackey, Mercedes. *Children of the Night.* New York: TOR, 1990. Pb. [V, 1]

Lambourne, John (John Lamburn). *The Unmeasured Place.* London: J. Murray, 1933. Hb. [V, 1]

Lansdale, Joe R. *Dead in the West.* New York: Space and Time, 1986. Tr. Pb. London: Kinnell, 1990. Hb. [V, We, 1, C]

Laws, Stephen. *The Wyrm.* London: Souvenir, 1987. Hb. London: New English Library, 1988. Pb. [Fo, We, 1.]

————*Darkfall.* London: New English Library, 1992. Hb. [V, 1]

————*Gideon.* London: New English Library, 1993. Hb. Rpt. 1994. Pb. [V, 1]

Laymon, Richard. *The Stake.* London: Headline, 1991. Hb. Rpt. 1991. Pb. New York: St. Martin's, 1991. Hb. [V, 1]

LeBlanc, Richard. *The Fangs of the Vampire.* New York: Vantage, 1979. Hb. [V, 1]

Le ale, Errol (Wilfred McNeilly). *Castledoom.* London: New English Library, 1974. Pb. [V (MacGlennie), 4, 7]

————*The Deathbox.* London: New English Library, 1974. Pb. [V, 4, 7]

————*Zombie.* London: New English Library, 1975. Pb. [V, 4, 7]

————*Blood of My Blood.* London: New English Library, 1975. Pb. [V (MacGlennie), 4, 7]

Lee, Edward (Lee Seymour). *Ghouls.* New York: Pinnacle, 1988. Pb. [Fo (ghoul), 1]

————*Succubi.* New York: Diamond 1992. Pb. [Su, 1]

Lee, Tanith. *Sabella.* New York: DAW, 1980. Pb. London: Unwin, 1987. Pb. [Al, Bl, Po, 2]

————*The Beautiful Biting Machine.* New Castle, VA: Cheap Street, 1984. Hb. Story. [Al, Bl, Ps, 2]

————*The Blood of Roses.* London: Legend, 1990. Hb. Rpt. 1991. Tr. Pb. [V, We, 3]

————*Dark Dance.* London: Macdonald, 1992. Hb. New York: Abyss, 1992. Pb. New York: Warner, 1994. Pb. London: Warner, 1994. Pb. [Blood Opera #1. V, 1, 10]

————*Personal Darkness.* London: Little Brown, 1993. Hb. New York: Dell, 1994. Pb. [#2.]

Le Fanu, Joseph Sheridan. *Carmilla.* New York: Scholastic, 1971. Pb. Story. First published in 1872; revised, 1873. [V ("Carmilla" Karnstein), 1, 9, C, M]

Leinster, Murray (William Fitzgerald Jenkins). *The Brain-Stealers.* New York: Ace, 1954. Pb. Ace Double #D79. New York: Ace, n.d.. Pb. German edition titled: *Vampire aus dem All* (Vampire from Space). [En, 2]

Lemias, Brooke. *The Summer Visitors.* New York: Signet, 1980. Pb. [En, 1]

Leroux, Gaston. *The Kiss That Killed.* New York: Macaulay, 1934. Hb. Trans. from the French. [V, 2]

Lewis, Richard. *David Cronenberg's Rabid.* London: Mayflower, 1977. Pb. [V, We, 1, M]

Lichtenberg, Jacqueline. *House of Zeor.* Garden City, NY: Doubleday, 1974. Hb. New York: Pocket Books, 1977. Pb. Revised edition. See also: Jean Lorrah. [Sine/Gen #1. En, We, 2]

————*Unto Zeor, Forever.* Garden City, NY: Doubleday, 1978. Hb. New York: Playboy, 1980. Pb. New York: Berkley, 1985. Pb. [#2]

————*Mahogany Trinrose.* Garden City, NY: Doubleday, 1981. Hb. New York: Playboy, 1982. Hb. New York: Berkley, 1986. Pb. [#4]

————*Rensime.* Garden City, NY: Doubleday, 1984. Hb. New York: DAW, 1984. Pb. [#6]

————*Those of My Blood.* New York: St. Martin's, 1988. Hb. [Luren #1. V, Al, 2]

————*Dreamspy.* New York: St. Martin's, 1989. Hb. [#2]

Lichtenberg, Jacqueline, and Jean Lorrah. *Zelrod's Doom*. New York: DAW, 1986. Pb. See also: Jacqueline Lichtenberg. [Sine/Gen #8. En, We, 2]

Linssen, John. *Tabitha Ffoulkes* New York: Arbor House, 1978. Hb. New York: Berkley, 1980. Pb. [V, 12]

Linzner, Gordon. *The Spy Who Drank Blood*. New York: Space and Time, 1984. Hb. and Tr. Pb. [James Blood series, continued from SPACE & TIME. V, 7, 12]

———*The Troupe*. New York: Pocket Books, 1988. Pb. [En, 1]

Little, Bentley. *The Summoning*. New York: Zebra, 1993. Pb. London: Headline, 1993. Hb. Rpt. 1994. Pb. [Fo (Chinese, cup hu girngisi), 1]

Logston, Anne. *Shadow Hunt*. New York: Ace, 1992. Pb. [Shadow series #2. V, 3]

Long, Frank Belknap. *The Horror From the Hills*. Sauk City, WI: Arkham House, 1963. Hb. Rpt. in: Long, Frank Belknap. *Night fear*. New York: Zebra, 1979. Pb. Story. [Cthulu Mythos series. Al, 1, 2]

Long, John Luther. *The Fox-Woman*. London: J. Mac-Queen, 1900. Hb. [Fo (Japanese fox-woman), 3]

Longstreet, Roxanne. *The Undead*. New York: Zebra, 1993. Pb. [Va, 1]

Lorrah, Jean. *Ambrov Keon*. New York: DAW, 1986. Pb. See also: Jacqueline Lichtenberg. [Sine/Gen #7. En, We, 2]

Lorrah, Jean, and Jacqueline Lichtenberg. *First Channel*. Garden City, NY: Doubleday, 1980. Hb. New York: Playboy, 1981. Pb. [Sine/Gen #3]

———*Channel's Destiny*. Garden City, NY: Doubleday, 1982. Hb. New York: DAW, 1983. Pb. [#5]

Lortz, Richard. *Children of the Night*. New York: Dell, 1974. Pb. Retitled: *Dracula's Children*. Sagaponack, NY: Permanent, 1981. Hb. London: J. Landesman, 1981. Hb. [Bl, We, 1]

Lory, Robert. *Dracula Returns*. New York: Pinnacle, 1973. Pb. London: New English Library, 1973. Pb. [Dracula Horror series #1. D, 1]

———*The Hand of Dracula*. New York: Pinnacle, 1973. Pb. London: New English Library, 1973. Pb. [#2]

———*Dracula's Brothers*. New York: Pinnacle, 1973. Pb. London: New English Library, 1974. Pb.]#3]

———*Dracula's Gold*. New York: Pinnacle, 1973. Pb. London: New English Library, 1975. Pb. [#4]

———*Drums of Dracula*. New York: Pinnacle, 1974. Pb. London: New English Library, 1976. Pb. [#5]

———*The Witching of Dracula*. New York: Pinnacle, 1974. Pb. London: New English Library, 1977. Pb. [#6. With Elizabeth Bathory]

———*Dracula's Lost World*. New York: Pinnacle, 1974. Pb. [#7]

———*Dracula's Disciple*. New York: Pinnacle, 1975. Pb. [#8]

———*Challenge to Dracula*. New York: Pinnacle, 1975. Pb. [#9]

Love at First Bite. Los Angeles, CA: Fotonovel, 1979. Pb. Fumette. [D, 12, M]

Lovell, Mark (Mark McShane). *An Enquiry into the Existence of Vampires*. Garden City, NY: Doubleday, 1974. Hb. Retitled: *Vampire in the Shadows*. London: Hale, 1976. Hb. London: Coronet, 1974. Pb. [V, 1]

Lowder, James. *Knight of the Black Rose*. Lake Geneva, WI: TSR, 1991. Pb. [Ravenloft series. V, 3, 8]

———*The Screaming Tower*. Lake Geneva, WI: TSR, 1991. Pb. [Ravenloft series. V, 3, 8]

Lumley, Brian. *Necroscope*. London: Grafton, 1986. Pb. New York: TOR, 1988. Pb. New York: TOR, 1994. Hb. [Necroscope #1. Al, 1, 2, C]

———*Necroscope II: wamphyri!* London: Grafton, 1988. Pb. Retitled: *Necroscope II: vamphyri!* New York: TOR, 1989. Pb. [#2, C]

———*Necroscope III: the source*. London: Grafton, 1989. Pb. New York: TOR, 1989. Pb. [#3]

———*Necroscope IV: deadspeak*. London: Kinnell, 1990. Hb. London: Grafton, 1990. Pb. New York: TOR, 1990. Pb. [#4]

———*Necroscope V: deadspawn*. London: Grafton, 1991. Pb. New York: TOR, 1991. Pb. [#5]

———*Blood Brothers*. New York: TOR, 1992. Hb. Rpt. 1993. Pb. Retitled: *Vampire World 1: blood brothers*. London: ROC, 1992. Pb. [Vampire World #1. Al, 1, 2]

———*The Last Aerie*. New York: TOR, 1993. Hb. Retitled: *Vampire World II: the last aerie*. London: ROC, 1993. Pb. [#2]

———*Bloodwars*. New York: TOR, 1993. Hb. Retitled: *Vampire World II: bloodwars*. London: ROC, 1993. Pb. [#3]

Lupoff, Richard A. *Sandworld*. New York: Berkley, 1976. Pb. [Al, 2]

Lutz, John. *Shadowtown*. New York: Mysterious Press, 1988. Hb. Rpt. 1989. Pb. [Ps, 4]

Lytton, E. K. (House Pseud.). *Dracula's Daughter*, 1977. See: Carl Dreadstone (House Pseud.), *Dracula's Daughter* (1980)

MacMillan, Scott. *Knights of the Blood*. New York: ROC, 1993. Pb. [Knights of the Blood #1, V, 3]
——*At Sword's Point*. New York, ROC, 1994. Pb. [#2]

Madison, J. J. *Ohhhhh, It Feels Like Dying*. New York: Peacock, 1971. Pb. Retitled: *The Thing*. New York: Belmont, 1974. Pb. [V, 4]

Mann, Jack (E. Charles Vivian). *Maker of Shadows*. London: Wright & Brown, n.d. (1938). Hb. [En, 4, 7]

Mannheim, Karl (Pseud.). *Vampires of Venus*. Manchester, U.K.: World Distributors, 1950. Pb. New York: Pemberton, 1952. Pb. Manchester, U.K.: Five Star, 1972. Pb. [Ps, 2]

Marley, Stephen. *Shadow Sisters*. London: Legend, 1993. Tr. Pb. [V, 3]

Marryat, Florence. *The Blood of the Vampire*. London: Hutchinson, 1897. Hb. [En, 1]

Martin, George R. R. *Fevre Dream*. New York: Poseidon, 1982. Hb. London: Gollancz, 1983. Hb. New York: Pocket Books, 1983. Pb. London: VGSF, 1989. Pb. [V, 1]

Martindale, T. Chris. *Nightblood*. New York: Warner, 1990. Pb. [V, 1, 8]

Matheson, Richard. *I am Legend*. New York: Fawcett, 1954. Pb. New York: Walker, 1970. Hb. New York: Bantam, 1964. Pb. New York: Berkley, 1971. Pb. London: David, Bruce & Watson, 1974. Hb. London: Corgi, 1977. Pb. [V, 1, 2, C, M]
——Earthbound (1982 and 1989). See: Logan Swanson, Pseud. of Richard Matheson.

Maturin, Charles Robert. *Melmoth the Wanderer*. London: Hurst & Robinson, 1820. Hb. University of Nebraska, 1961. Hb. Ed. by William F. Azton. Harmonsworth, Middlesex, U.K., Penguin, 1977. Pb. Ed. by Andrea Hayes. [Im, 4]

McCammon, Robert R. *They Thirst*. New York: Avon, 1981. Pb. London: Sphere, 1981. Pb. New York: Pocket Books, 1988. Pb. London: Kinnell, 1990. Hb. Arlington Hts, IL: Dark Harvest, 1991. Hb. [V, 1]

McCuniff, Mara, and Traci Briery. *The Vampire Memoirs*. New York: Zebra, 1991. Pb. See also: Traci Briery. [The Vampire Memoirs #1. V, 1]

McDaniel, David. *The Vampire Affair*. New York: Ace, 1966. Pb. Retitled: *The Man from U.N.C.L.E. #9*. London: Souvenir. Pb. [The Man from U.N.C.L.E. #6. D (cameo), Ps, 7]

McMahan, Jeffrey M. *Vampires Anonymous*. Boston, MS: Alyson, 1991. Tr. Pb. [Andrew series. V, 7, 10]

Merritt, A. *The Moon Pool*. New York: G. P. Putnams, 1919. Hb. New York: Avon, 1951. Pb. Net York: Collier, 1961. Pb. [Al, In, Po, 2]

Metcalfe, John. *The Feasting Dead*. Sauk City, WI: Arkham House, 1954. Hb. [En, 1]

Miller, Linda Lael. *Forever and the Night*. New York: Berkley, 1993. Pb. [Aidan Tremayne #1. V, 1, 9]
——*For All Eternity*. New York: Berkley, 1994. Pb. [#2]

Minns, Karen Marie Christa. *Virago*. Tallahassee, FL: Naiad, 1990. Tr. Pb. [V, 1, 10]

Monette, Paul. *Nosferatu: the vampyre*. New York: Avon, 1979. Pb. London: Picador, n.d.. Tr. Pb. [D (Count Orlock), 1, C, M]

Monohan, Brent. *The Book of Common Dread*. New York: St. Martin's, 1993. Hb. Rpt. 1994. Pb. [V, 1]

Monteleone, Thomas F. *Lyrica*. New York: Berkley, 1987. Pb. [La, 1]

Morgan, Robert. *Some Things Never Die*. New York: Diamond 1993. Pb. [V, 4, 7]

Moriarity, Timothy. *Vampire Nights*. New York: Pinnacle, 1988. Pb. [V, 1]

Morrell, David. *The Totem*. New York: Maurice Evans, 1979. Hb. New York: Fawcett, 1980. Pb. London: Pan, 1981. Pb. Restored edition: West Kingston, RI: Donald M. Grant, 1994. Hb. [Me (for rabies), 1]

Morrow, H. H. (Leo Giroux, Jr.). *The Black Madonna*. New York: Dell, 1990. Pb. [Su, We, 1]

Murdoch, Mordecai (Pseud.). *The Wroclaw Dracula*. Whitby, U.K.: Caedmon, 1985. Tr. Pb. [D, 4]

Myers, Robert J. *The Virgin and the Vampire*. New York: Pocket Books, 1977. Pb. [V, 9]

Myles, Douglas. *Prince Dracula: Son of the Devil*. New York: McGraw-Hill, 1988. Hb. [D (Vlad Tepes), 6]

Navarro, Yvonne. *Afterage*. New York: Bantam, 1993. Pb. [V, 1]

Neiderman, Andrew. *Bloodchild*. New York: Berkley, 1990. Pb. [V, 1]
——*The Need*. New York: Putnam's, 1992. Hb. New York: Berkley, 1993. Pb. [V, 1]

Newman, Kim. *Bad Dreams*. London: Simon & Schuster, 1990. Hb. London: Grafton, 1992. Pb. [V, 1]

———*Anno Dracula*. London: Simon & Schuster, 1992. Hb. New York: Carroll & Graf, 1993. Hb. London: Pocket Books, 1993. Pb. [D, 1, 3, 12]

Nile, Dorothea (Michael Avallone). *The Vampire Cameo*. New York: Lancer, 1968. Pb. [Ps, 9]

Nuetzel, Charles. *Queen of Blood*. San Diego, CA: Greenleaf, 1966. Pb. [Al, Bl, 3, M]

Ohnet, Georges (Georges Hénot). *A Weird Gift*. London: Chatto & Windus, 1890. Hb. New York: G. Munro, n.d. (c. 1895). Pb. Trans. as *Peter's Soul*. Chicago, IL: Donohue, Henneberry, n.d. (c. 1895). Pb. Trans. as *The Soul of Pierre*. New York: F. M. Lupton, n.d. (c. 1895). Pb. Trans. from the French of 1890. [Po, 4]

Olsen, Paul F. *Night Prophets*. New York: Onyx, 1989. Pb. [V, 1]

Owen, Dean (Dudley Dean McGaughy). *The Brides of Dracula*. Derby, CT: Monarch, 1960. Pb. [V (Baron Meinster, not Count Dracula), 1, M]

Parry, Michel. *Countess Dracula*. London: Sphere, 1971. Pb. New York: Beagle, 1971. Pb. [Bl (Elizabeth Bathory), 1, 6, M]

Paul, F. W. (Paul W. Fairman). *The Orgy at Madam Dracula's*. New York: Lancer, 1968. Pb. [D (cameo), Ps, 10, 12]

Perucho, Joan. *Natural History*. New York: A. A. Knopf, 1988. Hb. New York: Ballantine, 1990. Pb. Trans. from the Catalan of 1960. [V, 1]

Peterson, Gail. *The Making of a Monster*. New York: Dell Abyss, 1993. Pb. [V, 1]

Peterson, Margaret. *Moonflowers*. London: Hutchinson, 1926. Hb. [V, 1]

Pierce, Meredith Ann. *The Darkangel*. Boston, MS: Little, Brown, 1982. Hb. New York: TOR, 1984. Pb. [Darkangel #1. Al, En, 3]

———*A Gathering of Gargoyles*. Boston, MS: Little, Brown, 1984. Hb. New York: TOR, 1984. Pb. [#2]

———*The Pearl of the Soul of the World*. Boston, MS: Little, Brown, 1990. Hb. [#3]

Pike, Christopher. *The Season of Passage*. New York: TOR, 1992. Hb. Rpt. 1993. Pb. New English Library: London, 1994. Pb. [Al, 2]

Pinkney, John. *Thirst*. Melbourne, Australia: Circus, 1979. Pb. [Bl, 1, M]

Polidori, John. *The Vampyre*. 1819. See: Anon., *The Vampyre* (1819)

Popescu, Petru. *In Hot Blood*. New York: Fawcett, 1989. Pb. [V, 9]

Porter, Barry. *Dark Souls*. New York: Zebra, 1989. Pb. [V, 1]

Powers, Tim. *The Stress of Her Regard*. Lynbrook, NY: Charnel House, 1989. Hb. New York: Ace, 1989. Hb. Abridged. Rpt. 1991. Pb. London: Gollancz, 1993. Hb. Abridged. London: Grafton, 1993. Pb. Abridged. [La, 1]

Pozzessere, Heather Graham. *This Rough Magic*. New York: Silhouette Intimate Moments, 1988. Pb. [V, 9]

Praed, Mrs. Campbell. *The Soul of Countess Adrian*. London: Trischeler, 1891. Hb. [Po, 4]

———*The Insane Root*. London: T. Fisher Unwin, 1902. Hb. [Po, 4]

Thomas Preskett Prest (Attribution). See: Anon., *Varney the Vampyre* (1847)

Ptacek, Kathryn. *Blood Autumn*. New York: TOR, 1985. Pb. [Kristonosis Sisters #1. La, 1]

———*In Silence Sealed*. New York: TOR, 1988. Pb. [#2]

Raisor, Gary. *Less Than Human*. New York: Diamond, 1992. Pb. Woodstock, GA: Overlook Connection, 1994. Hb. [V, 1]

Randolph, Arabella (Jack Younger). *The Vampire Tapes*. New York: Berkley, 1977. Pb. London: Futura, 1978. Pb. [V, 1]

Raven, Simon (Arthur Noel). *Doctors Wear Scarlet*. London: A Blond, 1960. Hb. New York: Simon & Schuster, 1961. Hb. London: Panther, 1966. Pb [V, Bl, 4, 10, M]

Rechy, John. *The Vampires*. New York: Grove, 1971. Hb. Rpt. n.d. Pb. [Me (for the idle rich), 1]

Reeves, Stevens, Garfield. *Bloodshift*. Toronto, Ont., Canada: Virgo, 1981. Pb. Toronto, Ont., Canada: Seal, 1988. Pb. New York: Popular Library 1990. Pb. London: Pan, 1993. Pb. [V, 1, 3]

Reeves, Stevens, Garfield, and Judy Reeves, Stevens. *Nightfeeder*. New York: ROC, 1991. Pb. [V, 1, 3]

Reynolds, G. W. M. *Faust*. G. London: Vickers, 1847. Hb. [Im, 4]

———*The Necromancer*. London: J. Dicks, 1857. New York: Arno, 1876. Hb. [Im, 4]

Reynolds, Kay. *American Vampire*. White Rock, B.C., Canada: Transylvania Press, 1994. Hb. [V, 1, 3]

Rice, Anne. *Interview with the Vampire*. New York: A. A. Knopf, 1976. Hb. London: Macdonald, 1976. Hb. New York: Ballantine, 1977. Pb. London: Futura, 1977. Pb. [The Vampire Chronicles #1. V, 1, C, M]

————*The Vampire Lestat.* New York: A. A. Knopf, 1985. Hb. London: Macdonald, 1986. Hb. New York: Ballantine, 1986. Pb. London: Futura, 1986. Pb. [#2, C]

————*The Queen of the Damned.* New York: A. A. Knopf, 1988. Hb. New York: Ultramarine A. A. Knopf, 1988. Hb. 3 states. London: Macdonald, 1988. Hb. New York: Ballantine, 1989. Pb. London: Futura, 1990. Pb. [#3, C]

————*The Vampire Chronicles.* New York: A. A. Knopf, 1988. Hb. 3 vol. Includes *Interview with the Vampire, The Vampire Lestat,* and *The Queen of the Damned.*

————*The Tale of the Body Thief.* New York: A. A. Knopf, 1992. Hb. Rpt. 1993. Pb. London: Chatto & Windus, 1992. Hb. London: Penguin, 1993. Pb. [#4]

Rice, Jeff. *The Night Stalker.* New York: Pocket Books, 1973. Pb. Retitled: *The Kolchak papers #1: the night stalker.* Massapequa Park, NY: Cinemaker, 1993. Tr. Pb. [V, 1. 7, M]

Rich Douglas. *The Night that Never Ended.* London: Digit, 1961. Pb. [V, Ps, 1]

Rives, Amélie (Princess Troubetzkoy). *The Ghost Garden.* New York: F. A. Stokes, 1918. Hb. [En, In, 1]

Robbins, Clement. *Vampires of New York.* New York: Published for the proprietor, 1831. [Ps, 7]

Robbins, David. *Blade #3: Vampire Strike.* New York: Leisure, 1989. Pb. Rpt. in *Double Blade: Vampire Strike (and) Pipeline Strike.* New York: Leisure, 1992. Pb. [V, 2, 8]

Robeson, Kenneth (House Pseud, Written by Ron Goulart). *The Blood Countess.* New York: Warner, 1975. Pb. [Ps (Elizabeth Bathory), 8]

Rohmer, Sax (Arthur Sarsfield Ward). *Grey Face.* New York: Doubleday Page, 1924. Hb. London: Cassell, 1924. Hb. New York: A. L. Burt, 1926. Hb. [Bl, Im, 4, 7]

Romero, George A., and Susanna Sparrow. *Martin.* New York: Stein and Day, 1977. Hb. London: Futura, 1977. Pb. New York: Day Books, 1980. Pb. [Bl, Me, Ps, 1, M]

————*Dawn of the Dead.* New York: St. Martin's, 1978. Tr. Pb. See also: John Russo. [Night of the Living Dead #2. V, We, 1, M]

Romine, Mary C., and Aden F. Romine. *The Fellowship.* New York: Leisure, 1984. Pb. [D, 1, 4]

Romkey, Michael. *I, Vampire.* New York: Fawcett, 1990. Pb. [V, 1]

————*The Vampire Papers.* New York: Fawcett, 1994. Pb. [V, 1]

Ronson, Mark. *Blood-Thirst.* London: Hamlyn, 1979. Pb. New York: Lorevan, 1986. Pb. [V (Eliabeth Bathory), 1]

Ross, Clarissa (William Edward Daniel Ross). *Secret of the Pale Lover.* New York: Lancer, 1969. Pb. [V, 1, 9]

————*The Corridors of Fear.* New York: Avon, 1971. Pb. [V, 1, 9]

Ross, Marilyn (William Edward Daniel Ross). *Barnabas Collins.* New York: Paperback Library, 1968. Pb. [Dark Shadows #6. V (Barnabas Collins), 9, C]

————*The Secret of Barnabas Collins.* New York: Paperback Library, 1969. Pb. [#7]

————*The Demon of Barnabas Collins.* New York: Paperback Library, 1969. Pb. London: Coronet, 1969. Pb. [#8]

————*The Foe of Barnabas Collins.* New York: Paperback Library, 1969. Pb. [#9]

————*The Phantom and Barnabas Collins.* New York: Paperback Library, 1969. Pb. [#10]

————*Barnabas Collins Versus the Warlock.* New York: Paperback Library, 1969. Pb. London: Coronet, 1969. Pb. [#11]

————*The Peril of Barnabas Collins.* New York: Paperback Library, 1969. Pb. London: Coronet, 1969. Pb. [#12]

————*Barnabas Collins and the Mysterious Ghost.* New York: Paperback Library, 1969. Pb. London: Coronet, 1970. Pb. [#13]

————*Barnabas Collins and Quentin's Demon.* New York: Paperback Library, 1970. Pb. [#14]

————*Barnabas Collins and the Gypsy Witch.* New York: Paperback Library, 1970. Pb. [#15]

————*Barnabas, Quentin and the Mummy's Curse.* New York: Paperback Library, 1970. Pb. [#16]

————*Barnabas, Quentin and the Avenging Ghost.* New York: Paperback Library, 1970. Pb. [#17]

————*Barnabas, Quentin and the Nightmare Assassin.* New York: Paperback Library, 1970. Pb. London: Coronet, 1970. Pb. [#18]

————*Barnabas, Quentin and the Crystal Coffin.* New York: Paperback Library, 1970. Pb. London: Coronet, 1970. Pb. [#19]

————*Barnabas, Quentin and the Witch's Curse.* New York: Paperback Library, 1970. Pb. London: Coronet, 1970. Pb. [#20]

————*Barnabas, Quentin and the Haunted Cave.* New

York: Paperback Library, 1970. Pb. London: Coronet, 1970. Pb. [#21]

———*Barnabas, Quentin and the Frightened Bride.* New York: Paperback Library, 1970. Pb. London: Coronet, 1970. Pb. [#22]

———*Barnabas, Quentin and the Scorpio Curse.* New York: Paperback Library, 1970. Pb. London: Coronet, 1970. Pb. [#23]

———*Barnabas, Quentin and the Serpent.* New York: Paperback Library, 1970. Pb. London: Coronet, 1970. Pb. [#24]

———*House of Dark Shadows.* New York: Paperback Library, 1970. Pb. London: Coronet, 1970. Pb. [Barnabas Collins series. V, 9, M]

———*Barnabas, Quentin and the Magic Potion.* New York: Paperback Library, 1971. Pb. London: Coronet, 1970. Pb. [#25]

———*Barnabas, Quentin and the Body Snatchers.* New York: Paperback Library, 1971. Pb. [#26]

———*Barnabas, Quentin and Dr. Jekyll's Son.* New York: Paperback Library, 1971. Pb. London: Coronet, 1971. Pb. [#27]

———*Barnabas, Quentin and the Grave Robbers.* New York: Paperback Library, 1971. Pb. [#28]

———*Barnabas, Quentin and the Sea Ghost.* New York: Paperback Library, 1971. Pb. [#29]

———*Barnabas, Quentin and the Mad Magican.* New York: Paperback Library, 1971. Pb. [#30]

———*Barnabas, Quentin and the Hidden Tomb.* New York: Paperback Library, 1971. Pb. [#31]

———*Barnabas, Quentin and the Vampire Beauty.* New York: Paperback Library, 1972. Pb. [#32]

———*The Vampire Contessa.* New York: Pinnacle, 1974. Pb. [V, 9]

Ruddy, Jon. *The Bargain.* New York: Knightsbridge, 1990. Pb. [D, 1]

Rudorff, Raymond. *The Dracula Archives.* London: David, Bruce & Watson, 1971. Hb. New York: Arbor House, 1971. Hb. New York: Pocket Books, 1973. Pb. London: Sphere, 1973. Pb. New York: Warner, 1975. Pb. [D, V (Elizabeth Bathory), 1]

Rusch, Kristine Kathryn. *Sins of the Blood.* New York: Dell Abyss, 1994. Pb. [V, 1]

Russo, John. *Night of the Living Dead.* New York: Warner, 1974. Pb. See also: George R. Romero and Sussana Sparrow. [Night of the Living Dead #1. V, We, 1, M]

———*Return of the Living Dead.* New York: Dale, 1978. Pb. [V, We, 1, M]

———*The Awakening.* New York: Pocket Books, 1983. Pb. [V, 1]

James Malcolm Rymer (Attribution). See: Anon., *Varney the Vampyre* (1847)

Davy S. (Pseud.). *Gay Vampire.* New York: 101 Books, 1969. Pb. [V, 10]

Saberhagen, Fred. *The Dracula Tape.* New York: Warner, 1975. Pb. New York: Ace, 1980. Pb. New York: TOR, 1989. Pb. [The Dracula Tape #1. D, 1, 12]

———*The Holmes-Dracula File.* New York: Ace, 1978. Pb. New York: TOR, 1990. Pb. [#2. Vs. Sherlock Holmes.]

———*An Old Friend of the Family.* New York: Ace, 1979. Pb. New York: TOR, 1987. Pb. [#3]

———*Thorn.* New York: Ace, 1980. Pb. New York: TOR, 1990. Pb. [#4]

———*Dominion.* New York: TOR, 1982. Pb. [#5]

———*A Matter of Taste.* New York: TOR, 1989. Hb. Rpt. 1992. Pb. [#6]

———*A Question of Time.* New York: TOR, 1992. Hb. Rpt. 1993. Pb. [#7]

———*Seance for a Vampire.* New York: TOR, 1994. Hb. [#8. Vs. Sherlock Holmes.]

Saberhagen, Fred, and James V. Hart. *Bram Stoker's Dracula.* New York: Signet, 1992. Pb. London: Pan, 1992. Pb. [D, 1, C, M]

Sackett, Jeffery. *Blood of the Impaler.* New York: Bantam, 1989. Pb. [D, 1]

Salamanca, J. R. *Lilith.* New York: Simon and Schuster, 1971. Hb. New York: Bantam, 1962. Pb. [Ps, 5]

Salem, Richard (Pseud.). *New Blood.* London: Futura, 1981. Pb. New York: Signet, 1982. Pb. [Bl, 1]

Samuels, Victor. (Victor J. Banis). *The Vampire Women.* New York: Popular Library 1973. Pb. [V, 1]

San Souci, Robert D. *The Dreaming.* New York: Berkley, 1989. Pb. [V, 1]

Saralegui, Jorge. *Last Rites.* New York: Charter, 1985. Pb. [V, 1]

Sargent, Karl, and Marc Gascione. *Nosferatu.* New York: Penguin ROC, 1994. Pb. [V, 1]

Savory, Gerald. *Count Dracula.* London: Corgi, 1977. Pb. [D, 1]

Sawbridge, M. C. *The Vampire.* London: G. Allen and Unwin, 1920. Hb. [V, 1]

Saxon, Peter (Wilfred McNeilly). *The Torturer.* London: Mayflower, 1966. Pb. New York: Paperback Library, 1967. Pb. Manchester, U.K.: Five Star, 1976. Pb. [En, 1]

———*The Disoriented Man.* London: Mayflower, 1966. Pb. London: H. Baker, 1967. Hb. Retitled: *Scream and Scream Again.* New York: Paperback Library, 1967. Pb. [Al, Bl, We, 1, M]

———*Brother Blood.* 1970. Published as *Vampire's Moon* (1970, 1972).

———*The Vampires of Finistere.* London: H. Baker, 1970. Hb. Manchester, U.K.: Five Star, 1972. Pb. Retitled: *The Guardians: #4 the vampires of Finistere.* New York: Berkley, 1970. Pb. [V, 8]

———*Vampire's Moon.* New York: Unibook, 1970. Pb. Manchester, U.K.: Five Star, 1972. Pb. [V, 1]

Scarborough, Elizabeth. *The Goldcamp Vampire.* New York: Bantam, 1987. Pb. [V, 1, 8]

Scott, Alan. *Project Dracula.* London: Sphere, 1971. Pb. Retitled: *The Anthrax Mutation.* New York: Pyramid, 1976. Pb. [Ps, 2]

Scott, Jody. *I, Vampire.* New York: Ace, 1984. Pb. London: Women's Press, 1986. Pb. [V, 2, 12]

Scram, Arthur N. (Leo Guild). *The Werewolf vs. the Vampire Woman.* Beverly Hills. CA: Guild-Hartford, 1972. Pb. [V, 1, 10, 11, 12, M]

Selby, Curt (Doris Piserchia). *Blood County.* New York: DAW, 1981. Pb. [V, 1]

Seymour, Miranda. *Count Manfred.* New York: Coward, McCann & Geoghegan, 1976. Hb. New York: Popular Library n.d. Pb. [V (Lord Ruthven), 1, 9]

Shayne, Maggie (Margaret Benson). *Twilight Phantasies.* New York: Silhouette Shadows. 1993. Pb. [Wings in the Night #1. V, 9]

———*Twilight Memories.* New York: Silhouette Shadows. 1993. Pb. [#2]

Sheffield, Charles, and David Bischoff. *The Selkie.* New York: Macmillan, 1982. Hb. New York: Signet, 1983. Pb. [Fo (selkie), 1]

Shepard, Lucius. *The Golden.* Shingletown, CA: Zeising, 1993. Hb. 2 states. New York: Bantam, 1993. Pb. London: Millenium, 1993. Hb. Rpt. 1994. Tr. Pb. [V, 3, 7]

Sherman, Jory (Charlotte A. Sherman). *Chill #3: The bamboo demons.* Los Angeles: Pinnacle, 1979. Pb. [Fo (aswang), 4, 7]

———*Chill #4: Vegas vampire.* Los Angeles: Pinnacle, 1980. Pb. Retitled: *Vampire.* London: New English Library, 1981. Pb. [V, 4, 7]

Shirley, John. *Dracula in Love.* New York: Zebra, 1979. Pb. [D, 1, 4]

———*Wet Bones.* Shingletown. CA: Zeising, 1992. Hb. 2 states. [En, We, 4, 10, 11]

Siciliano, Sam. *Blood Farm.* New York: Pageant, 1988. Pb. [Bl, We, 1, 4]

———*Blood Feud.* New York: Pinnacle, 1993. Pb. [V, 1]

Simmons, Dan. *Carrion Comfort.* Arlington Heights, IL: Dark Harvest, 1989. Hb. New York: Warner, 1990. Pb. London: Headline, 1990. Pb. [En, 1]

———*Children of the Night.* New York: G. P. Putnam's, 1992. Hb. Northridge, CA: Lord John Press, 1992. Hb. London: Headline, 1992. Hb. Rpt. 1992. Pb. New York: Warner, 1993. Pb. [D, 1]

Skipp, John, and Craig Spector. *Frightnight.* New York: TOR, 1985. Pb. [V, 1, 12, C, M]

———*The Light at the End.* New York: Bantam, 1986. Pb. [V, 1]

Smith, Guy N. *The Blood Merchants.* London: New English Library, 1982. Pb. [Bl, Su (Lilith), 8]

———*The Knighton Vampires.* London: J. Piatkus, 1992. Hb. [Ps, 1]

Smith, Robert Arthur. *Vampire Notes.* New York: Fawcett, 1990. Pb. [V, 1]

Sohl, Jerry. *The Transcendent Man.* New York: Rhinehart, 1953. Hb. New York: Bantam, 1959. Pb. Italian edition titled: *Vampiri della morte* (Vampires of death). [Al, 2]

Somtow, S. P. (Somtow Sucharitkal). *Vampire Junction.* Norfolk, VA: Donning Starblaze, 1983. Hb. New York: Berkley, 1984. Pb. London: Macdonald, 1986. Hb. New York: TOR, 1991. Pb. London: Gollancz, 1992. Pb. [Timmy Valentine #1. V, 1]

———*Valentine.* London: Gollancz, 1992. Hb. Revised edition. [#2]

The Spectre (Pseud.). *Ye Vampyres.* Boston, MA: A. W. Lovering, 1897. Hb. [Me (for gambling)]

Stableford, Brian. *The Empire of Fear.* London: Simon & Schuster, 1988. Hb. New York: Carroll & Graff, 1991. Hb. New York: Ballantine, 1993. Pb. [V, 3]

———*Young Blood.* London: Simon & Schuster, 1992. Hb. London: Pocket, 1993. Pb. [V, 1]

Stanwood, Brooks (Susan Stanwood Kaminsky). *The Glow.* New York: McGraw-Hill, 1979. Hb. New York: Fawcett, 1979. Pb. London: Futura, 1980. Pb. [Bl, 1]

Steakley, John. *Vampire$.* New York: ROC, 1990. Tr. Pb. Rpt. 1991. Pb. [V, 1, 8]

Stenbock, (Count) Eric. *The True Story of a Vampire*. Edinburgh, Scotland: Tragara Press, 1989. Paper. Story. A.K.A. *The Sad Story of a Vampire*. First published in 1894. [En, 1, 10]

Stevenson, Florence. *Moonlight Variations*. New York: Jove, 1981. Pb. [V, 9]

Stewart, Desmond (Sterling). *The Vampire of Mons*. New York: Harper & Row, 1976. Hb. London: Hamish Hamilton, 1976. Hb. New York: Avon, 1977. Pb. [Ps, 5]

Stewart, Fred Mustard. *The Mephisto Waitz*. New York: Coward, McCann & Geohagen, 1969. Hb. London: Tragara Press, 1969. Hb. New York: Signet, 1970. Pb. New York: Berkley, 1978. Pb. [Im, Po, 1, 4, M]

Stockbridge, Grant (House Pseud. Written by Norvell Page). *Death Reign of the Vampire King*. New York: Pocket Books, 1975. Pb. London: Mews, 1976. Pb. Rpt. from *The Spider* #26, Nov. 1935. [Ps (Vampire bats), 8, C]

Stockholm, John. *Succubus*. London: Sphere, 1985. Pb. [Su, 1]

Stoker, Bram. *Dracula*. Westminster, U.K.: Constable, 1897. Hb. First edition. Rpt. n.d., 1899, 1904, and 1920 (9th edition). Other important editions include: New York: Doubleday & McClure, 1899. Hb. First American edition. Westminster, U.K.: Constable, 1901. Tr. Pb. Abridged by Bram Stoker. Rpt. White Rock, B.C. Canada: Transylvania Press, 1994. Hb. New York: A. Wessel's, 1901. Pb. First limited edition. London: Rider, 1912. Corrected edition. New York: Limited Editions Club, 1965. Hb. Annotated editions include: *The Annotated Dracula* (1975). Ed. by Leonard Wolf. *The Essential Dracula* (1979). Ed. by Raymond McNally and Radu Florescu. London: Penguin, 1993. Pb. Ed. by Maurice Hindel. [D, 1, C, M]

———*The Jewel of the Seven Stars*. London: Heinemann, 1903. Hb. New York: Harper & Row, 1904. Hb. London: Rider, 1905. Hb. London: Arrow, 1962, Pb. London: Jarrolds, 1966. Hb. New York: Carroll & Graf, 1989. Hb. New York: Scholastic, 1972. Pb. Abridged. Rpt. in *Dracula's Curse and The Jewel of the Seven Stars*. New York: Tower, 1968. Pb. [We, 1]

———*The Lady of the Shroud*. London: Heinemann, 1909. Hb. London: Rider, 1925. Hb. London: Arrow, 1962. Pb. London: Jarrolds, 1966. Hb. [Ps, 1]

———*The Lair of the White Worm*. London: Rider, 1911. Hb. London: W. Foulsham, n.d. (1925). Hb. Abridged. Rpt. n.d. Pb. London: Arrow, 1960. Pb. Abridged. London: Jarrolds, 1966. Hb. Abridged. Retitled: *The Garden of Evil*. New York: Paperback Library, 1966. Pb. Abridged. New York: Zebra, 1979. Pb. Abridged. Rpt. in Dalby, Richard, ed. *Dracula (and) The Lair of the White Worm*. London: W. Foulsham, 1986. Hb. [Fo, 1, M]

Straub, Peter. *Ghost Story*. New York: Coward, McCann & Geoghegan, 1978. Hb. London: J. Cape, 1979. Hb. London: Futura, 1979. Pb. New York: Pocket Books, 1980. Pb. [En, Su, Ps, We, 1, M]

Strieber, Whitley. *The Hunger*. New York: Morrow, 1981. Hb. New York: Pocket Books, 1982. Pb. New York: Avon, 1988. Pb. [V, 1, M]

Sturgeon, Theodore (Neé Edward Hamilton Waldo). *Some of Your Blood*. New York: Ballantine, 1961. Pb. London: Sphere, 1967. Pb. New York: Carroll & Graf, 1994. Pb. [Bl, Me, 1]

Süskind, Patrick. *Perfume*. New York: A. A. Knopf, 1986. Rpt. 1987. Pb. Trans. from the German of 1985. [Me, We (scent-draining), 5]

Swanson, Logan (Richard Matheson). *Earthbound*. New York: Playboy, 1982. Pb. Rpt. as Matheson, Richard. *Earthbround*. London: Robinson, 1989. Hb. Restored edition. [Po, 1]

Swanwick, Michael. *In the Drift*. New York: Berkley, 1985. Pb. [Bl, 3]

Symons, Julian. *The Players and the Game*. New York: Harper & Row, 1972. Hb. London: Collins, 1972. Hb. New York: Avon, 1975. Pb. Harmonsworth, Middlesex, U.K: Penguin, 1984. Pb. [Bl, Ps, 7]

Talbot, Michael. *The Delicate Dependency*. New York: Avon, 1982. Pb. [V, 1]

Taylor, C. Bryson. *In the Dwellings of the Wilderness*. New York: H. Holt, 1904. Hb. [V, We, 4, 8]

Taylor, Karen. *Blood Secrets*. New York: Zebra, 1994. Pb. [The Vampire Legacy #1. V, 1]

———*Bitter Blood*. New York: Zebra, 1994. Pb. [#2]

Tedford, William. *Liquid Diet*. Diamond, 1992. Pb. [V, 1]

Tigges, John. *The Immortal*. New York: Leisure, 1986. Pb. [Im (Saint-Germain), 4]

———*Venom*. New York: Leisure, 1988. Pb. [La, 1]

———*Vessel*. New York: Leisure, 1988. Pb. [Bl (Elizabeth Bathory), 1]

Tilton, Lois. *Vampire Winter*. New York: Pinnacle, 1990. Pb. [V, 1]

————*Darkness on the Ice*. New York: Pinnacle, 1993. Pb. [V, 1]

Tonkin, Peter. *The Journal of Edwin Underhill*. London: Hodder and Stoughton, 1981. Hb. London: Coronet, 1983. Pb. [V, 4]

Travis, Tristan, Jr. *Lamia*. New York: E. P. Dutton, 1982. Hb. [Ps, 7]

Tremayne, Peter (Peter Berresford Ellis). *Dracula Unborn*. Folkstone, U.K.: Bailey Brothers and Swinfen, 1977. Hb. London: Corgi, 1977. Pb. Retitled: *Bloodright*. New York: Walker, 1979. Pb. New York: Dell, 1980. Pb. [Dracula Unborn #1. D, 1]

————*The Revenge of Dracula*. Folkstone, U.K.: Bailey Brothers and Swinfen, 1978. Hb. West Kingston, RI: Donald M. Grant, 1979. Hb. New York: Walker, 1979. Hb. London: Magnum, 1979. Pb. New York: Dell, 1981. Pb. [#2]

————*Dracula, My Love*. Folkstone, U.K.: Bailey Brothers and Swinfen, 1980. Hb. London: Magnum, 1980. Pb. New York: Dell, 1981. Pb. [#3]

————*Dracula Lives!*. London: Signet, 1993. Pb. Includes *Dracula Unborn*, *The Revenge of Dracula*, and *Dracula Lives*.

Upton, Smyth. *The Last of the Vampires*. Weston-Super-Mare, U.K.: J. Whereat Columbian, 1845. Hb. Rpt. in *The Spectre Bridegroom and Other Horrors*. Arno: New York: 1976. Hb. [Im, 4]

Urquhart, M. *The Island of Lost Souls*. London: Mills & Boon, 1910. Hb. [V, 4, 8]

Valdemi, Maria. *The Demon Lover*. New York: TOR/ Pinnacle, 1981. Pb. [V, 1]

The Vampire: or, bride of the isles. London: J. Bailey, 1821. Hb. [V (Lord Ruthven), 1]

The Vampire: or, detective Brand's greatest case. New York: N. N. Munro, 1885. Pb. [Ps, 4]

Vampire I. New York: HarperCollins, 1994. Pb. [V, 1]

The Vampyre. London: Sherwood, Neeley, and Jones, 1819. Hb. Written by Dr. John William Polidori. Oxford, U.K.: Woodstock Books, 1990. Hb. Rpt. in Bleiler, E. F., ed. *Three Gothic Novels*. New York: Dover, 1966. Tr. Pb. Rpt. in Adams, Donald K., ed. *The Vampyre: a tale written by Dr. Polidori*. Pasadena, CA: G. Dahlstom, 1968. Hb. Rpt. in Ash, Russell, ed. *The Vampyre*. Tring, Herts., U.K.: Gubblecote, 1974. Hb. Phila

delphia, PA: International Publications, 1974. Hb. Story. First publication, 1819. [V (Lord Ruthven), 1, C]

Varney the Vampyre: or, the feast of Blood. London: E. Lloyd, 1847. In parts. As by The Author of Grace Rivers . . . (Pseud.), Rpt. 1853. In parts. New York: Arno, 1970. Hb. 3 vol. As by Prest, Thomas Preskett. Ed. by Devendra P. Varma. Erratum: Omits Chapter 74. New York: Dover, 1972. Tr. Pb. 2 vol. As by Rymer, James Malcolm. Ed. by E. F. Bleiler. [V, 1]

Van Over, Raymond. *The Twelfth Child*. New York: Pinnacle, 1990. Pb. [V, 1]

Van Vogt, A. E. *Supermind*. New York: DAW, 1977. Pb. London: Sidgwick and Jackson, 1978. Hb. [Al, En, 2]

Veley, Charles. *Night Whispers*. Garden City, NY: Doubleday, 1980. Hb. New York: Ballantine, 1981. Pb. London: Granada, 1981. Pb. [Bl (and drugs), Im, 1]

Verne, Jules. *The Castle of the Carpathians*. London: Sampson, Low, Marston, Searle & Rivington, 1893. Hb. New York: Merian, 1894. Hb. Akron, OH: Sanfield, 1906. Hb. Retitled: *Carpathian Castle*. London: Arco, 1963. Hb. Abridged. New York: Ace, 1963. Pb. Trans. from the French of 1892. [Ps, 2]

Vershoyle, Catherine M. *Oldham*. London: Longmans, Green, 1927. Hb. [En (youth), 1]

Vidal, Gore. *A Search for the King*. New York: E. P. Dutton, 1950. Hb. New York: Pyramid, 1968. Pb. [V, 3]

Viereck, George Sylvester. *The House of the Vampire*. New York: Moffat, Yard, 1907. Hb. New York: Arno, 1976. Hb. [En (creativity), Me, 1]

Walker, Robert. *Killer Instinct*. New York: Leisure, 1992. Pb. [Ps, 7]

Wallace, Patricia. *Monday's Child*. New York: Zebra, 1989. Pb. [V, 1]

Wallace, Robert (House Pseud.). *The Vampire Murders*. San Diego, CA: Popular Library, 1965. Pb. [Ps, 7]

Walters, R. R. *Ludlow's Mill*. New York: TOR Pinnacle, 1981. Pb. [La, 1]

————*Lily*. New York: TOR, 1988. Pb. [Su (Lilith), 1]

Warne, Philip S. *Despard, the Duelist: or, the mountain vampires*. New York: Beadle and Adams, n.d. (c. 1900). Paper. Story. [V, 3]

Warrington, Freda. *A Taste of Blood Wine*. London: Pan, 1992. Hb. and Tr. Pb. Rpt. 1993. Pb. [A Taste of Blood Wine #1. V, 1, 3]

———*A Dance in Blood Velvet*. London: Pan, 1994. Hb. and Tr. Pb. [#2]

Watt-Evans, Lawrence. *Nightmare People*. New York: Onyx, 1990. Pb. [V, 1]

Waugh, Michael. *Fangs of the Vampire*. Sydney Australia: Cleveland, 1954. Story. [V, 1]

———*Back from the Dead*. Sydney, Australia: Cleveland, 1955. Paper. Story. [V, 1]

———*The Living Dead*. Sydney, Australia: Cleveland, 1955. Paper. Story. [V, 1]

Weathersby, Lee. *Kiss of the Vampire*. New York: Zebra, 1992. Pb. [V, 1]

Webber, Chales Wilkins. *Spiritual Vampirism*. Philadelphia, Pa: Lippincott, Grambo, 1853. Hb. [En, 4]

Whalen, Patrick. *Monastery*. New York: Pocket Books, 1988. Pb. [Monastery #1. V, 1]

———*Night Thirst*. New York: Pocket Books, 1991. Pb. [#2]

Whitten, Leslie H. *Progeny of the Adder*. Garden City, NY: Doubleday, 1965. Hb. London: Hodder and Stoughton, 1966. Hb. New York: Ace, n.d. Pb. New York: Avon, 1975. Pb. Rpt. in *Moon of the Wolf (and) Progeny of the Adder*. New York: Leisure, 1992. Pb. [V, 1, 7]

Wilde, Kelley. *Mastery*. New York: Dell, 1991. Pb. [V, 1]

Williams, Sidney. *Night Brothers*. New York: Pinnacle, 1989. Pb. [V, 1]

Williams. Thad. W. *In Quest of Life*. London: F. T. Neely, 1898. Hb. [Bl, En, 3]

Williamson, Chet. *Mordenheim*. Lake Geneva, WI, 1994. Pb. [Ravenloft series. V, 3, 8]

Williamson, J. N. (Gerald Neal Williamson). *Death-Coach*. New York: Zebra, 1982. Pb. [Lamia Zacharius #1. V, 1, 4]

———*Death-Angel*. New York: Zebra, 1982. Pb. [#2]

———*Death-School*. New York: Zebra, 1982. Pb. [#3]

———*Death-Doctor*. New York: Zebra, 1982. Pb. [#4]

Wilson, Colin. *The Mind Parasites*. London: A. Barker, 1967. Hb. Sauk City, WI: Arkham House, 1967. Hb. New York: Bantam, 1968. Pb. London: Panther, 1969. Pb. [Al, En, In, 2]

———*The Return of the Lloiger*. London: Village, 1974. Paper. Story. [Al, En]

———*The Space Vampires*. London: Hart-Davis and MacGibbon, 1976. Hb. New York: Random House, 1976. Hb. London: Panther, 1977. Pb. New York: Pocket Books, 1977. Pb. Retitled:

Lifeforce. New York: Warner, 1985. Pb. London: Panther, 1985. Pb. [Al, En, 2, M]

Wilson, F. Paul. *The Keep*. New York: Morrow, 1981. Hb. Rpt.. Tr. Pb. New York: Berkley, 1982. Pb. Note: The vampire theme is not continued in subsequent books in this series. [En, Ps, We, M]

———*Midnight Mass*. Eugene, OR: Axolotl Pulphuose, 1990. Hb. Tr. Pb. Story. [V, 1]

Winston, Daoma (Dorian Winslow). *The Vampire Curse*. New York: Paperback Library, 1971. Pb. London: Severn House, 1993. Hb. [Ps, 9]

Worth, Margaret (Helen Arvonen). *Red Wine of Rapture*. New York: Avon, 1973. Pb. [V, 1]

Wright, T. Lucien. *The Hunt*. New York: Pinnacle, 1991. Pb. [V, 1]

———*Blood Brothers*. New York: Pinnacle, 1992. Pb. [V, 1]

———*Thirst of the Vampire*. New York: Pinnacle, 1992. Pb. [V, 1]

Yarbro, Chelsea Quinn. *Hotel Transylvania* New York: St. Martin's, 1978. Hb. New York: Signet, 1979. Pb. London: New English Library, 1979. Pb. New York: TOR, 1988. Pb. Revised edition. [Saint-Germain #1. V, 1]

———*The Palace*. New York: St. Martin's, 1978. Hb. New York: Signet, 1979. Pb. London: New English Library, 1979. Pb. New York: TOR, 1988. Pb. Revised edition. [#2]

———*Blood Games*. New York: St. Martin's, 1979. Hb. New York: Signet, 1980. Pb. New York: TOR, 1989. Pb. [#3]

———*Path of the Eclipse*. New York: St. Martin's, 1981. Hb. New York: Signet, 1981. Pb. New York: TOR, 1989. Pb. [#4]

———*Tempting Fate*. New York: St. Martin's, 1982. Hb. New York: Signet, 1982. Pb. [#5]

———*A Mortal Glamour*. New York: Bantam, 1985. Pb. White Rock, B.C., Canada: Transylvania Press, Restored version. Forthcoming, 1995. [Su, 1]

———*The Saint-Germain Chronicles*, 1986. [Saint-Germain #6]

———*A Flame in Byzantium*. New York: TOR, 1987. Hb. Rpt. 1988. Pb. [Atta Olivia Clemens #1. V, 1]

———*Crusader's Torch*. New York: TOR, 1987. Hb. Rpt. 1988. Pb. [#2]

———*A Candle for D'artagnan*. New York: TOR, 1989. Hb. New York: TOR Orb, 1994. Tr. Pb. [#3]

——*The Spider Glass.* Eugene, OR: Pulphouse, 1991. Paper. Story, Originally published in 1991. Saint-Germain series.

——*Out of the House of Life.* New York: TOR, 1991. Hb. New York: TOR Orb, 1994. Tr. Pb. [Madelaine de Montalia #1. V, 1]

——*Darker Jewels.* New York: TOR, 1993. Hb. [Saint-Germain #7. V, 1]

——*Better in the Dark.* New York: TOR, 1993. Hb. [#8]

——*Mansions of Darkness.* New York: TOR. Forthcoming. [#9]

——*In the Face of Death.* Forthcoming. [Madelaine de Montalia #2.]

Yeovil, Jack (Kim Newman). *Warhammer: Drachenfels.* Brighton, East Sussex, UK: GW Books, 1989. Tr. Pb. London: Boxtree, 1993. Pb. [Genevive #1. V, 3]

——*Warhammer: Genevive Undead.* London: Boxtree, 1993. Pb. [#2]

Zachary, Fay. *Blood Work.* New York: Berkley, 1994. Pb. [Ps, 7]

ANTHOLOGIES AND COLLECTIONS

Ackerman, Forrest J, and Jeane Marie Stine. *I, Vampire.* Forthcoming.

A. L. G. (Pseud.), ed. *A vampire and other stories.* London: Society for Promoting Christian Knowlege, 1984. Hb. Coll. Title story only. [Me (for laziness and the welfare state)]

Blaisdell, Elinore, ed. *Tales of the Undead: vampires and visitants.* New York: T. Y. Crowell, 1947. Hb.

Brite, Poppy Z. *Love in Vein.* New York: HarperCollins, 1994. Tr. Pb.

Burton, (Captain) (Sir) Richard F., trans. *Vikram & the Vampire: or, tales of Hindu devilry.* London: Longmans, Green, 1870. Hb. London: Tylston & Edwards, 1893. Hb. Abridged. London: Constable, 1969. Tr. Pb. New York: Dover, 1969. Tr. Pb. New Delhi, India: Oriental Reprint Corporation, 1985. Hb. Retitled: *Kind Vikram and the Vampire.* Rochester, VT: Park Street Press, 1992. Tr. Pb. Coll. Trans. from the Sanskrit. [Fo]

Carter, M. L. ed. *The Curse of the Undead.* Greenwich, CT: Fawcett, 1970. Pb.

Chetwynd-Hayes, R., ed. *Dracula's Children.* London: Kimber, 1987. Hb. Coll. [Dracula's Children #1.]

——*The House of Dracula.* London: Kimber, 1987. Hb. Coll. [#2]

Collins, Barnabas, and Quentin (Pseuds.), eds. *The Dark Shadows Book of Vampires and Werewolves.* New York: Paperback Library, 1970. Pb. Some werewolf stories.

Collins, Charles M., ed. *A Feast of Blood.* New York: Avon, 1967. Pb.

Dalby, Richard, ed. *Dracula's Brood: rare vampire stories by friends and contemporaries of Bram Stoker.* n.p. U.K: Park Street, 1987. Tr. Pb. London: Equation, n.d. Tr. Pb. New York: Dorset, 1991. Hb.

——*Vampire Stories.* London: Michael O'Mara, 1992. Hb. Avenal, NJ: Castle, 1993. Hb.

Datlow, Ellen, ed. *Blood Is Not Enough: 17 stories of vampirism.* New York: Morrow, 1989. Hb. New York: Berkley, 1990. Pb. [Blood Is Not Enough #1]

——*A Whisper of Blood.* New York: Morrow, 1991. Hb. New York: Berkley, 1992. Pb. [#2]

Dickie, James, ed. *The Undead.* London: N. Spearman, 1971. Hb. London: Pan, 1973. Pb. New York: Pocket Books, 1976. Pb.

Edwards, Wayne, ed. *Vlad the Impaler: volume one.* Lynn, IN: Merrimack, 1992. Paper. [Vlad the Impaler #1. D]

Edward, Wayne, and Tamara Price, eds. *Vlad the Impaler: volume two.* Lynn, IN: Merrimack, 1992. Paper. [#2]

——*Vlad the Impaler: volume three.* Lynn, IN: Merrimack, 1992. Paper. [#3]

Evans, E. Everett. *Food for Demons.* San Diego, CA: Shroud, 1971. Tr. Pb. Posthumous Coll. North Hollywood, CA: Fantasy House, 1974. Tr. Pb. Abridged.

Fox, Leslie H. *The Vampire and Sixteen Other Stories.* London: Alliance, n.d. (c. 1940–1945). Pb. Title story only.

Frayling, Christopher, ed. *The Vampyre: Lord Ruthven to Count Dracula.* London: Gollancz, 1978. Hb. Retitled: *The Vampyre: a bedside companion.* New York: Scribner's, 1978. Hb. Retitled: *Vampyres: Lord Byron to Count Dracula.* London: Faber, 1992. Hb. Revised edition. Rpt. 1993. Tr. Pb. Includes an extensive bibliography.

Ghidalia, Victor, ed. *Dracula's Guest and Other Stories.* Middletown, CT: Xerox, 1972. Pb.

Gladwell, Adele Olivia, and James Havoc, eds. *Blood & Roses: the vampire in 19th century literature.* London: Creation Press, 1992. Tr. Pb.

Greenberg, Martin H., ed. *Dracula: Prince of Darkness.* New York: DAW, 1992. Pb. Coll. [D]

————*A Taste for Blood: fifteen great vampire novellas.* New York: Dorset, 1992. Hb.

————*Vampire Detectives.* New York: DAW. 1994. Pb.

————*100 Vicious Little Vampire Stories.* New York: Barnes and Noble. Forthcoming, 1995.

Greenberg, Martin H., and Charles G. Waugh, eds. *Vamps: an anthology of female vampire stories.* New York: DAW, 1987. Pb.

Haining, Peter, ed. *The Midnight People: being eighteen terrifying and bizarre tales of vampires.* London: L. Frewin, 1968. Hb. Manchester, U.K.: Ensign, 1974. Pb. London: Everest, 1975. Pb. New York: Popular Library n.d.. Pb. Retitled: *Vampires at Midnight.* New York: Grosset & Dunlap, 1975. Hb. London: Warner, 1993. Pb.

————*Vampire: chilling tales of the undead.* London: Severn House, 1985. Hb. London: Target, 1985. Tr. Pb.

Johnson, Caroline, ed. *Legends in Blood.* West Los Angeles, CA: FantaSeas Press, 1992. Paper.

Jones, Stephen, ed. *The Mammoth Book of Vampires.* London: Robinson, 1992. Tr. Pb. New York: Carroll & Graf, 1992. Tr. Pb.

Keesey, Pam, ed. *Daughters of Darkness: Lesbian Vampire Stories.* Pittsburgh, PA: Cleis Press, 1993. Tr. Pb.

Kilpatrick, Nancy, ed. *Love Bites.* New York: Pocket Books, 1994. Tr. Pb.

Le Fanu, J. Sheridan. *The Vampire Lovers.* London: Fontana, 1970. Pb. Coll. Title story (i.e., "Carmilla") only. [M]

Leitch, Lavinia (Mrs. W. A. Hynd), ed. *A Vampire: and other stories.* Boston, MA: Christopher Publishing House, 1927. Hb. Coll. Title story only.

Lindner, Karl, ed. *Vampire.* Mt. Sterling, IL: Spoon River Poetry Press, 1977. Paper. Poetry.

McCammon, Robert R. *Under the Fang.* New York: Pocket Books, 1991. Pb. Baltimore, MD: Borderlands, 1991 Hb. Shared-world vampire anthology presented by the Horror Writers of America.

McNally, Raymond T., ed. *A Clutch of Vampires: these being among the best in history and literature.* Greenwich, CT: New York Graphic Society, 1974. Hb. New York: Warner, 1975. Pb. London: New English Library, 1976. Pb.

Moore, Steven, ed. *The Vampire in Verse: An Anthology.* New York: Dracula Press, 1985. Tr. Pb. Poetry.

Parry, Michel, ed. *The Rivals of Dracula: a century of vampire fiction.* London: Corgi, 1977. Pb. London: Severn House, 1978. Hb.

Petrey, Susan C. *Gifts of Blood: the collected stories of Susan C. Petrey.* Portland, OR: OSFCI, 1990. Hb. Posthumous Coll. Ed. by Paul M. Wrigley and Debbie Cross. New York: Baen, 1992. Pb.

Pickersgill, Frederick, ed. *No Such Thing as a Vampire.* London: Corgi, 1964. Pb. Title story only.

Perkowski, Jan L., ed. *Vampires of the Slavs.* Cambridge, MA: Slavica, 1976. Tr. Pb.

Preiss, Byron, David Keller, and Megan Miller, eds. *The Ultimate Dracula.* New York: Dell, 1991. Tr. Pb. London: Headline, 1992. Hb. Coll. [D]

Ryan, Alan, ed. *Vampires: two centuries of great Vampire stories.* Garden City, NY: Doubleday, 1987. Hb. Retitled: *The Penguin Book of Vampire Stories.* London: Penguin, 1988. Tr. Pb. London: Bloomsbury, 1991. Hb.

Shepard, Leslie, ed. *The Dracula Book of Great Vampire Stories.* Secaucus, NJ: Citadel, 1977. Hb. Rpt. n.d. Tr. Pb. New York: Jove, 1978. Pb. Rpt. in Shepard, Leslie, ed. *The Book of Dracula.* New York: Wings, 1991. Hb.

Tales of Ravenloft. Lake Geneva, WI, 1994. Pb. [Ravenloft series.]

Tolstoy, Alexis. *Vampires: stories of the supernatural.* Harmondsworth, Middlesex, U.K., 1946. Pb. New York: Hawthorn, 1969. Hb. Rpt. Tr. Pb. Posthumous Coll.

Trevistan, Dalton. *The Vampire of Curitiba and other stories.* New York: A. A. Knopf, 1972. Hb. Coll. Trans. from the Portuguese. Title story only.

Underwood, Peter, ed. *The Vampire's Bedside Companion: the amazing world of vampires in fact and fiction.* London: L. Frewin, 1975. Hb. London: Coronet, 1976. Tr. Pb.

Roger Vadim, Ornella Volta, and Valeria Riva, eds. *The Vampire: an anthology.* London: N. Spearman, 1963. Hb. London: Pan, n.d. Pb. Trans. from the abridged French edition of 1961, which was edited by Roger Vadim. Originally published in Italian (1960).

Van der Elst. *Death of the Vampire Baroness: and other thrilling stories*. London: The Van der Elst Press, n.d. (c. 1940). Paper. Coll. Title story only.

Varma, Devendra P., ed. *Voices from the Vaults: authentic tales of vampires and ghosts*. Toronto, Ont., Canada: Key Porter, 1987. Hb. Toronto, Ont., Canada: Seal, 1988. Pb.

Von Degen ([Baroness] Ann Crawford von Rabe), ed. *A Mystery of the Campagna and A Shadow on a Wave*. London: T. Fisher Unwin, 1891. Hb. Coll. Title story only.

Weinberg, Robert, Stefan R. Dziemianowicz, and Martin H. Greenberg, eds. *Weird Vampire Tales: 30 Blood-chilling stories from the weird fiction pulps*. New York: Gramercy, 1992. Hb.

Weisskopf, Tina, and Greg Cox, eds. *Tomorrow Sucks*. New York: Baen, 1994. Pb.

Yarbro, Chelsea Quinn, ed. *The Saint-Germain Chronicles*. New York: Pocket Books, 1973. Pb. Coll. Rpt. in *The Complete Vampire Stories of Chelsea Quinn Yarbro* (1994). [Saint-Germain series.]

———*The Complete Vampire Stories of Chelsea Quinn Yarbro*. White Rock, B.C., Canada: Transylvania Press, 1994. Hb. Coll. Includes *The Saint-Germain Chronicles* (1983).

Yolen, Jane, and Martin H. Greenberg, eds. *Vampires*. New York: HarperCollins, 1991. Hb. New York: Harper Trophy, 1993. Tr. Pb.

Youngson, Jeanne, ed. *The Count Dracula Book of Classic Vampire Tales*. Chicago, IL: Adams, 1981. Tr. Pb.

———*The Count Dracula Fan Club Book of Vampire Stories*. Chicago, IL: Adams, 1980. Tr. Pb.

———*Freak Show Vampire & The Hungry Grass*. Chicago, IL: Adams, 1981. Pb.

STUDIES

Barber, Paul. *Vampires, Burial, and Death: folklore and reality*. New Haven, CT: Yale, 1988. Hb. Rpt. Tr. Pb. [Fo]

Bhalla, Alok. *Politics of Atrocity and Lust: the Vampire tale as a nightmare history of England in the nineteenth century*. New Delhi, India: Sterling, 1990. Hb. [Me]

Biondi, Lt. Ray, and Walt Hecox. *The Dracula Killer*. New York: Pocket Books, 1992. Pb. London: Mondo, 1993. Pb. [Ps, 7 (true crime)]

Brokaw, Kurt. *A Night in Transylvania: the Dracula scrapbook*. New York: Grosset & Dunlap, 1976. Tr. Pb.

Bunson, Matthew. *The Vampire Encyclopedia*. New York: Crown, 1993. Tr. Pb.

Calmet, (Dom) Augustine(e). *Dissertations Upon the Apparitions of Angels, Demons, and Ghosts, and Concerning the Vampires of Hungary, Bohemia, Moravia, and Silesia*. London: M. Cooper, 1759. Hb. Retitled: *The Phantom World*. London: R. Bentley, 1859. Hb. 2 vol. Trans. from the French of 1746.

Carter, Margaret L. *Shadow of a Shade: a survey of vampirism in literature*. New York: Gordon Press, 1975. Hb. Bibliography.

———ed. *Dracula: the vampire and the critics*. Ann Arbor, MI: U.M.I. Research Press, 1988. Hb. [D]

———*The Vampire in Literature: a critical bibliography*. Ann Arbor, MI: U.M.I. Research Press, 1989. Hb. Bibliography.

Copper, Basil. *The Vampire: in legend, fact and art*. London: Hale, 1973. Hb. Rpt. Tr. Pb. Secaucus, NJ: Citadel, 1974. Hb. London: Corgi, 1975. Pb.

Cox, Greg. *The Transylvanian Library: a consumer's guide to vampire fiction*. San Bernardino, CA: Borgo Press, 1992. Hb. and Tr. Pb. Annotated bibliography.

Dawidziak, Mark. *Night Stalking: a 20th anniversary Kolchak companion*. New York: Image Publishing, 1991. Tr. Pb. [M]

Dresser, Norine. *American Vampires: fans, victims & practitioners*. New York: Norton, 1989. Hb. New York: Vintage, 1990. Tr. Pb.

Dworkin, Susan, ed. *Coppola and Eiko on Bram Stoker's Dracula*. San Francisco, CA: Collins, 1992. Hb. Rpt. 1993. Tr. Pb. [M]

Eighteen-Bisang, Robert. *Dracula: an annotated bibliography*. White Rock, B.C., Canada: Transylvania Press, 1994. Hb. Dracula bibliography. [C, M]

Finné, Jacques. *La Bibliographie de Dracula*. Laussane, Switzerland: L'age D'Homme, 1986. Tr. Pb. In French. Vampire bibliography.

Florescu, Radu [R.], and Raymond T. McNally. *Dracula: a biography of Vlad the Impaler, 1431–1476*. New York: Hawthorn, 1973. Hb. Reprinted in *The Complete Dracula*. New York: Copley, 1985. Tr. Pb. See also: McNally and Florescu. [In Search of Dracula #2. D (Vlad Tepes)]

———*Dracula: Prince of many faces; his life and his*

times. Boston, MS: Little, Brown, 1989. Hb. Rpt. Tr. Pb. [#3]

Flynn, John L. *Cinematic vampires: the living dead on film and television, from The Devil's Castle (1896) to Bram Stoker's Dracula (1992)*. Jefferson, NC: MacFarland, 1992. [M]

Frost, Brian J. *The Monster with a Thousand Faces: guises of the vampire in myth and literature*. Bowling Green. OH: Bowling Green, 1989. Hb. and Tr. Pb. Bibliography.

Glut, Donald F. *True Vampires of History*. n.p.: Castle, 1971. Hb. Rpt. n.d. Pb.

———*The Dracula Book*. Methuen, NJ: Scarcrow, 1975. Hb. Dracula bibliography. [D, C, M]

Gross, Edward, and Marc Shapiro. *The Vampire Interview Book*. New York: Image, 1991. Tr. Pb. [M]

Guiley, Rosemary Ellen. *Vampires Among Us*. New York: Pocket Books, 1991. Pb. London: Titan, 1993. Pb. Romania: Editura Venus, 1993. Pb.

Haining, Peter, ed. *The Dracula Scrapbook*. New York: Bramhall House, 1976. Hb. Stamford, CT: Longmeadow, 1992. Hb. [D]

———*The Dracula Centenary Book*. London: Souvenir, 1987. Hb. [D]

Haworth-Maden, Clare. *The Essential Dracula*. New York: Crescent, 1992. Hb.

Hillyer, Vincent. *Vampires*. Los Banos, CA: Loose Change, 1988. Tr. Pb.

Hoyt, Olga (Gruhzit). *Lust for Blood: the consuming story of vampires*. New York: Stein and Day, 1984. Hb. Rpt. n.d. Pb. Chelsea, MI: Scarborough, 1990. Tr. Pb.

Hurwood, Bernhard J. *Terror by Night*. New York: Lancer, 1963. Pb. Revised as *The Vampire Papers*. New York: Pinnacle, 1976. Pb.

———*Vampires*. New York: Quick Fox, 1981. Tr. Pb.

Jones, Stephen. *The Illustrated Vampire Movie Guide*. London: Titan, 1993. Tr. Pb. [M]

Kaplan, Stephen. *In Pursuit of Premature Gods and Comtemporary Vampires*. Long Island, NY: Vampire Research Centre, 1976. Pb.

Kaplan, Stephen, and Carole Kane. *Vampires Are*. Palm Springs, CA: ETC Publications, 1984. Tr. Pb.

Landau, Diana, ed. *Bram Stoker's Dracula: the film and the legend*. New York: Newmarket, 1992. Hb. and Tr. Pb. [D, M]

Leatherdale, Clive. *Dracula: the novel & the legend, a study of Bram Stoker's gothic masterpiece*. Wellingborough, Northhamptonshire, U.K.: Aquar-

ian, 1985. Tr. Pb. London: Desert Island, 1993. Hb. Revised edition. [D]

———ed. *The Origins of Dracula: the background to Bram Stoker's gothic masterpiece*. London: Kimber, 1987. Hb. [D]

Manchester, Sean. *The Highgate Vampire*. London: British Occult Society, 1985. Tr. Pb. London: Gothic Press, 1991. Hb. Revised edition.

Marigny, Jean. *Vampires: restless creatures of the night*. New York: Abrams, 1994. Tr. Pb.

Marrero, Robert G. *Vampires: Hammer style*. Key West, FL: RGM Publications, 1982. Paper. [M]

———*Dracula: the vampire legend*. Key West, FL: Fantasma, 1993. Tr. Pb. [M]

———*Vampire Movies*. Key West, FL: Fantasma, 1994. Hb. Rpt. 1995. Tr. Pb.

Mascetti, Manuela Dunn. *Vampire: the complete guide to the world of the undead*. New York: Viking, 1992. Hb.

Masters, Anthony. *The Natural History of the Vampire*. London: Rupert Hart-Davis, 1972. Hb. New York: Putnam's, 1972. Hb. London: Mayflower, 1974. Pb. New York: Berkley, 1976. Pb.

McNally, Raymond T. *Dracula Was a Woman: in search of the Blood Countess of Transylvania*. New York: McGraw-Hill, 1983. Hb. London: Hale, 1984. Hb. London: Hamlyn, 1985. Pb. Dracula and Elizabeth Bathory. Includes an extensive bibliography. [D]

McNally, Raymond (T.), and Radu Florescu. *In Search of Dracula*. Greenwich, CT: New York Graphic Society, 1973. Hb. New York: Warner, 1973. Pb. London: New English Library, 1979. Hb. Rpt. in *The Complete Dracula*. New York: Copley, 1985. Tr. Pb. Revised as *In Search of Dracula: twenty years later*. Boston, MA: Houghton, Mifflin, 1994. Hb. See also: Florescu and McNally. [In Search of Dracula #1. D (Vlad Tepes)]

———eds. *The Essential Dracula: a completely illustrated & annotated edition of Bram Stoker's classic novel*. New York: Mayflower, 1979. Hb. Inculdes: "Dracula's Guest" and *Dracula*. [D]

Melton, J. Gordon. *The Vampire and the Comic Book*. New York: Dracula Press, 1993. Paper. [C]

Meyers, William. *Vampires or Gods?* San Francisco, CA: III Publishing, 1993. Tr. Pb. [Me]

Monaco, Richard, and Bill Burt. *The Dracula Syndrome*. New York: Avon, 1993. Pb. [Ps, 7 (true crime)]

Murphy, Michael J. *The Celluloid Vampires: a history and filmography, 1897 to 1979.* Ann Arbor, MI: Peirean, 1979. Hb. [M]

Nance, Scott. *Bloodsuckers: vampires at the movies.* Las Vegas, NV: Pioneer, 1992. Tr. Pb. [M]

Noll, Richard. *Vampires, Werewolves, and Demons: twentieth century reports in the psychiatric literature.* New York: Brunner Mazel, 1992. Hb. Rpt. 1993. Tr. Pb.

Page, Carol. *Bloodlust: conversations with real vampires.* New York: HarperCollins, 1991. Hb. New York: Dell, 1993. Pb.

Pattison, Barrie. *The Seal of Dracula.* London: Lorrimer, 1975. Hb. New York: Bounty, 1975. Hb. [M]

Penrose, Valentine. *The Bloody Countess.* London: Calder & Boyars, 1970. Hb. London: New English Library, 1972. Pb. Trans. from the French of 1957. [Elizabeth Bathory]

Perkowski, Jan L. *The Darkling: a treatise on Slavic vampirism.* Cambridge, MA: Slavica, 1989. Tr. Pb. [Fo]

Pirie, David. *The Vampire Cinema.* New York: Crescent, 1977. Hb. [M]

Ramsland, Katherine. *The Vampire Companion: the official guide to Anne Rice's "The Vampire Chronicles."* New York: Ballantine, 1993. Hb.

Reed, Donald A. *The Vampire on the Screen.* Inglewood, CA: Wagon & Star, 1965. Paper. [M]

Riccardo, Martin V. *The Lure of the Vampire.* New York: Dracula Unlimited, 1983. Tr. Pb.

————*Vampires Unearthed: the complete multi-media vampire and Dracula bibliography.* New York: Garland, 1983. Hb. Bibliography. [C, M]

Ronay, Gabriel. *The Dracula Myth.* London: Allen, 1972. Hb. London: Pan, 1975. Pb. Retitled: *The Truth About Dracula.* New York: St. Martin's, 1972. Hb. New York: Stein and Day, 1974. Tr. Pb. [D]

Senf, Carol A. *The Vampire in Nineteenth-Century English Literature.* n.p.: Bowling Green State University Popular Press, 1988. Hb. and Tr. Pb.

Senn, Harry A. *Were-wolf and Vampire in Romania.* New York: Columbia, 1982. Hb. [Fo]

Skal, David J. *Hollywood Gothic: the tangled web of Dracula from novel to stage to screen.* New York: Norton, 1990. Hb. Rpt. Tr. Pb. [D, M]

————ed. *Dracula: the ultimate, illustrated edition of the world-famous Vampire play.* New York: St. Martin's, 1993. Hb. and Tr. Pb. [D]

————ed. *V is for Vampire.* New York: Plume, 1995. Tr. Pb.

Summers, Montague. *The Vampire: his kith and kin.* London: Kegan Paul, Trench, Trubne, 1928. Hb. New York: Dutton, 1929. Hb. Hyde Park, NY: University Books, n.d. (1960). Hb. London: Jenkins, 1963. Hb. New York: Dorset, 1991. Hb. Includes a pioneering but unreliable vampire bibliography.

————*The Vampire in Europe.* London: Keagan Paul, Trench, 1929. Hb. New York: Dutton, 1929. Hb. Hyde Park, NY: University Books, n.d. (1960). Hb. London: Jenkins, 1963. Hb. Wellingborough, U.K.: Aquarian, 1980. Tr. Pb.

Stoicescu, Nicolae. *Vlad Tepes: Prince of Walachia.* n.p., Romania: Editura Academiei Republicii Socialiste, 1978. Hb. Trans. from the Romanian. [D (Vlad Tepes)]

Sullivan, John, ed. *Monarch Notes on Bram Stoker's Dracula.* New York: Simon & Schuster, 1980. Paper. [D]

Treptow, Kurt W., ed. *Dracula: essays on the life and times of Vlad Tepes.* Columbia: New York, 1991. Hb. [D (Vlad Tepes)]

Toufic, Jalal. *Vampires: a post-modern vision of the undead in film and literature.* New York: Station Hill, 1993. Tr. Pb. [M]

Twitchell, James B. *The Living Dead: a study of the vampire in romantic literature.* Durham, NC: Duke, 1981. Hb. Rpt. Tr. Pb.

Umland, Samuel J., ed. *Dracula Notes.* Lincoln, NE: Ciffs Notes, 1983. Paper. [D]

Ursini, James, and Alain Silver. *The Vampire Film.* New York: A. S. Barnes (and) London: Tantivy, 1975. Hb. Cover says: Alain Silver & James Ursini. [M]

Volta, Ornella. *The Vampire.* New York: Award (and) London: Tandem, n.d. Pb. Trans. from the French of 1962.

Waller, Gregory A. *The Living and the Undead: from Stoker's "Dracula" to Romero's "Dawn of the Dead."* Urbana, IL: University of Illinois, 1986. Hb. [M]

Weiss, Andrea. *Vampires and Violets: lesbians in the cinema.* London: J. Cape. 1993. Tr. Pb. [Me, M]

Wolf, Leonard. *A Dream of Dracula: in search of the living dead.* Boston, MS: Little, Brown, 1972. Hb. New York: Popular Library, n.d., Pb. London: New English Library, 1976. Pb. [D]

————ed. *The Annotated Dracula.* New York: C.N.

Potter, 1975. Hb. New York: Ballantine, 1976. Tr. Pb. Revised as *The Essential Dracula*. New York: Plume, 1993. Tr. Pb. Includes *Dracula*. [D]

Wright, Dudley. *Vampires and Vampirism*. London: Rider, 1914. Hb. London: Rider, 1924. Hb. Revised edition. New York: Gordon Press, 1970. Hb. New York. Gale, 1973. Hb. Retitled: *The Book of Vampires*. New York: Causeway, 1973. Hb. New York: Dorset, 1987. Tr. Pb. Thornhill, Dumfriesshire, U.K.: Tynron Press, 1991. Pb. Retitled: *The History of Vampires*. New York: Dorset. 1993. Hb.

ROBERT EIGHTEEN-BISANG

Blood and Celluloid: The Vampire Legend as Recorded by the Silver Screen

The following is a list of films with themes of a vampiric nature as part, or the main ingredient, of their plots. The list is arranged chronologically with the films appearing in alphabetical order within each year. Please note that for foreign productions, the U.S. and foreign release date may differ. The date given is the one that is the most pertinent to the film's recognition in the marketplace. A name in quotes following a film's title refers to a specific vampire episode in an anthology film. Other titles the film was released under or foreign titles follow the films best known title in parentheses. Furthermore, where the information was available, the directors and vampiric actors have been noted. Directors are given first on the left, actors and actresses on the right. Finally, note that the following symbols appear as appropriate in the listings:

(+)   more than one vampiric creature
(c)   comedy
(TV)   originally made for television

(v)   available on video
(a)   animation

1921: *Drakula*, Hungary

1922: *Nosferatu: A Symphony of Horror*, German (v), F. W. Murnau/Max Schreck

1927: *London After Midnight*, U.S., Tod Browning/ Lon Chaney

1931: *Dracula*, U.S. (v), Tod Browning/Bela Lugosi

1932: *Vampyr*, Germany-France (v), Carl Theodore Dreyer/Henriette Gerard

1933: *Vampire Bat*, U.S. (v), Frank Strayer/Lionel Atwill

1935: *Condemned to Live*, U.S., Frank Strayer/Ralph Morgan
Mark of the Vampire (*London After Midnight*), U.S., Tod Browning/Bela Lugosi

1936: *Dracula's Daughter*, U.S., Lambert Hillyer/ Gloria Holden

1941: *Devil's Bat*, U.S. (v), Jean Yarbough/A bat

1942: *Dead Men Walk*, U.S., Sam Newfield/George
   Zucco
   Dr. Terror's House of Horrors, "Vampyr," U.S.,
   Carl Theodore Dreyer/Unknown
   The Return of the Vampire, U.S. (**v**), Lew
   Landers/Bela Lugosi
   Son of Dracula, U.S. (**v**), Robert Siodmak/Lon
   Chaney, Jr.

1944: *House of Frankenstein*, U.S., Erle C. Kenton/
   John Carradine

1945: *House of Dracula*, U.S., Erle C. Kenton/John
   Carradine
   The Vampire's Ghost, U.S., Lesley Selander/
   John Abbott

1948: *Abbott and Costello Meet Frankenstein*, U.S. (**v**),
   Charles T. Barton/Bela Lugosi

1952: *My Son the Vampire* (*Old Mother Reily Meets the
   Vampire: Vampire over London*), U.K., John
   Giling/Bela Lugosi

1953: *Drakula Istambulda*, Turkey

1955: *La Fantasma de la Opereta*, Argentina

1956: *Not of This Earth*, U.S. (**v**), Roger Corman/
   Paul Birch
   El Vampiro (*The Vampire*), U.S., Fernando
   Mendez/German Robles

1957: *El Ataud del Vampiro* (*The Vampire's Coffin*),
   Mexico, Fernando Mendez/German Robles
   Blood of Dracula, U.S., Herbert L. Strock/
   Sandra Harrison
   Dendam Pontianak (*Revenge of the Vampire*),
   Malaysia, B. N. Rao/Maria Menado
   Pontianak (*The Vampire*), Malaysia, Unknown/
   Maria Menado
   The Vampire (*Mark of the Vampire*), U.S., Paul
   Landres/ John Beal
   The Vampiri, U.S., Riccardo Freda/Gianna/
   Maria Canale

1958: *Blood of the Vampire*, U.K., Henry Cass/
   Barbara Shelley
   El Castillo de los Monstrous (*The Castle of the
   Monsters*), Mexico, Julian Soler/German
   Robles
   The Horror of Dracula, U.K. (**v**), Terence Fisher/
   Christopher Lee

Return of Dracula (*Curse of Dracula*), U.S., Paul
   Landres/Francis Lederer
Sumpah Pontianak (*The Vampire's Curse*), Mal-
   aysia

1959: *Curse of the Undead*, U.S., Edward Dein/
   Michael Pate
   First Man into Space, U.K. (**v**), Robert Day/
   Unknown
   Onna Kyuketsui (*Male Vampire; Vampire Man*),
   Japan, Nobo Nakagawa/Shigeru Amachi
   Plan 9 from Outer Space, U.S. (**v**), Edward D.
   Wood, Jr./Bela Lugosi
   Tempi Duri Per I Vampiri (*Uncle Was a Vampire;
   Hard Times for Vampires*), Italy (**c**), Stefano
   Steno/Christopher Lee

1960: *Atom Age Vampire*, Italy-U.S., Anton Guilo
   Masano/Susanne Loret
   Brides of Dracula, U.K., Terence Fisher/David
   Peel
   La Maldicion de Nostadamus (*The Curse of Nos-
   tradamus; Blood of Nostradamus*), Mexico,
   Federico Curiel/German Robles
   Le Maschera del Demonio (*Black Sunday*), Italy,
   Mario Bava/Barbara Steele
   El Mourir de Plaisir (*Blood and Roses*), France-
   Italy (**v**), Roger Vadim/Mel Ferrer
   El Mundo de los Vampiros (*World of the Vam-
   pires*), Mexico (**v**), Alfonso Corona Blake/
   Mauricio Garces and Siliva Fournier
   L'Ultima Preda Del Vampiro (*Playgirls and the
   Vampire; Curse of the Vampire*), Italy.
   Piero Regnoli/Walter Brandi

1961: *Ahkea Kkots* (*The Bad Flower*), Korea, Yongmin
   Lee/Unknown
   L'Amaote Del Vampiro (*Vampire and the Bal-
   lerina; The Vampire Lover*), Italy, Renato
   Polselli/Walter Brandi
   The Blood Drinkers, Philippines, Gerardo de
   Leon/Ronald Remy and others
   Frankenstein, el Vampiro y Cia (*Frankenstein, the
   Vampire and Co.*), Mexico, Benito Alazraki/
   Manuel Valdes
   Maciste Contra il Vampiro (*Maciste vs. the Vam-
   pire; Goliath and the Vampires*), Italy, Gia-
   como Genilomo and Sergio Corbucci/
   Gianna Maria Canale

Il Vampiro dell'Opera (*The Vampire of the Opera*), Italy, Renato Polselli/Giuseppe Addobati

1962: *La Invasion de los Vampiros* (*Invasion of the Vampires*), Mexico, Miguel Morayta/Carlos Agosti

Nostradamus y el Genio de las Tinieblas (*Nostradamus and the Genie of Darkness; Genie of Darkness*), Mexico, Frederick Curiel/German Robles

Santo contra las Mujeres Vampiras (*Santo vs. the Vampire Women; Samson vs. the Vampire Women*), Mexico, Alfonso Corona Blake/Lorena Velazquez

La Strage dei Vampiri (*Slaughter of the Vampires; Curse of the Blood Ghouls; Homme ou Femme?*), Italy (**v**), Roberto Marri/Dieter Eppler

El Vampiro Sangriento (*The Bloody Vampire*), Mexico (TV), Miguel Morayta/Carlos Agosti

1963: *Der Fluch der Grunen Augen* (*The Curse of Green Eyes; Night of the Vampires; Cave of the Living Dead*), Germany-Yugoslavia, Akosvon Rathony/Adrian Hoven

Kiss of the Vampire (*Kiss of Evil*), U.S., Don Sharp/Noel Willman

La Maldision de los Karnsteins (*La Cripta el Incubo; The Crypt of Horror; Terror in the Crypt; The Curse of the Karnsteins*), Italy-Spain, Thomas Miller and Camillo Mastrocinque/Christopher Lee

Pontianak Kembali (*The Vampire Returns*), Malaysia, R. Estellia/Maria Menado

I Tre Volti della Paura, "The Wurdalak" (*The Three Faces of Fear; Black Sabbath*), Italy (**v**), Mario Bava/Boris Karloff

1964: *Dr. Terror's House of Horror*, "Vampire," U.K. (**v**), Freddie Francis/Jennifer Jayne

Echenme a Vampiro (*Throw Me to the Vampire; Bring Me the Vampire*), Mexico, A. E. Crevenna/Borolas

Kiss Me Quick, U.S., Russ Meyer/Jackie DeWitt

The Last Man on Earth, U.S.-Italy (**v**), Sidney Salkow/+

MGA Manugang ni Drakula, Philippines

Pontianak Gua Musang (*The Vampire of the Cave*), Malaysia, B.N. Rao/Suraya Haron

Le Vampire de Dusseldorf, France-Italy-Spain, Robert Hossein/Peter Kurten

1965: *Devils of Darkness*, U.K., Lance Comfort/Hubert Noel

The Hand of Night (*Beast of Morocco*), U.K., Frederic Goode/Diana Clare

El Santo contra el Baron Brakola (*Santo against Baron Brakola*), Mexico, Jose Diaz Morales/Fernando Oses

Terrore Nello Spazio (*Terror in Outer Space; Planet of the Vampires; The Demon Planet*), Italy-Spain, Mario Bava/+

Un Vampiro Para Dos (*A Vampire for Two*), Spain, Pedro Lazaga/Gracita Morales

1966: *Billy the Kid vs. Dracula*, U.S., William Beaudine/John Carradine

The Blood Drinkers (*The Vampire People*), Philippines, Gerardo deLeon/Ronald Remy

Carry on Screaming, U.K., Gerald Thomas/Fenella Fielding

Devil's Mistress, U.S., Orville Mazer/Joan Stapleton

Dracula—Prince of Darkness, U.K., Terence Fisher/Christopher Lee

Munster, Go Home, U.S. Earl Bellamy/Al Lewis

Nightmare Castle, Italy (**v**), Mario Caiano/Helga Line

Orgy of the Dead, U.S., Stephen C. Apostoloff/Fawn Silver and Criswell

Planet of the Vampires (*Prehistoric Planet; Queen of Blood; Planet of Blood*), U.S., Curtis Harrington/Florence Marly

Wild World of Batwoman (*She Was a Hippie Vampire*), U.S., Jerry Warren/Katherine Victor

1967: *Blood of Dracula Castle* (*Dracula's Castle*), U.S. (**v**), Al Adamson/Alex D'Arcy

El Charro de las Calaveras (*The Rider of the Skulls*), Mexico, Alfredo Salazar/Dagoberto Rodriquez

Dr. Terror's Gallery of Horrors, "King Vampire", (*Return from the Past; The Blood Drinkers; The Blood Suckers*), U.S., David L. Hewitt/John Carradine and Lon Chaney

Fearless Vampire Killers (*Dance of the Vampires; Pardon Me, But Your Teeth Are in My Neck*), U.K. (**v**), Roman Polanski/Ferdy Mayne

El Imperio de Dracula (*The Empire of Dracula; Les Mujeres de Dracula*), Mexico, Federico Curiel/Eric del Castillo

Mad Monster Party, U.S. (**a**, **v**), Jules Bass/ voices of Boris Karloff and others

Die Schlangengrube und das Pendel (*The Snake Pit and the Pendulum; The Blood Demon*), Germany, Harald Rein/Christopher Lee

Taste of Blood (*The Secret of Dr. Alucard*), U.S. (**v**), Herschell G. Lewis/Bill Rogers

Las Vampiras (*The Vampire Girls*), Mexico, Federico Curiel/John Carradine

Le Viol du Vampire (*The Rape of the Vampire; Les Femmes Vampires; Sex and the Vampire; La Reine des Vampires; Queen of the Vampires*), France, Jean Rollin/Solange Pradel

1968: *Dracula Has Risen From the Grave*, U.K., Freddie Francis/Christopher Lee

Kuroneko, Japan, Kaneto Shindo/Kichiemon Nakamura

Sangre de Virgenes (*Blood of the Virgin*), Mexico, Emilo Vieyra/Ricardo Bauleo

Um Sonho de Vampiros (*A Dream of Vampires; A Vampire's Dream*), Brazil, Ibere Cavalcanti/ Ankito

The Vampire Beast Craves Blood, U.K., Vernon Sewell/Wanda Ventham

1969: *Blood Beast Terror*, U.K. (**v**), Vernon Sewell/ Wanda Ventham

Blood-Spattered Bride, Spain (**v**), Vincente Aranda/Maribel Martin

Dracula, the Dirty Old Man, U.S. (**c**), William Edwards/Vince Kelly

El Hombre Que Vino de Ummo (*Dracula vs. Frankenstein; Dracula Hunts Frankenstein*), Spain-Germany-Italy, Tulio Demicheli and Hugo Fregonese/Michael Rennie

Men of Action Meet the Women of Drakula, Philippines, Artemio Marquez/Eddie Torrente

One More Time, U.K. (**c**), Jerry Lewis/ Chrisopher Lee

El Vampiro de la Autopista (*The Vampire of the Highway; The Vampire of Castle Frankenstein*), Spain, Jose Luis Madrid/Valdemar Wohlfahrt

La Vampire Nue (*The Naked Vampire; The Nude Vampire*), France, Jean Rollin/Christine Francois

El Vampiro y el Sexo (*The Vampire and Sex; Santo and Dracula's Treasure*), Mexico, Rene Cardona/Carlos Agosti

1970: *Assignment Terror* (*Dracula vs. Frankenstein*),

The welcoming committee at the After Dark Club in *Vamp* (New World Pictures)

Spain-Germany-Italy, Tulio Demicheli/ Michael Rennie

Beiss Mich, Liebling (*Bite Me, Darling*), Germany, Helmut Foernbacher/Eva Renzi

Bloodsuckers (*Incense for the Damned*), U.K., Robert Hartford-Davis/Patrick Mower

The Body Beneath, U.K., Andy Milligan/Gavin Read

Count Dracula, U.K.-Italy-Spain-Germany (**v**), Jesus Franco/Christopher Lee

Count Yorga, Vampire, U.S., Robert Kelljan/ Robert Quarry

Countess Dracula, U.K., Peter Sasdy/Ingrid Pitt

Curse of the Vampires (*Blood of the Vampires*), Philippines, Gerardo De Leon/Amelia Fuentes

Dracula's Lusterne Vampire Dracula's Vampire Lust), Switzerland, Mario D'Alcala/Des Roberts

Le Frisson des Vampires (*Vampire Thrills; Shudder of the Vampire*), France, Jean Rollin/Jacques Robiolles

Garu the Mad Monk, U.K., Andy Milligan/Neil Flanagan

Guess What Happened to Count Dracula, U.S., Laurence Merrick/Des Roberts

House of Dark Shadows, U.S. (**v**), Dan Curtis/Jonathan Frid

Jonathan, Germany, Hans W. Geissendorfer/Jurgen Jung

Le Rouge aux Levres (*The Promise of Red Lips; Daughters of Darkness*), Belgium-France-Germany-Spain, Harry Kumel/Delphine Seyrig

Scars of Dracula, U.K. (**v**), Roy Ward Baker/Christopher Lee

Taste the Blood of Dracula, U.K., Peter Sasdy/Christopher Lee

Vampire Doll, Japan, Michio Yamamoto/Kayo Matsuo

Vampire Lovers, U.K. (**v**), Roy Ward Baker/Ingrid Pitt

1971: *Blood Thirst*, Philippines, Newt Arnold/Robert Winston

Chanoc contra el Tigre y el Vampiro (*Chanoc vs. the Tiger and the Vampire*), Mexico, Gilberto Martinez Solares/German Valdes

Chi O Suv Me (*Lake of Dracula; Dracula's Lust for Blood; Blood-Thirsty Eyes*), Japan, Michio Yamanoto/Mori Kishida

Count Erotica, Vampire, U.S., Tony Teresi/John Peters

Daughters of Darkness, Belgium (**v**), Harry Kumel/Elizabeth Bathory

Dracula vs. Frankenstein, U.S. (**v**), Al Adamson/Zandor Vorkov

House That Dripped Blood, "The Cloak," U.K. (**v**), Peter Duffell/Jon Pertwee

Let's Scare Jessica to Death, U.S. (**v**), John Hancock/Gretchen Corbett

Love: Vampire Style, Germany (**c**), Helmut Foernbacher/Patrick Jordan and Herbert Fuchs

Lust of Dracula (*To Love a Vampire*), U.K., Jimmy Sangster/Yvette Stensgaard

Return of Count Yorga, U.S., Bob Kelljan/Robert Quarry

Twins of Evil, "Vampire Lovers," U.K. (**v**), Roy Ward Baker/Ingrid Pitt

Vampire Happening, Germany (**c, v**), Freddie Francis/Ferdy Mayne

Vampire Men of the Lost Planet (*Horror of the Blood Monsters*), U.S., Al Adamson/+

The Velvet Vampire, U.S. (**v**), Stephanie Rothman/Celeste Yarnall

1972: *Baron Blood*, Italy (**v**), Mario Bava/Joseph Cotton

Dracula, U.S. (**v**), William Crain/William Marshall

Captain Kronos, Vampire Hunters, U.K. (**v**), Brian Clemens/Ian Hendry and others

Les Chemins de la Violence (*Lips of Blood*), France, Ken Ruder/Michel Flynn

Crypt of the Living Dead, Turkey (**v**), Ray Danton/Teresa Gimpea

Daughter of Dracula, France-Spain-Portugal, Jesus Franco/Howard Vernon

The Death Master, U.S., Ray Danton/Robert Quarry

Dracula A.D. 72 (*Dracula Today*), U.K. (**v**), Alan Gibson/Christopher Lee

Dracula vs. Dr. Frankenstein, Spain-France, Jesus Franco/Howard Vemon

Grave of the Vampire (*Seed of Terror*), U.S. (**v**), John Hayes/Michael Pataki

La Invasion de los Muertos (*The Invasion of the Dead*), Mexico, Rene Cardona/The Blue Demon

Legend of Blood Castle, Spain-Italy, Jorge Grau/Lucia Bose

Night Stalker, U.S. (TV, **v**), Dan Curtis/Barry Atwater

La Noche de Walpurgis (*The Night of the Walpurgis; The Werewolf vs. the Vampire Woman*), Spain-Germany, Leon Klimousky/Gaby Fuchs

Pastel de Shangre (*Cake of Blood*), Spain, Jose Maria Valles and Emilo Martinezo Lazaro/Romy, Franciso Bellmunt, and others

Saga of Dracula, Spain, Leon Kilmouski/Narciso Ibanez Menta

Santo and the Blue Demon vs. Dracula and the Wolfman, Mexico, Miguel M. Delgado/Aldo Monti

Vampire Circus, U.K., Robert Young/David Prowse

Vierges et Vampires (*Virgins and Vampires*), France, Jean Rollin/Marie Pierre Castel

Werewolf vs. the Vampire Woman Germany-Spain (**v**), Leon Klimovsky/Andres Resino

1973: *Blood Couple* (*Ganja and Hess*), U.S. (**v**), Bill Gunn/Duane Jones

Cercmonia Sangrienta (*Blood Ceremony; Ritual of Blood*), Spain-Italy, Jorge Grau/Lucia Bose

Devil's Wedding Night, Italy (**v**), Paul Solvay/Sara Bay

Dracula, U.S. (TV, **v**), Dan Curtis/Jack Palance

Dracula's Great Love (*Vampire Playgirls*), Spain, Javier Aguirre/Paul Naschy

Horrible Sexy Vampire, Spain, Jose Luis Madrid/Waldemar Wolfahrt

Lady Dracula (*Lemora-Lady Vampire*), U.S., Richard Blackburn/Cheryl Smith

Lake of Dracula, U.S.-Japan, M. Yamamoto/Mori Kishida

Legend of the Seven Golden Vampires (*Seven Brothers Meet Dracula*), Hong Kong (**v**), Roy Ward Baker/John Forbes Robertson

Santanic Rites of Dracula (*Count Dracula and His Vampire Bride*), U.K., Alan Gibson/Christopher Lee

Santo y Blue Demon contra Dracula y el Hombre Lobo (*Santo and the Blue Demon vs. Dracula and the Wolfman*), Mexico, Alfonso Corona Blake/Aldo Monti

Scream Blacula Scream, U.S., Bob Kelljan/William Marshall

Vampire's Night Orgy, Spain, Leon Kilmousky/+

Veil of Blood, Swiss, Joe Sarno/Olinka Borova

1974: *The Bat People*, U.S., Jerry Jamerson/John Beck

Blood!, U.S., Andy Milligan/Eve Crosby

Blood Drinker, Germany-France, Pierre Grunstein/Peter Cushing

Blood for Dracula (*Andy Warhol's Dracula*), Italy-France (**v**), Paul Morrissey/Udo Kiere

Count Dracula: The True Story, Canada

Dead of Night, U.S. (**v**), Bob Clark/Richard Backus

Grave of the Vampire, U.S., John Hayes/William Smith

Son of Dracula (*Young Dracula*), U.K. (**c**), Freddie Francis/Harry Nilsson

Tender Dracula or Confessions of a Thirsty Dead, Philippines (**v**), Terry Becker/John Considine

Vampira (*Old Dracula*), U.K., Clive Donner/David Niven

1975: *Deafula*, U.S., Peter Wechsberg/Gary R. Holmstrom

Vampyres—Daughters of Darkness, U.S., Joseph Larraz/Marianne Moore and Anulka

1976: *In Search of Dracula*, U.S.-Swiss, Calvin Floyd/Documentary

Martin, U.S. (**v**), George A. Romero/John Amplas

Nightmare in Blood, U.S. (**c**, **v**), John Stanley/Jerry Walter

The Sleep of Death, U.S., Calvin Floyd/Curt Jurgen

1977: *Dr. Dracula*, U.S., Al Adamson/John Carradine

1978: *Count Dracula*, U.K., Philip Seville/Louis Jordan

Dracula Sucks, U.S. (**v**), Philip Marshak/John Holmes

Dracula's Dog, U.S. (**v**), Albert Band/Michael Pataki

Nocturna (*Granddaughter of Dracula*), U.S. (**v**), Harry Tampa/John Carradine

1979: *Dracula*, U.S. (**v**), John Badham/Frank Langella

Dracula and Son, France (**v**), Edward Molinaro/Christopher Lee

Dracula Blows His Cool, Germany, Carlo Ombra/Gianni Garko

Love at First Bite, U.S. (**c**, **v**), Stan Dragoti/George Hamilton

Nightwing, U.S. (**v**), Arthur Hiler/Bats

Nosferatu—The Vampire, Germany (**v**), Werner Herzog/Klaus Kinski

Salem's Lot, U.S. (TV, **v**), Tobe Hooper/Reggie Nalder

Thirst, Australia (**v**), Rod Hardy/David Hemmings

Vampire, U.S. (TV), E. W. Swackhammer/Richard Lynch

Vampire Hookers (*Sensuous Vampires*), Philippines (**v**), Circo H. Santiago/John Carradine

World of Dracula, U.S. (TV), Kenneth Johnson/Unknown

1980: *Dracula's Last Rites* (*Last Rites*), U.S. (**v**), Domonic Paris/Gerald Fielding and Victor Jorge

Mamma Dracula, France-Belgium (**v**), Boris Szulzinger/Louise Fletcher

The Monster Club, U.K. (**v**), Ray Ward Baker/Vincent Price

1981: *Dracula Exotica*, U.S., Warren Evans/Jamie Gillis

Munster's Revenge, U.S. (TV, **v**), Don Weiss/Al Lewis

Two Faces of Evil, U.K. (**v**), Alan Gibson/Gary Raymond

1983: *Ferat Vampire*, Czechoslovakia, Juraz Herz/A car

The Hunger, U.S. (**v**), Tony Scott/Catherine Deneuve

The Keep, U.S. (**v**), Michael Mann/Molasar

1984: *Dracula*, Japan (**a**, **v**), Minori Okazaki/None

1985: *Dracula, the Great Undead*, U.S. (documentary, **v**)

Fright Night, U.S. (**v**), Tom Holland/Chris Sarandon

Lifeforce, U.S.-U.K. (**v**), Tobe Hooper/Mathilda May

Once Bitten, U.S. (**v**), Howard Storm/Lauren Hutton

Transylvania 6-5100, U.S. (**c**, **v**), Rudy DeLuca/Geena Davis

Vampire Hunter, Japan (**a**, **v**), Tayoo Ashida/None

Vampires in Havana, Cuba (**a**, **c**), Juan Padron/Unknown

1986: *Vamp*, U.S. (**v**), Richard Wenk/Grace Jones

1987: *Graveyard Shift*, U.S., Gerard Ciccoritti/Silvio Oliviero

The Lost Boys, U.S. (**v**), Joel Schumacher/Kiefer Sutherland and brothers

The Monster Squad, U.S. (**v**), Fred Dekker/Duncan Regher

Near Dark, U.S. (**v**), Kathryn Bigelow/Lance Henriksen and others

Return to Salem's Lot, U.S. (**c**, **v**), James Dixon/Andrew Duggan

1988: *Dance of the Damned*, U.S., Katt Shea Ruben/Starr Andreeff

Dracula's Widow, U.S. (**v**), Christopher Coppola/Sylvia Kristel

Graveyard Shift II—The Understudy, U.S., Gerard Ciccoritti/Silvio Oliviero

The Jitters, U.S. (**v**), John Fasano/James Hong and others

Lair of the White Worm, U.K. (**v**), Ken Russell/Amanda Donohoe

My Best Friend Is a Vampire, U.S. (**c**, **v**), Jimmy Huston/Robert Sean Leonard

Not of This Earth, U.S. (**v**), Jim Wynorski/Arthur Roberts

Waxwork, U.S. (**v**), Anthony Hickox/Miles O'Keeffe

1989: *Beverly Hills Vamp*, U.S. (**c**, **v**), Fred Olen Ray/Britt Ekland

Fright Night II, U.S. (**v**), Tommy Lee Wallace/Traci Linn

Nick Knight, U.S. (TV), Farhad Mann/Rick Springfield

Nightlife, U.S. (**v**), Daniel Taplitz/Ben Cross

Rockula, U.S. (**c**, **v**), Luca Bercovici/Dean Cameron

To Die For, U.S. (**v**), Dean Sarafian/Sydney Walsh and Scott Jacoby

Vampire's Kiss, U.S. (**v**), Robert Bierman/Jennifer Beals

A vampire (Doug Wert) rises from his coffin in Roger Corman's *Dracula Rising*

1990: *Red Blooded American Girl*, U.S. (**v**), David Blyth/Christopher Plummer

Sundown: The Vampire Retreat, U.K. (**v**), Anthony Hickox/David Caradine and cast

Vampyre, U.S. (**v**), Bruce G. Hallenbeck/Cathy Seyler

1991: *Children of the Night*, U.S., Tony Randel/Angus Scrimm

Subspecies, U.S. (**v**), Ted Nicolaou/Angus Scrimm and Michael Watsen

To Die For II—Son of Darkness, U.S. (**v**), David F. Price/Scott Jacoby and Michael Praed

1992: *Bram Stoker's Dracula*, U.S. (**v**), Francis Ford Coppola/Gary Oldman

Buffy the Vampire Slayer, U.S. (**v**), Fran Rubel Kuzui/Rutger Hauer and Paul Rubens

Dracula Rising, U.S. (**v**), Fred Gallo/Christopher Atkins

From Dusk Till Dawn, U.S., Robert Kurtzman/Unknown

Heart Stopper, U.S. (**v**), John Russo/Kevin Kindlin

Innocent Blood, U.S. (**v**), John Landis/Anne Parillaud

Moonrise (*My Grandpa Is a Vampire*), New Zealand (**v**), David Blyth/Al Lewis

Reluctant Vampire, U.S., Malcolm Marmostein/Adam Ant

Sorority House Vampires, U.S., Geoffrey de Valois/Robert Buchholz

Stephen King's Sleepwalkers, U.S. (**v**), Mick Garris/Alice Kriger and Brian Krause

To Sleep with a Vampire, U.S., Adam Friedman/Scott Valentine

Vampires and Other Stereotypes, U.S. (**v**), Kevin Lindenmuth/William White and Ed Hubbard

1993: *Midnight Kiss*, U.S. (**v**), Joel Bender/Greg Greer

Project Vampire (U.S.) (**v**), Peter Flynn/Myron Natwick

Subspecies II: Bloodstone, U.S. (**v**), Ted Nicolau/ Anders Hove

A Vampire Tale, U.K. (**v**), Shimako Sato/Julian Sands

1994: *Bats*, U.S., Tony Randel/Not cast at press time

Interview with a Vampire, U.S., Neil Jordan/ Brad Pitt, Tom Cruise, and others

The Immortals, U.S., Uli Edel/Not Cast

Charlie Colfax: Vampire Hunter, U.S., Alex Diaz/ Adam Tucker and others

Dragula, Canada, Bashar Shibib/Matt Denver

Subspecies III: Bloodlust, U.S. (**v**), Ted Nicolau/ Anders Hove

Vampire Babes from Outer Space, U.S., Brett Piper/Peni Lotoza and others

Vampire Conspiracy, U.S., Geoffrey de Valois/ Floyd Irons and others

Vampire in Brooklyn, U.S., Wes Craven/Eddie Murphy

The Vampire Embrace, U.S., Anne Goursand/ Pending

J. B. MACABRE

Vampire Date Book: An Annual Calendar of Dates to Remember

$\mathfrak{h}$ere is a selection of annual dates of note and anniversaries that should be on every vampire afficionado's calendar!

January

Sunday	Monday	Tuesday	Wednesday	Thursday	Friday	Saturday
1 In first trial three women accomplices and a man-servant of Elizabeth Bathory faced judgesfor following orders (1611) Frank Langella, Dracula actor, born (1940)	**2**	**3**	**4** Ramsey Campbell, British author, born (1946)	**5**	**6** In Kitzingen, West Germany, U.S. soldiers gathered in front of tomb awaiting the emergence of Count Dracula.	**7** In second trial of E. Bathory, Arnold Paole was beheaded and burned as a result of inquiry (1732)
8 Wilkie Collins born (1824)	**9**	**10** Karloff opened as Jonathan in *Arsenic and Old Lace* (1941)	**11** TV movie *The Night Stalker* debuted; written by Richard Matheson (1972)	**12**	**13** *New York Times* reported U.S. athlete's use of blood-packing (1985) Clark Ashton born (1893)	**14** *New York Times* reported vampire in Indonesia who bit the necks of twenty-one young women (1984)
15	**16**	**17** *San Francisco Chronicle* reported that Weldon Meade Kennedy believed he was a vampire and ate raw meat and blood to survive (1973)	**18** In French town of Dole, Gilles Garnier confessed to werewolfism and was buried alive	**19** Edgar Allen Poe, author, born (1908)	**20** Film, *The Invisible Ray*, debuted with Boris Karloff and Bela Lugosi (1936)	**21**
22	**23** Robert E. Howard, American author, born (1906)	**24** Erzsi Majorova, an accomplice of Elizabeth Bathory, was found guilty and executed	**25**	**26**	**27**	**28** *Son of Frankenstein* premiered in New York (1939)
29	**30**	**31**				

February

Sunday	Monday	Tuesday	Wednesday	Thursday	Friday	Saturday
1	2 *New York World* reported outbreak of vampirism in Rhode Island (1896) Boris Karloff died (1969)	3	4	5 Basil Copper, author, born (1924)	6	7 Mrs. Ann Radcliff, author, died (1823) J. Sheridan Le Fanu, author, died (1873)
8	9	10 Lon Chaney, Jr., actor, born (1906)	11	12	13 *New York Times* reported on the ideology of Dracula (1977)	14 *Dracula*, the play, opened in London to longest historical run (1927) *Dracula*, the movie, debuted (1931)
15 *The Daily Telegraph* reported that a farmer staked and stuffed garlic in the mouth of a vampire to stop visitations	16	17	18 John George Haigh killed Mrs. Durand-Deacon and drank some of her blood (1949) Jack Palance, actor, born (1920)	19	20	21 Mary Shelley, author, died (1851)
22 Dwight Frye, actor, born (1899)	23	24 August Derleth, actor, born (1906)	25	26 Dom Augustin Calmet, author, born (1672) Theodore Sturgeon, author, born (1918)	27	28 Premier issue of *Famous Monsters of Filmland* arrived on newstands (1958)
29						

March

Sunday	Monday	Tuesday	Wednesday	Thursday	Friday	Saturday
1 *Le Vampire*, a comedy by M. J. Mengals, opened at the Ghent Theatre, Paris (1826)	**2** Horace Walpole died (1797)	**3** Stockton State College presented Ted Tiller's *Count Dracula* (1977)	**4** The film *Nosferatu* premiered at the Berlin Zoo (1922)	**5** The film *Nosferatu* released in Germany (1922)	**6**	**7**
8 Bram Stoker wrote first outline for *Dracula* Peter Saxon born (1921)	**9**	**10**	**11** John George Haigh left for prison (1949)	**12** Mihnea, son of Vlad Tepes, stabbed to death in Sibiu (1510) Count Eric Stenbock born (1860)	**13**	**14** Dr. Zoltan Meder claims Dracula was a woman (1975) Vampire hunt in Highgate Cemetery, London (1970) Algernon Blackwood, author, born (1869)
15 H. P. Lovecraft, author, died (1937)	**16**	**17** Christopher Lee, actor, married Brigit Kroencke (1961)	**18** *Pittsburgh Press* reported that the real-life Dracula declared a hero in Romania (1984)	**19** In Indonesia, vampire blamed for the death of five successive husbands, all due to acute anemia (1984)	**20**	**21**
22	**23** Peter Lorre, actor, died (1964)	**24**	**25** In St. Cloud, Minnesota, four teens arrested for murder; one drank blood (1988)	**26**	**27** Bela Lugosi spoke about his new role of Dracula via radio (1931)	**28** *Der Vampyr*, an opera, opened in Leipzig, Germany (1928)
29	**30**	**31**				

April

Sunday	Monday	Tuesday	Wednesday	Thursday	Friday	Saturday
1 *The Vampyre* by Byron published in *The New Monthly Magazine* (1819) Lon Chaney, Sr., actor, born (1883)	**2** Vlad Tepes partied with thousands neatly arranged on stakes (1459) Peter Haining born (1940)	**3**	**4**	**5** Robert Bloch, author, born (1917) Roger Corman, director, born (1926)	**6**	**7**
8	**9**	**10** NBC studios in New York was picketed by "Dark Shadows" fans hoping to save the series (1991) Montague Summers born (1880)	**11**	**12**	**13** Trial opened for the Vampire of Dusseldorf, Peter Kurten (1931)	**14** "Dark Shadows" TV series debuted (1967)
15 Fritz Haarmann, the Hannover Vampire, executed by decapitation (1925)	**16** Gaston Leroux, author, died (1927)	**17** Newspaper reported on removal of Haarmann's brain for study (1925)	**18** API reported that Angela Papas burned at the stake for vampirism in a small Greek fishing village (1959)	**19** Bats attacked humans in Mexico City; victims recognized features as belonging to recently dead villagers (1965)	**20** Bram Stoker died (1912)	**21**
22 Lionel Atwill, actor, died (1946)	**23** Peter Kurten, real-life vampire, condemned to die "nine times for every killing," as is German law (1931)	**24**	**25**	**26**	**27**	**28** Johann Ludwig Tieck died (1853)
29	**30** Stoker dined with Prof. Arminius Vambery who related Dracula story, and idea for novel evolved (1890)	**31**				

May

Sunday	Monday	Tuesday	Wednesday	Thursday	Friday	Saturday
1	**2** William Beckford died (1844)	**3** Bela Lugosi's second stage opening as Dracula (1943)	**4**	**5** The play *Dracula* opened in Boston (1943) *Vampyr* screened at Olympia Theatre in New York at midnight (1972) TV series "Forever Knight" premiered on CBS (1992)	**6** The film *The Bride of Frankenstein* released (1935)	**7** The film *The Black Cat*, with Karloff and Lugosi, debuted (1934). Darren McGaven, actor, born (1922)
8 Elizabeth Bathory betrothed to Count Ferencz Nadasdy; she was 15 (1575)	**9** Newspapers reported that "Dark Shadows" fans rallied nationwide to save the remake (1991)	**10** The film *Bedlam*, with Karloff, released (1946) Matthew Lewis died (1818)	**11**	**12**	**13**	**14**
15	**16**	**17** *New York Times* reported that death among sheep in West Pakistan town was attributed to vampires (1969)	**18** *Dracula* debuted on the stage of the Lyceum; only one to be seen by Bram Stoker (1897)	**19** The stage play *Dracula*, starring Lugosi, closed after 261 performances (1928)	**20** Publisher's contract to print *Dracula* dated today (1897)	**21**
22 Christopher Lee, actor, born (1922) Arthur Conan Doyle, author, born (1859)	**23**	**24**	**25**	**26**	**27**	**28**
29 William Beckford born (1760)	**30** Dr. David Dolphin claimed porphyria is a link to vampirism (1985) R. Chetwynd Hayes, author, born (1919)	**31** Johann Ludwig Tieck born (1773)				

June

Sunday	Monday	Tuesday	Wednesday	Thursday	Friday	Saturday
1	**2** Marquis De Sade born (1740)	**3** *Chicago Tribune* reported that Romania goes to bat for Dracula (1979)	**4**	**5** Thomas Presket Prest died (1859)	**6**	**7**
8	**9**	**10** Vienna paper reported castle, located in Carpathian Mountains burned by populace due to mortality of peasant youth (1910)	**11** Court told of naked girls dancing among coffins in Highgate cemetery (1974)	**12** Hans Heinz Ewers died (1943) M. R. James, author, died (1936) Robert E. Howard, author, died (1936)	**13** John Polidori's *The Vampyre* staged in Paris (1820)	**14**
15 Newspaper reported that Allan David Farrant denied allegations of Highgate cemetery rituals (1974)	**16**	**17**	**18** In France, Joseph Vacher killed a thirteen-year-old by hacking and biting body, one of a series of brutal murders (1897)	**19** *The Vampire*, in three acts, opened at Princes' theatre in London (1852)	**20**	**21**
22	**23**	**24** Ambrose Bierce, author, born (1842)	**25** *La Morte Amoreuse* (The Dead Lover), play by Theophile Gautier, opened in Chrinique de Paris (1836)	**26** Lugosi opened as Dracula on London stage (1951) Peter Lorre, actor, born (1904) Colin Wilson, actor, born (1931)	**27**	**28**
29	**30** Sam Moskowitz born (1920)					

July

Sunday	Monday	Tuesday	Wednesday	Thursday	Friday	Saturday
1 Orson Welles' radio production of *Dracula* for the Mercury Theatre aired (1938)	**2** Peter Kurten, Vampire of Duesseldorf, executed by decapitation (1931)	**3** In North Sumatra an elderly barber accused of sucking the blood of babies (1967)	**4** August Derleth, author, died (1971)	**5**	**6** The film *Frankenstein 1970*, with Karloff, opened (1958) Guy De Maupassant died (1893)	**7** Arthur Conan Doyle, author, died (1930)
8	**9** Mrs. Ann Radcliff born (1764) Matthew Lewis born (1775)	**10** Military investigated Sgt. Bertrand (1849) Carl Jacobi born (1908)	**11**	**12** In Wallachia, proclamation made that peasants may no longer exhume bodies of suspected vampires if done twice before (1801)	**13** John Badham's film *Dracula*, starring Frank Langella, opened (1979) Lon Chaney, Jr., actor, died (1973)	**14**
15	**16**	**17**	**18** A. D. Ferrant sentenced to four years, 8 months for Highgate cemetery incidents (1974) Sydney Horler born (1888)	**19** John George Haigh, real-life vampire, sentenced to death by hanging (1949).	**20**	**21**
22 The film *The Raven*, with Karloff and Lugosi, opened (1935)	**23**	**24** John George Haigh born (1910) E. F. Benson born (1867)	**25** Vlad Tepes and Prince Steven Bathory hold council of war in Turda (1476)	**26** Author Vincent Hillyer spent the night in Castle Dracula (1977)	**27**	**28**
29	**30** *London Times* reported elderly barber behaving like a vampire and sucking blood of two babies (1969)	**31** Elizabeth Bathory wrote her last will and testament (1614)				

August

Sunday	Monday	Tuesday	Wednesday	Thursday	Friday	Saturday
1 *London Times* reported charred, headless body of a woman found in Highgate cemetery (1970) M. R. James, author, born (1862)	**2** F. Marion Crawford born (1854)	**3** *Daily Mirror* reported local vampires in North Wales fined and warned not to drink any more cattle blood (1971)	**4**	**5** Lugosi appeared in stage play *Arsenic and Old Lace* (1943) Guy De Maupassant born (1850)	**6** Vampire of Nuremburg tried for sucking the blood of those he killed (1974)	**7**
8 Prof. Leonard Wolf's vampire course entered its third year (1973)	**9** Lugosi on cover of *Hollywood Filmograph* named as possible lead in *Dracula* film (1930)	**10** John George Haigh, real-life vampire, executed by hanging (1949) Montague Summers, author, died (1948)	**11**	**12**	**13** H. G. Wells, author, died (1946) Alfred Hitchcock, writer/director, born (1899)	**14** E. Bathory died imprisoned in Cachtice Castle (1614) Clark Ashton Smith, author, died (1961)
15 *The Vampyre* written by R. Reece, with music, opened at the Royal Strand Theatre in London (1872)	**16** Bela Lugosi, actor, died (1956)	**17**	**18**	**19**	**20** H. P. Lovecraft, author, born (1890)	**21** Another date given for the death of E. Bathory after three-and-a-half years in seclusion (1614)
22 Ray Bradbury, writer, born (1920)	**23** Peter Kurten killed first victim by slitting throat (1929)	**24** Vampire Festival in Padua, Italy (1985) Some 30,000 people killed by Vlad Tepes in Brasov (1460)	**25** A freely adapted version of *Der Vampyr* opened at the Lyceum theater and ran for sixty nights (1829)	**26** Lon Chaney, Sr., actor, died (1930)	**27**	**28** J. Sheridan Le Fanu, author, born (1814)
29	**30** Allan David Farrant arrested for penetrating an enclosed area of Highgate cemetery (1970)	**31** Mary Shelly, author, born (1797) Theophile Gautier born (1811)				

September

Sunday	Monday	Tuesday	Wednesday	Thursday	Friday	Saturday
1	2	3	4	5	6	7 John Polidori, author, born (1795)
8	9	10	11	12	13 "Seer" Veronica Leuken claimed a vampire was busy organizing covens throughout the U.S. for his blood (1977)	14 In London, 250th performance of the play *Dracula* (1927)
15	16	17	18 TV series "The Addams Family" debuted (1964)	19 The stage version of *Dracula* opened at the Shubert Theatre in America (1927)	20 Romania issued stamp depicting Vlad Tepes in honor of the 500th anniversary of the founding of Bucharest (1959)	21 H. G. Welles, author, born (1866) Stephen King, author, born (1946)
22 TV program starring Karloff debuted (1949)	23 Stage production of *Dark Shadows*, part of the Dance Theater Workshop, debuted in New York (1988)	24 TV series "The Munsters" premiered (1964) TV series "Dracula: The Series" debuted (1991) Horace Walpole born (1717)	25 John Landis's film *Innocent Blood* opened (1992)	26	27 "The Vampire," a two-scene sketch, appeared at the Paragon Theatre opening in England (1909)	28
29 Filming of *Dracula* began (1930)	30	31				

October

Sunday	Monday	Tuesday	Wednesday	Thursday	Friday	Saturday
1 The *New York Daily News* reported of vampire hunt begun by Stephen Kaplan (1980)	**2**	**3**	**4**	**5** Bela Lugosi appeared in his first stage portrayal of *Dracula* (1927)	**6**	**7** Edgar Allen Poe died (1849) Micahel Parry born (1947)
8 David Farrant arrested by Police for ceremonies in Highgate Cemetery (1971)	**9**	**10**	**11**	**12**	**13** *Ogden Standard Examiner* reported of M. H. Singh, murderer, who said vampires sucked his blood (1985)	**14**
15	**16**	**17** *Daily Telegraph* reported of operation Dracula in which former President of Argentina was removed from grave (1974)	**18** Klaus Kinski, actor, born (1926)	**19**	**20** Frank Langella debuted as Count Dracula on stage in New York (1977) Bela Lugosi, actor, born (1882)	**21**
22 TV series "Monsters" debuted (1988)	**23** James P. Riva II, told of smothering grandmother and sucking her blood as told by a vampire in Massachusetts (1981)	**24** Fritz Haarmann, The Hanover Vampire, born (1879)	**25** Newspapers reported that Vampira said Elvira stole her character (1987) Vampires discovered in Rhode Island history (1979)	**26** Reported that James P. Riva was charged with the murder and drinking of victim's blood to survive (1981)	**27** Court of inquiry held against Elizabeth Bathory (1610) Sydney Horler died (1954)	**28** *News of the World* reported that in England a priest alleged to have been attacked by a human vampire with a history of attacks (1973)
29 Mircea, son of Vlad Tepes, elected prince of Wallachia (1509)	**30** Objections to Hallmark's production of Transylvania T-shirts (1987)	**31**				

November

Sunday	Monday	Tuesday	Wednesday	Thursday	Friday	Saturday
1 Iles of Scotland ritual of candles lit in windows to show dead the way back home (late 1800s)	**2** California Ballet offered *Dracula* (1987)	**3** Hans Heinz Ewers born (1871)	**4**	**5**	**6**	**7** Dwight Frye, actor, died (1943)
8 In the novel *Dracula*, Jonathan killed Count Dracula (1887) Bram Stoker born (1847)	**9** In 1987, AL-COMIX Dracula Liquer introduced (*AD Week*)	**10**	**11** The film *The Mad Genius*, with Karloff, opened (1931)	**12**	**13** "Thriller," TV program hosted by Karloff, debuted and ran for 66 shows (1960) Francis Ford Coppola's film *Bram Stoker's Dracula* opened (1992)	**14**
15 Filming of *Dracula* completed in a little over two months (1931)	**16** Serial killer Ed Gein arrested (1957) Vlad Tepes recaptured most of Walla in battle (1476)	**17** The film *Tower of London*, with Karloff, Rathbone, and Price, debuted (1939)	**18**	**19**	**20** Dracula Weekend began at Boston College (1975)	**21** The film *Frankenstein* previewed (1931)
22	**23** Boris Karloff, actor, born (1887)	**24**	**25** Klaus Kinski, actor, died (1991)	**26**	**27**	**28** John Carradine, actor, died (1988)
29	**30**	**31**				

December

Sunday	Monday	Tuesday	Wednesday	Thursday	Friday	Saturday
1 First victim of Jack the Ripper found (1887) Marquis De Sade died (1740)	**2** Brian Lumley, actor, born (1937)	**3**	**4** *Frankenstein* the movie premier (1931)	**5**	**6**	**7** *Dark Shadows* actress Joan Bennett died (1990)
8	**9** Pope Innocent VII issued a Papal bull warning against sexual encounters with demons (1484)	**10** Algernon Blackwood, author, died (1951)	**11** Maila "Vampira" Nurmi born (1921)	**12** Dr. Johannes Fluckinger ran public enquiry regarding vampire reports in Austria (1731) Karl Edward Wagner, author, born (1945)	**13**	**14**
15	**16**	**17**	**18**	**19**	**20** Bela Lugosi's American stage debut in the title role of *Dracula* (1922) Dr. J. Youngson, CDFC president, born (1923)	**21**
22	**23**	**24** *Castle of Otranto* by Horace Walpole published (1764)	**25**	**26** Richard Chase committed suicide by biting wrists and sucking blood (1980)	**27**	**28** F. W. Murnau, director, born (1889)
29	**30** Castle of Elizabeth Bathory raided and all arrested due to unusual findings (1610)	**31** G. S. Viereck born (1884)				

Gather Round a Shallow Grave: Vampire Organizations, Clubs, and Publications

The Anne Rice's Vampire Lestat Fan Club
P.O. Box 5827
New Orleans, LA 70158-8277
Publish a quarterly newsletter and offer a pen pal service.

Blooddreams
1312 West 43rd St.
No. Little Rock, AR 72118
Gunter Atlas, Editor
A quarterly journal of fiction, poetry, and articles devoted to the legends of vampires and werewolves. Send an SASE for subscription information and writer's guidelines.

The Bram Stoker Memorial Association
Penthouse North, Suite H
29 Washington Sq. West
New York, NY 10011
Dr. Jeanne Youngson, founder
Lifetime membership is $10.

The Bram Stoker Society
c/o Albert Power
227 Rochester Ave.
Dun Laoghaire, County Dublin
Ireland
Leslie Shepard, founder

The Vampyre Society
38 Westcroft
Chippenham, Wilts

England, SN14 OLY
Allen J. Gittens, honorable chairman
Publish a quarterly journal, For the Blood Is the Life.

The Collinsport Record, the Collinswood Journal, and the Friends of "Dark Shadows"
P.O. Box 213
Metraire, LA 70004
Sharida Rizzuto, editor
Publications for "Dark Shadows" fans.

The Count Dracula Fan Club
Penthouse North, Suite H
29 Washington Sq. West
New York, NY 10011
Dr. Jeanne Youngson, president

Count Dracula Society
334 West 54th St.
Los Angeles, CA 90037
Dr. Donald Reed, national president

Count Ken Fan Club
18 Palmer St.
Salem, MA 10970
Ken Gilbert, president
Monthly newsletter.

The Dracula Society
36 Elliston St.
Woolwich, London

England, SE18
Bernard Davies, honorable chairman
Membership applications are approved by the board. They hold meetings, dinners, film screenings, and other special events. Their periodical of commentaries, articles, and reviews is Voice from the Vault.

The Miss Lucy Westerna Society of the Undead
125 Taylor St.
Jackson, TN 38301
Lewis Sanders, founder
Membership is $10 annually, and they publish a newsletter three to four times a year.

Necropolis
P.O. Box 77693
San Francisco, CA 94107
A quarterly fact/fiction newsletter for fans of the undead. Subscriptions are $10 a year, and they are also open to submissions.

Nocturnal Extacy Vampire Coven
4527 South Troy
Chicago, IL 60632
Darlene Daniels, president
Open membership at the cost of $15 a year ($20 outside the U.S.).

Onyx
P.O. Box 137
Uniontown, OH 44685
Mark Williams, editor
Newsletter devoted to all aspects of vampirism. Single issue is $1.50; yearly subscription costs $5.50.

Secret Order of the Undead
155 East "C" St., Suite 323
Upland, CA 91786
T. J. Teer, president
Currently looking for members, submissions, and correspondents. For information, send a SASE to the above address.

Shadows of the Night
P.O. Box 17006
Rochester, NY 14617
A new publication that hopes to cater to the "mature" fan. For information on membership and submission, send a SASE to the above address.

The Society for the Acquisition & Preservation of Vampire Lore
Penthouse North, Suite M

29 Washington Sq. West
New York, NY 10011
Fern S. Miller, executive director
This organization collects, catalogues, and preserves factual data regarding the vampire throughout history. They welcome contributions of newspaper and magazine clippings. Please send your name and address with each piece.

Vampire Archives
2926 W. Leland
Chicago, IL 60625
Publishes a newsletter that tries to keep readers up to date on the happenings in the world of vampirism. Subscriptions cost $35 a year ($45 foreign).

Vampire's Crypt
105 Phipps Lane
Annapolis, MD 21403
Margaret L. Carter, editor
Newsletter with fact and fiction pieces. Issues cost $7.50 each.

The Vampire Guild
127 Reforne
Portland, Dorset
England DT5 2AP
Phill White, founder
A relatively new organization that hopes to publish a newsletter. For membership information, send a SASE to the above address.

The Vampire Information Exchange
P.O. Box 328
Brooklyn, NY 11229-0328
Eric Held, director
This organization serves as an information clearing house. They also publish a newsletter six times a year, Vampire Information Exchange Newsletter.

The Vampire Journal
P.O. Box 994
Metrairie, LA 70004
Thomas Schellenberger, president
Publish journals and newsletters.

The Vampire Pen Pal Network
Penthouse North
29 Washington Sq. West
New York, NY 10011
Ann Margaret Hart, executive director

The Vampire Research Foundation
Penthouse North, Suite E

---

29 Washington Sq. West
New York, NY 10011
Robert J. Clark, executive director
Issue a yearly listing of recommended books on vampire research. Copies are available without cost or obligation if you send your request with a SASE to the above address.

Vampire Studies
P.O. Box 151
Berwyn, IL 60402
Martin V. Riccardo, president
Founded in 1977, this organization is not open to membership. They are interested in hearing about vampire fantasies and serve as a clearing house for information and conduct lectures. Their publication is the Journal of Vampirism.

The Vampirism Research Institute
P.O. Box 21067
Seattle, WA 98111
This organization is more of a study group, consisting of psychologists, parapsychologists, astrologers, etc., that examines vampirism as it relates to their different fields of study. For a sample issue, send a SASE to the above address.

Vamps
% de Lioncourt
P.O. Box 21067
Seattle, WA 98111
Newsletter/magazine with numerous fact/fiction pieces. Cost is $1 per issue, and checks should be made out to McMahon.

Vampire Junction
c/o Books
114 N.W. 13th St. Gator Plaza
Gainesville, FL 32601
Nonprofit fanzine devoted to original artwork, poetry, short stories, book and movie reviews, and articles.

Inquisition Ink
30-40 45th St., Suite 1-D
Astoria, NY 11103
Andrew Henning, in association with The Mind's Eye Theatre and White Wolf Studios, organizes vampire role playing parties at various clubs around New York City.

Thy food is the food of ghosts; thy drink is the drink of ghosts.
—ASSYRIAN INCANTATION AGAINST VAMPIRES

Index

Italic page references indicate boxed text.

Incubi, 4, 6
Industrial rock, 163–64
Interview with the Vampire (novel), 64, 71, 85–86, 123, 155
Irving, Henry, 74–75, 82, 104
Italian films, 113

J

Jaeger, Denny, 168
J. B. Macabre's Macabreotorium (radio program), 132
J. Geils Band, 169
Johnson, Crane, 105
Johnston, Ben, 108, 170
Jonathan (film), 118–19
Jones, Russ, 152
Journey into Fear (comic book), 151
"Jungle" genre, 147

K

Kane, Bob, 146
Keats, 54
Keel, John A., *20–21*
Keep, The (film), 116–17
Keep, The (novel), 116
Kelly, Tim, 106
Killing vampires, 37–38, 40
Killough, 69
King, Stephen, 63, 69
Kirby, Jack, 146
Kiss of the Vampire (film), 166
Kitzingen (Germany), 50
Kolchak Papers, The (novel), 137
Komeda, Krzysztof, 166, 167
Kondoleon, Harry, 105–06
Krasyy, 24
Krueger, Freddy (character), *120*
Kuzul, Fran Rubel, 125–27

L

L.A. Guns, 162
Lajthay, Karoly, 110

Lamia, 7, 24
"La Morte Amoureuse" (story), 58
Landis, John, 129–30
Langella, Frank, 68, 104, 116, 168
Langsuyar, 24
Last Man on Earth, The (film), 113–14
Laymon, Richard, 65
Leach, Wilford, 108
Lee, Christopher, 112, 113, 114
Lee, Stan, 154
Le Fanu, Joseph Sheridan, 58, 108, 112, 114, 115, 170
Leiber, Fritz, 138
Lerici (Italy), 49
Lestat (character), 64, 71, 87, 123, 155
"Le Vampire" (play), 103
Lifeforce (film), 118
"Ligeia" (story), 60
Light sensitivity, 30
Literary vampires. *See also* Novels; specific authors and titles
    action/adventure genre and, 66
    anthologies/collections and, 216–18
    classic literature and, 54
    classic vampire novels and, 63–64
    Dracula (Stoker novel) and, 89
    early vampire stories and, 58, 65
    energy-draining vampires and, 59, 61, 65
    female vampires and, 58–59
    first vampire stories and, 54–55, *56–57*
    forms of, 59
    genres of, 65, 66, 137
    horror genre and, 137
    in 1700s, 18–19
    in early lateeighteenth and early-nineteenth centuries, 60–61
    in 1930s, 61
    in 1950s, 62–63
    in 1960s, 63
    in 1970s, 62, 63–64
    monster movie magazines and, 62–63
    mystery/suspense genre and, 65–66
    overview of, 197–98
    popularity of, 53–54
    possession by vampires and, 59–60